The Pontifical Biblical Commission

WHAT
IS
MAN?

A JOURNEY THROUGH
BIBLICAL ANTHROPOLOGY

The Pontifical Biblical Commission

WHAT
IS
MAN?
(Psalm 8:5)

A JOURNEY THROUGH
BIBLICAL ANTHROPOLOGY

Translated by Fearghus O'Fearghail *and* Adrian Graffy

Presentation by Cardinal Luis Ladaria SJ
President of the Pontifical Biblical Commission

DARTON·LONGMAN+TODD

Darton, Longman and Todd Ltd
1 Spencer Court,
140-142 Wandsworth High Street
London SW18 4JJ

Translated from *Che cosa è l'uomo? Un itinerario di antropologia biblica*,
Liberia Editrice Vaticana 2019 by Fearghus O'Fearghail and Adrian Graffy.

ISBN 978-1-913657-14-7

A catalogue record for this book is available from the British Library

Designed by Judy Linard.
Printed and bound by Scandbook AB, Sweden

"What is Man?" (Psalm 8:5)

TABLE OF
CONTENTS

BIBLICAL REFERENCES

Old Testament

Gen	Genesis
Ex	Exodus
Lev	Leviticus
Num	Numbers
Deut	Deuteronomy
Josh	Joshua
Jdg	Judges
Ruth	Ruth
1 Sam	The First Book of Samuel
2 Sam	The Second Book of Samuel
1 Kgs	The First Book of Kings
2 Kgs	The Second Book of Kings
1 Chr	The First Book of Chronicles
2 Chr	The Second Book of Chronicles
Ezr	Ezra
Neh	Nehemiah
Tob	Tobit
Jdt	Judith
Est	Esther
1 Macc	The First Book of Maccabees
2 Macc	The Second Book of Maccabees
Job	Job
Ps	Psalms
Prov	Proverbs
Qoh	Ecclesiastes/Qoheleth
Song	The Song of Songs
Wis	Wisdom
Sir	Ecclesiasticus/Ben Sira
Is	Isaiah
Jer	Jeremiah

11

Lam	Lamentations
Bar	Baruch
Ezek	Ezekiel
Dan	Daniel
Hos	Hosea
Joel	Joel
Am	Amos
Obad	Obadiah
Jon	Jonah
Mic	Micah
Nah	Nahum
Hab	Habakkuk
Zeph	Zephaniah
Hag	Haggai
Zech	Zechariah
Mal	Malachi

The New Testament

Mt	The Gospel according to Matthew
Mk	The Gospel according to Mark
Lk	The Gospel according to Luke
Jn	The Gospel according to John
Acts	The Acts of the Apostles
Rom	Romans
1 Cor	1 Corinthians
2 Cor	2 Corinthians
Gal	Galatians
Eph	Ephesians
Phil	Philippians
Col	Colossians
1 Thess	1 Thessalonians
2 Thess	2 Thessalonians
1 Tim	1 Timothy
2 Tim	2 Timothy
Phlm	Philemon
Heb	Hebrews
Jam	James
1 Pt	1 Peter
2 Pt	2 Peter
1 Jn	1 John
2 Jn	2 John
3 Jn	3 John
Jude	Jude
Apoc	The Apocalypse

PRESENTATION

"There is nothing truly human that does not find an echo in the hearts of the disciples of Christ". The Pastoral Constitution *Gaudium et Spes* (§ 1) thus expresses itself, when enunciating the hermeneutical principle of its pronouncements, while paying due attention to the history of humanity in the light of the mystery of the Kingdom of God. This commitment is fundamental for the mission of the Church in the contemporary world, faced as it is with new demands, new issues and new challenges. Already by the end of the Second Vatican Council in 1965, it was evident that modern society had undergone profound changes, especially in the areas of science and technology, but also in that of human relationships, which have produced "a true social and cultural transformation, that has repercussions also on religious life" (*Gaudium et Spes* § 4). On the one hand, imbalances and discrepancies have arisen between actions and normative thinking, between practical efficiency and moral conscience, between growing specialisation and a universal vision of reality; and in addition to unexpected conflicts between generations, a different relationship has emerged between man and woman, with a vision of sexuality that contrasts with traditions that were once seen as binding and established. On the other hand, there is growing evidence of an increasingly strident aspiration towards an existence that conforms fully to the nature of the human being, in which the equal dignity of every person is recognised, without distinction of race, sex or ideology; the supernatural dimension is sometimes obscured in favour of purely earthly hopes, and choices of a religious nature no longer appear relevant to the truth of the human being. Because of this ensemble of factors *Gaudium et Spes* states (§ 10) "in the face of the present evolution of the world, a growing number of people ask themselves or feel with a new intensity the most fundamental questions", the first of which is "What is man?"

In recent decades the change alluded to above has gathered pace, with questions and behaviour of an anthropological nature that require serious discernment. The desire of the Church, faithful to the commandment of its Lord, is to be at the service of humanity, providing those elements of truth that lead to authentic progress, according to God's plan. It is by having recourse to the divine Revelation attested in the Sacred Scriptures that the Church fulfils its mission, bringing to the questioning and the searching of human beings that light that comes from the inspired Word of God, and that can bring about a heartfelt appreciation of the value and the vocation of the human being created in the image of God (*Gaudium et Spes* § 12).

The initiative of Pope Francis in entrusting to the Pontifical Biblical Commission the task of preparing a Document on *biblical anthropology* is to be seen in this light, its purpose being to provide an authoritative basis for developments in the disciplines of philosophy and theology, in the renewed awareness that Sacred Scripture constitutes "the supreme rule of faith" (*Dei Verbum* § 21) and "the soul of sacred theology" (*Dei Verbum* § 24).

The Document which we present represents an innovation, both in relation to its content and to its method of exposition. Such an approach, which in an organic way expounds all the principal elements in the Old and New Testaments that together define what a human being is, has not hitherto been undertaken. Themes developed for the most part in isolation are here brought together into a coherent whole. This approach is based on a method of exposition that takes Gen 2-3 as a basic text of reference (combined with the other accounts of origins), since these pages of Scripture are considered fundamental in the literature of the New Testament and the dogmatic tradition of the Church. In these inaugural chapters the sacred author sets out in an exemplary manner, even if succinct for the most part, the constitutive elements of the human person, included from the beginning in a dynamic process in which the human creature assumes a role that is decisive for its future. All this is seen in relationship with the active and loving presence of God, without which one cannot understand either the nature of humanity or the sense of its history.

As is indicated in the Introduction to the Document, each of the significant elements announced in the foundational narrative is then developed, using the whole of biblical literature; the various traditions of the Old Testament (the Torah, the sapiential writings and the prophetic collections) and the New Testament (the gospels and the letters of the Apostles), each in its own way, combine to present the complexity of the human person both as a mystery to be explored and as one of the wonders of the divine work that raises perpetual praise to the Creator (Ps 8).

The intention of the present Document, therefore, is to make visible the beauty and the complexity of divine Revelation in relation to the human person. The beauty leads one to appreciate the work of God, and the complexity invites one to take on a humble and unceasing labour of research, of deepening knowledge and of communication. The Document is offered as an aid to members of theological faculties, to catechists and to students of the sacred sciences, to promote an overall vision of the divine project, which began with the act of creation, and is realised in the course of time until it reaches fulfilment in Christ, the new man, who constitutes "the key, the centre and the goal of all human history" (*Gaudium et Spes* § 10). In fact, "only in the mystery of the incarnate Word is light truly shed on the mystery of the human person" (*Gaudium et Spes* § 22), and this is given as a sure principle of hope for all people as they journey towards that Kingdom of justice, love and peace that every heart desires and awaits.

Cardinal Luis Ladaria, S.J.
President of the Pontifical Biblical Commission
30 September 2019, Feast day of St. Jerome.

Introduction

1. The history of humanity is marked by its incessant activity of enquiry. A wise man of Israel once said: "I, Qoheleth, have been king of Israel in Jerusalem. I have applied myself to seek out and investigate in wisdom everything under the sun. It is a wearisome business that God has given to human beings to occupy them" (Qoh 1:12-13). The desire to know constitutes without doubt one of the characteristics of the human being, recognised and valued already by the ancient philosophers because it enhances existence itself and makes it creative and useful. To the aspect of weariness underlined by Qoheleth should be added also therefore the illuminating discovery of truth and goodness (Wis 7:25-30). An ancient Hebrew proverb envisages for the king, as a symbol of the wise man, a task that is certainly onerous but at the same time glorious: "To conceal a matter is the glory of God, to sift it thoroughly, the glory of kings" (Prov 25:2). For his part Ben Sira praises the diligent work of the scribe who "delves into the wisdom of all the Ancients; he occupies his time with the prophecies, [...] researches into the hidden sense of proverbs; he ponders the obscurities of parables. [...] He travels in foreign countries; he has experienced human good and human evil" (Sir 39:1-4). The wise person strives to understand the sense of events, which at times take a dramatic turn, and at times are invested with hope; and in the mysterious process of history this person asks questions about the role of human beings, their origin, their duty and their destiny.

What is man?

2. Human beings examine the skies to understand their secrets and deduce omens from them; they travel the highways of the world searching for resources for one's life and wonders to contemplate; they investigate everything, continually asking questions. But in this continuous search the fundamental question is always the same: What is man?

The responses have been many, and as a consequence the books that have come down to us even from the distant past are numerous. They contain the fruits of the noble efforts of so many researchers bearing witness to a ray of the truth. In this literary heritage one particular work stands out. It is a work composed by a plurality of authors, the product of the same source of inspiration, and it displays a unique coherence, even though it was redacted by various hands over many centuries and subjected to the varied manifestations of contingent cultural values. The *Holy Bible* is a book which for believers has a value beyond compare because of its divine wisdom, capable of stirring up in the human heart a free and loving assent to the fullness of truth. This is because it is a book that comes from the reflective struggles of wise people, that testifies to conflicts, sufferings and great joys, that springs from the fruitfulness of the human heart, but that above all has its ultimate source in the inspiring breath of God. Sacred Scripture as a whole is "prophecy" which reveals to all, in illuminating truth, what a human being is (*Dei Verbum* § 21; *Gaudium et Spes* § 12).

Over the course of its extensive history, humanity has progressed in scientific knowledge, and has gradually refined its awareness of "human rights", showing a growing concern for minorities, the defenceless, the poor and the marginalised, fighting for the protection of the environment and for the historical heritage, and proposing ever more appropriate forms of civil coexistence. Notwithstanding the progress that can be seen above all in the technological sphere, and notwithstanding the continuous and marvellous rise of beneficial forces that are the leaven of universal society, it is clear to the attentive observer that today's society is going through a moment of spiritual crisis.

Gaudium et Spes (§§ 4-10) already recognised this, and underlined the difficulties and questions that need to be subjected to the light of the Word of God.

3. In a well known passage of the letter to the Romans regarding the impiety and injustice of human beings, Paul sees the root of moral degradation in the distortion of the relationship with God, which replaces devotion to the true Lord with acceptance of wretched and counterfeit beings: "claiming to be wise, they became foolish and exchanged the glory of the immortal God for the likeness of the image of a mortal human being, or of birds or animals or reptiles" (Rom 1:22-23). In our days this worship of worldly realities does not take the form of cultic idolatry; but the abandonment of the true God, presented even as a liberation and an achievement of which to boast, results in people becoming subject to false and unjust principles and rules (Rom 1:25). The lack of respect for God leads, according to Paul, to confusion in how one perceives the significance of the sexual human body, with the acceptance of unseemly passions (Rom 1:24, 26-27); and the whole of society is pervaded by disorder, violence, rebellion and ruthlessness (Rom 1:28-31). Such painful and dramatic phenomena characterise our world too, where the anthropological value of sexual difference is brought into question, and where the fragility of marital relationships and the spread of domestic violence are experienced; more generally one notes the increasing display of self-centred and domineering kinds of behaviour that give rise to cruel wars, as well as leading to instability on the planet, and disastrous forms of poverty and segregation.

Paul concludes his analysis saying that "those who behave like this [...] not only do it, but even applaud others who do the same" (Rom 1:32). But the desire for good that must animate every responsible person urges one to "speak", to pronounce that "truth" that is "suffocated by injustice" (Rom 1:18), rediscovering so to speak what human beings are, in their dignity and in their duties, beginning from the words that come to us from God himself.

The Catholic Church has used and continues to use every means to help people of good will to have the right perspective on what is good. In line with this, Pope Francis asked the Pontifical Biblical Commission to prepare a document on the theme of Biblical Anthropology. The Church has always founded its message on Scripture (*Dei Verbum* § 24), but until now no official writing has appeared that offers a complete panorama on what the human being is according to the Bible. The assignment of this important task demanded careful consideration of the best way to put forward what the Scriptures affirm on the theme of biblical anthropology.

A journey through biblical anthropology

4. This Document aims to present a faithful interpretation of the whole of Scripture on the theme of anthropology. This requires, on the one hand, that the directing principles guiding the study are set out, and, on the other, that the arrangement of the study be briefly presented so as to be of assistance to the reader.

Some hermeneutical principles

A synthesis of what the Bible says about anthropology requires that one keeps in mind some fundamental hermeneutical principles. Respect for the particular character of the sacred text studied must go hand in hand with the soundness of the methodological procedure.

Obedience to the Word of God

5. The Bible is the Word of God; it is prophecy to be heard and to be heeded with profound obedience (*Dei Verbum* § 5). This requires that one must neither "add" to nor "take away" from what has been revealed (Deut 4:2; 13:1; Jer 26:2; Apoc 22:18-19), and, in addition, that one interprets the sacred text with the same Spirit with which it was written (*Dei Verbum* § 12).

Interpretation is, or rather should be, an act of obedience. Obedience to what the author wished to communicate implies that one should know how to distinguish between what in the Bible is an integral part of Revelation and what is *provisional*, bound up with the mentality and customs of a specific historical period. It is rather easy to recognise that ritual prescriptions because of their symbolic nature undergo variations within the same biblical tradition and should be accepted for what they intended to signify and not according to the letter; the same can be said of legal norms, especially in the area of penal regulations, which have undergone many adjustments down the centuries up to the present day. The New Testament's contribution in relation to such points is clearly innovative, and for Christians has normative value. Discernment is more difficult in the case of concepts of an anthropological nature that do not match with what the human sciences have gradually discovered and theorised about. It is, therefore, a matter of being attentive to what the biblical text seeks to promote while bearing in mind the historical and cultural "conditionings" in which its pronouncements are rooted. In this challenging interpretative process one is naturally guided by the Spirit, who is active throughout the evangelical and apostolic tradition, by the *sensus fidei* of the Church, and by the authoritative insights of theologians, faithful to the utterances of the biblical text.

6. Obedience to Sacred Scripture is not to be restricted to its content alone, but is expressed also in the reception of the literary form in which the divine message was transmitted. The Bible is first and foremost the account of God's history with human beings, the story of the covenant, from the origins of the world up to the eschatological fullness. Scripture should not be seen as a collection of dogmatic assertions on God and humanity, but rather as the testimony of Revelation in history. What it expresses belongs mainly to the *symbolic* rather than the merely conceptual world; for this reason it facilitates and promotes a never ending work of interpretative actualisation, always faithful and always new (Mt 13:52).

This document on biblical anthropology, then, does not take the form of a conceptual grid predisposed a priori, based on theological schemes or according to principles dictated by the human sciences, but has as its programmatic base the *account of Gen 2-3* (read together with Gen 1), because of its paradigmatic value: this text condenses, in a certain sense, what is detailed in the rest of the Old Testament, and is seen as normative by Jesus and by the Pauline tradition. This account of the origins is to be read as a "*figure*" (*typos*), that is to say, as an attestation of an event of symbolic value that prophetically announces the sense of history up to its perfect fulfilment. The approach adopted will be one of *narrative theology*, an approach no less rigorous than that used in systematic theology.

Since it prefigures what will come to pass, the narrative of Gen 2-3, with its own literary form, introduces various thematic motifs which combine to delineate the profile of the human being according to the design of God and to envisage the global sense of human history. As we follow the narrative readings of the foundational text, then, the constitutive aspects of the human being gradually emerge; and, in an act of fidelity to Scripture, such aspects will be thematised, making use of the testimony of the Bible as a whole, and taking care to respect the different literary forms that contribute to the richness of the sacred text.

The totality of Scripture

7. If one wants to be obedient to the Word of God it is not appropriate to limit oneself to one part of Scripture, or to a text that is particularly suggestive or seen as more suited to the mentality of today. On the other hand, because of the variety of the Bible's literary genres and the different ideological perspectives that emerged in different epochs, it appears an absolutely impossible task to set out the anthropology of the *entire* Bible. Some are of the view that the complexity of the Bible rules out any attempt at creating an acceptable synthesis. And yet, if one values the truth of the Word of God, one should carry through the project of a *biblical theology* which, in a respectful and articulated way, expounds the message of the entire "prophecy" from the book of Genesis to the Apocalypse, from narrative prose to legal collections, from prophetic oracles to wisdom sayings, from the Psalter to the gospels and the apostolic letters.

The method with which the present document expresses its fidelity to the total message of Scripture is that of setting out how a specific aspect of anthropology, dictated by the narrative of Gen 2-3, is treated thematically in the principal sections in which the biblical books are organised. These sections will not be presented in the Document according to a diachronically developed scheme, which would be difficult to prove in any case, but as parts of the same whole, as pieces of the mosaic of Revelation. For the Old Testament, the tripartite division is traditional: (1) *Torah* (Pentateuch), with its specifically normative character; (2) *Prophets*, who reveal the sense of the history of the covenant, calling for conversion and revealing the divine intervention in human affairs; and (3) *Wisdom writings,* of a generally universal character, in which we find an important contribution to the understanding of human nature, with useful wise counsels. In this document, we have also, in a systematic way, paid special attention to (4) the *Psalter*, since certain values of great importance for anthropology are expressed in prayer. Consideration of the Old Testament will predominate in our discussion, not only because it is the larger part, from a textual point of view, but also because the New Testament accepts the principal anthropological affirmations of the ancient Scriptures. As regards the New Testament, we have adopted a simple two-part approach: on the one hand (1) we have considered the contribution of the *Gospels*, taking into account the example and teaching of Jesus, the teacher, highlighting especially their innovative aspects; on the other hand (2) we have presented in summary form what was transmitted by the *tradition of the Apostles*, especially by Paul, in the letters attributed to him, as a development and actualisation of the biblical message. Thus the aim of fidelity to the Word of God respects the significant particularities of the biblical text, and welcomes them to present them to the people of today as a salvific way of life.

The question "What is man?" is an example of our method of procedure.

8. The question "What is man?" is the title given to the present Document. With this one intends to express fidelity to the biblical text by adopting one of its formulae as well as its call to interrogate ourselves. We must begin from the question that sets in motion a process of investigation that will find its fulfilment in hearing what the Word of God suggests in the complexity of the inspired text, since the general question leads to a series of questions relating to each of the aspects in which the question of man is articulated.

If we limit ourselves to the precise formulation of the question "What is man?" we see that it occurs repeatedly and is interpreted in various ways, depending on the situations and the issues of the various human speakers. The foundation text, because of its liturgical roots, seems to be that of Ps 8:5: here, through the use of the interrogative form, the person praying expresses joyous wonder when considering how small the human creature is when compared with the sky (Ps 8:4), and yet this person is cared for by the Creator and crowned "with glory and honour", because the "son of man" dominates all living things (Ps 8:6-9): praise for the sublime Name of God is the beginning and the end of the entire contemplation (Ps 8:1, 10).

The same question is, in a certain sense, taken up in Ps 144:3; this time, however, it is not a basis for praise, but a support for the supplication, since the person praying is contemplating the fragile and precarious aspects of the human being (Ps 144:4; cf. also Sir 18:8-10), and thus making explicit the need to be helped in order to have life (Ps 144:5-8). We have before us, then, a form of "re-reading" of an identical literary motif, through which a fresh contribution is made to the understanding of faith.

The Wisdom tradition offers other aspects of meaning in relation to the same question, the fruit of various experiences. Citing Ps 8 indirectly, Job, in a certain sense, turns the perspective on its head (Job 7:17). Focussing on the weakness of every creature, he asks God to suspend that "visit", which to him appears as an investigation that is excessively scrupulous and even disrespectful of human misery (Job 7:18-21). In response, Eliphaz takes up the same question (Job 15:14), but to affirm that no one is pure before God, disputing, therefore, every claim for justice on the part of his friend (Job 15:15-16). And Sirach, echoing the questioning of the book of Job (Sir 18:8), reaffirms the dimension of the human being's weakness and insignificance but concludes with a reverential attitude of trust in the "mercy" of the Lord (Sir 18:11-14).

9. The examination could be extended to other Old Testament texts, which, though not formally presenting the question "What is man?", pose an analogous question. One thinks, for example, of the glorious figure of the king (Is 14:13-14), shameless in his proud arrogance (Is 14:16: "Is this the man who made the world tremble?"); or, by contrast, the questioning that arises from the contemplation of the face of the suffering and glorified Servant (Is 52:13-14). In the New Testament we see the question being put by Jesus to his disciples in relation to his own person: "who do people say the Son of man is?" (Mt 16:13), "But you, who do you say I am?" (Mt 16:15). The expression "son of man" present in Ps 8:5 evokes in the gospel a messianic dimension, as is evident from Peter's reply (Mt 16:16); the letter to the Hebrews, citing Ps 8, confirms this, declaring that the "crown of glory" is achieved in the death of Christ for the benefit of all (Heb 2:6-9). When Pilate presented Jesus, tortured to death, to the crowd, and exclaimed "Behold the man" (Jn 19:5), he attested, without realising it, the fulfilment of Revelation. In fact weakness and glory, instead of being opposed to one another, are joined already in the divine act of creation (Ps 8), and they find their perfect fulfilment in the salvific mystery of Christ, who is the exemplary revelation of the true sense of the human being. Believers welcome this sense in their own life, being called to be "conformed to the image of his Son", so that they are also "glorified" (Rom 8:29-30).

The human being in relationship

10. The Bible does not provide a definition of the essence of the human being, but rather an articulated consideration of what human beings are, involved as they are in multiple relationships. In other words, one can only grasp what Scripture reveals about the human being if one explores their relationships with the whole of reality. *Laudato Sì* of Pope Francis (§ 66) speaks of three fundamental relationships: with God, with our neighbour and with the earth. Others derive from these, such as the relationship to time, to work, to the law, to social institutions, and so on. It is certainly useful, therefore, to consider the constituent parts of the human being in itself, but this should always be seen in the context of a series of relationships, so that the human being is not considered only under those aspects that characterise one as a single individual, but also as a "son" or "daughter", of God and of humankind, and as a "brother" or "sister", and a collaborator responsible for the destiny of all. In this way the human being is understood in his or her "vocation", because only in justice and in love is the nature of the person realised. Such a consideration will be kept constantly in mind in the course of the present Document.

The human being in history

11. The Bible, as has been said, narrates the history of humanity with God, or better, of God with humanity. To account for this expository method and to grasp its meaning, it is not sufficient to make a presentation of biblical anthropology according to a static scheme, even one set at the original moment; it is essential rather to see the human being as the protagonist of a process, in which one is a receiver of favours and an active subject of decisions that determine the very meaning of one's being. Human beings can only be understood in the context of their global history. And, in this regard, one should not adopt a naive evolutionary model, that supposes never-ending progress, much less resort to contrary schemes, from the golden age to the present misery; nor should one assume the idea of cyclical repetition, that would attest the continual return of the same. Scripture speaks of a *history of the covenant*, and in it nothing is taken for granted; it is indeed the astonishing revelation of the unexpected, the incredible, the marvellous and even of the impossible, humanly speaking (Gen 18:14; Jer 32:27; Zech 8:6). Various journeys and different routes give us a glimpse of the meaning of history in the divine forging of a new covenant, in which the divine action accomplishes its masterpiece, because the human being freely consents to being made a participant in the divine nature. The Bible not only has the task of describing reality or of defining truths in an abstract way; it is the Word of God in so far as it is directed to human beings, so that they will make decisions, orientating their lives to the good that is God. Scripture welcomes the questions that arise from the human heart, examines them, directs them and brings them to the threshold of the choice that every single person is called to make. This decisive choice brings the complete fulfilment of the service of loving truth which belongs to the divine Word. The historical dimension and its fulfilment will be evoked in the various chapters of our Document. The fourth chapter in particular will present biblical anthropology in the form of a history of salvation.

A guide to the reading of the Document

12. The present Document is divided into four chapters. Its subdivision is dictated by the narrative reading of Gen 2-3.

The first chapter presents the human being as a *creature of God*. This is the first and fundamental "relationship" that draws attention both to the fact that the human being is made of "dust", and through the divine "breath" is a living being.

The second chapter illustrates the condition of the human being *in the garden*. Here are developed the themes of food, of work, and of the relationship with other living beings. In this way a series of important relationships contributes to the spelling out of the responsibility of the human being to adhere to the divine plan.

The general topic of the third chapter is the *interpersonal relationship*, which has its fundamental nucleus in marriage and which is developed in the complex web of family and social links. Many questions will be treated, such as the meaning of sexuality and its forms, at times imperfect or incorrect, the relationship between parents and children, the ethics of fraternity, in opposition to domination and wars. Some of these issues have received the attention of the Magisterium, as in the recent post-synodal Exhortation *Amoris Laetitia*. However, we have decided that in a general presentation of biblical anthropology an ordered synthesis of issues relating to the family should not be lacking.

The fourth chapter considers the *history of the human being* who disobeys the divine command, choosing the path of death; this episode, however, is linked to the divine intervention, which makes history an event of salvation.

The Introduction furnishes some principles that justify the expository nature of the Document, while the Conclusion completes the survey with some notes of a spiritual and pastoral character.

In practice, a passage of Gen 2-3 (in bold) is cited in each chapter, followed by a brief exegetical comment (in italics) which aims to highlight the thematic motifs that are to be developed. The treatment of the individual themes comes next, following systematically the indications of the various constitutive parts of Scripture, from the Old to the New Testaments. Additional developments will frequently be inserted (in a smaller font), to help the reader who wishes to explore matters further. For the biblical citations we adopt the text of the Revised New Jerusalem Bible with slight variations to reflect more faithfully the original text.

The reader may be interested in a particular biblical theme and, using the Thematic Index, may go immediately to the pages where it is discussed. It should be kept in mind, however, that each single aspect constitutes a part of the general treatment of biblical anthropology, which is adequately understood only in the work as a whole.

The spirit of the Document

13. The Word of God is light: it illuminates horizons of hope, because it reveals God who acts in history with his infinite power for good. When it admonishes, the Word effects healings; when it commands, it transforms hearts; when it makes promises, it brings joy. Anyone who welcomes the Word of God is showered with consolation, because that person hears the words of the prophet, who, as interpreter of the Saviour's merciful intent, proclaims "Console, O console my people [...] grass withers, a flower fades; but the word of our God stands firm for ever" (Is 40:1, 8).

A person's heart is gladdened not by a self-satisfied gaze at the world, but by humble adherence to the divine message. Consolation is received and passed on not by human pride in ingenious striving, but by the work of the Lord: "Blessed be the God and Father of our Lord Jesus Christ, the Father of mercies and the God of all consolation, who consoles us in all our affliction, so that we are able to console those in every hardship with the consolation with which we ourselves are consoled by God" (2 Cor 1:3-4).

This is the intention of the Word of God, and this is the spirit with which we offer this Document on biblical anthropology; contemplating the human being on whom God has lavished the inestimable riches of his grace gives us joy.

CHAPTER ONE

THE HUMAN BEING CREATED BY GOD

14. From "the beginning" (Gen 1:1) Sacred Scripture introduces the protagonist of its narrative exposition: God, seen in his creative action, especially in his privileged relationship with the human creature (*'ādām*). In Gen 1, in fact, the man and the woman constitute the summit of creation (Gen 1:31), while in the parallel and complementary account of Gen 2 *'ādām* is presented as the first work of the Creator, to whom all is subordinated. As a consequence, understanding the nature and calling of the person demands, according to the Bible, that one sets out firstly the human being's foundational relationship with the Lord, so as to explore the richness of its meaning.

> When speaking of the work of God, the origin of all things, the account of Gen 2 does not use the verb "to create" (*bārā'*), which occurs in the first account (Gen 1:1, 21, 27; 2:3), but makes use of synonyms such as "to make" (*'āśāh*: Gen 2:4, 18; cf. Gen 1:7, 16, 25-26, 31; 2:2-4) and "to form" (*yāṣar*: Gen 2:7, 8, 19; cf. Is 29:16; 43:7; 45:18; 64:7; Jer 10:16; Am 4:13; Ps 95:5). The biblical text, as has been said, certainly gives particular prominence to the creation of humanity; however, one should not overlook the importance of all the other works of the Creator, which in other texts are recalled as material for sapiential inquiry (Job 38-41), for admiring wonder (Sir 42:15-43:33), for contemplation and for praise (Ps 8; 104).

15. In Gen 2, in the account which, as stated in the Introduction, serves as a guide text for our exposition, God is the subject of two creative actions in relation to 'ādām, "forming" (v. 7a) and "breathing" (v. 7b). These two acts dictate the structure of the present chapter that will focus on two constitutive aspects of humankind: on the one hand, the origin of the human being "from the dust of the earth", and on the other, as a "living being" through the divine "breath".

The first motif, that of the precariousness of the human being, is experienced in modern western society with feelings of anguish and revolt, sometimes even with cynicism or desperation; in other cultures a sense of fatality and resignation has developed. The second motif, which points towards the specific quality of the human creature, has undergone a speculative development in philosophy through the concept of soul and spirit; today, with the progress of the neuro-sciences, there is the danger of reducing the person to a simple functional organ, explicable in terms of chemistry and biology. Biblical tradition has a message to communicate in relation both to human finiteness and to the spiritual worth of the person. In this regard it is necessary to keep the Creator always in mind, because without this original relationship it is not possible to account for the mystery of the human creature.

Gen 2:4-7

⁴At the time when the Lord God made earth and heaven, ⁵there was as yet no wild bush on the earth nor had any wild plant yet sprung up, for the Lord God had not sent rain on the earth, nor was there anyone to till the soil. ⁶Instead, water came up from the ground and watered all the face of the earth. ⁷The Lord God shaped man from the dust of the ground and breathed the breath of life into his nostrils, and man became a living being.

16. *In this account of creation, the first observation of the narrator indicates that in the beginning there was no vegetation (vv. 4b-5a); this lack is justified by the absence of*

rain and especially by the absence of a man ('ādām) capable of cultivating the soil ('ădāmāh) (v. 5b). The intention is thus to suggest that without man the other created realities are not significant. Moreover, through the play on words 'ādām and 'ădāmāh, which may be rendered with "human" and "humus", a close relationship is suggested between the earthly human being and the earth; this constitutive relationship, seen first and foremost in its functional aspect (in the task of cultivation), is then specified with a reference to the origin of man ('ādām), affirming that the human being was "formed" by the Lord God, with "the dust [taken] from the ground ('ădāmāh)" (v. 7). In this way the biblical narrator situates the "earthly" creature in the place where it exists, according to the saying "the heavens, the heavens belong to the Lord, but to the children of Adam he has given the earth" (Ps 115:16); at the same time allusion is made from the beginning to the insubstantiality of the human being, to human frailty, and to human mortality, which, as we shall see, is attested also in other biblical texts where dust is often associated with finiteness and death (Gen 3:19; 18:27). It is the hands and the breath of God that give cohesion and life to what is ephemeral, fragile and insubstantial (Gen 2:7b).

17. In this sense, the image of the potter, evoked by the verb "to shape" (yāṣar), used to describe the Lord's work, assuredly recalls the delicacy of the gestures and the very close attention of the creator towards the creature he has formed (Is 29:16; Jer 18:1-6; Sir 33:13). This leads the reader to accept a fundamental truth: although created from the earth and made for it, the human being is not simply a child of the earth, nor the result of chance, because one's origin and one's vocation lie in the loving design of God, creator and saviour.

Such a truth is expressed, with different terminology, also in the first account of creation, where the triple use of the verb bārā' (to create) in reference to humanity (Gen 1:27) highlights the unique character of the human being with respect to the rest of creation, as if, with such a work, God had made something totally new. In support of this interpretation it should, on the one hand, be noted that the biblical narrator makes the reader a participant in the secret divine deliberation ("Let us make humankind ['ādām]", Gen 1:26), the sign of a narrative turning point of great importance; on the other hand, it is said that humanity is created at the end of the sixth day, after God had prepared everything for them, so that humanity is the masterpiece of the creatures made by God.

18. In Gen 2, after the first act of forming man from the dust (making use probably of the "water [that] came up from the ground", v. 6), the narrative mentions another divine action: "he breathed the breath of life (nišmat ḥayyîm) into his nostrils; and man became a living being (nepeš ḥayyāh)"(v. 7b). This "breath of life" is not simply the breathing that permits the human being to live; the fact that it is not said that the animals, also formed from the soil (Gen 2:19), possess it, leads the reader towards another interpretation: this special "breath of life" establishes a fundamental distinction between the animal world and human beings. The latter can live only by receiving the divine breath, and its acceptance gives them a unique status. But, as we shall see, there are other characteristics that distinguish the human being from the other creatures with which one has to live in harmony: the human being, privileged interlocutor of God and custodian of a special mission (Gen 2:15), is the beneficiary of that special divine gift that makes one a relational being (Gen 2:18, 22-24), endowed with speech (Gen 2:20, 23), liberty and responsibility.

Finiteness and greatness characterise the biblical authors' vision of the human being, who is recognised as a creature – not therefore a creator of oneself – bound to the dust and the earth, fragile and threatened by death, yet joined to the Creator by a special and unique relationship. A creature among the other creatures, the human being is nevertheless in a relationship of responsibility towards the other beings that form part of one's world: this also is the greatness of the human being.

Terminology
19. In the present Document we will sometimes use the term "man", inclusive of both male and female, as a synonym for

"human being". The context will clarify the sense to be attributed to this term that in itself is ambiguous. In any case even in the Hebrew Bible the term *'ādām* sometimes refers to the human being in general (Gen 1:27) and sometimes to the male (Gen 2:19, 23); this also holds true for the noun *'îš*, which for the most part designates "man" in contrast to "woman" (*'iššāh*) (Gen 2:24), but in certain cases has the sense of "whoever", and consequently indicates every human person (Gen 9:5).

The biblical tradition generally considers man as a being that exists in the body and is unthinkable outside it. Even if in some texts, as in the account of Gen 2:4-7, *'ādām* (that is, the human being) is described through the juxtaposition of two constitutive elements, dust and breath, these cannot be considered autonomous and separate entities. It is in the flesh that human beings live that spiritual experience that marks them out from all other living beings.

20. In the *Hebrew Bible*, to designate the (human) person, terms are used that refer to the body, its organs and to its various bodily manifestations. The term "flesh" (*bāśār*) is used, as in Gen 2:23; 6:12-13, 17, not to indicate a part of the human being, but rather the very nature of the person as a weak, vulnerable and mortal being (Is 40:6-7). The term "blood" (*dām*) is used as a synonym for "life" (Gen 9:4; Lev 17:11, 14), and in many cases it defines a person, especially from the aspect of one's vulnerability (Ps 72:14; Prov 1:18). The noun *nepeš*, translated sometimes with "soul", has in reality as its prime significance "the throat", the breathing organ and the seat of the experience of thirst. Accordingly it is the noun used as a symbolic expression of desire (Ps 42:2) and of "life" itself (Gen 1:30; 9:5; Ps 16:10). Another anthropological term often associated with *nepeš* (1 Sam 1:15; Is 26:9; Job 7:11; 12:10) is *rûăh*, which designates in the first place the "wind" and in derived fashion the life-giving "breath". When it refers to the human being it indicates the divine breath that makes it live, as is said in the psalm: "You hide your face, they are dismayed; you take away their breath (*rûăh*), they die, returning to the dust" (Ps 104:29). Something analogous is valid for other organs of the body such as the heart (*lēb*), kidneys, bones, and entrails, which point to the intimate and hidden principle of feelings, decisions and spiritual experiences. In the poetic texts, in fact, such terms are often used together and in parallel to signify the person, especially from the point of view of one's greatest value, that of the relationship with God. And so the person praying affirms: "My soul (*nepeš*) is longing and yearning for the courts of the Lord. My heart (*lēb*) and my flesh (*bāśār*) cry out to the living God" (Ps 84:2); "Therefore my spirit (*rûăḥ*) fails, my heart (*lēb*) is desolate within me" (Ps 143:4); "At night my soul (*nepeš*) longs for you and my spirit (*rûăḥ*) within me eagerly seeks you" (Is 26:9).

21. With the translation into Greek of the Hebrew Bible (LXX), and especially with the *literature of the New Testament*, one encounters innovation in terminology and some semantic movement all due to a different linguistic system, and to lexical and conceptual borrowings from contemporary philosophical currents. Firstly, we find the term "body" (*sōma*), which on occasions is identified as "flesh" (*sarx*) (2 Cor 4:10-11); the latter noun can be equivalent to "human being" (Gal 2:16), and is often used to suggest elements of human fragility (Rom 6:19; 2 Cor 4:11; Gal 4:13; Eph 2:14), sometimes even of impulsive attractions contrary to the spirit (Jn 6:63; Rom 8:5-8; Gal 3:3; 5:16-19; 6:8; Eph 2:3). The term "soul" (*psychē*) indicates not so much the immaterial element of the person, as in Greek philosophy, but rather the living dimension of the human being (Mt 10:28; 1 Cor 15:44). The noun *pneuma*, on the other hand, is used, as much in Paul as in other writings of the New Testament, both of the divine Spirit and of the human spirit in so far as it is capable of a relationship with the transcendent (Mt 5:3; 1 Cor 6:17). Alongside the more markedly intellectual terms such as "mind" (*nous*) and "conscience" (*syneidēsis*) (1 Cor 1:10; Rom 7:23; 1 Cor 8:7-13), we find the term "heart" (*kardia*), which, in continuity with the Hebrew concept, designates the centre of the person, as the seat of feelings (Rom 9:2; 10:1; 2 Cor 2:4; 6:11; Phil 1:7), of innermost thoughts (Rom 8:27; 1 Cor 4:5; 14:25; 1 Thess 2:4) and of religious and moral decisions (Mk 7:21; Rom 10:9; 1 Cor 7:37; 2 Cor 9:7).

1. THE HUMAN BEING MADE OF EARTH

22. The Genesis account, briefly commented upon above, evokes, in a few lines, some defining elements of the human being, whose specific nature is later illustrated by the biblical tradition with a great richness of terms and images. Basically, however, the idea remains that the human being is a mystery, an amazing wonder (Ps 71:7; 139:14-15), the object of continuous reflective enquiry, precisely because it brings together contrasting and paradoxical traits. The human being, image of God (Gen 1:26-27), placed as lord in the garden of Eden (Gen 2:9, 15), is in fact made of dust, because taken from the earth and destined to return to it (Gen 2:7; 3:19). The human being is "flesh", in other words, fragile and ephemeral (Gen 6:3; Is 40:6; Jer 17:5; Ps 56:5; 78:38-39; Sir 14:17-18; 17:1), and yet dominates over other living beings. A privileged creature, destined to subdue the earth (Gen 1:26-28), the human being is nevertheless bearer of a life that is constantly threatened. Humankind, in fact, is structurally confronted with death. Of this the Scriptures give abundant testimony.

The experience of human perishability

23. It is the *wisdom tradition* that makes plain, with much insistence, the drama of human perishability (Sir 40:1-11; 41:10); in this literature thoughts and feelings take shape that arise from the human being's concrete earthly experience.

Particularly significant in this regard is the book of *Job*, which presents the protagonist as a typical representative of one who grapples with the meaning of suffering. Introduced with no details of space and time, merely that he is from Uz, Job is a paradigmatic figure, in whom each person can recognise oneself. Struck by a remarkable series of calamities which deprive him of all his possessions, his children and finally his health, and bring him to the threshold of death, Job begins his lament and his argument with God, refusing the destiny that is assigned to him, and desiring never to have been born or to be already at peace in Sheol (Job 3:11-16; 10:18). Life, Job asserts, is marked by trouble and pain (Job 3:24-26; 7:1-3; 14:1-2; cf. also Sir 40:1-8), and finally by death (Job 7:6-10).

> **24.** In the oldest wisdom texts, as also in the traditions of the Old Testament as a whole, we find no explicit reference to the text of Gen 3:19, where, according to a rather common interpretation (based on Gen 2:17), death would be presented as a consequence of the sin committed by the first man. Only in the late text of Wis 2:24 is it noted that "death came into the world through the devil's malice", without, however, implying, as will happen in some areas of Pauline theology, a universal involvement in guilt. If in Scripture it is asserted that "the wages of sin are death" (Rom 6:23), this does not imply that every death, or all suffering, should be seen as a consequence of some personal guilt (cf. Lk 13:1-6; Jn 9:2-3). The friends of Job seek to justify the misfortunes that befall their friend in a line of thought based on the strict law of retribution (Job 4:7-9, 17-20; 8:20; 11:11; 15:14-16; 22:4-9; etc.), but they receive from the protagonist a reasoned refutation (Job 7:20; 9:29-31; 16:17-19; 29-31); God himself, in any event, will approve the words of his "servant Job" (Job 42:7).

25. Death is in fact the real problem of the human being, who alone is capable of painfully perceiving one's own precariousness; and it is against this reality, masterfully defined as "the king of terrors" (Job 18:14), that Job struggles and debates. In his dialogues with the three friends, the anguished vision of the human being as mortal, perishable and ephemeral repeatedly emerges. Various images are used in the book to express this reality: the life of the human being is like a breath (Job 7:7, 16), a flower of brief duration (Job 14:1-2), a fleeting shadow (Job 8:9; 14:2); a creature formed of clay and destined for the dust (Job 10:9), the human being goes towards death like a cloud that vanishes (Job 7:9). One's days "pass more swiftly than a runner; they flee away with never a glimpse of happiness, they skim past like a reed canoe, like an eagle swooping on its prey"

(Job 9:25-26). They slip by swifter than a weaver's shuttle, and come to their end without hope (Job 7:6). Suffering, the anticipation of death, forces one to confront one's own precariousness and, removing every illusion, places each one before a destiny essentially marked by the end. Even if religious tradition had reiterated that God uses the rod as a corrective tool (Prov 3:11-12; Job 5:17-18; 33:19; Heb 12:7-11; Apoc 3:19), suggesting in this way that pain can have a beneficial purpose (Prov 13:24; 22:15; 23:13-14; 29:15), the fact remains that death contradicts a positive pedagogical intent (Job 14:7-10; 17:15-16).

26. For *Qoheleth*, too, death is the great enigma, a reality that seems to undermine everything: "vanity of vanities; all is vanity" is the book's refrain (Qoh 1:2, 14; 2:1, 11; etc.). Everything seems useless, because all equally die (Qoh 3:18-20), indeed they are already dying, given that human life is nothing but a moving towards death (Qoh 1:4; 6:3-6; 9:10; 12:5); in synthesis, "everything comes from the dust, everything returns to the dust" (Qoh 3:20; cf. also Sir 17:1-4; 40:11; 41:10), and no memory will remain of the departed (Qoh 1:11; 2:16). If the human being, although experiencing multiple and original expressions of vitality, is in reality walking towards death, then every difference with other beings disappears, the world becomes senseless, and wisdom and length of days are useless, because the same inevitable fate has already marked every living being (Qoh 2:15-16; 3:19; 8:10, 14; 9:2). The sage invites one to accept with simplicity and gratitude the passing joys of a life marked by the ephemeral (Qoh 2:24; 3:12-13, 22; 5:17; 8:15; cf. also Sir 14:14), but this does not take from human life its intrinsic tragic nature. The poetic sophistication with which the end of human life is described in the final chapter of Qoheleth does not eliminate the bitterness of knowing oneself to be mortal (Sir 41:1). The images are of a rare beauty but suffused with deep melancholy:

"Remember your Creator while you are still young,
before the bad days come [...]
before the silver thread snaps
or the golden bowl is cracked,

> or the pitcher shattered at the fountain,
> or the pulley broken at the well head –
> the dust returns to the earth from which it came
> and the spirit returns to God who gave it."
>
> (Qoh 12:1, 6-7)

With death, silence invades everything. Certainly, there is the justice of God who distinguishes between the wicked and the just (Qoh 3:17; 11:9; 12:14), and the book teaches that human beings must live in fear of the Lord (Qoh 3:14; 5:6; 7:18; 8:12-13; 12:13; cf. also Prov 14:26-27), but death, already imprinted on the human journey, seems nevertheless to have the power to render everything vain.

27. However, the wisdom tradition goes on to say, death does not have the last word. The horror experienced in the face of the inexorability of the end reveals in reality that the human being is made for life; and the sage, who poses questions on the meaning of existence, discovers finally that the human being is destined for immortality. It is the book of *Wisdom*, the final contribution to the reflective tradition of the Old Testament, that makes explicit this bright future of hope for the just. The author, who by a literary fiction presents himself as the wise king Solomon, speaks in particularly perceptive terms of his reality as a creature:

> "I too am mortal like everyone else,
> a descendant of the first man formed from the earth.
> I was modelled in flesh inside a mother's womb [...]
> I too, when I was born, drew in the common air,
> I fell on the same ground that bears us all,
> and crying was the first sound I made like everyone else [...]
> for there is only one way into life and one way out of it."
>
> (Wis 7:1, 3, 6)

But unlike the fools who, with the excuse of the brevity of life, give themselves over to the carefree enjoyment of the "good things that are", without any respect for the poor and the just (Wis 2:1-20; cf. also Ps 73:3-12), the true sage is aware of possessing an immortal destiny (3:4; 4:1; 8:13, 17; 15:3). The just one, in fact, even if persecuted and condemned by the wicked to a shameful and painful death (Wis 2:19-20), even dying before due time (Wis 4:7), is in fact secure in the hands of God (Wis 3:1), who is the "lover of life" (Wis 11:26). From here there is an opening to eternity:

> "No! God created us (*ton anthrōpon*) for immortality,
> made us as the image of his own eternity;
> death came into the world through the devil's malice
> as those on his side must discover.
> But the souls (*psychai*) of the righteous are in the hands of God,
> and no torment can touch them. [...]
> and if in human eyes they were being punished,
> their hope was rich with immortality."

(Wis 2:23–3:1, 4)

28. Already in the drama of Job an opening appeared that allowed a glimpse of a response to the great question of the suffering of the just, and death. At the end of the book (Job 38-41), in fact, when God presents to his opponent the picture of the creation of all things, before the eyes of Job the consoling vision of the created world unfolds there where human existence continues and where that explosion of life is displayed that can only have originated from an omnipotent and wise God (Job 42:2-3). In this way the individual who suffers can emerge from the darkness of anguish, becoming reconciled to an existence marked even by death. And, while confessing one's own insignificance (Job 40:4), can bring out the greatness of the human being as an interlocutor of God. It is in fact by accepting one's own finiteness, no longer perceived as a threat, but as a place of truth and of relationship, that human beings, fleeting breath and ephemeral flower that lasts just a day, can finally recognise themselves as such, and recognise God as God: "I knew you only by hearsay, but now my own eyes have seen you" (Job 42:5). Qoheleth declared with more humility: "God is in heaven, you on earth" (Qoh 5:1), but this affirmation contains implicitly a seed of hope, because the God of the heavens has "the power of life and death"; he leads mortals "to the gates of Hades and back again" (Wis 16:13; cf. also Deut 32:39; 1 Sam 2:6; 2 Kgs 5:7; Tob 13:2); "for God did not make death, he takes no pleasure in the destruction of the living. He created all things to exist. The generative forces of the world bring salvation; in them there is no fatal poison, nor is Hades king of the world" (Wis 1:13-14).

The people of Israel in the desert

29. For the biblical writer the consciousness of human fragility is rooted in the experience of the people of Israel, with whom the Lord is bound in a privileged relationship (called "covenant"). A well-defined period of history, narrated in the *Torah*, played a determining role in this realisation, which came about after the crossing of the Red Sea when the liberated slaves made a long journey in the desert to the land of Canaan. The great events and the dramas that for forty years dotted this pilgrimage in a desolate and hostile world will have a lasting place in the memory of Israel, and will constitute a fundamental theological reference point of the biblical tradition and something of a symbol of the whole of human existence. Even if the people down the centuries progress in making everyday life less precarious, constructing houses in place of tents, and cultivating the soil instead of gathering the manna (Deut 6:10-12; 8:11-16; Josh 5:12), the desert must always be remembered (Deut 8:2), because the human being remains a pilgrim on this earth (Lev 25:23; Ps 39:13; 1 Chr 29:15; Heb 11:13), and one's authentic life depends not on "bread", but rather on the breath that comes from the mouth of God (Deut 8:3).

In the time of the desert the "fathers" suffered day after day because of the precariousness of life, dependent as they were on the presence or absence of a well, reliant on an improbable meal, exposed to the risks of their nomadic lifestyle and to encounters with dangerous enemies (Ex 17:8-16; Deut 8:15); in a place from which they could not escape unless they remained united and supportive of one another, the Hebrews experienced recriminations, divisions and rebellions. And yet, they will never forget that it is in this very place of fear and death that their ancestors experienced the solicitous presence of their God, without which they would not have survived (Jer 2:2-3, 6). Thus the episode of the manna and the quails (Ex 16:1-35), or that of the waters of Meribah (Num 20:1-11), when the water gushed from the rock in abundance for the community and the animals, will remain forever imprinted in the memory of Israel, clear instances of the providence of the one who, in the desert, responded to insecurity and danger with the daily gift of food and with unfailing protection (Deut 8:2-4; 29:4-7; 32:10-12).

30. Limiting oneself to this consoling memory, however, signifies undervaluing the fact that amidst the trials and difficulties of the journey, the one-time slaves began to pine for "the fish [...], the cucumbers, melons, leeks, onions, and garlic" which they ate in Egypt (Num 11:4-5), as if they preferred the limited benefits of past oppression to the stupendous liberty that had been granted them. In the desert they accused God and his envoys (Moses and Aaron, in particular) of having dragged them into a deadly venture (Num 14:2-4), demonstrating in this way that in the face of deprivation or the unexpected, it is not easy to accept insecurity and to advance on the journey of faith. The episode of the golden calf, with the request directed to Aaron: "Come, make us a god to go at our head" (Ex 32:1), is a dramatic illustration of this. The idol that was made and venerated revealed their desire to escape the unknown and to evade dependence on God. While the image of the bull calf is reassuring, it reduces the divinity to a degraded image of the living God (Ps 106:20).

Such an experience of weakness is part of the human story; and, according to the biblical tradition, the "fathers" died in the desert because of their rebellion. But for the "children" the promise sworn by the Lord was fulfilled, and they were able to enter the good land, symbol of a full life (Deut 1:39). All this is then put forward by Scripture as a collective symbol of the entire course of human existence (Is 48:21).

The prayer of the mortal human being

31. In the biblical tradition, and in particular in the *Psalter*, the fragility of the human being is taken up in prayer that becomes a desire directed to the eternal and good God, attentive to human weakness. In several psalms the awareness of human perishability is often expressed through poetic images that echo those of the wisdom tradition: the human being is only a breath (Ps 39:6, 7, 12; 62:10; 144:4), a gust of wind (Ps 78:39), grass of the field and a flower that immediately fades (Ps 37:2; 90:5-6; 102:12; 103:15-16), an unreal dream (Ps 90:5), a sigh (Ps 90:9), a fading shadow (Ps 102:12; 109:23; 144:4), dust (Ps 103:14) that returns to dust (Ps 104:29).

Ps 90 is a particularly significant example of such an anthropological vision. In the opening verses, having proclaimed the powerful and provident eternity of God (vv. 1-2), the psalmist contrasts with it the perishability and inherent fragility of the human being:

> "You turn people (*'enôš*) back to dust,
> and say, 'Return, O children of Adam (*bᵉnê 'ādām*)' [...]
> You sweep them away like a dream,
> like grass which is fresh in the morning.
> In the morning it springs up fresh,
> by evening it withers and fades [...]
> All our days pass away in your wrath.
> Our years are consumed like a sigh.
> Seventy years is the span of our days,
> or eighty if we are strong.
> And most of these are toil and pain.
> They pass swiftly and we are gone."

(Ps 90:3, 5-6, 9-10)

Human life is marked by limits, the human being is dust and into dust returns, in obedience to the command of God: "Return, O children of Adam". These, in fact, are the only words that God utters in the psalm, almost an echo of Gen 3:19. However, acknowledgement of one's mortal condition is for the person praying a reason for wise reflection: "teach us to number our days, that we may gain wisdom of heart" (v. 12; cf. also Ps 39:5; Job 38:21; Sir 17:2; 18:9-10). To recognise ourselves as perishable, different from God, as creatures marked by finiteness, this indeed is true wisdom. At the same time, the short-lived human beings entrust themselves to the power of the Lord.

> "At dawn, fill us with your merciful love;
> we shall exult and rejoice all our days.
> Give us joy for all the days of our affliction,
> for the years when we looked upon evil. [...]
> Let the favour of the Lord our God be upon us."
>
> (Ps 90:14-15, 17)

32. The human being who prays is conscious of being weak and mortal, and on this condition weaves a lament and a tearful supplication (Ps 42:4; 56:9; 102:10). The condition of precariousness is experienced in particular by those who live in economic poverty (Ps 74:19; 86:1), those who are alone and without help (Ps 22:12; 25:19; 38:12), who are weakened by old age (Ps 71:9, 18), or surrounded by numerous and cruel enemies (Ps 3:2-3; 22:17; 69:5). When the threat of death becomes real, imminent, dramatic (Ps 22:15-16), the prayer to God becomes a desperate "cry" (Ps 13:2-3; 22:2-3), which, however, never ceases to be a confident appeal (Ps 22:23-25), open to the certainty that in the end the life-giving power of the benevolent God will triumph (Ps 27:13; 49:16; 73:23-24; 116:9). This is typically expressed in Ps 16:

> "And so, my heart rejoices, my soul is glad;
> even my body shall rest in hope.
> For you will not abandon my soul to Sheol,
> nor let your faithful see corruption.
> You will show me the path of life,
> the fullness of joy in your presence,
> at your right hand, bliss for ever."
>
> (Ps 16:9-11)

A creature of clay, terrified by death, the human being is made for immortality (Wis 2:23). The God who created the human being is the faithful God who accompanies his creature as the generations take their course (Ps 27:13; 116:9; 142:6), revealing himself as refuge, help and saviour (Ps 18:3; 30:11; 55:17; 63:8; etc.). It is in fact the evildoers who are like chaff scattered by the wind (Ps 1:4), vanishing like smoke (Ps 37:20); the righteous are given lasting vitality (Ps 1:3; 92:13-15). In prayer the human being opens up to a promise of eternity, because in confessing one's faith the mortal being surrenders to the Lord of life (Ps 30:4; 49:16).

God makes known the way of life

33. The *prophetic tradition* transmits the revelation of God to those who question themselves about the reason for a life that is short and marked by death; at the same time, the voice of the Lord offers a consoling promise to those who in their plight pray for heavenly assistance. The prophetic literature made two main contributions in relation to the theme of human precariousness.

Against foolish human pride

The first contribution of the prophets presents itself in sapiential form as a *warning* directed to the powerful. It takes the form of an invitation to consider the contingency of every human being as the essential truth that gives access to the "fear of God", the principle of wisdom and therefore of life (Prov 1:7; 9:10; 15:33; Job 28:28; Sir 1:14). The failure to recognise the "created" nature of the human being is made explicit in history as an arrogant presumption and even as contempt for the work of God. For this reason, Isaiah, opposing the pseudo-wisdom of the sages of Jerusalem and criticising their foolish claim of impunity, evokes the image of the clay and the potter:

> "Woe to those who burrow deep
> to conceal their plans from the Lord,
> whose deeds are in the dark so they say,

'Who can see us? Who knows about us?'
How perverse you are!
Is the potter no better than the clay?
As if what was made could say of its maker,
'He did not make me.'
Or a pot say of the potter,
'He does not know his job.'"

(Is 29:15-16; cf. also Is 45:9; Ps 94:8-11)

34. An extraordinary endowment of intelligence, wealth and power gives the human being the illusion of being equal to God. To expose this deception of conscience the Lord predicts the inglorious end of the arrogant (Is 47:7-11; Zeph 2:15). This is admirably announced by Ezekiel in an oracle against the king of Tyre:

"Thus says the Lord God:
Because your heart has grown proud
and you have said,
'I am a god;
I am divinely enthroned in the heart of the seas.'
Though you are human and no god, [...]
see, I am bringing foreigners against you,
the most barbarous of nations. [...]
Will you insist on saying, 'I am a god',
in the face of your killers?
You will be human and no god
in the hands of those who strike you down!"

(Ezek 28:2, 7, 9; cf. also Is 14:10-15; 51:12;
Ezek 31:1-14; Acts 12:21-23)

The wise and salvific action of the Lord will be shown therefore in history as a systematic humiliation of the proud (Is 2:17, 22) and as a raising up of the humble (Is 29:19; cf. 1 Sam 2:3-10; Ps 138:6; Job 22:29; Sir 11:12-13; Lk 1:51-53). This is not a simple historical application of the law of retaliation but an affirmation of the truth of the human being in relation to the revelation of God's glory

(1 Sam 2:3-8; Is 26:5-6; Lk 1:52-53). God in fact chooses what is small, weak and incapable precisely because in it can be revealed the quality of mercy of the omnipotent Lord of life (Is 41:14; 52:13-15; cf. Mt 11:25-27).

The promise of life

35. The second contribution of prophecy comes accordingly as a word of *consolation* (Is 40:1) to those who experience the precariousness of existence, as happened in the case of the people of Israel when exiled in a foreign land. The image of the grass of the field, symbol of ephemeral life, is contrasted with the manifestation of an irrepressible force for life:

> "All humanity is grass
> and all its beauty like the wild flower. [...]
> Grass withers, a flower fades,
> but the word of our God stands firm for ever."
>
> (Is 40:6, 8)

The glory of God reveals itself (Is 40:5) wherever weakness welcomes in faith the power of the Lord, which manifests itself as a regenerating word; sent by the Most High, the word does not return to him without having accomplished what it was sent to do (Is 55:10-11). The desert will bloom (Is 35:1), the blind, the deaf and the lame will recover full vitality (Is 35:5-6). Even when the afflicted believe that all hope is lost (Ezek 37:11), the prophetic voice rings out to announce the coming of a Spirit capable of giving life back to dry bones (Ezek 37:1-10). God in fact promises: "I am now going to open your graves; I shall raise you from your graves, my people, [...] and put my spirit in you, and you shall live" (Ezek 37:12-14). The breath of the Lord, which in the beginning had formed from the dust a living being (Gen 2:7), is at work in history giving life to an exhausted people. Isaiah, too, interprets the miracle of a wonderful rebirth when he writes:

> "Your dead will come back to life,
> their corpses will rise again.

Wake up and sing, you dwellers in the dust,
for your dew will be a radiant dew,
and the earth will give birth to the shades."

(Is 26:19)

Future generations will find nourishment in this consoling
announcement; Daniel will reiterate it with the announcement of
the resurrection of the just (Dan 12:2-3); and the mother of the
Maccabees will attest it at the very moment in which her sons are
subjected to torture (2 Macc 7:20-23). The revelation of the New
Testament follows the same prophetic trail (Acts 3:24-26; 23:6-8).
The person of Elijah, taken up by the Lord in a chariot of fire (2
Kgs 2:11), will become the prefiguration of the glorious destiny of
the saved (1 Thess 4:17).

The help of Jesus of Nazareth in the face of human weakness

36. The New Testament welcomes, as just mentioned, the religious
legacy of the ancient scriptures, and adds to them the gift of a
new and decisive revelation, when it attests that in Christ all the
promises of life predicted by the prophets are fulfilled (Mt 8:16-
17; Lk 24:27, 44; Acts 3:18). Indeed it is he the Word who gives
life to all flesh (Jn 1:4; Jam 1:18; 1 Pt 1:23-25); it is he who pours
out the Spirit through which mortals rise to new and imperishable
life (Rom 8:11). Only God can work wonders of such a nature (Jn
3:2; 9:33); because of this Jesus of Nazareth, a man among human
beings, is recognised as "Son of God" (Mt 14:33; Mk 1:1; Lk 1:35;
Jn 11:27; etc.).

In the *gospel accounts* the fragility and precariousness of the
human being are expressed in different ways; they are constantly
presented by the evangelists with the intention of exalting, by
way of contrast, the divine power (*dynamis, exousia*) of the Lord
Jesus (Mt 9:8; Lk 5:17; 24:19; Jn 17:2), and of pointing out to those
who have lost heart (Mt 11:28) a source of sure hope. Human
perishability is illustrated above all by *sickness*, a presentiment of

death when it takes the form of fever (Mk 1:30), dropsy (Lk 14:1-4), "weakness" (*astheneia*), a symptom of endangered health (Mk 6:56; Lk 9:2; Jn 4:46), the loss of blood (Mk 5:25-29) or the terrible plague of leprosy (Mk 1:40; Lk 17:11-19). There are also situations of *disability* such as blindness (Mk 8:22-25; 10:46-52), deafness (Mk 7:31-37), paralysis of the hand (Mk 3:1-5) or feet (Mk 2:1-12), sometimes over an extended period (Jn 5:5) and in certain cases congenital (Jn 9:1), situations that make it impossible to carry out activities worthy of the human being: the quality of life is so radically undermined here as to condemn such persons to a miserable existence. In other gospel accounts *situations of grave danger* are narrated, as when the crowds find themselves in the desert, hungry and deprived of resources (Mk 6:36-44; 8:1-9), or when the boat with the disciples is violently struck by the storm (Mk 4:35-41); the hostility of enemies towards the followers of Jesus also constitutes a specific threat to life (Mt 10:17-25; Jn 16:2). Finally, people can live in the condition of *slavery* when they are subjected to insidious forces (Mt 17:15), identified as evil spirits, which take possession of the human being (Mt 9:32-34; Mk 5:1-13; 9:14-27; Lk 8:2; 13:10-17).

37. Christ "visits" (Lk 7:16) this diversified weakness, curing the sick, healing the maimed, saving from mortal danger, liberating the possessed, and even *raising the dead* (Mk 5:35-43; Lk 7:11-17; Jn 11:38-44). In the history of Israel other men of God had received similar powers from the Lord: to Moses was given the power to heal lepers (Num 12:9-15), Elijah and Elisha performed various miraculous deeds (1 Kgs 17:10-16; 2 Kgs 4:1-7, 38-44; etc.) and raised the dead (1 Kgs 17:17-24; 2 Kgs 4:18-37); it is also said of Isaiah that he cured King Hezekiah with a strange poultice of figs (2 Kgs 20:7). But what the gospel tradition attests above all is that Jesus' work of healing and regeneration is not limited to an occasional intervention but constitutes the essence of his mission (Mk 2:17; Lk 4:16-21; Acts 2:22; 10:38) and the daily exercise of his ministry (Mk 1:32-34; 6:54-56; Mt 9:35). The various infirmities and weaknesses are healed by the Saviour; and the vulnerable people, Jews or pagans (Mk 7:24-30; Mt 8:5-13), are given back their lives, if their prayer is animated by authentic faith (cf. Mt 13:58). Moreover, Christ's divine power is handed on by him to his disciples, who are sent into the world with the same powers of healing, liberation and regeneration, so that history is forever marked by the salvific action of God (Mt 10:1, 8; Acts 2:43; 3:1-10; 9:36-41; etc.).

All this is astonishing (Mk 2:12) and so is declared by the evangelists to be the "messianic" fulfilment, the coming of the Kingdom of God (Mt 11:2-5; Lk 11:20). The human person, fearful of the prospect of dying and depressed by weakness, is lovingly healed in the flesh, but above all internally revived: faith in Christ liberates people from fear (Mk 5:36; 6:50; Mt 10:26, 28, 31; Jn 14:1, 27; Heb 2:15) and fills them with hope, enabling them to praise God in a sincere and enduring way (Mt 9:8; Mk 2:12; Lk 5:25-26; etc.), provided that they understand the meaning of the activity of Jesus, and his apostles, and attribute to the saving events accomplished in history the significance of a *"sign" (sēmeion)*.

38. This is a category used by the evangelists – in a critical sense also (cf. Mt 12:38-39) – and is highlighted especially by John (Jn 2:11, 23; 4:54; 6:2, 14; etc.). In healing a man blind from birth, Jesus did something unheard of (Jn 9:32), but his action was intended primarily to manifest himself as the light of the world, so that only belief in him truly gives access to life (Jn 1:9; 8:12; 9:5; 12:36). Lazarus came out of the tomb, but returned there, as is the destiny of every mortal; through the extraordinary miracle of the raising of a dead person, Christ revealed that he is "the resurrection and the life" (Jn 11:25). Similarly, the healing of a paralytic is a sign of the forgiveness of sins (Mt 9:1-8), the multiplication of the loaves in the desert is a prophetic type of the gift itself of Christ in his body (Jn 6:51), and so on. It is indeed "eternal life" that Christ gives (Mk 10:30; Mt 25:46; Jn 3:15-16, 36; 10:28; etc.), not just a passing remedy for illness or a deferral of the tragic epilogue of existence. As long as history lasts, therefore, there are concrete and eloquent signs of the power of God which sustains the fragile human being; but this does not at all exhaust the salvific work of God. The evangelists guide us to make the transition in faith from sign to reality, embracing the eschatological meaning of what is attested in the specific act of grace. This, moreover, is realised as a primary and foundational sign in the very person of Jesus, the crucified one risen from the dead for an immortal life. Every person of every race and time is called to recognise in the event of his resurrection the miracle of life given for ever to mortal flesh.

39. The evangelists tell us that Jesus of Nazareth presented himself frequently as "the Son of Man" (Mt 11:19; 12:8; 16:13; Mk 2:10, 28; etc.). This title, not without apocalyptic significance, conserves however the idea that the Messiah, by his own declaration, belongs to the human race and shares with his brothers and sisters the same condition of fragility and mortality (Mt 8:20; 12:40; cf. also Rom 8:3; Phil 2:7; Heb 2:17; 4:15). He too experienced from birth the poverty of the pilgrim (Lk 2:7) and the threat of death from those in power, such as King Herod (Mt 2:13), he suffered exile (Mt 2:14-15), he submitted in obedience to his parents (Lk 2:51), he suffered hunger in the desert (Mt 4:2), he felt the fatigue of travelling on foot and the burning of thirst (Jn 4:6; 19:28), he sensed the weariness of his prophetic ministry (Mt 17:17; Mk 3:20; 6:31-32), he wept at the death of his friend Lazarus (Jn 11:35) and for Jerusalem's approaching destruction (Lk 19:41). A target of hostility and derision, he was threatened (Lk 4:28-29), persecuted (Mk 3:6), and finally tortured and condemned to a cruel and ignominious punishment. He lived therefore all the suffering and humiliation of human life (Phil 2:7-8) up to death and burial. Faced with the prospect of a premature and painful end (Mt 26:37-38; Mk 14:33-34; Lk 22:44), he experienced anguish in his heart, and, like all those who suffer, "during the days of his flesh, he offered up prayer and entreaty, with loud cries and with tears, to the one who had the power to save him from death" (Heb 5:7); indeed "he learnt obedience, Son though he was, through his sufferings" (Heb 5:8).

But this fate, apparently senseless because it was unjust, even if freely willed by Christ in an act of love for the Father and for his brothers and sisters (Mk 8:31-33; Lk 9:51; Jn 12:27) is the way that leads to glory (Lk 24:26; Phil 2:9). Because Jesus, abandoning himself fully to God "was heard" (Heb 5:7): raised from the dead on the third day, as he had predicted (Mk 8:31), he became "the first-born from the dead" (Col 1:18; cf. also Rom 8:29; 1 Cor

15:23; Apoc 1:5). In him, the Risen One, death has lost all power, in him the powers of the underworld are definitively defeated (1 Cor 15:26; Apoc 20:14; 21:4).

The believers in Christ truly share in his mystery of life (Rom 6:9-10; 2 Tim 1:10; Heb 2:14-15); to them also it is given to make real the paschal event of the passage from the suffering perishability of this world to the perpetual joy of eternal life (Jn 14:3, 19; Apoc 7:13-17). It is this consoling truth that is taken up in the letters of Paul and the other apostles.

The Pauline praise of weakness and the hope of resurrection

40. The mystery of Christ, who died and rose, constitutes the kerygmatic nucleus of the apostolic preaching (Acts 2:23-24; 3:13-15; 4:10; etc.). *Paul*, in his letters, also concentrates all his "gospel" in this announcement (1 Cor 15:1-4; 2 Tim 2:8); and constructs his theology of universal salvation on the two words "Crucified-Risen". The two elements that define the Christological event are inseparable, so that the Apostle can assert that his only knowledge is that of "Christ crucified" (1 Cor 2:2), without thereby disregarding the glorification of the suffering servant. This, in synthesis, is the aspiration of Paul: "that I may come to know him and the power of his resurrection, and partake of his sufferings by being moulded to the pattern of his death, if somehow I may reach the goal of resurrection from the dead" (Phil 3:10-11).

Boasting of weakness

41. It is in light of the very mystery of Christ, crucified and risen from the dead, that Paul paradoxically takes on, as a reason for boasting (1 Cor 1:31; 2 Cor 11:30; 12:5), human perishability, which for the sages constitutes an unsolved problem, and for the people "of this world" an object of abhorrence (1 Cor 1:18-25). Weakness (*astheneia*), in its aspects of fragility, humiliation, sacrifice, suffering and defeat, instead of being abhorred as contrary to God and to humankind, is seen in faith as the place where the life-giving power of God is clearly revealed (1 Cor 4:9-13). The Apostle, minister of Christ and his imitator (1 Cor 11:1), not only accepts, but even more freely chooses the way of the Master (1 Cor 2:3; 2 Cor 10:10), trusting in the word of the Lord which says to him: "My grace is enough for you: for power is at the full (*teleitai*) in weakness" (2 Cor 12:9). For this reason Paul asserts: "So I am happy to boast about my weaknesses so that the power of Christ may dwell in me; therefore I am content with weaknesses, insults, constraints, persecutions and distress for Christ's sake. For whenever I am weak, then am I strong" (2 Cor 12:9-10). The ideal of stoic heroism is not in view here, nor a radical contempt for the values of life; what is indicated as the experience of the believer lived out by the Apostle in his mission for Christ is rather the triumph of the divine power which is accomplished in the very misery of mortal flesh, which is compared to a "clay pot" (2 Cor 4:7). This is why human life is presented in a paradoxical way: "We are subjected to every kind of hardship, but not hindered; we see no way out but we are not at a loss; we are pursued but not abandoned, knocked down, but not destroyed; at every moment we carry with us in our body the death of Jesus so that the life of Jesus, too, may be made visible in our body" (2 Cor 4:8-10).

42. Some texts of Paul reveal a certain relativisation of earthly reality, motivated in certain cases by the conviction of an imminent return (*parousia*) of the Lord (1 Cor 7:29-31); in other cases we find a critique of the "flesh" (*sarx*), seen as an expression of sinful concupiscence (Rom 8:6-8; 1 Cor 3:3; Gal 5:16-17, 19-21; 6:8). This does not mean the loss of the Christian's daily commitment: because "the present pattern of the world is passing away" (1 Cor 7:31), it is more urgent to carry out works of salvation deployed in charity (1 Cor 13:8-13; 1 Thess 5:8). The apostolic teaching reiterates in synthesis that one should not attribute absolute value to any passing reality; consolation does not come from what is passing, but from the courageous announcement of the resurrection: Christ "was crucified out of weakness, but lives by the power of God. We too are weak in him, but will live with him through the power of God" (2 Cor 13:4).

Hence the Pauline affirmation: "I reckon that the sufferings of the present time are nothing in comparison with the glory which is destined to be disclosed to us" (Rom 8:18; cf. 2 Cor 4:17).

The hope of the resurrection of the body

43. The resurrection of Jesus, attested to by numerous witnesses (1 Cor 15:5-8), becomes for Paul the foundation of faith in the "resurrection of the dead" (1 Cor 15:13-14). Christ in fact is the new Adam: "The first man, Adam, became a living being, the last Adam, a life-giving spirit" (1 Cor 15:45); if all die because of the former, "so in Christ will all be brought to life" (1 Cor 15:22; cf. also 2 Tim 1:10; 2:11).

How this miracle comes about remains shrouded in mystery. Paul makes use of the image of the seed, found also in the gospel of John, to speak about Christ's saving act (Jn 12:24): the metaphor is used by the Apostle to suggest the marvellous *transformation* of the human body: "what is sown is corruptible, but what is raised is incorruptible; it is sown in contempt but raised in glory; it is sown in weakness but raised in power; it is sown a physical body (*sōma psychikon*), and it is raised a spiritual body (*sōma pneumatikon*)" (1 Cor 15:42-44).

> Paul speaks of "body" to indicate that in the eschatological event the identity of every single individual will persist without any fusion or absorption into a confused mass; on the other hand, he uses an oxymoron to define as a "spiritual body" the person transformed by the Spirit of God, made similar to Christ, the new Adam, become "the heavenly man" (1 Cor 15:9) on account of the resurrection from the dead.

44. The resurrection, therefore, does not eliminate the body; on the contrary, it exalts it, making it immortal and glorious. And this destiny is not only for the individual human creature. With the image of the woman in labour – used by Jesus in Jn 16:21 – Paul evokes a life process that involves the whole of creation, which is subject to perishability and corruption, suffering because of the pain of giving birth, but awaiting a bodily "redemption" that will constitute the glorious fulfilment of salvation through the work of God and of his Spirit of life (Rom 8:18-23, 28-30). God in fact says "Look, I am making everything new" (Apoc 21:5), and therefore what is announced is not only a "new man" (Eph 2:15; 4:24), but also a "new creation" (2 Cor 5:17; Gal 6:15), "new heavens and a new earth" (2 Pt 3:13; Apoc 21:1), in which "death will be no more, and sadness and crying and pain will be no more. The first things have passed away" (Apoc 21:4) This is the mystery of faith and of hope awaited with perseverance by believers who "possess the first fruits of the Spirit" (Rom 8:23), the beginning of eternal life.

2. THE "DIVINE" BREATH IN THE HUMAN BEING

45. The motif of the human being as a *"creature"* of God is often mentioned in the Scriptures to highlight the profound difference from the Creator, and to encourage in the human heart that humility which is the way of truth. But the same motif has another aspect in a certain sense opposed to it when it evokes in the act of creation the care shown by the Lord (Is 64:7) and the spiritual endowment that characterises the human being (Sir 17:3-11).

In this respect, as was mentioned at the beginning of this chapter, the creation account in Gen 2 uses the image of the *"breath"* of God which, entering into the dust moulded by the Creator, transforms it into a *"living"* being, different from all other creatures (Gen 2:7). In this passage one of the many modes of expression is used which in Scripture attempt to give an idea of the special, indeed unique, status of the human being. In the Bible we find in fact a rich variety of expressions, metaphors and concepts, aimed at illuminating the mystery of a being made of earth, yet endowed with potential that is in a certain sense "divine". From this gift flows also the "vocation" of the human being, understood as the personal and communal role to be carried out in history, in obedience to the plan of the Creator. All this is "revealed" by God, so that human beings are enlightened about the truth of their wonderful nature. Let us see now how the motif just described is treated in the various literary traditions of Scripture.

The human being in the image of the living God

46. The first account of creation in Gen 1 spells out in different terms what is said in Gen 2:7 by means of the "breath" of God; it recognises in fact the special nature and extraordinary dignity of the human person, affirming that 'ādām was "created in the image, according to the likeness" of God (Gen 1:26).

Explanation of terms

It should be noted first of all that in Gen 1:26 it is not said that God created the human being "in his image *and* likeness", as we usually say, but literally: "in the image according to the likeness", which in a dynamic translation could be rendered as "in a similar image". To speak of the same event in Gen 1:27 only the term "image" is used, while in Gen 5:1 only the term "likeness" is used.

The term "image" (ṣelem) refers to a painting or statue (1 Sam 6:5, 11; Ezek 23:14), articles intended to make visible what is absent or even invisible (cf. Wis 14:15-17). The noun generally has a negative connotation. Indeed in some passages it denotes the idol (Num 33:52; 2 Kgs 11:18; Ezek 7:20; 16:17; Am 5:26), a reality, which, being "dead" (Wis 13:18; 15:5), does not hear, does not speak, cannot act (Ps 115:5-7); and this highlights by way of contrast the quality of the human being, who, according to the affirmation of Gen 2:26, is deputed to "represent" God by the very fact of being a living being, capable of having relationships with other spiritual subjects. Even if it is true that in the Psalter the term ṣelem is applied to the human being as an ephemeral creature (Ps 39:7; 78:20), this nuance does not contradict what is foreshadowed by the book of Genesis; the human creature is in fact a "figure" of

57

God in the fragility of the flesh and in the contingency of history.

The abstract noun "likeness" (*dᵉmût*) makes explicit the relationship of similarity between two realities, as happens between a specific subject and its pictorial or sculpted representations (Ezek 23:15). When the biblical authors received from God the privilege of the sensory perception of superior beings or events, they were forced to say that what they saw was "similar" to an earthly reality (Ezek 1:5, 26; 10:21-22; Dan 10:16). Now God is certainly "incomparable"; nothing can be compared to him (2 Sam 7:22; Is 40:18; Jer 10:6-7; Ps 86:8); and yet, Scripture says, human beings carry within themselves characteristics of the divine. Not a few commentators have suggested that the term "likeness" intends to lessen the force of the noun "image", specifying that the copy (man), cannot possibly be considered identical to the original (God). It seems more likely that with such a term the author of Gen 1 wanted rather to underline the privileged likeness between the human being and the Creator, which constitutes the original foundation of the historical dialogue between the two. That God wished to make *'ādām* in his image would indicate in other words that he intended to enter into a personal covenant relationship with him (Sir 17:12; 49:16; see also Ps 100:3).

As far as the Hebrew Bible is concerned, the expression "in the image of God" is attested only in a few passages of the *book of Genesis*, and they also provide significant insights into the meaning of the term.

The human being shepherd of the living

47. In Gen 1:26 the announcement of the divine project to "make man" in the "image" of the divinity is immediately linked with a phrase that is often translated with an imperative (or jussive), but which could perhaps be better rendered with a consecutive (or final) clause: "so that they may be masters of the fish of the sea, the birds of heaven, the cattle, all the wild animals and all the creatures that creep along the earth". In this text *'ādām* is seen in the role of ruler because endowed with the power of governing all other living beings. This important dimension is reaffirmed immediately afterwards, and almost with the same words, in the bestowal of the divine blessing (Gen 1:28).

The universal and exclusive dominion of human beings over the animals cannot be identified with a selfish and violent despotism, both because, in this paradigmatic narrative, all the living are given plants as their food (Gen 1:29-30), and above all because such exercise of power would not be in keeping with the image of God: the Creator in fact exercises authority to protect and promote the life of his creatures (Ps 36:7; see also Gen 7:1-3; Gen 4:11; Ps 145:9; Sir 18:13; Wis 11:24), giving them existence, nourishment, fruitfulness and an instinct for survival. The human being, as a representative of God on earth, receives the task of supporting the divine activity in a way that is favourable to other living beings.

We can ask ourselves then how one expresses in concrete terms this capacity to govern and this mission to "dominate" the animals. It is to be excluded that dominating is synonymous with "subjugation" to human needs because this does not correspond to God's way of working. Domination according to the divine model is better understood if one looks at it from a symbolic perspective using the image of the "shepherd" found in various biblical texts to characterise God's action towards human beings (Is 40:11; Jer 31:10; Ezek 34:11-16; Sir 18:13; Jn 10:1-18); by analogy human beings are called upon to use their potential to take care of the living beings entrusted to them, working with humility, so that every animal, according to its species, can live in a harmonious relationship with all creation. This requires great wisdom from human beings, as they show respect for the divine work and display an ecological responsibility that in the course of history, especially recent history, has not always been apparent.

The human being called to generate life

48. In Gen 1:27 it is twice stated that God created 'ādām in his "image", thus describing the human being, without distinction of gender, ancestry or culture, as a result of God's work. Precisely because human beings are different from the animals, which are created each "in their own kind" (Gen 1:21, 24-25), and because of their unique nature, human beings are the image of the one God (Deut 6:4).

The sacred author then adds a clarification, which is surprising in this context: "male and female he created them"; in this way the aspect of plurality is introduced, with the specification of different sexual identities, whereby each person will be in the image of God in a specific bodily form, with all that this implies, and in a relationship with the other, who is different from oneself. Sirach notes that God created all things "in pairs, by opposites" so that "one thing complements the excellence of another" (Sir 42:24-25); for every human individual, therefore, reference to the other sex will recall the limit inscribed in the flesh, and will bring out at the same time the desire for the union from which life flows, an act in which an important aspect of being in the image of God is realised. If human beings are in fact similar to animals because like them they are "male and female", they are nevertheless also similar to God because they are capable of giving life in love and for love: human generation cannot therefore be described simply as the fruit of a carnal relationship, because it is able to express a "divine" quality when it takes place according to the way in which God gives life to every person, that is, in gratuitous generosity. This theme will be developed extensively in chapter three of the Document.

The human being as a child of God

49. The relationship between the image of God and the act of generation is confirmed by another passage from Genesis. Further on in the account of the origins, the sacred writer repeats once again that "On the day that God created Adam he made him in the likeness of God" (Gen 5:1). And this affirmation introduces the act of human generation, presented in the same terms (even if literarily inverted), that had characterised the divine work in Gen 1:26: "Adam [...] fathered a son (Seth), *in his likeness, after his image*" (Gen 5:3). Here it is clear that the quality of "similar image" is what the child receives from the father at birth; each person, in fact, bears within the body the imprint of the parent. And that very brief note gives rise to the motif of the human being as "child of God" (Lk 3:38; Acts 17:28-29), a motif which, as we shall see, will receive a development of extraordinary anthropological and theological importance in the Scriptures.

The human being responsible for life

50. The final passage of the book of Genesis in which the expression "in the image of God" appears is to be found in Gen 9. The narrator had previously affirmed that humanity's unbridled wickedness, especially in the form of immorality and "violence" (Gen 6:11, 13), had risked putting an end to the plan of the Creator (Gen 6:5); the human being, called to give life and protect it, had paradoxically proved to be a destroyer of the divine work. The intervention of God then became necessary and is presented in two phases: on the one hand, the dramatic aspect of the terrible punishment of the flood that puts an end to the guilty, and involves all living beings; on the other hand, the salvific aspect represented by Noah and his family and all the kinds of animals, producing a kind of new creation with a new humanity. All this is crowned by an eternal covenant between the Creator and all the living, in which God undertakes never again to punish with a flood (Gen 8:21), and in which he again pours out his blessing on humanity, which involves fertility and dominion over the animals (Gen 9:1, 2, 7). Precisely because a new creation is announced, it is not surprising that it is recalled that the human being was made "in the image of God" (Gen 9:6).

This new creation is not, however, a simple repetition of the old. And the biblical author presents two significant variants with respect to Gen 1, which should be read always in light of the image of God. They are in practice two new "commandments" which commit the human partner of the covenant to the protection of life (symbolised by "blood").

51. The first variant relates to diet: the human is offered not only the vegetable nourishment of "every seed-bearing plant" and of every "tree with seed-bearing fruit" (Gen 1:29) but is also given the flesh of animals as food (Gen 9:3), with, however, the important exception, "you must not eat flesh, with life, that is to say blood, in it" (Gen 9:4). This regulation was interpreted as a concession to the violence that was by now inexorable; however, it must also be pointed out how the commandment expresses something about the human being in the likeness of God. What the attitude of the human being in history should be is indicated *symbolically* under the form of a *ritual* law: one can kill the animal to the extent that such an act sustains one's existence, and this will not be considered a reprehensible act of violence if conducted in such a way as not to destroy life (forever). The distinction between the two acts (killing and respect), is not easy to grasp. It may be useful in this regard to recall a minor commandment of Deuteronomy which allows the eggs of a bird to be taken, but lets the mother go (Deut 22:6-7); this norm makes it clear how human beings are to use creation ("to eat"), provided that the vital principle ("blood") is not affected. All this could be seen as a metaphor for the judicial action.

52. The second variant, undoubtedly the more important one, is formulated like a *juridical* axiom in sapiential style, remarkable for its sophisticated literary construction, which emphasizes, through paronomasia, the relationship between "blood" and "the human being" (Gen 9:6a):

> "whoever sheds
> > the blood (*dām*)
> > > of a human being ('*ādām*),
> > > by a human being ('*ādām*)
> > his blood (*dām*)
> shall be shed"

The human being is here given the task of meting out justice through the application of a punishment proportionate to the crime; in practice, unlike what was prescribed in Gen 4:15 in the case of Cain, the human being is given the power to put to death the assassin, and this with the purpose of protecting life. This very rule is immediately connected to the motivation "for in the image of God he made the human being" (Gen 9:6b). And with this last phrase, on the one hand, the fundamental value of human life, because of its special provenance from God, is affirmed, so that whoever does not respect it insults God himself (Prov 14:31); but, on the other hand, it is also recognised that the human being is the image of God in punishing in a proportionate way whoever extinguishes a human life. The act of justice is an authoritative and necessary act, which is entrusted to those who in history represent God in punishing evil (cf. Is 11:4; Ps 82:1-6; 101:3-8).

53. In the text we are considering the behaviour of the human being is universally marked by the principle of "deterrence": it is, in fact, "fear and dread" that express the power of the human being towards the animals (Gen 9:2), while the extreme threat of capital punishment was used historically as a constraint on the violence of humans (Gen 9:6). Although presented as part of a covenant of peace (Gen 9:8-16), this norm, ritual and juridical, is only an imperfect figure of the "new covenant" which will be established in the blood of Christ, to be celebrated in the bloodless ritual of bread and wine, and regulated not by the threat of punishment, but by the loving spirit of forgiveness, in obedience to what the Son willed and acted upon in universal reconciliation.

The human being "like God" in the practice of justice

54. After offering an overview on all humanity (Gen 1-11), with a decided emphasis on human transgressions, the biblical narrator focuses on the story of the people of Abraham. It is through understanding the sense of this particular story and adhering to its message that the reader understands what it is that makes the human being "similar" to God himself. This is the contribution of the literary tradition of the *Torah*, beginning from chapter 12 of Genesis.

Every person, as a child of *'ādām*, is able to listen to the divine voice that speaks in the secrecy of conscience (cf. Rom 2:14-15), demonstrating in this way one's nature of being intelligent, free, and called to an obedient and loving relationship with God. Such a potential, inscribed in human nature, has been realised, according to the Scriptures, in the course of history in certain individuals with whom the Lord established a covenant, as in the case of Noah (Gen 9), of Abraham (Gen 15 and 17) and of his descendants (Ex 2:24). It is above all the people of Israel that enter into a permanent relationship with the Lord (Ex 19-20; Deut 5), committing themselves to a covenant (Ex 24:3,7; Deut 26:17-18), which despite the asymmetry of the contracting parties, presupposes elements of likeness and spiritual communion. One of the metaphors that expresses such a relationship is that of sonship: Israel is called "son" (Deut 14:1; 32:5-6, 19-20; Is 1:2; Jer 3:19; 31:20; Hos 2:1; 11:1; Mal 1:6; etc.), or "firstborn" of the Lord (Ex 4:22; Jer 31:9).

55. The filial nature is realised in practice when Israel *imitates* God (cf. Eph 5:1: "as God's dear children, then, take him as your pattern"). It is in this way that the similarity to God is displayed in the Torah. If the Lord loved the fathers (Deut 4:37; 10:15), their descendants are as a consequence called to respond to God with the same attitude (Deut 6:5; 10:12; 11:1, 13; etc.). The Lord rested on the Sabbath day and Israel will do the same (Ex 20:10-11); God liberated the people from the slavery of Egypt, and the father of the family must therefore on the Sabbath day do the same for his dependents; analogously, every master will free his slaves in the seventh year. The Lord loves the foreigner (Deut 10:18), and acting in the same way Israel acts like God (Deut 10:19). And so on. The similarity with God will be real in the measure in which Israel follows God on the way of justice (Deut 6:25) and of holiness; Leviticus in fact repeats: "You shall be holy to me, for I, the Lord, am holy" (Lev 20:26; cf. 11:44-45; 19:2; 21:8; cf. also Ex 19:6; Deut 26:19).

Wisdom, bringer of life and of authority

56. The *wisdom texts*, as is the nature of this literature, take on a universal perspective, drawing upon the treasures of the revelation known to them and communicating them to all the nations. The sages act truthfully when they put human beings in their rightful place as part of creation:

"The Lord fashioned human beings from the earth,
to consign them back to it.
He gave them so many days and so much time,
he gave them authority over everything on earth.
He clothed them in strength like himself
and made them in his own image.
He filled all living things with dread of human beings,
making them masters over beasts and birds.
He made them a tongue, eyes and ears
and gave them a heart to think with.
He filled them with knowledge and intelligence,
and showed them what was good and what was evil.
He put his own light in their hearts
to show them the magnificence of his works."

(Sir 17:1-8)

On the one hand, as we have mentioned, the sages insist on the limitations of the human creature (Sir 18:8), and so on the necessity of the "fear of God" as the radical principle of wisdom (Prov 1:7; 2:5; Qoh 5:6; Sir 1:14, 16, 18, 20); on the other hand, they remind us that "the human spirit is the Lord's lamp – searching the innermost being" (Prov 20:27; cf. 1 Cor 2:10-11), and point out to anyone ready to listen what an inexhaustible source of life and dignity flows from the wisdom given by God to the human being (Prov 2:7-22; 3:13-26; Sir 4:12-13; 6:18-37; 15:1-6; Wis 7:7-14; 8:5-8, 18), called by the Creator to the role of ruler of the world.

57. If it is true that the sages of Israel transmit the fruits of their age-old tradition, enriched by the specific experience of some distinguished master (Prologue of Sirach 7-14), they also, at the same time, constantly insist that God is the source of wisdom (Sir 39:6; Wis 8:21), and it is therefore from him that one draws intelligence, instructions and the fruits of life (Sir 51:13-14; Wis 8:21). Now God wished the human being to participate in his intimate spiritual nature (Wis 7:7; 9:1-18), that with which he created the world and with which he governs it (Prov 8:22-31; Sir 24:3-22; Wis 8:1), so that, through this fundamental endowment, the human being comes to resemble the Creator and Lord. It is really in the wisdom tradition, in fact, and specifically by reason of the gift of wisdom, that one is reminded that human beings were created in the image of God (Sir 17:3; Wis 2:23), and given the power to rule over the earth (Prov 8:15-16; Sir 4:15; Wis 6:20-21; 8:14).

The divine breath, which according to Gen 2:7 brought the human being to life, is identified in the wisdom literature with the "spirit" of wisdom (Wis 1:5-6; 7:22-30) which makes the creature "immortal" (Wis 2:23; 4:1; 5:5, 15; 6:18; 8:13, 17), a characteristic this of exact similarity with God. And in conformity with the image of *'ādām* to whom is entrusted responsibility for the living, the sages of Israel remind the human being of the vocation as ruler; the task of governing can be exercised with justice (Wis 1:1), in conformity therefore with the divine "dominion" of the world, only with the wisdom that is bestowed by the Lord on those who desire and invoke it (Sir 51:13-14; Wis 8:21–9:17).

The man of God

58. While not making use of the expression "(in) the image of God", the *prophetic books* present the readers with the ideal figure of the human being according to God's design; and this not only confirms what the foundational texts say in relation to the project of the Creator, but attests to its concrete realisation in history. The "spiritual" condition of the human being in the likeness of the Lord is manifested in two figures, for both of which the prophecy of the Old Testament refers not only to their historical appearance, but also to their perfect eschatological fulfilment.

The king according to the heart of God
Many biblical characters are presented as exemplary leaders of the people of God: Moses, Joshua, Deborah, Samuel, etc. Their role as "shepherds" of Israel likens them to the Lord. But it is above all the king that is singled out, not without some resistance (1 Sam 8), as the one in whom the divine gift is more fully realised. And it is above all King David, "the man according to the heart of God" (1

Sam 13:14; cf. also Acts 13:22), prefiguration of the Messiah (Jer 3:15; 30:9), who is identified as the subject of a special covenant with the Lord and the beneficiary of the promise of an eternal kingdom (2 Sam 7:8-16; Ps 89:20-38). From the tribe of David, in fact, will arise the one who, gifted with extraordinary virtues by God, will have the power to reign for ever over the earth and bring universal peace. The prophet Isaiah gives voice to this promise in the book of Emmanuel when he announces:

> "dominion has been laid on his shoulders;
> and this is the name he has been given,
> 'Wonder-Counsellor, Mighty-God,
> Eternal-Father, Prince-of-Peace'."

> (Is 9:5)

Here are the "divine" qualities given to the human being which in the reality of history make the creature the image of the saving God. And these qualities are the fruit of the "spirit" (*rûăḥ*) poured out by the Lord on his king:

> "On him will rest the spirit of the Lord,
> the spirit of wisdom and insight,
> the spirit of counsel and power,
> the spirit of knowledge and fear of the Lord."

> (Is 11:2)

What the sages of Israel hope and call for is promised by the prophets, and will find a full realisation in the history of Israel when there will appear the perfect image of the Lord, the "son of David" (Is 11:1; Jer 23:5; 30:9; 33:15-16; Mic 5:1-3; Mt 1:1; Rom 1:3), who with wonderful wisdom and with divine power will bring blessing on the whole world.

The prophets, men of God

59. There is, however, according to the prophetic tradition, another manifestation of the human reality that makes one similar to God; and this is not only a promise ideally for a distant future, but is declared to be constantly present in the history of the people of God. It is the figure of the prophet, the man of the Word, the man of the divine Spirit.

The man of the Word. According to the account of Gen 1, God, from the beginning, "speaks", and his words constitute the basis of everything, of every living being, of every spiritual reality. This original Word marks the beginning of the history, into which the Creator will continue to send it to give life (Is 55:10-11). Now, the human being was created as the subject capable of understanding and communicating the divine speech; and such potential is realised when a person freely adheres to the Word and assumes the task of transmitting it. God in fact reveals himself through actions and words, and these words are communicated by human beings. The transmitter of the Word is designated with the title "man of God" (Josh 14:6; 1 Sam 2:27; 9:6; 1 Kgs 12:22; 17:24; 2 Kgs 5:8; etc.), "servant of the Lord" (Ex 14:31; Num 12:7; Josh 24:29; 2 Sam 3:18; 2 Kgs 9:7; Jer 7:25; Am 3:7; etc.), and "prophet" (Gen 20:7; Deut 18:15; 34:10; 1 Sam 3:20; Jer 1:5; Am 2:11; Mal 3:23; etc.). These qualifications highlight the human role of authoritatively "representing" the divinity. Since the prophets when they speak represent the voice of God, their words are Word of God; they possess the same power as the Ruler of the world "to knock down" and "to build" (Jer 1:10; 18:7), to unleash punishment (1 Kgs 17:1) and to give rise miraculously to salvation (1 Kgs 17:16). The person of the prophet highlights, therefore, in exemplary fashion how the human being can be and is in fact in God's similar image.

60. *The man of the Spirit.* In Gen 1:2 the Spirit that hovers over the water presides over the work of creation, while in Gen 2:7 we are told that *'ādām* was made a living being because the Creator breathed into his nostrils the "breath" of life. The terms "spirit" (*rûăḥ*) and "breath" (*nᵉšāmāh*) are synonyms (Is 42:5; Job 27:3; 33:4; cf. also Zech 12:1), even if the first has a broader range of meanings and a greater use. The image of the divine breath that penetrates the respiratory organ (Job 27:3), the flesh (Gen 7:15, 22), the bones (Qoh 11:5), thus bringing life (Ps 104:30), is revisited by the prophetic tradition, for not only is it applied to the biological dynamic, but it is used above all as a symbol of the gift of a "spiritual" life that confers on the creature the perfect state desired by the Creator. The sacred writer speaks both of the "spirit" of God that regenerates an entire people that had been reduced to dry bones, making them stand on their feet like an immense army (Ezek 37:10), and of the divine gift that heals the heart (Ezek 36:26-27), that takes possession of human creatures, conferring on them a superhuman power (Deut 34:9; Jdg 3:10; 6:34; 11:29; 1 Sam 16:13; 1 Kgs 18:12; Is 42:1), and makes people "prophets" (Num 11:16-17; 2 Kgs 2:9; Is 61:1; Ezek 11:5; Joel 3:1-2; Zech 7:12; Neh 9:30). Such profusion is not limited to single individuals, since the entire people of God is destined to receive the spirit of God (Num 11:29; Joel 3:1-2); this promise will be fulfilled for the community of believers in Christ in the event of Pentecost (Acts 2:1-21; 1 Cor 2:10-16), thus fully realising in history the original design of the Creator.

Meditation on the human being "crowned with glory and honour"

61. Sacred Scripture gives a voice to the sages and the prophets but welcomes also in the *Psalter* the voice of those who pray, presenting it as a precious inspired legacy. And among the treasures of these ancient prayers shines the jewel of Ps 8, attributed to David, a figure of every individual elected to royal status. In the context of praise of God as the Lord of all the earth (Ps 8:2, 10), the psalmist gives the reason for astonished praise at the particular situation of the human being:

> "When I see the heavens, the work of your fingers,
> the moon and the stars which you arranged,
> what is man (*'ĕnôš*) that you should keep him in mind,
> or the son of man (*ben 'ādām*) that you care for him?

> Yet you have made him little lower than the angels;
> with glory and honour you crowned him,
> gave him power over the works of your hands.
> You put all things under his feet,
> all of them, sheep and oxen,
> yes, even the cattle of the fields,
> birds of the air, and fish of the waters
> that make their way through the seas."
>
> (Ps 8:4-9)

The question "What is man?" recurs also in Ps 144:3. But whereas with the request for God's salvific intervention in this psalm (Ps 144:5-7) it introduces the motif of human fragility (Ps 144:4; cf. also Sir 18:7-9), in Ps 8 it constitutes an exclamation of surprise which leads into the song of praise. The smallness of the "son of man", highlighted by comparison with the majesty of the heavens, paradoxically becomes a factor of joyful recognition, because the one praying feels filled with the "care" (literally, the "visit"), of the Lord, who has clothed his modest creature with "glory and honour", conferring a *regal* status, slightly lower than that of God, so that the human being can exercise on earth the "power" to subdue all the living. Such an image of victorious triumph (Ps 110:1-3; 113:7-8) is not evoked by the one praying as an excuse for boasting, but to celebrate the Name of the Lord (Ps 8:2, 10), author of such a wonder.

62. In other hymns of the Psalter the element of praise is associated with the expression of supplication (Ps 20:2-3; 71:1-9), that the "king" may be given the possibility of actually exercising in history his role as ruler, obtaining victory over all hostile forces (Ps 2:8-9; 18:33-49). This is achieved always in a climate of great confidence, because the human prayer unites with the design and the will of God to have ruling on earth (Ps 21:4) the one whom he proclaimed his "child" (Ps 2:7; 89:27-28; 110:3).

A very expressive example of prayerful filial trust is to be found in Ps 71:

"It is you, O Lord, who are my hope,
my trust, O Lord, from my youth.
On you I have leaned from my birth;
from my mother's womb, you have been my help.
At all times I give you praise."

(Ps 71:5-6)

Jesus of Nazareth, true man, image of God

63. At the time of the emperor Caesar Augustus (Lk 2:1), a man appeared on earth, destined to be the heir to the throne of his father David, for a kingdom that will have no end (Lk 1:32-33; 2:11). For this reason he will receive the title of "Son of the Most High" (Lk 1:32). All that the Creator had wished to give to the human creature with the "breath" breathed into the nostrils of '*ādām*, all that the sages had desired and the prophets had promised, what the Psalmist had admired as a wonder wrought on the "son of man", all this was realised in the person of Jesus, son of Mary. A man among men, the true man.

His life is narrated in the *Gospels*, which through a detailed genealogy insert his story into the history of his people and of the entire human race. Matthew's gospel underlines in particular that Jesus is "son of David" and "son of Abraham" (Mt 1:1): beneficiary of covenants in which God freely elects and bestows, this "son" with a humble and obedient heart (Mt 11:29; Jn 4:34; 5:30; 6:38) becomes mediator and architect of a new and more perfect communion with God; his kingship extends to all peoples, and his blessing is a source of eternal life for everyone (Mt 25:31-34; Eph 1:3,10). For the evangelist Luke, however, Jesus is placed in a complete sequence of generations that goes back to "Adam, son of God" (Lk 3:38); all human history, not just that of the Jewish people, has its fulfilment in this son of man who brings humanity back to the splendour of its first origins.

64. The various episodes of the gospels outline the figure of a person who is revealed to be the *Christ* (Mk 8:29; Lk 9:20; Jn 1:41), the *Holy One* (Lk 1:35; Jn 6:69), the *Son of God* (Mt 14:33; 16:16;

27:54; Mk 1:1). From this narrative we are taught how to recognise in him the image of God, so that through him we may come to know the Father (Jn 6:46; 14:7-9), and obtain eternal life (Jn 17:3). All that Jesus said, all his actions, reveal God to the world; for, like the Creator (Gen 1:31), "everything he does is good" (Mk 7:37). In him are present all the qualities that a person can desire and all the gifts that God can bestow (Eph 3:8; Col 2:3), so that everyone can be enriched by his incomparable spiritual riches (Eph 2:7; cf. 2 Cor 8:9).

Jesus is the true *king*, capable of subduing all hostile forces (Jn 10:28-29; 12:31; 16:33; Heb 2:8): in the desert he is with wild beasts (Mk 1:13), he imposes obedience on unclean spirits (Mk 1:27), and he placates the fury of the stormy sea (Mk 4:39-41). These are figurative anticipations of his final triumph, "when he hands over the Kingdom to God the Father, when he has done away with every ruler, every authority and power. For he must reign until he has put all his enemies under his feet, and the last enemy to be done away with is death, for he has put all things under his feet" (1 Cor 15:24-27; cf. Eph 1:22; Apoc 20:14). Being the perfect realisation of the dominion promised to 'ādām (Gen 1:26), the kingdom of Christ does not come about according to the earthly model (Jn 18:36); the rulers of the world exercise dominion over their people by oppressing and exploiting them (Mt 20:25); they deprive their subjects of their possessions to the point of turning them into slaves (1 Sam 8:10-17), while the "good shepherd" puts himself at the service of his brothers and sisters (Mt 20:28) and gives his own life for them (Jn 10:11, 15, 18). For Jesus, the title of king is placed on his cross (Jn 19:19-22). This is the true kingly image that Christ reveals in the "completion" of his life (Jn 19:30); in response to the governor Pilate, he declares: "You say that I am a king. I was born for this, I came into the world for this, to bear witness to the truth" (Jn 18:37). In the letter to the Hebrews it is said that Christ was "crowned with glory and honour" (cf. Ps 8:6), "because he submitted to death" (Heb 2:9); he was "made perfect through suffering" (Heb 2:10), because in it he showed supreme love towards those whom "he is not ashamed to call brothers and sisters" (Heb 2:11). The same dynamic is attested in the hymn of Phil 2:8-11.

65. Such a style of ruling, surprising or even paradoxical as it is, is characteristic of the "Spirit"; it is in fact the way of the Most High, Creator and origin of all that is good, who exercises authority always with respect for his creatures and with great lenience (Wis 11:22-23; 12:18). Jesus of Nazareth was "conceived" by the Spirit of God (Mt 1:20; Lk 1:35), and the whole of his mission is guided by the Spirit who comes down on him (Mt 3:16) and rests on him (Jn 1:32). "What is born of the Spirit is spirit" (Jn 3:6) and therefore everything in Christ has a spiritual nature, and divine power, which is infinitely efficacious and at the same time supremely respectful. The Apostle says: "The Lord is the Spirit and, where the Spirit of the Lord is, there is freedom" (2 Cor 3:17). If the rulers of the earth impose their dominion with coercive force, Christ by contrast exercises his power by the gentle attraction of the grace of his words (Lk 4:22; Jn 12:32), and with the humble offer of truth which fosters a free response. One of the titles frequently used of Jesus is that of "*Master*" (Mt 8:19; 19:16; 22:16; Mk 9:17; Lk 7:40; 11:45; Jn 3:10; 11:28; 13:13; etc.) or "*Rabbi*" (Mt 26:25, 49; Mk 9:5; 10:51; Jn 1:38, 49; 4:31; etc.). This leads us to see in Jesus a sapiential quality, which is revealed in a regular way in his teaching, that is, in his offer of the truth that saves. Nevertheless he is not like the human teachers (Mt 7:28-29; Mk 1:22), because his wisdom is "inspired" by God (Jn 6:63; 12:49-50) and he possesses therefore a unique and universal authority. His is the wisdom of the true ruler, of the king endowed with the spirit of God (Is 11:2; 61:1; Wis 9:1-4), it is the only wisdom that gives life (Jn 6:63, 68; Wis 9:18). It is by teaching in fact that Christ comes to the help of the sheep who have no shepherd (Mt 9:35-36; Mk 6:34); it is with his voice that he leads them to the sheepfold and to the pasture (Jn 10:3-4, 16).

66. Since Jesus is the one filled with the Spirit of the Lord, his life will be that of a *prophet* (Mt 21:11; Mk 6:4; Lk 4:24; 7:16; 13:33; Jn 4:19; 6:14; 7:40; 9:17), "powerful in action and speech" (Lk 24:19). Everything in Christ is revelation of the Father (Mt 11:27); his words express the definitive and perfect communication of God to humanity; he is, in the flesh, the same Word that makes known the one whom no one can see (Jn 1:18). "Anointed with the Holy Spirit and with power" (Acts 10:38), he represents the spiritual summit of human history and the realisation of every expectation (Mt 11:2-6).

Made "alive" by the Spirit, Jesus of Nazareth will show the world the intimate principle that makes it live, for he will reveal to all the *love* of the Father which, in him, becomes the source and driving force of his saving work, defined by the apostle Paul as "the glorious ministry of the Spirit" (2 Cor 3:8). Like God Christ forgives sinners (Mk 2:7, 10), like God he inaugurates a new covenant (Mk 14:22-24), like God he "breathes" on the disciples to communicate the Spirit to them (Jn 20:22), like God he bestows eternal life (Jn 10:28). For this reason the apostles and evangelists testify that Jesus is "the Son of God" (Mk 1:1; 15:39; Rom 1:4; Heb 1:5; 3:6), "the only-begotten Son" of the Father (Jn 1:8), the firstborn of the children of God (Rom 8:29; Col 1:15, 18); he and the Father are one (Jn 10:29). For this same reason, the theological tradition, developed in particular by Paul and his school, will reintroduce the metaphor of the "image of God", giving it its full meaning in attributing it to Jesus Christ (Rom 8:29; 2 Cor 4:4; Col 1:15; Heb 1:3).

The Christian, image of God

67. Jesus puts before his disciples the way of perfection (Mt 19:21), that is, the full realisation of the human being, taking as a model God himself in his capacity to love: "be perfect as your heavenly Father is perfect" (Mt 5:48), "be compassionate just as your Father is compassionate" (Lk 6:36). The likeness to God, inscribed in the act of creation, is presented here not as a given fact, but as a duty, a call of liberty, a challenge entrusted to human endeavour. On the other hand, the Master offers himself as the figure to be imitated, and always in terms of love: "learn from me, for I am gentle and humble in heart" (Mt 11:29), "I have given you an example so that as I have done to you, you also should do" (Jn 13:15), "you also must love one another just as I have loved you" (Jn 13:34; 15:12). The "new commandment"

(Jn 13:34) has already been practised by a person, Jesus. It is not only possible (Deut 30:11-14), but has become reality, and is, therefore, the inspiring principle for human behaviour; it is a luminous example to imitate (1 Thess 1:6).

Being like God, or being like Christ, is not only a precept, nor a simple orientation of the desire for a life more and more worthy of human beings. Love has been given. In fact, the Spirit was poured out on the community on the day of Pentecost (Acts 2:1-4), and all believers received the Spirit of the Son in their hearts (1 Cor 6:19; Gal 4:6; 1 Jn 4:13) so as to become conformed to Christ (Rom 8:29), sharing in the "divine nature" (2 Pt 1:4), children of God in truth (Jn 1:12; Rom 8:14-17; 1 Jn 3:1).

> The title of "son of God" which was applied metaphorically to the king of Israel (2 Sam 7:14; Ps 2:7; 1 Chr 22:10), to the righteous (Wis 2:16) and to the people of the covenant (Ex 4:22; Deut 14:1; Jer 31:9, 20; Wis 18:13; Sir 4:10; Rom 9:4) becomes actual reality through "filial adoption" (*hyiothesia*) (Rom 8:15; Gal 4:5; Eph 1:5) and is conferred on those who, in faith and through baptism, are associated with Christ, the only Son of the Father (1 Jn 4:9).

Similar to the earthly human being, Christians are similar also to the Lord (1 Cor 15:49): "all of us, with our faces unveiled, seeing the glory of the Lord as in a mirror, are being transformed into the same image, from one degree of glory into another, as by the Spirit of the Lord" (2 Cor 3:18).

CONCLUSION

68. One of the principal contributions of the biblical tradition, constantly repeated in the pages of the Bible, is the assertion that the human being is to be considered a *creature of God*. This challenges all the cultural tendencies, widely diffused today, which in their anthropologies ignore any reference to the divinity, believing that in this way they are defending human autonomy and dignity that would be suffocated by the religious perspective.

Scripture, by introducing into the definition of the human person the element of a constitutive *relationship* with the Creator, introduces insights of profound wisdom (Ps 119:73). First of all, it liberates every creature from the naive pretension of being the origin of itself, and at the same time calls for an appreciation of the fact that every person has been desired and loved by the Father of life who "keeps in mind" and "cares for" every child of man (Ps 8:5). Moreover, the biblical tradition promotes in the conscience a principle of responsibility that is firmly rooted in one's personal freedom, in a project that from the beginning cannot disregard the relationship with all other human beings, who share the same origin and the same destination (1 Cor 8:6; 1 Tim 2:4-5). Finally, the Word of God, far from being an obstacle, promotes all the inventive qualities of the human being, recognised as bearer of a "spirit" that makes the creature similar to the Creator.

CHAPTER TWO

THE HUMAN BEING IN THE GARDEN

69. According to the foundational account of Gen 2, the human being was placed by the Creator in a "garden", deliberately "planted" by God for his creature (Gen 2:8). The phraseology used brings immediately to light the positive aspects of such a location: a garden, in fact, naturally evokes fertility, beauty and usefulness, while its situation "in Eden", because of the significance of the Hebrew name (*'ēden*), offers delight and enjoyment.

As we shall see when commenting on the biblical text of Gen 2:8-20, three principal motifs combine to describe the situation of *'ādām*, defining in particular his task in relation to the earth, his natural *habitat* (Ps 115:16). The first motif is that of *food*: the human being draws from the ground what nourishes existence day by day, and this reality provides material for reflection for the entire biblical tradition. The second motif is the call to *work* for the safeguarding and development of the heritage received, so as to enhance the sustenance and the quality of life of human beings. This theme, like the previous one, is also of great importance in the contemporary social situation, and the Bible offers valuable and decisive contributions in this regard. The third motif is that of the *relationship between human beings and animals*: these, located in the same environment as *'ādām*, contribute, among other things, to food and human work. This apparently less significant theme receives extensive treatment in the account of Gen 2, as well as having considerable resonance in the whole of biblical literature. One must accept on this point too, therefore, the guidance of the sacred text, so as to have a more faithful understanding of the nature and vocation of human beings.

These three motifs are intertwined, being in fact complementary expressions of the relationship between human beings and their earthly world. This does not prevent them from being treated separately in their specificity, each revealing to us its own richness of meaning. A particularly significant theme, that of the divine ban on eating the fruit of the tree of the knowledge of good and evil (Gen 2:16-17), will be treated at length in the fourth chapter of our Document.

Gen 2:8-20

⁸The Lord God planted a garden in Eden in the east, and there put the man he had shaped. ⁹From the soil, the Lord God caused to grow every kind of tree, pleasant to look at and good to eat, with the tree of life in the middle of the garden, and the tree of the knowledge of good and evil. ¹⁰A river flowed from Eden to water the garden, and from there it divided to make four streams. ¹¹The name of the first is Pishon, and this winds all through the land of Havilah where there is gold. ¹²The gold of this country is pure; bdellium and cornelian stone are found there. ¹³The name of the second river is Gihon, and this winds all through the land of Ethiopia. ¹⁴The name of the third river is Tigris, and this flows to the east of Ashur. The fourth river is the Euphrates.

¹⁵The Lord God took the man and settled him in the garden of Eden to cultivate and keep it.

¹⁶Then the Lord God gave the man this command, 'You may eat of all the trees in the garden. ¹⁷But of the tree of the knowledge of good and evil you are not to eat; for the day you eat of that you shall die.'

¹⁸The Lord God said, 'It is not good that the man should be alone. I shall make him a helper as a partner.' ¹⁹So from the soil the Lord God shaped all the wild animals and all the birds of heaven. These he brought to the man to see what he would

call them, and whatever the man called each living creature, that was its name. [20]The man gave names to all the cattle, all the birds of heaven and all the wild animals, but no helper was found as a partner for the man.

70. *Aware now of the greatness of the human being, created in the image of God and therefore destined to exercise dominion over the earth (Gen 1:26-28), the reader of the biblical text is surprised to find that, instead of 'ādām (Gen 2:5), it is the Lord God who plants the garden, making all sorts of good and beautiful trees sprout, including the tree of life and that of the knowledge of good and evil (Gen 2:9). With this literary surprise, the idea of the gift, already suggested in the original act of the creation of man, is reaffirmed, and now illustrated with the provision of the treasures of the earth. From being a "potter", the Lord God, with a change of metaphor, now becomes a "farmer", and as "master" of the garden generously provides for his creature all sorts of goods that are necessary and useful for life: fruit trees that provide nourishment are joined by plants to be admired also for their beauty (Gen 2:9); rivers ensure fertility for the soil (Gen 2:10-14), which in secret places hides precious minerals (Gen 2:11-12). Compared to the account of Gen 1, there is no mention of "heaven"; the focus, in fact, is on the "earth", and on its life-giving riches. The location of the garden, with the names of known territories and rivers, leads us to understand that Eden is really this earth of ours, entrusted to the responsibility of humanity.*

71. *The divine activity of the origins has as its initial purpose to provide the living with the nourishment necessary for survival and growth: the fruits of the trees are "good to eat" (Gen 2:9), and human beings are allowed to take advantage of all of them (Gen 2:16), and so also of the "tree of life", excluding only the tree of the knowledge of good and evil (Gen 2:17). This limitation does not lessen the divine liberality nor human potentialities; on the contrary it is an element that is necessary to define the proper status of the human being, called to discern between good and evil, so as to receive freely, in wisdom and obedience, the gift of God.*

72. *On two occasions the narrator states that the Lord placed the man in the garden (Gen 2:8, 15): the first time to prepare him to* *appreciate the quality of the divine gift (Gen 2:9-14); the second, to introduce the tasks of work and care entrusted to 'ādām. Since the creature becomes protagonist in Gen 2:15, the sacred text inserts a more specific description of the divine action, using the verbs "to take" and "to place". The verb "to take" (lāqaḥ) expresses the act of divine election in various cases (Gen 24:7; Ex 6:7; Num 8:16, 18; Deut 4:20; 32:11; Josh 24:3; 1 Kgs 11:37; Ezek 17:22; 36:24; Am 7:15; Hos 11:3; etc.) as a foundation of the covenant relationship; we can, therefore, discern this significance also in Gen 2:15 (cf. Sir 17:12). The original covenant between the Creator and his creature has its foundation in the divine choice; and from it, as in every covenant, emanates the duty of the human being's proportionate response. The verb translated as "to place" (nûăḥ), on the other hand, not only expresses a material arrangement, but also implies the connotation of "rest" (as in Ex 20:11; 23:12; Is 14:7; 57:2; Job 3:13; Est 9:22; Neh 9:28). An atmosphere of peace thus pervades the description of the garden of Eden.*

The man's task is also formulated by means of two verbal roots that have as complementary object a feminine pronoun, which refers to the "earth" (Gen 2:15; cf. also Gen 3:23). The first root ('ābad) expresses the duty of work, already evoked in Gen 2:5, with the nuance of fatigue and even a certain servile condition; the second (šāmar) belongs to the terminology of "guarding", and underlines, on the one hand, the duty of respect for what has been received, and, on the other, the task of defending it from harm. At this stage of the biblical story, there is no sense of punishment or of humiliation for the human being; on the contrary, what is stated here is the privilege bestowed on the creature to be the means responsible for making life flourish. These two roots, moreover, are widely used in religious language to indicate respectively the worship of God (Ex 3:12; 4:23; 7:16; Deut 6:13; 10:12; etc.) and the observance of the commandments (Gen 17:9-10; 18:19; 26:5; Ex 12:17; Deut 4:2; 10:13; etc.); the duties that, in the history of the covenant, will have as their object the Lord and his Law, are prefigured, in a certain sense, in the diligence of agricultural work. As in certain gospel parables (Mt 20:1-7; 21:28), working in the vineyard symbolises fundamental obedience to the divine command, and the life of hard work is comparable to a "divine service" (cf. Num 8:24-26) in the great temple of the cosmos.

73. A new narrative development is marked by the divine observation expressed in the rather surprising phrase: "It is not good (lō' ṭôb) that the man should be alone" (Gen 2:18). Compared to the parallel text of Gen 1, in which the expression "And God saw that it was good (ṭôb)" resounded repeatedly (Gen 1:3, 10, 12, 18, 21, 25, 31), we have in Gen 2 a different system of expression, which begins with what is incomplete and inadequate and shows how creation progressively reaches its complete fulfilment. What is imperfect is the fact that 'ādām is "alone". The Hebrew adverbial expression lebaddô, translated with the adjective "alone", if attributed to God, indicates his status as a unique and salvific being (Ex 22:19; 1 Sam 7:3-4; Is 2:11,17; Ps 72:18; Job 9:8), but, if referred to the human being, it expresses isolation and powerlessness (Gen 32:25; 42:38; 2 Sam 17:2). For this reason, the Creator comes to the aid of 'ādām, providing him with a "helper" ('ēzer), or better perhaps an "ally" (cf. 2 Kgs 14:26; Is 31:3; Ps 30:11; Job 29:12; Sir 36:24), who not only frees him from the presumptuous idea of being the only living person on earth, but above all works with the man in carrying out the task assigned to him by God. It is specified that the Creator wants a helper that is, literally, "as in front of him" (keneḡdô). The Hebrew phrase, attested only in Gen 2:18, 20, has been translated and interpreted in various ways; since it was not adequately realised with the creation of animals (Gen 2:20), the term is indirectly applied to the relationship between man and woman (Gen 2:23) to express equality and reciprocity. In the context on which we are commenting, and thus in reference to the divine work of forming the animals, it seems for the moment that one can more simply affirm that the Creator intends helping the human being by putting in front of him a visible, actual helper, to enable him to escape at least in some way from his "solitude".

74. God begins his work as potter again, and through his creative power he gives life to the different species of animals and birds; he then presents to the man the results of his activity (Gen 2:19). Immediately afterwards we have another significant narrative variant in comparison with Gen 1. In the first account *it was the Creator who named (Gen 1:5, 8, 10) and evaluated his works (Gen 1:31), while in Gen 2 it is the man who is called to name the various living creatures (Gen 2:19-20a) and to judge their suitability for his life (Gen 2:20b). Giving a specific name to each type of animal constitutes, in the first place, an exercise in sapiential discernment, which knows how to recognise similarities and differences between beings, how to classify groups and species, and how to place each one in order of usefulness (Wis 7:15-21); Solomon is celebrated for his ability to "discourse on plants from the cedar in Lebanon to the hyssop growing in the wall" as well as on "animals and birds and reptiles and fish" (1 Kgs 5:13; cf. Wis 7:20). Secondly, the imposition of the name represents for the ancients a form of power; and in our account this expresses, therefore, what was conveyed in Gen 1:26, 28 with the terminology of "dominating", with the clarification that this power is exercised through knowledge and the word.*

This narrative section ends with the affirmation that "no helper was found as a partner for 'ādām" (Gen 2:20); this heralds the new and definitive creative act with the establishment of the human being as man and woman (Gen 2:21-25). The completion of the work, which will be the subject matter of chapter three, does not in any event diminish the richness of what the Lord has done previously, as we will now show.

The angels

75. The focus on earth and on humanity explains perhaps the fact that we do not find in the creation stories (Gen 1–2) any allusion to the creation of "heavenly" beings close to the throne of God (Is 6:2-3; Mt 18:10; Lk 15:10), singers of praise to the Creator (Ps 148:2; Dan 3:58; Apoc 5:11-13) and faithful executors of his commands (Ps 103:20-21). They are frequently mentioned in biblical history, though, as messengers, hence the name "angels", and ministers of salvation (Gen 16:7; 22:11, 15; 28:12; 31:11; Ex 3:2; 14:19; 23:20, 23; Mt 1:20; 28:2; Lk 1:26; 2:9, 13-14; Acts 12:7; Gal 3:19; Heb 1:14; Apoc 5:2; etc.); in certain cases they receive specific qualifications, such as Cherubim, Seraphim, Principalities, Powers, etc., and are also called by their own names, e.g. Gabriel, Michael, Raphael.

The human creature will constantly experience their beneficial presence, through which the Father intervenes for the benefit of his children (Ps 91:11-12).

1. FOOD FOR HUMANITY

76. Every living creature needs to feed itself in order to support its development and to stay alive for as long as possible. This obviously applies also to humans, who have always grappled with the basic need for food (Ps 104:27; Sir 39:26). In our days, the food issue takes on dramatic proportions for many poor populations due to huge natural disasters, but above all because of violence and the inequalities inflicted by those in power. For the rich, too, eating has great significance, with the craving for gastronomic delicacies, combined with the search for the ideal diet, considered a primary indication of quality of life.

The need to feed oneself is an innate feature of the body, which shows itself in the symptoms of hunger and thirst that reveal the powerful instinct for survival with which every living being is endowed. In this respect creatures appear to differ radically from the Creator, the only being who has a full and perennial life, and therefore does not need to feed himself (Ps 50:9-13); the pagan gods, imagined as desiring abundant banquets (Dan 14:1-22), display an improper image of the divinity (Ps 106:20).

Food for human beings

77. In their basic daily need for food and drink human beings resemble the animals. But many features are specific to the human relationship to food. First of all, it may be noted that while the animals were given "the foliage of the plants" (Gen 1:30) as food, to *'adām* the Creator said: "Look, to you I give all the seed-bearing plants [...] and all the trees with seed-bearing fruit; this will be your food" (Gen 1:29), thus indirectly suggesting that human beings will be called to sow and to reap, thereby nourishing themselves not only from the spontaneous produce of the land blessed by the Lord, but also from the fruit of their own labour.

Moreover, humans do not "devour" food for the sole purpose of satisfying the appetite; instead they are able to savour food, and consequently carefully engage in choosing, preparing and tasting it. Every form of gluttony and every manifestation of bulimia has the effect of destroying the organism; at the same time, the obsessive search for the pleasure of eating is a harmful vice for the individual and the community (Sir 37:29-31).

Another important and distinctive feature is that nourishment for human beings is not only a natural necessity, but represents also a cultural factor, since it is a vehicle for interpersonal relationships, and a starting-point for alliances and communion. The child receives from the parents a food specially "prepared" for their offspring and is invited to taste it; every mouthful is a gift, and this engenders a relationship of trust, founded on the experience of repeated acts of anticipated love. Anorexia, a serious eating disorder, expresses not only the refusal of food, but also an awkwardness in the reception of life itself. More generally, the human menu is enriched with a variety of products, the result of commercial exchanges, and in its quality it reflects the skilled inventiveness of those who have been able to enhance the nutritional value and the flavours of the foods, so as to provide nourishment and make the meal an enjoyable experience. The habit of eating together, sharing in a peaceful way what gives life, is a primary sign of fraternal communion (1 Cor 10:17). In contrast, it is reprehensible that some human beings are left to die of hunger due to the selfish indifference of others, while food is wasted and useless gastronomic refinements craved. The one who continues to feast while the poor person waits in vain at the door (Lk 16:19-21; cf. Sir 34:25-27) is to be morally condemned. Indeed feasting is to be commended only if experienced in hospitality, in conviviality, and in shared love.

One final element characterises food in the life of human beings: since they are able to recognise a symbolic dimension, they can give food a higher meaning of a spiritual nature. Bread that is broken becomes a sign of covenant; a lamb sacrificed on an altar is intended as an offering of oneself to God; the renunciation shown in fasting expresses the hunger of the heart; and things most desired by the human soul are compared to exquisite foods and refined drinks (Is 55:2; Ps 119:103; Prov 9:3-6). For human beings do not live on bread alone.

These summary notes help us to appreciate the complex message that Scripture gives regarding food in the life of human beings.

Food as a divine gift

78. In the opening pages of the Bible, which consider the origins, food is presented as a lasting provision on the part of the Creator for his creatures (Gen 1:29-30; cf. also Ps 104:14); and the vegetable food that nourishes living beings evokes the relationship of peace between them (Is 11:7; 35:9; 65:25). The primordial blessing of the Lord is expressed as the paternal act which ensures nourishment to sustain life (Gen 1:29; Lev 26:3-5; Deut 28:2-5, 8, 11-12; Mt 6:26-32), so that the human being, capable of understanding this universal and permanent *gift*, makes of it the culminating reason for thanksgiving (Ps 136:25-26).

The history narrated subsequently in the *Torah*, however, seems, at first sight, to deny the affirmation of this generous divine liberality, since in reality human beings experience instead famines and shortages of food. Three subsequent narrative sections provide the reader with a deeper understanding of how food is "regulated" (and not just "given") by the Lord for the good of his children.

79. The first section comes after the sin. The first parents disobeyed the divine command concerning the fruit of the forbidden tree (Gen 3:6), and one of the consequences is the cursing of the soil, with the pain and the hardship involved in obtaining bread to eat (Gen 3:17-19). Similarly, after Cain killed his brother, the curse intervenes, and the earth, as a result, will no longer give "its strength" (Gen 4:12). These accounts of the origins are composed with the intention of interpreting historical events in which one can or one must recognise that the sterility of the land is a sign of a divine curse caused by sin (Lev 26:16, 20, 26; Deut 28:16-18, 22-24, 30; 29:21-22). The prophetic voice, in particular, will link the phenomenon of famine with the divine sanction against the guilty (1 Kgs 17:1; Is 5:5-6; Jer 3:24; Ezek 4:16-17; Hos 2:11, 14; 8:7; Joel 1:7, 10-12, 15-20; Am 4:6; 7:4; Hag 1:6; 2:17). God, however, never ceases to be benevolent; his temporary withdrawal, in fact, has the purpose of producing the conversion of hearts (Hos 2:8-9), and consequently a more abundant provision of good things (Deut 30:8-9; Mal 3:10), in which the merciful goodness of the Father will be fully manifested.

80. A second narrative cycle of the Torah is that which traces the events of the patriarchal history. From Abraham to the family of Jacob, those who were destined for the blessing (Gen 12:2-3) repeatedly experience phenomena of drought and hunger (Gen 12:10; 26:1; 41:30-31, 36), without this being attributed, however, to some fault of their own, nor to the customs of the local inhabitants. The reader is then offered a different interpretative key, so as to understand the scarcity of resources not as a punishment, but rather as an opportunity for wisdom and benevolence, deployed this time by human beings in favour of other human beings. The patriarchs, because of the drought in the land of Canaan, had to go to Egypt (Gen 12:10; 42:1-2; 47:4); the people of this foreign land, as is said in Gen 12:3, will become blessed or cursed to the extent that they welcome or harm the foreigners (Gen 12:17). Abraham himself is the prototype of this saving "oikonomia": he feeds the wayfarers, and, because of his hospitality, his tent becomes a place of unexpected fruitfulness (Gen 18:1-16). It is in the story of Joseph, in particular, that we find an example of how a difficult situation can turn into a favourable opportunity for good: the wise man above all knows how to exploit the years of prosperity in preparation for lean times (Gen 41:28-31, 36; Sir 18:25); and because of his shrewd foresight, with savings in consumption and with the conservation of the harvest in barns, he becomes the "providential" protagonist of the family and national history. Moreover, those who find themselves with plenty are called in conscience to open their stores (Gen 41:56) for the benefit of the hungry. Instead of being a curse, poverty then becomes a source of ethically precious relationships, when good flourishes through the justice shown by the merciful. This special responsibility for feeding the hungry is given to the reader of the Bible as a permanent programme for life (Is 58:7; 2 Chr 28:15; Prov 25:21; Sir 4:1-6; Tob 1:17; Mt 25:35-36; Rom 12:20).

81. A third important narrative section of the Pentateuch is represented by the forty years in which Israel wandered in the desert, experiencing hunger (Ex 16:3; Deut 8:3), and suffering from the lack of the rich produce of the cultivated land (Num 11:5; 20:5). The message on food as a gift from God receives here three different nuances, all important because of the symbolic value attributed by Scripture to the period in the desert. (i) First of all, it is reaffirmed that being in an arid steppe is a consequence of the *sin* that consists in the refusal of the rich land given by God (Deut 1:35), in the rebellion against the charismatic leadership of Moses, and in idolatry. Every time, then, that human beings experience "desolation", they are urged to undertake a path of conversion, so that the Lord grants forgiveness and allows entry into the land flowing with milk and honey (Ex 3:8, 17; 13:5; 33:3; Deut 8:7-10; 32:13-14). (ii) And yet, in that long period of deprivation, Israel also experienced, despite its repeated rebellions, God's continuous *providence* (Deut 29:4-5; Neh 9:20-21), with the miracle of the water gushing from the rock (Ex 17:5-6; Num 20:11; Deut 8:15), and especially with the gift of manna (Ex 16:4, 16-21; Deut 8:3, 16), daily nourishment (Ex 16:35), dispensed without people having anything else to do but collect and cook (Ex 16:4; Num 11:8) the food that came from heaven (Ex 16:4, 16-21; Ps 78:23-25; 105,40; Wis 16:20). Such an event is recalled by the biblical narrator to encourage trust in God, especially in the difficult moments of deprivation; the Father of life will always feed the hungry multitude (Ps 33:19; 107:4-9; Is 49:10), renewing in the course of the centuries his beneficial intervention of love (Ps 146:7). (iii) Pondering on the period in the desert, Deuteronomy brings a further element for reflection, always with the aim of helping to understand the mystery of the love of the Lord in the bestowal of his life-giving gift. Moses states that the desert is a time of "*testing*" (Deut 8:2); it is not only a punishment, nor only the place where the miracle of unexpected heavenly aid takes place, since it is also a period of education, in which the human being is urged to discern (Deut 8:2), to "understand" (Deut 8:3, 5; 29:5) and to decide, starting from the very experience of hunger (Deut 8:3). In fact, what appears negative and worthless is the occasion for a discovery concerning life and concerning God: namely, that "human beings live not on bread alone, but on every word that comes from the mouth of the Lord" (Deut 8:3; Mt 4:4). Hunger, which is repulsive for the flesh, is nevertheless a wonderful opportunity for the "heart" (Deut 8:2, 5), which can reach the full meaning of existence, which cannot be reduced to mere biological functioning sustained by earthly nourishment. The real life of the human being is actually God himself (Deut 30:20), and what really nourishes is God's Word (Wis 16:26).

82. It is along these lines that one understands better why the covenant rituals with the Lord have in the *sacred meal* one of the most significant forms of expression: that human beings can experience communion with the Most High is signified in the consecrated food, taken in the presence of God (Ex 24:9-11). Grafted on to the memory of the founding event of the Sinaitic pact, the various symbolic acts, linked to food, are interwoven in the daily life of the believing Israelite. If life is being nourished by God and his Word, then the person of faith can paradoxically also fast: not only as a penitential act, but as a place for prayer and the assimilation of the Torah, as a moment in which it is reaffirmed that the Lord is the inexhaustible source of life. Always starting from the centre of this faith, the believer will also be able periodically to do without bread and the many products of the land being cultivated, both to consecrate them to God in an act of trust towards the giver of all that is good (Ex 22:28-29; 23:19; 34:26; Lev 27:30), and as a sign of goodness towards the poor, the Levite, the widow, the orphan, the immigrant (Deut 14:22-27; 16:11; 18:4; 26:11).

83. Even the *restrictive rules* such as to refrain from eating the kid cooked in its mother's milk (Ex 23:19; 34:26; Deut 14:21) and all the dietary prohibitions relating to impure foods (Gen 9:4; Ex 22:30; Lev 10:8-11; 11:1-47; 20:25-26; Deut 12:16; 14:3-

21) will be considered as symbolic acts to express the "holiness" of the people (Lev 11:44-45; Deut 14:2, 21); this is not because what God created is unworthy (1 Tim 4:4), but because the source of life is found only in obedience to divine norms, motivated by various reasons. We recall, in this regard, the episode of Daniel and his three companions, who, rejecting the food and drink of Nebuchadnezzar's royal table, and dining only on vegetables and water, not only looked "better and fatter" than the other youths, but they received the gift of a wisdom superior to that of all the magicians and fortune-tellers of the Chaldean kingdom (Dan 1:8-21). Indeed, it is by accepting the limit that the human being symbolically recognises God as God, and receives everything from him in unheard of abundance.

> Dietary laws have had a notable impact in promoting the identity of the Hebrew people in times when they risked being assimilated to the dominant cultures. In Scripture the observance of this kind of ritual norms is attested above all in later times, when Israel lost its full political autonomy or was in exile (in addition to Dan 1:8-21 cited above, see Tob 1:10-11; Jdt 10:5; 12:1-9, 19; Est 4:17x-y). In the book of Maccabees the refusal to eat pork is a cause of martyrdom (2 Macc 6:8-9, 18-31; 7:1-42).

Choose the right food

84. The *sages* of Israel, considering and evaluating what is given to human beings to live "under the sun" (Qoh 1:13; 2:3), cannot fail to appreciate among the gifts of God the basic gift of food (Sir 29:21; 30:25; 39:26). Qoheleth writes: "I know there is no happiness for a human being except in pleasure and enjoyment through life. And when we eat and drink and find happiness in all our achievements, this is a gift from God" (Qoh 3:12-13; cf. also Qoh 2:24; 5:17-18; 8:15; 9:7). Such a perspective may be considered too limited, perhaps, as there are, in addition to eating and drinking, other situations and experiences of potential happiness; the teaching of Qoheleth, however, can be accepted because of the fundamental and symbolic value that meals have in the life of human beings, as pleasurable assimilation of the fruit of one's work and, at the same time, as gratitude for what God has bestowed on his creatures.

85. The anthropological centrality of food should not, however, lead to its excessive exaltation. For this reason, the sages introduce in their counsels the healthy principle of *moderation* in eating (Prov 3:1-3, 20-21; 30:8-9; Qoh 10:16-17; Sir 31:16-21; 37:27-31), faithful to the saying: "Eat to your satisfaction what honey you may find, but not to excess or you will bring it up again" (Prov 25:16). Most of all, drinking wine or other alcoholic drinks, although an expression and means of festive joy (Jdg 9:13; Is 24:9; Ps 104:15; Qoh 10:19; Sir 31:27; 40:20), has to be controlled and limited (Prov 20:1; 31:4-5; Sir 31:25, 27-30; Tob 4:15), so as not to degenerate into drunkenness, stupefaction and contentiousness:

> "For whom is pity, for whom contempt,
> for whom is strife, for whom complaint,
> for whom blows struck at random, for whom the clouded
> eye?
> For those who linger over wine too long,
> ever on the lookout for the blended liquors.
> Do not gaze at wine, how red it is, how it sparkles in the cup!
> How smoothly it slips down the throat!
> In the end its bite is like a serpent's,
> its sting as sharp as an adder's.
> Your eyes will see strange things,
> you will talk nonsense from your heart."
>
> (Prov 23:29-33)

In developing a process of evaluation, with the aim of presenting "the ways of good (*ṭôb*)" (Prov 29), the author of the book of Proverbs downplays the pleasure of the palate, preferring to it the values of tranquillity and peace, without which the banquet itself becomes unpleasant: "Better (*ṭôb*) a dish of vegetables when love is there, than a fattened ox and hatred to go with it" (Prov 15:17);

"Better (*ṭôb*) a mouthful of dry bread with peace, than a house filled with festivities and quarrels" (Prov 17:1).

Even more, the sage knows that he can only really appreciate the delicious food on the table if it is the result of justice and generosity (Job 31:17; Prov 23:6-8; 28:27; Sir 4:1-6; Wis 2:1, 6-11), and not obtained at the expense of poor brothers and sisters (Prov 13:23; 22:9; Sir 34:25).

86. A further step, in which the wisdom of Israel reaches its climax, teaches that the food that gives life, growth and happiness is not so much earthly food, however abundant, tasty and nutritious, but *wisdom* (Sir 15:3). According to Prov 24:13-14, honey is only a symbolic figure of the true exquisite gift given to human beings: "Eat honey my child, since it is good (*ṭôb*): honey that drips from the comb is sweet to the taste; and so, for sure, will wisdom be to your soul". It is not in fact "the production of the various crops that provides nourishment"; it is rather the word of God, as a spiritual food, that gives life, strength and joy to believers (Wis 16:26; cf. also Ezek 3:3). Personified Wisdom then raises her voice, with an invitation to the banquet prepared by her:

"Come and eat my bread,
drink the wine which I have mixed!
Leave foolishness behind and you will live,
go forwards in the ways of insight" (Prov 9:5-6).
"Come to me, you who desire me
and take your fill of my fruits;
for the memory of me is sweeter than honey,
possession of me is sweeter than the honeycomb.
Those who eat of me will hunger for more,
those who drink me will thirst for more."

(Sir 24:19-21)

If physical food assuages hunger, the nourishment of wisdom stimulates desire (Sir 24:21; Wis 6:17), with a longing for truth that finds joy in the continuing process of assimilation. If food prolongs life, wisdom, by communicating itself, bestows immortality (Wis 8:13, 17).

The desire for life: from earthly food to spiritual nourishment

87. In prayer, the believer praises the Lord for the good things that nourish his existence, at the same time invoking from God a spiritual gift that fully satisfies one's aspiration for life.

Grateful praise

In the *Psalter* a first fundamental dimension of prayer consists in the joyful acknowledgement of the Creator and provident God, who distributes food continuously and universally to all the living (cf. Acts 14:17). In Ps 104, praise to the Lord bursts forth from the contemplation of the work of God, who, by renewing the miracle of creation, continuously makes the plants grow to feed the animals and especially human beings:

> "From your dwelling you water the hills;
> by your works the earth has its fill.
> You make the grass grow for the cattle
> and plants to serve human needs;
> that they may bring forth bread from the earth
> and wine to cheer the heart;
> oil, to make faces shine,
> and bread to strengthen the heart."
>
> (Ps 104:13-15)

As in Gen 2, the Creator is celebrated in his agricultural activity (Ps 65:10-11). A constant blessing then arises from those who pray (Ps 104:1, 35) to the one who "provides the cattle with their food, and young ravens that call upon him" (Ps 147:9), and "satisfies" his children with the "finest wheat" (Ps 147:14), because he "gives food to all living creatures" (Ps 136:25), helps the hungry (Ps 107:5-6,9; 146:7; cf. 1 Sam 2:5), and does not allow the poor to lack food (Ps 132:15). By making his thanksgiving with bread (Mk 6:41; Lk 24:30), Jesus becomes a model of such reverent acceptance of the Father's gift.

The prayer for spiritual nourishment

88. The prayer for bread is not prominent in the Psalter; the request emerges, so to speak, in an indirect way (Ps 144:13), and is as it were incorporated in the heartfelt recognition of a God who does not disappoint expectations:

> "All of these look to you
> to give them their food in due season.
> You give it, they gather it up;
> you open wide your hand, they are well filled."
>
> (Ps 104:27-28; cf. also Ps 33:18-19; 145:16).

For the Lord is a shepherd solicitous of his flock; on his own initiative he leads them to abundant pastures and restful waters (Ps 23:2), and, as master of the house, he prepares the table for his guests, anointing their heads with perfumes, and offering to all a cup that overflows (Ps 23:5).

Prayer, however, is desire; and the desire of the human being is not satisfied with food, however necessary it is for the sustenance of one's mortal flesh; the aspiration of being satisfied and of a full life broadens, and, relying on the traditions of wisdom, directs prayer towards a spiritual gift, towards God himself, towards his Word and his presence. The one who is suffering, who swallows tears instead of bread (Ps 42:4; 102:10), turns to the Lord saying: "My soul is thirsting for God, the living God; when can I enter and appear before the face of God?" (Ps 42:3); "O God, you are my God; at dawn I seek you; for you my soul is thirsting. For you my flesh is pining" (Ps 63:2). What gives joy is the fullness of grace, and not the abundance of wheat and wine (Ps 4:8; 63:4,6; 65:5). The request for heavenly blessing will certainly not exclude the daily help of food, but will be ready also to await a nourishment of a spiritual nature: "At dawn, fill us with your merciful love (*ḥesed*); we shall exult and rejoice all our days" (Ps 90:14). When Jesus, in the "Our Father", teaches us to ask for our daily "bread", he opens up the longing for "what is substantial", so that the believer recognises his condition as a child who lives from his relationship with the Father.

The prophets call for sharing and announce the eschatological banquet

89. The extensive *prophetic literature* takes up the directives provided by the Torah, bringing them into the reality of the history of Israel and of the world; it also takes up the counsels of the centuries-old traditions of wisdom, not however as simple advice, but as issues subject to the unavoidable nature of the divine judgment.

In relation to the specific theme of food, we can distinguish two literary forms: on the one hand, the biblical *narrative*, from the book of Joshua to the second book of Kings, where the saving deeds of the Lord are displayed; on the other hand, the *oracles* of the prophets, from Isaiah to Malachi, in which the sin of extravagant feasting in the absence of justice is denounced, and where, especially in the final part of this literature, there resounds the joyful announcement of the eschatological banquet promised to the poor.

The prophetic account

90. As in all beginnings, the history of Israel at the outset is clearly marked by the gift, represented by the ruler of the world (Ex 19:5) who gives to his people the "good land" (*ṭôbāh*) (Ex 3:8; Num 14:7; Deut 1:25; 3:25; 6:18; Jos 23:16; etc.), a land rich in all kinds of resources, characterised in particular by vineyards (Num 13:23-24; Jos 24:13), from which comes "the fermented blood of the grape for drink" (Deut 32:14), as a privileged symbol of gladness. When they reached the land of Canaan, the Israelites were able to eat "the produce of the land: unleavened bread and roasted ears of corn", putting an end to the austere food regime of the manna (Josh 5:11-12). According to the Deuteronomic tradition, the people of God even come to inherit, without effort (Deut 6:11; Jos 24:13) and without merit (Deut 9:4-6), a new Eden, since the Lord brought them into "a land of streams and springs, of waters that well up from the deep in valleys and hills [cf. Gen 2:10-14], a land of wheat and barley, of vines, of figs, of pomegranates, a land

94

of olives, of oil, of honey, a land where you will eat bread without stint, where you will lack nothing [cf. Gen 2:9], a land where the stones are iron and where the hills may be quarried for copper [Gen 2:11b-12]. You will eat and have your fill, and you will bless the Lord your God in the rich country which he has given you" (Deut 8:7-10).

Unfortunately, as stated in the Canticle of Moses, which outlines prophetically the whole history of the people of the covenant, Israel "grew fat, gross, and bloated. He disowned the God who made him" (Deut 32:15; cf. Jer 2:7; 5:7); abundance and satisfaction, instead of producing appreciation and faithfulness to the Lord, led in fact to forgetfulness and rebellion, with the consequent loss of the divine gift (Deut 32:23-25).

91. Nevertheless, God remains present at the heart of this total failure and manifests his fidelity in a discreet, focussed and exemplary manner with the same gift of food. This is paradigmatically illustrated in the Elijah cycle. This "man of God" (1 Kgs 17:18), zealous interpreter of the exclusive attachment to the Lord, in a time of drought caused by the sin of idolatry, is nourished in extraordinary fashion, first with the "bread in the morning and meat in the evening" that "the ravens brought him" (1 Kgs 17:6), then with the "scrap of bread" prepared for him by the widow of Zarephath (1 Kgs 17:7-16), and finally with the "cake baked on hot stones" offered by the angel to the fugitive prophet in the desert (1 Kgs 19:5-8). These episodes cease to be mere edifying anecdotes when they are understood as the revelation of the divine gift, which gives life not only to the prophet, but also to anyone who welcomes him, because "anyone who welcomes a prophet as a prophet will have a prophet's reward" (Mt 10:41). The widow's small handful of meal, which is miraculously multiplied, so as to feed the family indefinitely (1 Kgs 17:15; cf. also 2 Kgs 4:42-44), is in fact a symbol of how the blessing poured out by the Creator at the creation of the world is realised in history, conferring on the "seed", both plant and animal, the potential marvellously to produce a multitude of "fruits" (Jn 12:24). The miracle of multiplication, however, occurs only if there is faith and acceptance of the stranger, who is a figure of God himself (cf. Gen 18:1-10; Mt 25:35).

The prophetic words

92. As we know, the prophets echo the voice of the Lord who first denounces serious sin; as regards our theme, the fault lies in particular with the wealthy leaders of Israel, who, oblivious to their subjects, live carefree lives, banqueting and carousing:

> "Woe to those so comfortable in Zion
> and for those so confident on the hill of Samaria,
> the notables of this first of nations,
> those to whom the House of Israel has recourse! [...]
> Putting off the evil day, you speed the arrival of violence.
> You who lie on ivory beds and lounge on divans,
> dine on lambs from the flock and stall-fattened veal;
> sing to the sound of the lyre
> and, like David, improvise on musical instruments.
> They drink wine by the bowlful,
> anointed with the finest oils.
> For the ruin of Joseph they care nothing."

> (Am 6:1, 3-6)

93. This lively description of Amos, not without sarcasm, is echoed in other prophets, who deplore in particular the abuse of wine (Is 5:11-12, 22; 28:1, 7-8; Hos 4:11; 7:5), associated almost inevitably with disregard for the pursuit of justice (Is 5:23; cf. Prov 31:4-5) and with the abasement of every charismatic gift (Am 2:12; Mic 2:11). While criticism is directed at a deplorable excess in eating and drinking, much more blame is laid on behaviour that is injurious to the poor (Jer 5:28), because what feeds the powerful is in fact the flesh of their own fellow citizens (Is 56:11; Ezek 22:27; 34:3,10; Zech 11:5; Ps 14:4; Prov 28:15):

> "Listen, you leaders of the House of Jacob,
> you princes of the House of Israel.
> Surely it is for you to know what is right?
> Yet you hate what is good and love what is evil:
> skinning people alive, pulling the flesh off their bones,
> eating the flesh of my people, stripping off their skin,

breaking up their bones, chopping them up small
like flesh for the pot, like meat in the stew-pan"

(Mic 3:1-3).

When the prophets follow the denunciation with the threat of the
devastation of the earth (Is 5:5-6) and the failure of its produce
(Is 5:10; 24:7-9; Hos 2:11; Am 4:6), they seek to provoke a change
of lifestyle, not only through a dignified sobriety, but above all by
practical works of justice (Is 1:17), which involve sharing with the
hungry poor (Is 58:6-7; Ezek 18:7, 16).

94. Another complementary request from the prophets
urges the people to abandon idolatry, which is useless (Jer 2:8)
and pernicious, because idols "devour" instead of giving (Jer
3:24), and rather to take up the way towards the Lord, the one
giver of life-giving riches. Using a wisdom form and giving voice
to God, the prophet says:

"O you who are thirsty, come to the water!
You who have no money, come buy and eat!
Come buy wine and milk without money, free!
Why spend money on what cannot nourish
and your earnings on what fails to satisfy?
Listen carefully to me:
have good things to eat and rich food to enjoy.
Pay attention, come to me; listen, and you will live"

(Is 55:1-3).

The great and definitive promises, which constitute the
culmination of the prophetic tradition, often take the form of
the gift of food that is abundant, healthy, permanent and joyous
(Is 1:19; 7:22; 30:23-25; 65:13; Joel 2:23-26; etc.). Amos promises
that "the ploughman shall tread on the heels of the reaper" and
"the mountains shall run with new wine" (Am 9:13), and Hosea
confirms it by saying that the earth will give "the grain, the new
wine and oil" (Hos 2:24; 14:8); Isaiah announces that "on this
mountain, the Lord Sabaoth is preparing for all peoples a banquet
of rich food, a banquet of fine wines, of succulent food, of well-

strained wines" (Is 25:6), a meal so full of life as to eliminate death forever (Is 25:8). Jeremiah prophesies the restoration of the vineyards (Jer 31:5, 12) and satiety for the people of the covenant (Jer 31:14), while Ezekiel will evoke the benefits of the water that gushing out from the sanctuary will allow the growth of every kind of tree, whose fruits will always be ripe and whose leaves will serve as medicine (Ezek 47:12; cf. also Ezek 36:29-30). The new Eden and the perfect nourishment promised by God are in effect symbols of the sending of the Word (Is 55:1-3,10-11; Ezek 3:1-3; Jer 15:16; Am 8:11-12), of saving justice (Is 61:11; Zech 8:17; Ps 85:11-13) and, ultimately, of the very presence of the Lord giving fullness of life to those who hunger and thirst for justice (Mt 5:6).

The bread given by Christ

95. Jesus of Nazareth is presented by the *evangelists* not only as a great prophet (Mt 21:11; Lk 7:16; 13:33; 24:19; Jn 4:19; 7:40; 9:17), but above all as the one who fulfils all the prophetic words (Mt 1:22; 4:14; 5:17; 8:17; 12:17; 26:56; Lk 4:21; Jn 1:45; 6:14; 12:38; cf. Acts 3:18,21,24; etc.). This applies also to food, which the Master often makes the object of his teaching, both confirming the ancient Scriptures, and bringing the newness of eschatological fulfilment.

The daily bread

From the beginning of his preaching, Jesus invites the disciples to trust in God, who, as a loving father, will not fail to provide for his children. For this reason he warns them: "not to worry about your life, what you should eat [...]. Look at the birds in the sky. They do not sow or reap or gather into barns; yet your heavenly Father feeds them. Are you not worth much more than they are?" (Mt 6:25-26); and again: "Do not seek what you should eat and drink, and do not worry. It is the gentiles of this world who strive for all these things. Your Father knows you need them" (Lk 12:29-30). Anxious concern must be replaced by confident prayer; the Master therefore teaches us to pray confidently saying: "Father,

[...] give us each day our daily bread" (Lk 11:2-3; Mt 6:9,11), because, he stresses, "Everyone who asks receives; everyone who searches finds; to everyone who knocks the door will be opened. Is there anyone among you who, if your child asks for bread, would give a stone? Or, if your child asks for a fish, would give a snake? If you, then, evil as you are, know how to give your children what is good, how much more will your Father in heaven give good things to those who ask him!" (Mt 7:8-11).

96. There is no need, therefore, to worry, but simply to ask; moreover, the Lord, with a paradoxical piece of wise advice, also adds that goods must not be stored away, but shared. We read in the gospel: "do not store up treasures for yourself on earth, where moth and woodworm destroy" (Mt 6:19) because "life does not consist in abundance of possessions" (Lk 12:15). The choices of wisdom are not for self-enrichment, but "before God"; for this purpose the Lord tells the parable of the fortunate but foolish man who plans to build new barns to store an abundant harvest, and who dies that same night (Lk 12:16-21; cf. Ps 39:7; 49:14-15; Sir 11:18-19). The parable of the wealthy man who used to "feast magnificently every day", without concern for poor Lazarus, "who longed to fill himself with what fell from the rich man's table" (Lk 16:19-31), has the purpose of inviting the "sharing" of goods, the only way of life that conforms to the teaching of Moses and the prophets (cf. Lk 3:11). Finally, in the parable of the last judgment, Jesus will indicate in feeding the hungry and giving the thirsty a drink the first condition for admittance into the Kingdom of heaven (Mt 25:34-35), for "anyone who gives so much as a cup of cold water to one of these little ones ... will most certainly not go without the reward" (Mt 10:42). The appeal to give finds its maximum extension in the gospel, when Jesus calls for everything to be sold, even what, according to human wisdom, might be necessary for survival, to give the proceeds to the poor (Mk 10:17-22).

Perfection, which coincides with the path of a full life, consists in offering all that one possesses in an act of love. This is what the Lord Jesus did. The sacramental symbol of his total self-giving is constituted by the offering of bread to eat and wine to drink, as a handing over of his life for the life of his own (Mt 26:26-28). This was prefigured when he fed the crowd in the desert (Mt 14:13-21; 15:32-38), a sign of his loving care for the hungry (Mt 15:32), and, indirectly, an invitation to do the same (cf. Mt 14:16).

Food in religious rites

97. We have alluded to the fact that in the religious world of Israel the meal was considered to have symbolic value, expressed in liturgical rites; all this is accepted by Jesus with important new features.

Firstly, he takes up a position against the Jewish rule that distinguished legally between clean and unclean foods. The evangelist Mark says that Jesus "pronounced all foods clean" (Mk 7:19), since it is not what enters a person from outside that makes that person unclean, but what comes out of the heart as wickedness and debauchery (Mk 7:18-23). The episode narrated in the Acts of the Apostles, in which Peter is invited to eat animals prohibited by the Mosaic law, confirms that one must no longer consider profane or unclean what God has made clean (Acts 10:15). The Christian tradition will then accept with thanksgiving all the foods created by God (1 Tim 4:3-5), and "holiness" (cf. Deut 14:2-3) will be shown through good conduct marked by generous almsgiving (Lk 11:41), and no longer having recourse to the rules of clean and unclean.

Another point of evangelical innovation concerns the practice of fasting. The figure of John the Baptist, who had retired to the desert, feeding on locusts and wild honey (Mt 3:4; Mk 1:6), was at that time, and also later, considered an ideal of praiseworthy religious behaviour, to be imitated through austerity and abstinence (Mt 9:14). Taking up the experience of the people of Israel, Jesus spent an initial period in the desert, in order to live in truth the Lord's saying that one does not live on bread alone (Mt 4:4; Lk 4:4); in his public life, however, he adopted a different style, and was criticised by certain zealous (and hypocritical) contemporaries, because he "ate and drank", and what is more with sinners (Mt 9:11; 11:19; Lk 7:34). But the advent of the Kingdom of God, identified by the presence of the

Bridegroom, required an innovative sign to indicate the end of waiting and the joy of present salvation (Mt 9:15-17; Jn 2:1-11). This is why Jesus feasted, in order to express symbolically that in him was finally accomplished the participation of the redeemed in the eschatological banquet, foretold by the prophets, and inaugurated by the Messiah as the decisive event in history (Mt 8:11; 10:1-10; Lk 14:15-24; cf. also Apoc 19:7; 21:6).

To make clear that feasting should not be understood as mere sensory satisfaction, the Master shows what the spirit of the festive occasion should be. It is beneficial only when it expresses the free generosity of the heart; in fact those invited to the meal are people who are unable to reciprocate (Lk 14:12-14). The banquet, moreover, must be experienced in humility, by choosing the last place (Lk 14:7-11; cf. Mt 23:6). Finally, and paradoxically, one participates in the banquet with an attitude of service; for Jesus, presenting himself as a model, said: "Who is the greater: the one at table or the one who serves? The one at table, surely? Yet I am among you as one who serves!" (Lk 22:27; cf. Jn 13:1-17).

98. The most significant innovation brought by Christ is the perennial memorial of his death carried out in the eating of bread and the drinking of wine (Mt 26:26-29), in obedient conformity to what he commanded. In the sacrament of the Eucharist a new way of celebrating the Passover of liberation and life is, in fact, prescribed, no longer in the blood and meat of the lamb, but in the bloodless rite, which both restores the sign of the peaceful nourishment of the origins (Gen 1:29) and puts an end to the blood sacrifices of the ancient covenant, because of the perfectly redemptive offering of the Son of God (Heb 9:12-14). As we will see later, the breaking of the bread will become for Christians the sacrament that identifies them, not as a pure ritual sign, but as a sacrament of faith in Christ and as the realisation of authentic fraternal communion.

Spiritual food

99. When the disciples returned from buying provisions (Jn 4:8), they said to their master: "Rabbi, have something to eat" (Jn 4:31). Jesus replied: "I have food to eat that you do not know about [...].

My food is to do the will of the one who sent me" (Jn 4:32, 34). Inviting his hearers not to worry about their daily food, the Lord concluded: "Strive first for his kingdom, and righteousness, and all these other things will be given you as well" (Mt 6:33). And to Martha who was preoccupied with serving at table, Jesus pointed out the better situation of her sister Mary, who nourished herself with the Word of the Lord (cf. Lk 14:15-24). As was envisaged in ancient wisdom traditions, the disciple is invited by the Master to consider what the true life-giving food is, so as to seek it and digest it (cf. Lk 14:15-24).

The passage from the "sign" of the bread (Mt 14:13-21; 15:32-39) to the "reality" signified is not easy (Mk 8:14-21); for this reason the Lord admonished the crowd who had been fed with the bread of multiplication and thought they had obtained full satisfaction (Jn 6:26), saying to them: "Do not work for food that corrupts, but work for food that endures for eternal life, which the Son of man will give you" (Jn 6:27). For Christians, the food given for eternal life is identified with the sacrament of the Eucharist. It should be remembered, however, that it is itself a "sign" of welcoming the Lord, and his Word, which is spirit and life (Jn 6:63), and his total self-giving in love (Jn 6:51-57). Hence the evangelist Matthew will proclaim blessed "those who hunger and thirst for righteousness" (Mt 5:6); the promised fulness is indeed that which is reached in the joyful assimilation of the mystery of love of the Lord Jesus (Jn 6:35).

Food in the life of the Christian community

100. When we read the biblical texts that speak of the life of the first Christians, in the Acts of the Apostles and the Letters of Paul, two principal aspects deserve to be highlighted. The first concerns the actual food and the acts of justice and charity related to it, while the second concerns certain aspects of the sacred rituals, through which is specified what the path of faith and love should be.

In time of need

As often happens in history, there were also for the communities of the early Church times of scarcity, as well as enduring situations of economic hardship; consequently, measures had to be taken to come to the aid of the "hungry". In the book of Acts it is narrated that in Jerusalem Greek-speaking widows were neglected in the daily distribution; this led to the institution of the commission of "waiting at tables", which was entrusted to "seven men of good reputation" (Acts 6:1-3). The structure of the church will thus be permanently marked by the service to be provided to those in need of food. Subsequently, the entire Jerusalem community found itself in economic difficulties, so much so that Paul had to raise substantial funds to help the "poor" (Acts 24:17; Rom 15:25-28; 1 Cor 16:1; 2 Cor 8–9; Gal 2:10). The pagans who, coming to faith, had grafted themselves onto the trunk of Judaism, thus provided for the material needs of those who had given them spiritual gifts (Rom 15:27).

As James teaches in his letter, faith is manifested in good works, and primary among them is that of helping those without food (Jam 2:14-17); among other things, this charity becomes a builder of communion (*koinōnia*) among brothers and sisters. As we read in the Acts of the Apostles: "The whole group of believers was of one heart and mind; no one claimed private ownership of any possessions, but everything they owned was held in common (*koina*) [...]. None of their members was ever in want, as all those who owned land or houses sold them, brought the proceeds of the sale, and laid it at the feet of the apostles; it was then distributed to each as any had need" (Acts 4:32, 34-35; cf. also Acts 2:44-45). An ideal of fraternity is presented here (cf. Deut 15:4) which is to be implemented as a sign of the coming of the Kingdom, while taking account of the economic structures of the various historical periods.

The community meal

101. Communion between brothers and sisters in faith is expressed in the fact of participating at the same table. Among the Christians of the first century, problems and conflicts arose because of the different religious cultures, each with specific needs or dietary customs.

A first major difficulty was posed by the Judeo-Christians, scrupulous followers of the Mosaic norms concerning unclean foods in particular. Following a solemn meeting of the Church in Jerusalem, it was decided in this regard that the ritual prescriptions of Jewish law should not be imposed on uncircumcised brothers; they were asked only to "abstain from anything polluted by idols, from illicit marriages (*porneia*), from the meat of strangled animals and from blood" (Acts 15:20, 29). On the basis of the command given to Noah (Gen 9:4) and the rules prescribed for foreigners in the land of Israel (Lev 17:7-14), a sort of compromise was reached which, safeguarding some fundamental religious and ethical duties, would have allowed everyone to share the same table. Such issues are not relevant in Christian communities today; but the principle, prompted by the Holy Spirit (Acts 15:28), remains valid, that for the sake of communion everyone is called to take the needs of the brother and sister into account, renouncing out of love a non-essential traditional practice (cf. Col 2:22-23) or a personal expression of freedom (1 Cor 10:23).

This is theorised by Paul also in relation to another situation, pertaining to the common meal, and concerning the question of "idolotites", that is, those who consider it is lawful to eat meat from the sacrifices offered to pagan deities. The Apostle discusses this issue on several occasions and at length (Rom 14:1-15:13; 1 Cor 8:1-23; 10:14-33), which shows both the theoretical difficulty of the case and its impact on fraternal harmony. We can summarise Paul's arguments by saying that the principle of freedom, legitimate and appropriate in itself (Col 2:16-17; 1 Tim 4:3; Heb 9:10; 13:9), must, however, be subordinated to the duty of charitable care towards the one who is "weak" because he is tied to customs from which he is unable to free himself; remembering the brother or sister for whom Christ died (1 Cor 8:11), the Apostle concludes: "if food causes my brother or sister to fall, I will never eat meat again, to avoid causing such a fall" (1 Cor 8:13). The freedom of the "strong" is thus placed at the service of love: "Whatever you eat, then, whatever you drink, and whatever you do, do it all for the glory of God. Do not give offence, either to Jews or to Greeks or to the Church of God, just as I try to please everyone in everything, seeking not my own advantage, but that of many, so that they may be saved" (1 Cor 10:31-33).

102. What all Christians are called to eat in their sacred ritual is the "broken bread", the real sign of Christ (Mt 26:26; Lk 24:35; 1 Cor 11:24) and a sign of communion with him and with one's brothers and sisters (Acts 2:42, 46; 20:7, 11): "The bread which we break, is it not a fellowship in the body of Christ? As there is one bread, so we, though many, are one body, for we all share in the one bread" (1 Cor 10:16-17). The Apostle then rails against the divisions that distort "the Lord's supper" (1 Cor 11:20), when, in the meal taken in common, "one is hungry, while another is drunk" (1 Cor 11:21); this situation contradicts the mystery that is being celebrated (1 Cor 11:25), and consequently those who do not respect the needs of fraternal sharing, instead of being nourished by the very life of the Lord, "eat and drink their own condemnation" (1 Cor 11:29).

Finally, we must add that, already in the first summary that describes the life of the early Christian communities, eating the broken bread is associated with persevering in listening to the teaching of the apostles (Acts 2:42). Moreover, this teaching is compared to spiritual nourishment (1 Tim 4:6): it is like milk, when it concerns the first rudiments of faith, and then it is like solid food, necessary for those who have already progressed (1 Cor 3:1-2; Heb 5:12-13; 1 Pt 2:2). In continuity with the whole biblical tradition, it is stated that the nourishment that gives true life comes from God, and is indeed God himself (cf. 1 Cor 10:3-4).

2. THE TASK OF WORK ENTRUSTED TO THE HUMAN BEING

103. In Scripture, the motif of food is mainly linked to the gift of God (cf. Gen 1:29-30); the theme of work (Gen 2:15), though, highlights human activity, which is necessary not only to obtain food, but also to promote a better quality of life. The responsibility of working is formulated in Gen 2:15 in terms of a purpose, "to work and to keep", which is inherent in the very constitution of the human being; the reader of the Bible, asking questions about the human being, is invited to investigate the meaning and value of working and keeping the land in which *'ādām* was placed.

The human being as worker

104. The idea that work is a sort of condemnation from which one would like to have been relieved is very common; some even think of it as a consequence of sin (Gen 3:17-19), due to the fact that it intrinsically involves elements of hardship (Gen 3:17, 19; 5:29) and servitude (Job 7:1-2), evident above all in manual labour, and accentuated when working conditions are unjust, as for Israel in Egypt. In Scripture, however, not only is work assigned to *'ādām* before the transgression, but above all this directive is preceded by a series of actions of God, who, as if he were a craftsman grappling with formless matter, brings into existence what is "good" (Gen 1:4, 10, 12, 18, 21, 25, 31; 2:9, 12). By radically reversing the Mesopotamian myth which narrated how human beings were created to work in order to provide food for the gods (cf. Acts 17:25), the word of God testifies instead that it is God who serves his creatures by providing them with food and giving them an example. In the account of Gen 1–2, in fact, the Creator is presented as a father who teaches his child the right way of behaving (cf. Jn 5:19-20), so that the child, by behaving in this way, acts out in reality similarity to the father.

Of course, while the work of God is effortless, the creature grows weary and tired (Is 40:28-30); and while the Creator immediately achieves the result of his project (Is 48:3; Ezek 12:25; Ps 33:9), the human being must accept a time delay to see the fruit of one's work (cf. Mk 4:27-29). Despite these important differences, it must be recognised that the child of man has been given "power" to operate in the world, producing "good", so that creation itself, as it were, is brought to perfection by the dutiful contribution of the child of God. Unemployment and precariousness in employment, in addition to being factors of serious social disorder, go against the universal human vocation, the gift and duty of everyone to work together for the life of all.

The imitation of God's work, however, must not be restricted to mere practical activity, but will take on also the components of wisdom and love which are illustrated in exemplary form in the act of creation (Jer 10:12; 51:15; Ps 104:24; 136:5; Prov 3:19-20; 8:22-31). In fact, it is not work as such that is promoted by Scripture, but its purpose to do good. The spirit of wisdom, malleable and multiform (Wis 7:22-23), will therefore be visible in human work, in particular in the various professions and in the different occupations which, in history, enhance the intelligent creativity of human beings at the service of the common good (cf. 1 Cor 12:7-11); and the spirit of goodness, secretly powerful, will ensure that human activity produces life-giving fruit for the children and for the children's children, from generation to generation.

105. Every work in fact is intrinsically orientated towards producing fruit. This implies that there is a hierarchy and a coordination between activities, as is the case indeed in the divine creation, where everything happens at its precise moment (Gen 1), and every reality comes into being in relation to what comes next (Gen 2). For human beings this means that their productive activity must be organised (Prov 24:27), and in many cases coordinated, in grateful cooperation, with the work of another, who is perhaps not even present yet on the scene of history. This is not an "alienating" factor but should be understood rather as a legacy, freely given to those who will come to benefit from it and receive it as an ancestral inheritance. The proverb says: "one sows, another reaps" (Jn 4:37);

and thus, even without knowing it, each worker gives to others, as God gives to all humanity.

This does not contradict the fact that every service deserves a reward, expressed as "wages" in the event that the job has been requested or imposed by an employer. The public recognition conferred on every useful service is a source of gratification for every worker (Sir 38:32), and is expected as a *right*; while for those who have commissioned any work it is a *duty* to provide the right remuneration. Work, a vehicle for relationships between humans, is thus one of the privileged places of social justice, in which the aims of communion and life desired by all are realised.

From these summary reflections one can already perceive how the activity of work is full of anthropological meaning, and how it has therefore been the object of attention by the Church in its constant commitment to guiding consciences and promoting social justice. Since work is "human" activity, it is natural that it is also marked by imperfection and by sin; Scripture, with its rich patrimony of truth, helps by providing directives, and by encouraging appropriate decisions for an unceasing promotion of what is truly "good".

The human being as custodian of creation

106. There is no doubt that human work, in the likeness of divine action, carries within itself the character of transformative, even if not properly creative, activity; in fact, it constantly introduces innovative elements into history, sometimes radically changing the existing social structures, and as a result imposing new styles of life. The vibrant and overwhelming potential of "work" receives in the text of Gen 2:15 a kind of restraint, or limit, through the purpose given by the Creator to the human being to "keep" the earth, that is, the creation. Human work must not subvert, let alone destroy, the divine work. Such commitment can express a dimension of faith, when the person recognises that what is possessed is a sacred good coming from God. It will then have the value of an ethical decision, beyond any specific religious adherence, whenever action is taken to protect rather than to ravage or irresponsibly squander the wonderful common treasure. "Keeping" the land is therefore not a different activity from work, but rather an essential part of it. For this reason, we will not treat it specifically, and we will limit ourselves from now on to some brief notes starting from some suggestive passages of Scripture.

A wonderful biblical image of "keeping" life is depicted in the story of Noah. Just when the world seems destined for destruction due to the corruption and violence of human beings (Gen 6:5-7, 13), this righteous man is called by God to build an ark (Gen 6:14-16), symbol in reality of the earth, in which all living species can be saved (Gen 6:19-21), even those not immediately useful to humans, such as unclean animals (Gen 7:2, 8). The earth is not preserved without taking care of all forms of life.

107. Two minor commandments of the Torah can be mentioned at this point, to make it clear how care for creation should unfold; these are two precepts that symbolically trace the rather subtle boundary between consumption and conservation, between actions that are destructive and protective.

The first of these commandments has already been mentioned in chapter one in relation to human responsibility to protect life; it is found in Deut 22:6-7: "If, on the road, you come across a bird's nest, in a tree or on the ground, with chicks or eggs and the mother bird sitting on the chicks or the eggs, you shall not take the mother as well as the chicks. Let the mother go; the young you may take for yourself. Thus will you have prosperity and long life". Going beyond this specific rule for the hunter, this regulation makes it clear that the continuing path of happiness and life requires that one be able to exploit the resources of nature, without however affecting the life-giving principle; using a different metaphor, one is invited to benefit from the fruit without cutting down the tree.

This vegetable motif allows us to pass to the second prescription of the Torah found in the context of rules concerning the conduct to be followed during war, and specifically in laying siege to a city. The destructive urge, which inevitably arises from hatred of the enemy and which unfortunately is a feature of war, is to be controlled, so as to allow life to continue. The legislator writes: "If, when attacking a town, you have to besiege it for a long time before you capture it, you must not destroy its trees by putting the axe to them: eat their fruit but do not cut them down. Is the tree in the fields human, that you should besiege it too? Any trees, however, which you know are not fruit trees, you may destroy and cut down and use to build siege-works against the hostile town until it falls" (Deut 20:19-20). The fruit tree is distinct from the "enemy" here, and is seen in its life-giving aspect, since it is capable of nourishing those who are engaged in a just repressive action. Once again, the restraint of a destructive action has as its purpose the protection of an element which is beneficial to humans.

108. The close relationship between the Creator and the earth, formed by him as a gift useful to human beings, permits one also to understand that every act that devastates creation is an offence against the Lord. On the other hand, and less evidently perhaps, even if widely attested in the Bible, when one sins against God by transgressing his commands and therefore refusing his beneficial cosmic lordship, the land suffers, undergoing processes of drought, infertility, and destruction. By divine decree the world in its flourishing or in its languishing becomes, in a certain sense, the symptom of how right or how wrong the relationship of human beings is with the Lord of the cosmos (Lev 18:25, 28; Is 24:4-6; Hos 4:1-4; etc.). Even those who do not believe in God can still feel that the degradation of the environment is caused by ignorance and human selfishness; consequently, even for non-believers, the state of health of the planet is an indicator of the justice or injustice of human beings.

The Creator entrusts the earth to humankind. As in every divine commandment, and indirectly suggested in Gen 2:15, the Lord does not benefit from human obedience. The Torah is always directed exclusively to the good of the child, and is therefore intrinsically an act of love. Like every commandment of God, that of "keeping" the earth is also a call to love. It is a call to love not only things, however beautiful and useful, not only "nature", however indispensable for individual life, but also other people, who share the same natural *habitat*, and the children who will inherit the legacy left by their parents. The verb "to keep" has in itself also the sense of conserving, preserving and maintaining a specific good over the course of time; it is a verb that points towards the future, and therefore requires the individual and a specific society to think of and provide for generations to come, that they may find a "good land", and can thus live happily, in accordance with the desire of the Creator.

We conclude then that if "working" is limited by "keeping", care of the earth in turn requires the active stimulus of human intervention. The gift received is not protected by a passive attitude of inactivity. On the contrary, humankind is involved in projects and enterprises designed to defend the earth from the degradation of time and from the destructive threats of the wicked. The scrupulous maintenance of the eco-system requires a creative commitment, supported by love for human beings, both for the present poor who already suffer from the greed of the powerful few, and also for those innocent people who risk coming to live in a land devastated by the foolish neglect of our generation.

"Working" and "keeping" are therefore two joint activities. And both, as the Psalmist says, are taken on in "collaboration" with God himself, because without God human activity is a failure, while with God it is creative and beneficial:

> "If the Lord does not build the house,
> in vain do its builders labour [*work*];
> if the Lord does not guard the city,
> in vain does the guard keep watch [*keep*]."

(Ps 127:1)

Work and its laws

109. According to biblical tradition, it is in the *Torah* that one finds the normative instructions for human behaviour; these are suggested in the narrative part and then formalised in the legislative sections. This also applies to work, which must be regulated to respond to the design of the Creator and Lord.

Work-related problems

In the stories of the book of Genesis we see various aspects of working practice, marked in the main by ambiguity; from here, indirect criticism is addressed to methods of work that are apparently harmless or even commendable, but actually harmful.

Expelled from the Garden of Eden, 'ādām does not receive a different occupation; his task, in fact, remains "to work the soil" ('ădāmāh) (Gen 3:23), with the clarification, however, that the soil to be cultivated is the matter "from which he had been taken", thus explicitly referring to the mortality of human beings (Gen 3:19). Moreover, it is no longer the garden that is his place of work, but the "cursed" land, which will produce "brambles and thistles", and bread can be obtained only with "pain" and the "sweat of your face" (Gen 3:17-19). Such a description of the soil should not be generalised, because Scripture also speaks of fertile lands comparable to Eden (Gen 13:10; Deut 8:7-8) and blessed by God (Deut 11:11-12; 28:3-5).

110. However, we can see the perspective of Gen 3:17-18 illustrated in the story of Cain, the first son of Adam and Eve, who is actually presented as one who "worked the soil", unlike his brother Abel, who was instead "a shepherd and kept flocks" (Gen 4:2). This diversity of the professions of farmer and shepherd would seem motivated by the fact that agricultural activity was not sufficient to feed everyone; however, the difference in work also involves variations in culture and in religious practices (Gen 4:3-4); now, the particular lifestyle, combined with a different quality of life (Gen 4:4-5), inevitably leads to confrontations, jealousies and rivalries, as indeed the history of humanity attests. With this story, Scripture does not intend to teach that there is a good profession, such as that of shepherd, and a bad one, that of farmer, but rather that one must do good in one's work without affecting the right of those who have a different occupation.

Diversity in the professions continues in fact with the descendants of Cain: some of his "sons" were "tent-dwelling herdsmen" (Gen 4:20), which implies pastoral activity; others played "the harp and the pipe" (Gen 4:21), inaugurating the noble art of music; and still others dedicated themselves to working "copper and iron" (Gen 4:22), a practice that will improve working techniques, but will pave the way for increasingly destructive instruments of war, appropriate to the children of the vengeful

Lamech (Gen 4:23-24). Once again, what is praiseworthy is not the occupation itself, but the way it is exercised; even what is good can in fact be transformed by evil intentions of the heart into an occasion of abuse.

111. The account of Genesis adds that Cain became the "builder of a city" (Gen 4:17); the murderer who had been condemned to be "a homeless wanderer", threatened with death by anyone who met him (Gen 4:12-14), stands paradoxically at the origin of the city, a place of protection and a means of social life and of collaboration between human beings. The city, however, will not always receive a positive evaluation in the pages of the Bible. The very building of the great city, which will be called Babel (Gen 11:9), with its tower that sought to touch heaven (Gen 11:4), is judged by God as a mistaken project, perhaps because of its arrogance towards the Most High (Gen 11:6), perhaps because it is the expression of an imperialist intent that does not respect the differences between the various groups of people (Gen 10:5). The ambiguity of the city will subsequently be demonstrated in the story of Sodom, which displays violence towards foreigners, and for this reason will be annihilated by God (Gen 19:1-29).

112. As the narrative continues beyond the book of Genesis, the motif of the construction of the city returns at the beginning of the book of Exodus, putting before the reader reprehensible policies and executive procedures. Here the work of construction appears in its most brutal and most offensive form. At the start it was publicised by the Pharaoh as an initiative favourable to the Egyptians, because, on the one hand, "storage cities" needed to be built to guarantee future supplies of food (Ex 1:11b), and, on the other hand, it subjugated and weakened a foreign population, the Hebrews, who were considered dangerous (Ex 1:10-11a). The tyranny of the ruler, disguised by apparent motivations of shrewd prudence (Ex 1:10), produces in reality an oppressive system, based on working conditions which are intolerable for those forced to leave their land, change occupation (cf. Gen 47:5-6), and undergo servitude which was ever more demanding (Ex 1:13-14; 5:10) and vexatious (Ex 5:14). Biblical tradition will adopt the image of these working conditions as the symbol of "slavery", from which the Lord will free his people; and memory of this will be the basis of the legislation concerning, in particular, human work.

Labour laws

113. The Law given by the Lord to the liberated people concerns all areas of life, including working activity; it provides directives to the individual subject involved in work, and governs the relationships that arise from work and which must be regulated by justice. Four groups of laws deserve specific consideration.

(1) THE COMMANDMENT OF THE SABBATH

The motif of work is made clear above all in the Sabbath commandment, which is situated at the heart of the Decalogue, and developed with an unparalleled textual extension in comparison with the other adjacent precepts, which is a sign of its centrality for the faith of Israel. The very severe penalties for offenders (Ex 31:14-15; Num 15:32-36) aim to confirm this importance. Moreover, in the formulation of this commandment we find major differences between the two editions of the Decalogue, that in Ex 20:8-11 and that in Deut 5:12-15, further confirming the richness of meaning contained in the Sabbath precept.

The norm concerns what a person "does" (*'āśāh*), including any type of "service" (*melā'kāh*) (Ex 20:9; Deut 5:13). Describing it as "work" (*'ābad*), God commands it should last for six days, implicitly condemning idleness, therefore, while forbidding work on the seventh day, which is called the "Sabbath", that is "cessation". The Sabbath therefore takes on the function of the limit, becoming a "sign" (Ex 31:13,17; Ezek 20:12) both of the consecration of time ("to keep it holy": Ex 20:8; Deut 5:12), and of the relationship with God ("for the Lord": Ex 20:10; Deut 5:14).

114. The Decalogue does not develop further the duty of work, which is not addressed even in other legislative sections; it insists rather on the privileged day on which the Israelites are asked to suspend their activities, so as to express symbolically their belonging to the covenant with the God of creation and redemption. To adhere to the Lord is equivalent to welcoming reverently what the Lord gives. By renouncing the work of their hands, believers abandon every idolatrous work that foolishly might claim to be life-giving, when in actual fact it enslaves (Ex 20:4-5; Deut 5:8-9); in the radical passivity of their being, believers claim to live only because God works in them and in all creation.

On the other hand, the Sabbath is the day on which the faithful imitate their God, conforming to what the Lord did "at the beginning" of the world and of salvific history. The editing of Exodus thematises in a comprehensive way the idea of the imitation of the Creator, making reference to Gen 1 ("remember": Ex 20:8): as the temporal order of the week regulated the Creator's action, so it must be for his creature. In six days God made the universe (Ex 20:11a) and on the seventh day "he rested" (Ex 20:11b). Human beings will do the same: in their work they will make present the divine work, and on the Sabbath they will experience the peaceful enjoyment of all that has been "accomplished" by the Creator (Gen 2:1-2) and by themselves.

115. The motivation of the deuteronomic editor is different and complementary. By emphasising the verbal root that refers to work ('ābad), in which the "servile" component is clearly present, the legislator brings out the "memory" (Deut 5:15) of Egyptian slavery, from which the Lord redeemed Israel. The Sabbath is thus "observed" (Deut 5:12) when it is experienced as the day of liberty in respect of any form of servitude, especially that which human beings impose on themselves with idolatry. By placing a limit on one's own work, the person concretely achieves independence from any external obligation; freedom will then be found in enjoying free time, which escapes the need for economic profit and social approval.

Moreover, in imitation of God, the Sabbath is also the day of the act of liberation on the part of the *pater familias* towards those who are subject to his authority in the house, from the children to the servants, from the foreign labourer to the domestic animals that collaborate in the daily toil (Deut 5:14). The freedom obtained by the Lord is thus placed at the service of the enslaved. The hand, the power, of the father, who gives rest to his family members, accomplishes an effective saving action, comparable to that of the Lord who acted "with strong hand and outstretched arm". Unfortunately, the active and beneficial requirement of the Sabbath was not always understood even by the Jewish tradition (cf. Mt 12:11-12; Lk 14:5), which insisted unilaterally on abstaining from any form of work (cf. Is 58:13-14; Lk 13:14); Jesus, however, by carrying out healings precisely on the Sabbath day, brought out the full meaning of this sacred day: by freeing those who were held in slavery from an even stronger power than that of the Pharaoh he made it clear that "the Sabbath was made for man, not man for the Sabbath" (Mk 2:27), and above all he presented himself as "equal to God" (Jn 5:18, 23) and as the Saviour (Mk 3:4; Lk 6:9; Jn 5:34).

116. The spirit and the beneficial force of the Sabbath are further displayed in other legal prescriptions, with the effect of proving the salvific character of the norm. We remember the prescription of the so-called "sabbatical year" (Ex 23:10-11; Lev 25:2-7), during which the landowners refrained from cultivating the land, freely making available to the poor (Ex 23:11; Lev 25:6) the spontaneous produce of their fields. Similarly, the various festive celebrations are marked by the command "you will do no heavy work" (Lev 23:7, 8, 21, 25, 28, 31, 35-36; Num 28:18, 25, 26; Deut 16:8). On such days Deuteronomy invites people to "rejoice in the presence of the Lord", together with the son and the daughter, the serving men and women, with the foreigner, as on the Sabbath, and with the poor, in memory of being saved from slavery in Egypt (Deut 16:11-12). Each feast is like an annual Sabbath, in the common participation of Israel in the divine blessing.

Sunday, the day of the Lord

117. While recognising that on festive days there are people who are forced to work for the good of all, today it is more necessary than ever to rediscover the spirit of the biblical norm of the Sabbath, in a world in which the logic of economic gain threatens the dignity of people, and the quality of family relationships. The disciples of Christ, on the first day of the week, commemorate the fulfilment of the liberating salvation that took place in the resurrection of Jesus. A time of prayer, of generosity and of solidarity, Sunday contributes to the development of family relationships, as well as giving a human face to the working week. The time of "rest" should not therefore be filled with activities that end up being as stressful as professional activity, nor "consecrated" to entertainments that do not do credit to the greatness and the spiritual dimension of the human person. In this perspective, Sunday takes on a "prophetic" dimension, since it not only affirms the absolute primacy of God, but also the dignity of the human being that must prevail over any other economic or organisational concern. A symbolic anticipation of the "new heavens and new earth", the Lord's day (Apoc 1:10), a day of freedom and solidarity, will then truly be a day for the child of man (Mk 2:27).

(2) LAWS THAT PROTECT WORKERS

118. In Israel the legislation concerning the "slave" is significant and innovative compared to the customs of the contemporary world, for the slave is usually a fellow citizen who has become a "servant", forced to work for a master as compensation for an unpaid debt. Leviticus says: "If your kinsman becomes impoverished while with you and sells himself to you, you shall not make him do the work of a slave; you will treat him like an employee or member of the household, and he will work for you until the jubilee year" (Lev 25:39-40). On the one hand, therefore, respectful regard is to be shown towards an impoverished "brother", who is to be considered a collaborator, and not to be treated "harshly" (Lev 25:43), in contrast to the way the Egyptians treated the Israelites (Ex 1:13-14). On the other hand, he should be "released" at the end of the seventh year (Ex 21:2; Deut 15:12); indeed, in memory of what happened when the Lord redeemed his people from servitude (Deut 15:15), the brother should not be let go "empty handed" (Deut 15:13); and the legislator specifies: "You must provide liberally things from your flock, from your threshing-floor and from your winepress; you must make a present proportionate to the blessing which the Lord your God has bestowed on you" (Deut 15:14), so that the poor man can resume his activity with dignity, without resorting to begging.

The ban on practising any form of exploitation is extended

also to the relationships between employer and paid employee (Deut 24:14); in particular, the Law insists on wages being paid for work on the same day (Lev 19:13; Deut 24:15), taking into account primarily the need of the worker (Job 7:2). For this reason Sirach will say: "to deprive an employee of wages is to shed blood" (Sir 34:22); and James, heir of the Hebrew traditions (cf. Jer 22:13; Mal 3:5), will condemn the speculators with very harsh words: "See how the wages of the labourers mowing your fields, which you have held back, are crying out against you! The cries of the reapers have reached the ears of the Lord Sabaoth [cf. Deut 24:15] [...] You condemned and killed the righteous one; he does not resist you" (Jam 5:4, 6).

(3) RULES REGARDING PUBLIC OFFICE

119. In the Deuteronomic Code we find rules governing the "services" of authority in the Israelite community; these concern in particular the duties of the judges (Deut 16:18-20; 17:8-13), the king (Deut 17:14-20), the priests (Deut 18:1-8) and the prophet (Deut 18:9-22). Each of these professional categories faces the temptation of abusing its authority to obtain advantages; for this reason, both the Law (Ex 18:21; 23:2, 6-9; Deut 1:16-17; 16:19-20; 17:16-17), and the prophetic tradition (1 Sam 8:3; Is 1:23; 5:23; 33:15; 56:11; Jer 6:13; 8:10; Ezek 22:27-28; Am 5:12; Mic 3:5, 11) and the sapiential tradition (Prov 1:10-19; 15:27; 17:23; 28:16) will inculcate the need for honesty, impartiality and the exclusive search for justice in the exercise of these duties, especially when dealing with the defenceless. One may perhaps add that, in Deuteronomy, a particular "virtue" is recommended to each of the categories mentioned above: to the judge, justice (Deut 16:20), to the king, humility (Deut 17:16-17), to priests, trust in God, along with the renunciation of land ownership (Deut 18:2), and to prophets, respect for the truth (Deut 18:20).

(4) THE "SERVICE" DESTINED FOR GOD

120. It should not be forgotten that worship, in its various expressions and forms, is interpreted by Scripture as the provision of a service; in this regard use is made of the terms for "work", such as the verb ʿābad (Ex 3:12; 7:16; Deut 6:13; 10:12) and the noun ʿăbōdāh (Ex 12:25-26; 13:5; Num 3:7), to suggest that in this activity human beings live their vocation as "servants" for the Lord. There is no lack of ambiguity in this concept, which would seem to present the Most High as a "lord" desiring to be served out of necessity (cf. Is 43:23-24); however, one can draw from this a useful lesson for the understanding of life as a "liturgy", sacred activity which consists in giving thanks to God, the origin of everything and the universal provider of all good. For this reason the priests in the temple, even if they apparently violate the Sabbath (Mt 12:5), actually celebrate it with dignity.

Work and prayer

121. The relationship between work and prayer is indirectly present in the commandment about the Sabbath: in the actual application of the commandment the "sanctification" of the seventh day is accomplished through the practice of prayer and liturgical worship. Ps 92, for example, is introduced as "song of the Sabbath". More directly, the legislation concerning the celebration of the feasts of Israel, in addition to prescribing abstention from work, invites a sacrificial offering to the Lord in an atmosphere of praise and blessing.

The position of Sirach is more complex. He believes that the activity of the manual worker is already prayer (Sir 38:34), probably because such is the inevitable situation of the humble worker; nevertheless, he has special praise for the scribe who, free from servile duties, as a first task addresses to the Lord a prayer to obtain the spirit of understanding, in order to reflect adequately on the mysteries of God (Sir 39:5-7). King Solomon also invokes the gift of wisdom from the Most High to govern the people righteously (Wis 8:21-9:5; cf. also 1 Kgs 3:4-15). Every profession is good, therefore, insofar as it expresses, in a way proper to itself, a prayerful relationship with God.

122. It is in the *Psalter* that we find the most complete attestation of how Israel prayed in relation to the work done by human hands. Different aspects contribute to expressing how work is seen in the light of the relationship with God.

First of all, a quite peaceful acceptance of daily "toil" appears (Ps 104:23); inserted in the celebratory framework of creation, it is considered therefore an element that does not disturb the harmony of life but rather exalts the wisdom of the Creator (Ps 104:24). Blessedness is identified with being able to feed on the "labour of your hands", when parents and children gather around the table, welcoming the heavenly blessing (Ps 128:1-4).

The psalmist, however, does not rejoice in work, but recognises with a reverent prayerful attitude that tireless human activity, going on from morning to evening, produces a "bread of toil", while God gives what is necessary "in sleep" when all activity is suspended (Ps 127:2-3; cf. Prov 10:22). It is "in vain", that is, without real efficacy, that human beings build the house or watch over the city, if the Lord is not active where they toil (Ps 127:1). Such a divine presence, which takes the form of collaboration, is formulated in the Psalter as a cooperation of "hands", that of God Almighty coming to give vigour and perseverance to the weak human hand (Ps 89:22). From this truth arises the prayer that asks the Lord not to "discard" (Ps 138:8), but to "strengthen", that is to give perseverance and strength to the work of human hands (Ps 90:17; cf. also Ps 18:35; 80:16).

The hands of the believer are stretched out therefore in supplication (Ps 28:2; 77:3; 141:2; 143:6), in the expectation of receiving; but they are also raised in an attitude of praise (Ps 134:2) for the marvellous and tireless work of the hands of the Creator (Ps 8:4,7; 95:5; 102:26; 119:73) and Saviour (Ps 44:2; 78:42; 109:26-27; 139:10). This is how the Israelite celebrates the Sabbath of the Lord.

Necessity and limits of human work

123. It is not surprising that the *wisdom literature*, constantly concerned with promoting life (Prov 3:2,18,22; 4:13; 9:11; etc.), widely discusses the phenomenon of human work, outlining its implications with particular insight, and subjecting its various aspects to a subtle examination.

In the collections that we can consider to be an expression of "traditional" wisdom, we find observations and counsels that have parallels also in contemporary cultures. In these literatures the hardworking person is particularly exalted, above all if ready to combine diligence, astuteness and audacity. At the end of the book of *Proverbs*, the profile of the "woman of value" is presented, which some commentators believe is a personification of wisdom itself, to be sought and "found" (Prov 31:10) because of her talents and her priceless gifts. She is described in terms of her tireless activity (Prov 31:15, 18), comprised of manual work (Prov 31:13, 17, 19-20), resourcefulness in investments (Prov 31:14, 16, 22, 24), and practical kindness towards family members (Prov 31:11-12, 15, 21) and the poor (Prov 31:20).

On the one hand, therefore, the world of wisdom praises those who are industrious, because intelligent hard work produces wealth (Prov 10:4; 11:16; 12:27; 21:5) and power (Prov 12:24); on the other hand, and often with antithetical parallelism, the *lazy* person is systematically ridiculed, because indolence, justified because of false fears (Prov 22:13; 26:13), is not only useless for others (Prov 10:26; 18:9; Sir 22:1-2), but is damaging for the person (Prov 12:27; 15:19; 19:15; Qoh 10:18), causes poverty (Prov 10:4; 12:11; 20:4,13; 24:30-34) and ultimately leads to death (Prov 13:4; 21:25; Qoh 4:5). Mention deserves to be made of some of the wittiest sayings that criticise with irony those who live in idleness:

"Idler, go to the ant;
ponder her ways and grow wise:
no one gives her orders,
no overseer, no master,
yet all through the summer she gets her food ready,
and gathers her supplies at harvest time.
How long will you lie there, idler?
When will you rise from your sleep?
A little sleep, a little slumber,
a little folding of the arms to lie back,

and poverty comes like a vagrant
and want like a warrior armed"

(Prov 6:6-11)

"The door turns on its hinges,
the idler on a bed."

(Prov 26:14)

"Into the dish the idler dips his hand,
but cannot bring it back to the mouth."

(Prov 19:24; cf. also 26:15)

Being lazy is equivalent to being foolish; consequently, to become wise it is necessary to accept the need for effort, comparable to work in the fields (Sir 6:18-20). The sages of Israel promote as something beneficial the *hand* that produces wealth; but they do not fail to recommend moderation (Prov 30:8-9; Qoh 4:6; Sir 11:10-11), modesty (Prov 15:33; Sir 3:17-24; 10:26-27) and above all justice (Prov 11:5, 18; 12:28; Sir 11:21; 31:8-11) and generosity (Prov 11:24-25; Sir 4:1-10), because without these virtues the blessing of the Lord will be lacking (Prov 10:22).

124. In the book of *Sirach* we find a deeper reflection on work, through the presentation of different professions (Sir 38–39) which are assessed in the light of wisdom. The activity of the doctor (Sir 38:1-15) is described, and later the task of the farmer (Sir 38:25-26), the craftsman (Sir 38:27), the blacksmith (Sir 38:28) and the potter (Sir 38:29-30), with words of appreciation for the skills involved (Sir 38:31) and the useful contribution of their products to the life of the city (Sir 38:32a, 34). Sirach actually says that these workers "sustain the structure of the world" (Sir 38:34), thereby using a beautiful formulation to express the realisation of the "care of creation" entrusted to humanity by the Creator (Gen 2:15). Reservations, however, are expressed by the author regarding their exercise of wisdom, which is necessary to give counsel (Sir 38:32b) and to make judgements (Sir 38:33); and this prepares the eulogy of the activity of the scribe, who, not being engaged in practical activities (Sir 38:24), can be devoted to study (Sir 39:1-3), to journeys of learning (Sir 39:4) and to prayer (Sir 39:5), and can thus reach the highest form of wisdom (Sir 39:6-11; cf. also Wis 6:15-21), a source of beneficial teaching for all who desire life (Sir 24:30-34).

125. Traditional wisdom, present above all in Proverbs and Sirach, expresses, therefore, a substantially positive evaluation of work. A critical stance, however, is attested in other wisdom writings. *Qoheleth*, in a certain sense, is the most radical in posing the question about the "profit" (*yitrôn*) obtained by the unceasing toil of human beings (Qoh 1:3; 3:9; 5:15). He asserts that he personally deployed energy and wisdom in every type of activity, procuring for himself wealth and pleasures (Qoh 2:4-10), and he concludes: "I then reflected on all that my hands had achieved and all the effort I had put into its achieving. What vanity it all was, what chasing after the wind! There is nothing to be gained (*yitrôn*) under the sun" (Qoh 2:11). Bitterness becomes "hatred" of work, because the results will be left to others (Qoh 2:17-21), and even "hatred" of life (Qoh 2:17), because the days of the human being are nothing but sorrow and painful discomfort (Qoh 2:23). Such a vision, however, does not lead to apathy or depression. It constitutes rather a warning not to overestimate the "profit" of the works that everyone can perform "under the sun", since everything, though beautiful and wise, is subjected to the regime of "vanity" (Qoh 4:4), that is, of the ephemeral.

126. In the book of *Job*, too, there appears, though veiled, a critical assessment of human effort. In poetic form two activities are described, which are difficult and important: work in the mines (Job 28:1-11) and trade in precious metals (Job 28:15-19), both activities which seek things of great value. However, at the end of each of the two sections, the protagonist asks himself: "where is wisdom to be found?" (Job 28:12) and "where does wisdom come from?" (Job 28:20). Here then it is not simply stated, following tradition, that wisdom is more precious than gold and gems (Prov 3:15; 8:11; Wis 7:9), but rather that human activities, even the most daring and enterprising, can find jewels, but they do not reach the wisdom that is known only by God (Job 28:23-27). This is an invitation to avoid all *hybris*, finding instead in the fear of God (Job 28:28) the right path for human beings.

127. Finally, even the book of the *Wisdom* of Solomon, speaking in its own distinctive style of the most prestigious and refined kinds of work, brings out something that needs to be condemned, when the author sees the craftsman making an idol, a deceptive trap and a source of evil for society (Wis 13-15). A line of thought is developed here, already attested in the prophets (cf. Is 44:9-20; Jer 10:1-5) and in the Psalms (cf. Ps 115:4-8), which with irony derides the foolishness of the making of idols. From this there follows not only reproach of the fetishes and talismans that were venerated in ancient times, but also a warning to recognise and to repudiate whatever is idolatrous in the various works of human hands and hearts.

Wealth

128. Idols, the biblical texts say, are "gold and silver" (Ex 20:23; Deut 7:25; Hos 2:10; Hab 2:19; Wis 13:10; etc.); this simple consideration invites us to reflect more generally on the theme of wealth, usually seen as the welcome result of different forms of work, insofar as it provides guarantees for the future and attracts public honour. The Old Testament considers that prosperity is a blessing that the Lord pours out on the just (Gen 13:2; Deut 28:12; 1 Kgs 3:13; Ps 112:3; Prov 14:24; Wis 7:11); but it also warns against avarice and any form of excessive exaltation of riches, which inevitably take on an idolatrous aspect (Deut 7:25-26; cf. Eph 5:5). Scripture often speaks of rich people who are arrogant, abusive and oblivious of the poor, destined for the divine judgement of condemnation (Is 5:8-10; Jer 12:1-2; Ezek 27:25-27; Am 3:9-11; 8:4-6; Ps 49:17-18; 73:3-20; Job 21:7-18; Qoh 5:9-10; Sir 31:5-7; etc.). In the light of the New Testament, the believer is invited to recognise the "beatitude" of poverty (Mt 5:3; Lk 6:20), and not to aspire, with one's work, to the riches of this world, which are destined to be left behind (Lk 12:15-21); the Lord says that "you cannot serve both God and money" (Lk 16:13), and then urges one to seek and to find what is truly precious, the pearl of great price (Mt 13:45-46), for which it is worth leaving everything to acquire what gives eternal life.

Human work and divine "work"

129. The view of the *prophets* on the world of human activity is also somewhat critical. Although it starts from the good principle of industriousness and ingenuity and provides useful products, the work of human beings does not conform to the divine mandate when it conceals distortions of the heart and produces grave injustices.

The work of human beings

As mentioned in the paragraph on the world of wisdom, the relentless struggle of the prophets against idolatry is also expressed in a robust condemnation of the foolish and blasphemous process of forging an image and attributing to it divine power. With an element of sarcasm, the prophet describes a man who cuts a tree, takes part of it to light the oven and cook food, then with the rest carves an idol, which he invokes saying: "Save me, for you are my god" (Is 44:14-17). The deceit of this activity lies in the fact that the artisan commits energy (Is 41:6-7; 44:12) and great ability (Is 44:13) to the work of forging a cult object, making it beautiful and gleaming, for it is covered with gold (Is 40:19; Jer 10:4; Ezek 16:17; Hos 2:10; Bar 6:8-9) and adorned with splendid garments (Jer 10:9; Bar 6:10-11), so that it is extremely attractive and gives the impression of being alive and eternal. But the idol is a delusion (Is 44:20; Jer 10:14); it does not have breath (Jer 10:14; Bar 6:24); it is a useless thing (Is 41:23; 44:9; Jer 2:8,11; 10:5; Hab 2:18-19; Bar 6:34-39, 52-68), which will vanish in the light of truth (Is 41:29; 46:1-2; Jer 10:11). The mockery of the craftsmanship that results in an intolerable sacrilege is designed to denounce not only the manufacture of sacred fetishes, but every human enterprise that claims to guarantee salvation.

To the heartfelt denunciation of the "evil" inherent in idolatry (Jer 2:13, 19), which results in an exaltation of the unique status of the Lord, Creator and Saviour (Jer 10:1-16), the prophets add a severe criticism of those human activities that violate the rules of justice on the pretext of providing some economic progress or in the illusion of achieving great technological advancement. It will not be difficult to see how all this is echoed also in modern times.

130. The first point of reproof relates to *agricultural land*, a fundamental basis for the subsistence of families, who were always threatened by poverty. The intention of the powerful is to make the work of the defenceless impossible. As is narrated paradigmatically in the story of Naboth (1 Kgs 21:1-6), the rich man, in this case King Ahab, lord in Samaria, seeks to extend his property, to make himself "greater" by taking what belongs to another (Is 5:8). The excuses given can vary, such as improving production, diversifying the harvest, beautifying the property or simply demonstrating wealthy *status* by extending the estate, with the prestige that follows from it. The law forbids such covetous accumulation (Ex 20:17; Deut 5:21), prohibiting in particular the moving of the "neighbour's boundary mark, positioned by earlier generations", that is, those stones at the boundaries of the fields that define every family's inherited portion of the land given by God (Deut 19:14; 27:17; cf. Hos 5:10; Prov 22:28; 23:10; Job 24:2). In the book of Joshua it is said that the land of Canaan was distributed by means of drawing lots, intended as an expression of the divine will, among the various tribes, clans and families of the Israelites (Josh 13–21); this is certainly not the chronicle of a historical event, but rather a theological vision in narrative form, which affirms, first of all, that the land in which they live is a gift from God (Lev 25:23), and, secondly, that it must be shared, so that everyone is given the opportunity to "reside" as a citizen, providing for his or her livelihood and enjoying all civil rights. The prophets embody this perspective of justice, and therefore denounce the plots and usurpations of the landowners, who take possession of the fields of others, driving people out of their houses for the sole purpose of personal enrichment (Is 5:8-10; Mic 2:1-5). More generally, the prophetic voice criticises the violence of territorial conquests carried out by imperialist regimes, which use superior military force for their unjust purposes, and, without any respect for life, reduce entire populations to slavery (Am 1:3–2:3; Hab 1:5-10, 14-15, 17; 2:6-8, 15-17).

131. Another activity for denunciation identified by the prophets is that of *fraudulent trade*, which involves tampering with "weights and measures", which the Law seeks to maintain as a necessary guarantee of fairness (Lev 19:35-36; Deut 25:13-16). Various kinds of fraud lead to the poor being left hungry (Am 8:4-7; Mic 6:9-15; cf. also Hos 12:8-9). On the international front there are condemnations of kingdoms such as Tyre, which made trade an enormous economic success and achieved universal prestige (Ezek 27:3-36); their proud triumph has actually been based on injustice and violence (Ezek 28:15-18). Not every exchange of goods is reprimanded, and trade is indeed necessary to improve living conditions; only professional activity which enriches itself unduly at the expense of others is denounced.

132. Finally, the activity of *public works*, in particular that of important buildings, such as palaces, stately homes, wall defences, sanctuaries, bridges and roads, is subjected to scrutiny by the prophets. Grandiose undertakings, which give prestige to the rulers and are objects of admiration over the centuries, are indeed often the fruit of oppressive and abusive practices. Solomon had built palaces and completed the great Temple in Jerusalem, but his workers had paid the price, being subjected to harsh servitude, comparable to slavery in Egypt (1 Kgs 12:4), and his son Rehoboam made things worse (1 Kgs 12:14). "Woe", cries the prophet, "to one who builds a town with bloodshed and founds a city on wrong-doing" (Hab 2:12); disaster will fall on what is built and maintained by unacceptable injustices (Am 3:9-11; Mic 3:9-12; Zeph 3:1-8), including that of not paying workers their wages (Jer 22:13-17; Mal 3:5).

The work of God

133. In the account of Gen 1–2, the work of God, who creates, makes, divides, plants, and gives, is presented first, and then the task entrusted to human beings to work and keep the garden, with which history begins. In Gen 2:2-3 it is said that God "rested after all his work of creating"; in reality, as is affirmed in the rest of the biblical tradition, the Lord does not stop acting (cf. Jn 5:17): without God history does not exist, and it is not understood without seeing that the Lord, who is the origin of everything, is at work actually displaying his omnipotence (Is 46:10-11) and in his constant desire for what is good (Deut 32:4; Is 26:12).

It is above all the prophets who testify to the active presence of God in human affairs (Is 43:13), thus inspiring also the other sacred writers. In their pronouncements they use, in an obviously analogical way, the same terminology that is used to define "work", in particular the verbs "to do" (*'āśāh*), "to act" (*pā'al*), with nouns derived from these roots, and also the term "work" (*melā'kāh*) (Gen 2:2-3; Ps 73:28), all with substantially the same meaning. The prophets not only remember the act of creating the world (Is 45:12,18; Jer 10:12-13; 14:22; 27:5), but they take over the same vocabulary especially when they evoke an historical event such as Israel's election, with its associated benefits (Is 5:12; Hab 3:2). For this, in addition to the terminology indicated above, they have recourse to metaphors that relate to work, comparing, for example, God to a farmer who plants a vineyard and takes care of it (Is 5:1-7; 27:3; Jer 2:21; cf. also Ps 80:9-10), or to a potter who by moulding gives form to things (Is 29:16; 43:7; 44:2; 64:7; Jer 18:6).

134. The believer knows that God acts in a wonderful way in human history (Is 12:5; 25:1; Ps 77:13; 92:5; 143:5), not only at the beginning, but continuously, and especially when the world goes through a tragic phase of corruption caused by the wickedness of human beings. The prophets raise their voice precisely at that juncture to reveal that God is active, just when everyone would say that God is absent or impotent (Deut 32:27; Is 5:19). As will be developed more extensively in the fourth chapter of this Document, it is the constant attestation of the biblical authors that the work of God presents itself as a juxtaposition of two contrasting acts: it is said that he gives death and life (Deut 32:39; 1 Sam 2:6; Wis 16:13; Tob 13:2), breaks down and exalts (Ps 75:8; 2 Chr 25:8; Sir 7:11), wounds and heals (Deut 32:39), destroys and rebuilds (Jer 31:28), forms the light and creates darkness, makes peace and creates disaster (Is 45:7). The divine action is not easy to understand (Jer 9:11; Hos 14:10; Ps 92:6-7; 107:43), because of this very contrast. Yet each of the two contrasting acts is significant and expresses the salvific purpose of the Lord: in the negative act, he brings out the bad effects of the evil committed by human beings (Jer 2:19; Prov 16:4), while in the positive act, the one in which the "work" of God appears more clearly, the ultimate eschatological event is announced, in which the saving work of the Lord of history is manifested (Is 44:23; Am 9:12; Hab 1:5). Here, too, metaphors taken from human work are used, whereby God is compared to a refiner (Mal 3:2), a builder (Is 44:26; Jer 18:9; 31:4), a farmer (Is 60:21; Jer 24:6), etc., symbols that indicate the restoration of everything, a kind of new creation (Is 43:19; 66:22) brought about in forgiveness. Believers, enlightened by the prophetic word, will then be able, in full truth, to raise the song of praise, saying: "What great deeds the Lord worked for us" (Ps 126:3), "How great and wonderful are your works, Lord God Almighty; righteous and true are your ways, king of the nations" (Apoc 15:3; cf. Ps 111:2-3).

God makes his active presence known through the prophets: he does nothing if he does not first communicate his wise plan to his "servants" (Am 3:7; cf. also Gen 18:17), who, with their word, become the beginning of wisdom and the source of hope for the world. The prophets are witnesses, not properly bringers of salvation; they perform "signs"; they do not make "reality" exist, for this is the work of God alone. Without them, however, without their "work", faith could not be aroused in people's hearts, and the work of the Lord would remain unknown or would be rejected. The ancient prophets, whose oracles Israel preserved, will have as successors the prophets of the new covenant, permanent witnesses of the definitive and perfect work carried out by God in Christ.

Work, service, ministry

135. In the narratives and speeches of the *gospels* we do not find a particular concern to present projects of work intended to achieve tangible economic results. More precisely, we do not see that models are presented or directives provided that would introduce innovative elements with respect to the traditions of the Old Testament.

We are told that Jesus was a "craftsman" (*tektōn*) (Mk 6:3), "son of a craftsman" (Mt 13:55), in accordance with what usually happened in the passing on of various trades within families. His first disciples were fishermen (Mk 1:16-20); and another is said to have been a tax collector (Mk 2:14). This information suggests an appreciation for manual activities; but their main purpose is to highlight the transition from a profession taken over from the father and carried on to support the family to a role arising from a charismatic "vocation", which is fostered by God or by his spokesperson in order to encourage a new activity that will benefit many. As happened with Moses (Ex 3:1) and David (1 Sam 16:11; 17:34), who were called from shepherding to be leaders of Israel (Ex 3:10; 2 Sam 7:8), as with Gideon, Elisha and Amos, farmers or breeders (Jdg 6:11; 1 Kgs 19:19; Am 7:15), the first of whom became a leader and judge (Jdg 6:14) and the others prophets (1 Kgs 19:21; Am 7:14-15), so the apostles changed their way of life because of their encounter with Christ. All this should not be read as a sort of promotion according to human standards; rather, it is a question of the call to become the Lord's "servants" for work of a spiritual nature, which will entail persecution (Mt 5:11-12), humiliations (Mt 23:11-12) and even the giving of life itself (Mt 16:25; 23:34-35).

136. In the gospels, and especially in the parables, various kinds of work are mentioned, such as that of the sower (Mt 13:3), the labourer (Mt 20:1), the merchant of pearls (Mt 13:45), the steward (Mt 24:45), the manager (Lk 16:1), as well as that of the housewife who kneads the flour (Mt 13:33). These references do not provide specific teachings of a professional nature, but simply an encouragement to treasure work, along with diligence and wisdom, qualities that make the servant trustworthy (Mt 8:9; 24:45; 25:21). A sense of achievement in the assured result of a job well done is also fostered (Mt 7:24-25; 24:46; 25:29), without, however, claiming merit with God, because each one must consider oneself a "useless servant", content simply to have done one's duty (Lk 17:10).

In the gospels, however, the interpretation of the "ministry" of teaching and healing carried out by Jesus and his disciples in terms of "work" (Mt 9:37-38; Jn 5:17; 9:4) takes on great importance. The Master, with appropriate instructions and above all with his example, prepares the apostles for that particular work, which will be highly beneficial for the human community. This work "is like" (cf. Mt 13:24, 31, 33, 44-45, 47) that of the ploughman (Lk 9:62), the sower (Mt 13:3), the reaper (Mt 9:37-38; Jn 4:38), the shepherd (Jn 10:14), the fisherman (Mt 4:19; 13:47-48), in that it produces fruit, and perhaps expects payment, as a reward for work done (Mt 10:10; 20:2; Lk 10:7); all this of course must be seen as a metaphor. In addition to valuing occupations of a spiritual nature, as Sirach already did, the divine Master directs desire towards rewards that are heavenly, lasting and supremely fulfilling, thus going beyond Qoheleth's criticism of the vanity of human activity. On the other hand, since the work of Christ and his disciples imitates that of God himself (Jn 4:34; 5:17; 17:4), it becomes an inspiring model for every type and kind of human work, introducing in particular the principle of "service" (Lk 22:26-27; Jn 13:13-17), of "gratuitousness" (Mt 10:8; 2 Cor 11:7), of the renunciation of the accumulation of possessions (Mt 10:10), and of generosity in letting others share in the fruits of one's own work (Mt 19:21).

The apostolic work of Paul

137. The apostle *Paul in his letters* mentions some fundamental duties regarding work. We do not find, except in passing, reference to the duty of giving a fair wage to workers (cf. Rom 4:4); this theme, as already mentioned, is in fact highlighted in Jam 5:4-6 in the form of a vehement denunciation. In a social context in which perpetual subservience is expected Paul exhorts masters to show respect and even benevolence towards slaves (Eph 6:9; Col 4:1; Phlm 8-17); and the latter are encouraged to be gently submissive with the faithful performance of the works assigned to them (1 Cor 7:21-24; Eph 6:5-8; Col 3:22-25; 1 Tim 6:1-2; Tit 2:9-10; in relation to "domestic servants" cf. 1 Pt 2:18-20).

More significant is Paul's insistence on the duty of work.

The charitable distributions to the needy, which took place in the Christian community, and probably also the expectation of the Lord's imminent return, had led some, especially in Thessalonica, to adopt idle ways, with repercussions of social disorder. The Apostle corrects this improper conduct rather harshly; and already in his first letter to the Thessalonians he writes: "However, we do urge you, brothers and sisters, to abound in love even more, and to aspire to living quietly, attending to your own business and earning your living, just as we told you to, so that you behave decently to outsiders and are not dependent on anyone" (1 Thess 4:10-12). The relationship between work and the promotion of peace in society, to be kept in mind even in our day, is then amply reiterated in the second letter to the same community: "Now we hear that there are some of you who are living in idleness, doing no work themselves but interfering with other people's. In the Lord Jesus Christ, we command and urge such people to earn the food they eat by working quietly" (2 Thess 3:11-12). The rule to follow is summed up pointedly with the famous saying: "anyone who did not wish to work should not eat" (2 Thess 3:10). In the letter to the Ephesians we have a further clarification: "The thief must steal no longer; instead he should work with his own hands what is good so that he may have something to share with someone in need" (Eph 4:28): hard work is pointed out here as the opposite of injustice, which is described as "stealing", and it promotes love, because it can contribute to the needs of the poor (cf. Acts 20:35).

138. Paul not only indicates the conduct to follow, but he repeatedly presents himself as a model to be imitated (1 Thess 4:1; 2 Thess 3:7-9), for, despite being a minister of the gospel, and therefore having the right to a tangible reward (1 Cor 3:8; 9:7-14; Gal 6:6; 1 Thess 3:9), he preferred to support himself with the work of his hands (1 Cor 4:12; 1 Thess 2:9; 2 Thess 3:7-8). This course of action is confirmed also by the book of Acts (Acts 18:3; 20:34-35). This decision of Paul, who was concerned not to be a burden on his communities (2 Cor 11:9-10; 12:13-14, 16-18; 1 Thess 2:9; 2 Thess 3:8), was meant above all to highlight the gratuitousness of his apostolic service for the edification of all (1 Cor 9:18; 2 Cor 11:7). Following the gospel tradition, this ministry is clearly interpreted as an authentic "work" (2 Tim 2:15), undertaken with total dedication, even if extremely exhausting (Gal 4:11), a work taken on as "service" (*diakonia*) (1 Cor 3:5; 4:1) which is commanded by the Lord (1 Cor 9:17) for the benefit of all (1 Cor 9:22). Aware of the importance and urgency of such a precious task, Paul involves numerous "fellow-workers" (*synergoi*) in his ministry (Rom 16:3, 9, 21; 2 Cor 8:23; Phil 2:25; 4:3; 1 Thess 3:2; Phlm 24), calling them "fellow-workers of God" (1 Cor 3:9; cf. also Mk 16:20). Mindful of the prophetic tradition, he compares missionary service to agricultural activity (1 Cor 3:5-9) and to building (1 Cor 3:10, 14), recognising at the same time that it is always and only God who makes the plant grow (1 Cor 3:7), while only Christ is the solid foundation of the building that is the Church (1 Cor 3:11).

3. ANIMALS HELPING HUMAN BEINGS

139. As already indicated in the commentary on Gen 2:18-20, the intention of the Creator is to provide a help for 'ādām, a sort of ally who could soothe his "solitude" to some extent. After the flood, God made a covenant with Noah and his descendants, including, according to his words, "every living creature that is with you: birds, cattle and every wild animal with you; everything that came out of the ark, every living thing on earth" (Gen 9:10). The repetitive description of the variety and totality of the animals stresses that one should think not just of animals that make a real contribution to human beings. Other aspects too, of a different and higher nature, will be suggested by the scriptural tradition as useful service to humankind. Recently, some have criticised the anthropocentric perspective of the biblical narrative, and it has been put forward indirectly that animals should be accorded a status that is in some way equal to that of the human being.

Scripture, however, takes a different view, as Gen 2:20 states: "but no helper was found as a partner for the man". We must grasp the correct meaning of these words. If the Bible assumes the centrality of human beings, presenting it as a feature of God's design, it does not, however, attribute to them the right to exercise a despotic control over other creatures; on the contrary, it calls for a regime of "covenant" (cf. Gen 9:9, 12; Hos 2:20), with sympathetic respect for the value of every animal and action to protect this particular work of God.

> Today animal rights activists, vegetarians and vegans practise and campaign for lifestyles, which, with increasing demands, aim to eliminate the exploitation of animals. While this represents a just condemnation of behaviour that is cruel and exploitative, it would not be in conformity with biblical tradition to prevent animals being of service to human beings. To put it another way, it is not good for human beings to be deprived of the Creator's gifts.

In this final part of our chapter we will illustrate the most important elements of humanity's relationship with the animals. We will not, however, distinguish between the various sections of the Old Testament, nor will we introduce a special consideration on the New Testament; we will only indicate, where appropriate, the innovations brought by the gospel tradition.

A help for life

140. The human being has been called by God to take care of the garden. In the garden there are not only plants, but also the animals created by God for human beings; the vocation of the farmer is complemented then by that of the shepherd who takes care of the living beings entrusted to humanity.

This responsibility is seen above all in relation to domesticated animals. The Law of Israel provides valuable regulations in this regard, such as when it prescribes not to "muzzle an ox when it is treading out the corn" (Deut 25:4); or when it requires that, on the Sabbath day, neither the ox nor the donkey, nor any other beast should work, taking advantage of the rest together with all those who are at the service of the family (Ex 20:10; 23:12; Deut 5:14); or when it requires that in the sabbatical year the fruits of the uncultivated land be left for the poor and for livestock (Ex 23:11; Lev 25:6-7). One is asked to "take home" the animal that has strayed until one can restore it to its rightful owner (Deut 22:2), and to give aid to the ox or the donkey, of a neighbour and even of an enemy, that risks succumbing under the load (Ex 23:5; Deut 22:4). Undue violence against animals is condemned (Lev 24:18, 21), and, more generally, a curb is placed on greed that would endanger the future of a species (Deut 22:6-7).

141. Some of these laws should perhaps be understood as ways to discern and as instructions for regulating, according to an "analogical" procedure, the relationship between a "master", owner, one who benefits from a service, and a "servant", a subordinate, one who provides the service. The animal would then be a metaphor for the person entrusted to the ethical responsibility of its master. We know that the legislation concerning the ox that gores, causing injury to someone (Ex 21:28-32), can also be understood as a discipline concerning the duties of the master of an unruly servant, or even the father of a violent son. The apostle Paul, probably following a procedure recognised in the rabbinic environment, applies the norm of Deut 25:4, concerning the muzzle for the ox that threshes, to the recompense due to the missionary of the gospel (1 Cor 9:9; 1 Tim 5:18). Jesus, from the care given to domestic animals, draws a lesson about what should be done for those in need (Mt 12:11-12; Lk 13:15-16). The rest granted to cattle on the Sabbath (Ex 20:10; Deut 5:14) is intended to prohibit advantage being taken of the work of an animal on the day when the work of God is celebrated; however, the application of the norm can be extended to any type of service, even that of enslaved people, that would benefit a master. Rescuing the donkey burdened by too much weight (Ex 23:5; Deut 22:4) can point to the duty of helping the person forced into excessive and unjust work. Finally, the fast and the sackcloth imposed by the king of Nineveh even on animals (Jon 3:7-8) could perhaps suggest the involvement in a penitential rite of the whole population, including those who, being slaves, were treated like animals.

142. The shepherd does not abuse other living beings, but takes care of them (1 Sam 12:3). The wisdom tradition, in fact, teaches just that:

> "The righteous understands the needs of the livestock,
> but the response of the wicked is cruelty."
>
> (Prov 12:10; cf. also Sir 7:22)

The shepherd brings the flock to pasture (Ex 3:1; Ezek 34:14; Ps 23:2), waters it (Gen 24:11, 14, 19-20; Ex 2:16-19), defends it against predators (1 Sam 17:34-36; Jn 10:11-13), building fences and sheepfolds (Num 32:16, 36; Mic 2:12; 2 Chr 32:28). Even corrective activity, such as putting a bridle on a recalcitrant animal (Ps 32:9; Prov 26:3), is seen as beneficial to the animal itself, which is trained to give better service (Jer 31:18). In this activity of shepherding, human beings, as already stated, imitate God; moreover, a certain relationship of collaborative "alliance" is established between the individual and the animal that will also serve as a metaphor for the relationship between the king and his subjects.

The shepherd, of course, derives considerable advantages from taking care of the flock, and of this he should be aware and grateful:

> "Know well the condition of your flocks;
> take good care of your herds
> for riches do not last for ever:
> a crown continues from one generation to the next.
> The grass once gone, the aftergrowth appearing,
> the hay gathered in from the mountains,
> you should have lambs to clothe you,
> goats to the price of a field,
> goat's milk sufficient to feed you,

food for your household and to provide for your young
people."

(Prov 27:23-27)

Human beings are not only nourished by animals with milk and
meat, eggs and honey, but they also obtain wool for their clothing
and hides for various needs. The ox and the donkey help in the
work of the fields (1 Sam 8:16; 1 Kgs 19:19; Is 28:28; Prov 14:4) and
are used for the transport of people (Num 22:21; Jdg 5:10; Zech 9:9)
and goods (Gen 44:13; Ex 23:5; 1 Sam 25:18; 2 Sam 16:1), while the
horse is used for combat in war (Ex 15:1; 2 Kgs 18:23-24; Hos 14:4;
Am 2:15; Ps 20:8; 33:17). The dog in the story of Tobias seems to be
a prototype of the animal who provides company (Tob 6:1; 11:4).
Some of these functions are carried out today by mechanical means,
but human life is unthinkable without this useful presence of other
living beings. In this the religious person recognises a precious gift
of the Creator (1 Tim 4:4-5).

A help to become wise

143. There are many instances in the Bible where the behaviour
of animals is also shown to have much to teach human beings.
Thus another aspect of the help provided to *'ādām* by the Creator
is shown, through those very beings in whom God has placed
helpful forms of the spirit of wisdom.

Animals teach

The ant, for example, as indicated above, is a model of
industriousness (Prov 6:6-11; 30:25); and the bee, "small among
winged creatures", but with produce that is "the basis of sweetness"
(Sir 11:3), can teach human beings to appreciate the result of
actions without being influenced by how small the actor is. On the
other hand, smallness is not an obstacle to perfection, as shown
by ants, coneys, locusts and lizards, which teach everyone, even
the king, both how to organise and how to penetrate closed places
(Prov 30:24-28). The qualities inherent in the different species of

animals allow the biblical writers to use metaphors to illustrate the behaviour of God and of the just: God is compared to an eagle, which carries the young on its wings (Ex 19:4) and watches over its brood (Deut 32:11); Jesus said that he longed to gather together the children of Jerusalem "as a bird gathers her chicks under her wings" (Mt 23:37); the prophet speaks of being similar to a "lamb led to the slaughterhouse" (Is 53:7; Jer 11:19), and so on.

Some animals demonstrate a capacity for "discernment" superior to that of humans. The donkey of Balaam anticipates its master in seeing the angel of the Lord who stands in the way with drawn sword in hand (Num 22:22-34); this is not intended to be a mockery of pagan prophetism, but rather a criticism of humans who are sometimes less insightful than the animals they ride. This is confirmed by Isaiah, who writes:

> "The ox knows its owner
> and the donkey its master's crib;
> Israel does not know,
> my people do not understand"

> (Is 1:3)

Animals therefore know how to recognise who is in charge; they also know where to find food, while people who have received countless pieces of knowledge behave foolishly. This truth is reiterated by Jeremiah, who compares the useful instinct of migratory birds with the inability to change attitude that distinguishes by contrast the people of Jerusalem:

> "Even the stork in the sky knows its seasons;
> turtledove, swallow and crane observe their time of migration
> but my people do not know the Law (mišpāṭ) of the Lord"
> (Jer 8:7)

The witness of animals to the mystery of life

144. All this should move humans to "look" at the animals, carefully observing their behaviour, not only to draw from it suggestions on how to act (Mt 10:16), but, more radically, to understand the meaning of life. Jesus, to bring his listeners to an attitude of intelligent trust in God, addressed them saying: "Look at the birds in the sky. They do not sow or reap or gather into barns; yet your heavenly Father feeds them. Are you not worth much more than they are?" (Mt 6:26); "Are not two sparrows sold for a small coin? And yet not one of them falls to the ground without your Father [...]. So there is no need to be afraid; you are worth more than many sparrows" (Mt 10:29-31).

There is something enigmatic, "beyond comprehension", in the way the eagle crosses the sky or the snake slithers on the rock (Prov 30:19). The animal world is in fact one of the most mysterious places, where life expresses itself in an amazing and uncontrollable way. All this is opened up by God before the eyes of Job, so that he will cease claiming to know and to challenge everything, and become aware of the limits of his knowledge, while adopting an attitude of greater respect for the Creator:

> "Do you know when mountain goats give birth?
> Have you ever watched deer in labour?
> Who has given a wild donkey its freedom,
> who has undone the harness of a wild ass?
> Is the wild ox willing to serve you
> or spend a night at your manger?"
>
> (Job 39:1, 5, 9)

> "But look at Behemoth, my creature, just as you are! [...],
> Can you catch it with hooks
> or put poles through its nose? [...].
> Leviathan, too! Can you catch it with a fish hook
> or hold its tongue down with a rope?"
>
> (Job 40:15, 24-25)

The rhetoric of the book of Job multiplies examples, illustrates details, and emphasises actions of the animal in order to help the reader penetrate a world of exuberant vitality, and thus assist in a process of deepening the understanding of life and history. The one who "sees" with inner eyes the mystery of life lavished on the world, sees God (Job 42:5), and then, turning to the Creator with the words of Job himself, can declare:

"'I know that you are all-powerful:
no plan of yours can be thwarted.
Who is this that obscures the plan without knowledge?
So I have spoken without understanding,
about marvels beyond me, which I did not understand."

(Job 42:2-3)

Animals as signs of God's action

145. Finally, God uses animals to make his presence and his "judgement" felt in the history of humanity. In the first place, he uses them as a demonstration of beneficence, even if, at times, in a paradoxical way: he sends crows to feed the prophet Elijah (1 Kgs 17:4-6); he arranges for a large fish to swallow Jonah (Jon 2:1) and then speaks to the fish which vomits the prophet out on the beach (Jon 2:11); he also ensures that hungry lions spare Daniel and pounce instead on the false accusers of the just one (Dan 6:17-25). These stories, of a rather legendary character, illustrate, however, how animals are instruments in the hands of God to assist his providential care or to bring human beings to understand the good that they either do not want or are unable to grasp.

This last aspect appears as a mode of action used by the Lord in his punitive interventions. In the book of Exodus we read that in the face of Pharaoh's arrogance, God sends frogs to cover "the land of Egypt" (Ex 8:1-2), then mosquitoes (Ex 8:12-13) and horseflies (Ex 8:20), and finally the locusts that devour the vegetation (Ex 10:4-6,12-15). The book of Wisdom recalls these events (Wis 16:1, 3, 9; 17:9), interpreting them as one of the signs of divine moderation, which, in striking the wicked, gives them time for conversion (Wis 12:8-10, 19-21; 16:6). The same motif returns later in Israel's history; we find it attested in relation to the Canaanites, driven out with hornets (Ex 23:28; Deut 7:20; Josh 24:12; Wis 12:8), but it is also applied when Israel rebels against the Lord and is threatened with poisonous snakes (Num 21:6; Deut 32:24; Jer 8:17; Wis 16:5) or struck by swarms of locusts that devastate the countryside (Deut 28:38; Joel 2:25; Am 4:9; 7:1). The wild beasts sent by God against the people also have a similar meaning (Jer 2:15; 4:7; Hos 13:7-8; Am 3:12; Sir 39:30-31; etc.).

Wild animals

146. There are, of course, harmful beasts and ferocious animals, which humans fear and of which they are sometimes victims. This constitutes a problematic element in a harmonious vision of creation. In the first two chapters of Genesis there is no mention of rivalry between or a threat from wild animals, because in this section of the story the sacred author wants to show the totally beneficial gift made by the Creator to those who are moulded in his image. Only in the third chapter do we see the animal that tempts, in the form of a snake, which uses its cunning to harm the human being (Gen 3:1); we will discuss this in chapter four. It is quite common to say that the harmony between living beings was ruptured by the sin of Adam and Eve, and that one of the effects of this transgression would be the aggression of the animals, among themselves and towards humans. In actual fact, only the hostility of the serpent against the descendants of Eve is mentioned in Gen 3:15, and the sentence pronounced by God does not appear to support the theory of the unleashing of the ferocity of animals. What Scripture clearly assumes, however, is that human history is on the way to its fullness. During their lives human beings experience many phenomena of imperfection, including that of a conflict between living beings who are in the same territory. This is a cause of pain, and in it the human being has a real experience of fragility. Wild beasts will thus become one of the privileged metaphors for describing the threat of the ruthless enemy (Jer 4:7; Ps 17:12; 58:5-7; Dan 7:2-7; etc.). The believer, however, is animated by the hope that a cosmic redemption will be accomplished (Rom 8:19-25), in which all the living can peacefully coexist. This is the promise of the prophets (Is 11:6-8; 65:25; Hos 2:20), linked with the coming of the good shepherd who will make a covenant of peace, and cause dangerous animals to disappear from the country (Ezek 34:23-25). Perhaps in the image of Jesus, who "was with the wild animals" in the desert and was served by angels (Mk 1:13), we see not only the confirmation of the words of the Psalm which guaranteed protection

141

for the just (Ps 91:11-13), but also the symbolic inauguration of the Kingdom of God.

A help in ancient worship

147. The relationship of the human being to God, who is invisible, is expressed through a series of external, symbolic acts. One of the most frequent and most significant among these is the *offering* to the divinity of an important possession as a sign of reverent adoration, of supplication for a favour, and of thanksgiving for a grace obtained. Among these offerings, in all ancient civilizations and still today within some populations practising traditional religion, the *sacrifice of an animal* had and has a privileged place; sometimes it is consumed by fire as a burnt offering, and sometimes roasted and distributed among the participants in the sacred ritual as a sign of communion.

In these sacred ceremonies the mediation of what in a particular social and economic context is considered the most precious asset is used to signify the relationship with the Absolute. What is "sacrificed" to God is not in fact a wild beast caught in the forest; it is not a repulsive animal that human beings would not eat nor a maimed or useless animal (Lev 1:3; 3:1; 22:18-25; Mal 1:8, 14), but rather the perfect (Ex 12:5) and precious animal, raised specifically to be a worthy offering to the Most High God. The first born of the animal is consecrated to God (Gen 4:4; Ex 13:1-2, 11-12; 22:28-29; Deut 12:6; 15:19), the only gift that can be offered at that time, thus showing that one gives back to God all that was given by God.

The animal is "consecrated", therefore, in an action of religious significance of the highest importance. Ancient humans saw in this no violence, no betrayal of God's creative plan. However, like every sign, even that of animal sacrifice naturally has its ambiguities. Today, such a way of practising religion is challenged, paradoxically not from greater respect for God, but to safeguard the "dignity" of the animal and its "right" to life. The biblical tradition, although expressing respect for animals, moves in a different direction with regard to sacrifices.

148. In the prophetic writings in particular repeated criticisms are made not of the sacrificial rite in itself, but rather of the exterior nature of the acts, which are not matched by the justice of human behaviour (Is 1:11-17; 43:22-24; 58:3-5; Jer 6:20; 11:15; Hos 5:6-7; 6:6; Am 5:21-25; Mic 6:6-7; Zech 7:4-6). Instead of expressing an authentic religious attitude, sacrifice becomes a deceptive mask, a substitute for the commitment of the heart, even an attempt to deceive God in order to obtain some advantage (Sir 35:11-12) or to escape judgement (Ps 50:7-15). The very abundance of the sacrifices (Am 4:4-5), such as thousands of burnt offerings and rivers of oil (Mic 6:7), betrays the fact that the person has lost sight of their symbolic value, which is more adequately represented by the humble offering of two turtle doves (Lev 12:8; Lk 2:24). What matters is the contrite heart (Ps 51:18-19), the soul that desires good (Ps 40:7-9), not the externals of the action, however liturgically perfect.

Though severe, the prophetic critique did not lead to the abolition of the sacrificial rites; they are attested in the whole of biblical literature and are present also in the time of Jesus. The Master himself does not denounce this religious practice, but only subordinates it, as the prophets did, to the duty of fraternal reconciliation (Mt 5:23-24). He repeats, with Hosea (Hos 6:6), "My pleasure is in mercy, not sacrifice" (Mt 9:13; 12:6), but applies this saying to situations where it is not really a question of sacrificial rites. Furthermore, he celebrated Passover, centred on the sacrifice of the lamb (Lk 22:14-16). What Christ taught, and what became the religious discipline of his disciples, fits in to the prophetic tradition, bringing it to fulfilment: the Lord insists that it is the human being who must surrender to God in an offering of love (cf. Rom 12:1), it is the human person who by surrendering life expresses in total gift the truth that only in God does one live (Mt 16:24-25; Jn 10:17-18; 12:25). Going further, and to show clearly that the blood to be shed is his own and not that of another living being, Christ instituted a new rite of offering, the "memorial" that remembers, celebrates and makes present his sacrifice on the cross, in the gift of his flesh and blood, offered "once and for all" (Heb 7:27; 9:12; 10:10) for the multitude (Mt 26:26-28). The new rite not only abolishes the ancient sacrifices for ever, but also symbolically suggests the end of violence, because Christ is peace (Eph 2:14-18), and in him everything has been reconciled, brought back ideally, therefore, to the time of paradise (Gen 1:29-30), or rather projected, in faith, to the eternal Kingdom (Is 35:9; 65:25) of full communion with all living beings and with God.

CONCLUSION

149. The text of Gen 2:8-20 aims to encourage the contemplation of creation, seeing how it is "very good" (Gen 1:31), a divine gift that is free and permanent. The food that nourishes living beings and the animals given to help *'ādām* clearly point to the goodness of things, but above all to the generosity of God towards his creatures, and the work assigned to human beings must be seen as affirming the potential of the hand and heart of those who, on earth, have authority.

Each gift creates relationships; and from the original gift directions are implicitly proposed which the biblical tradition amply develops. Creation first of all establishes a fundamental relationship between humanity and God, a covenant that God will perpetually safeguard, and which human beings are freely called to assume in the days of their existence. They will do so by expressing gratitude, with the offering of the gifts received, and by giving themselves over to the Lord as a perpetual offering. They will also do so by preserving the earth and all it contains as a precious asset, making good use of the soil, but also of the talents received, with laborious but profitable and beneficial "work". Each gift is such only if shared and transmitted, and if it is used to promote the good of the other.

The text of Gen 2:8-20 ends on a somewhat incomplete note: "no helper was found as a partner for man". It is necessary therefore to continue reading the founding text to explore other dimensions of the gift of God, those which make explicit, in interpersonal relationships, and especially in the relationship between man and woman, the "very good" reality that the Creator wanted for humanity.

CHAPTER THREE

THE HUMAN FAMILY

150. God said: "it is not good that *'ādām* should be alone" (Gen 2:18). The fact that the Creator wished that "in the beginning" humanity should be constituted by man and woman (Gen 1:27; 2:21-23) invites us to consider carefully this fundamental human difference and to explore its meaning. It is not enough, even if it is essential, to stress the equal dignity of the two sexes. It is necessary also to examine the element of relationship, in particular in the ideal situation of a relationship of love. The divine breath which brought to life the dust shaped by the Creator shows its truth and its vital power in the consensual meeting between man and woman, from which life emerges. The goodness of creation coincides with the overcoming of "loneliness", which occurs in the act of welcoming the other, out of love. This transpires in ever widening spheres of relationship, from the couple to the children, and from family bonds to communion with all human beings.

We do not find in Scripture a systematic treatment of the relationship between man and woman. However, the theme is present from beginning to end of the Bible, both in its concrete expressions of the *marriage union*, and in its symbolic use as an image capable of expressing spiritual and transcendent covenants. The relevance of such a motif is evident not least from the numerous components implied here. First among these is the sexual body ("male and female he created them": Gen 1:27), of which one should consider not only the function of procreation, which appears to be given priority in Scripture, due to the primary value given to life, but also the psychological and emotional aspects, the importance of which for each person is known to all, even if it is not at all easy to be precise about the behaviour that is proper to each of the two sexes. When one speaks of love, with its values of dedication, fidelity and creativity, one automatically thinks of the image of marriage, since in it the emotional dimension combines with free choice, and because from such a union there emerges a particular story often rich in fruits. At the same time there is no shortage of hardships, transgressions, violence and failures. Spousal love, in fact, should not be identified with the first passionate attraction, which presents ambiguities and dangers, as the wisdom literature in particular warns. Moreover, the desires of men and women united in marriage will not always match. Tensions will come about at moments of decision, and the question of authority will arise, and how it might foster communion. These are some of the issues that will be developed in the first part of this chapter.

151. In Gen 1 the creation of the human couple (Gen 1:27) is immediately linked to the act of divine blessing which expresses itself as a call to fruitfulness (Gen 1:28). *Children are born of the couple* and they in turn are called upon to be fruitful and multiply; from the initial encounter innumerable offspring of humankind descend (Gen 5:1-32; 10:1-32). In the tradition of the patriarchs the condition of sterility seems, at first, to be at odds with the divine promise made to the whole human race and repeated in particular to Abraham (Gen 12:2; 17:5-6; Deut 7:13-14); however, the history of the people of the covenant, subject to the action of God, displays then a positive development that culminates in the remarkable proliferation of the children of Israel (Ex 1:7; Is 51:2). But the spontaneous growth in procreation risks appearing as a pure reflex of the instinct of survival of the species or of a particular "family", if it is not accompanied by the element of love, which not only creates new relationships, but also sustains them and brings them to fruition. The love of parents for their children – and Gen 22:2 marks the first occurrence in the Bible of the verb "to love" – is at the origin of the parental relationship, and from this foundational act flows the possibility that the one who is begotten and educated by love learns to love (1 Jn 4:19), beginning with a real affection for one's parents. The asymmetry in the relationship between parent and child, unlike the equal relationship between husband and wife, requires specific qualities of love, sometimes difficult to put into practice. Here too, as in every relationship where freedom is exercised, inappropriate and destructive actions can occur (1 Pt 2:16). This theme of the relationship between parents and children will occupy the second part of the present chapter.

The multiplication of humankind creates a large, growing, dynamic community. This is a positive factor in history, insofar as it brings out the love between the children of the same father, a love that is expressed in collaboration and harmony. But we know that there is not always harmony among *brothers*, as the Scripture narrates starting from Cain and Abel; rivalries, wars and massacres punctuate history. The appeal to fraternity, which is gradually extended from the blood family to the entire human community, becomes God's commandment to humanity, so that creation can reach its peak of perfection. This will be the subject of the third part of the chapter.

Gen 2:21-25

²¹Then the Lord God made the man (*'ādām*) fall into a deep sleep. And while he was asleep, he took one of his ribs and closed up the flesh in its place. ²²The Lord God built the rib he had taken from the man (*'ādām*), into a woman (*'iššāh*), and brought her to the man (*'ādām*). ²³And the man (*'ādām*) said: 'This one at last is bone of my bones and flesh of my flesh! She shall be called Woman (*'iššāh*), because she was taken from Man (*'îš*).'

²⁴This is why a man (*'îš*) leaves his father and mother and becomes attached to his wife (*'iššāh*), and the two become one flesh.

²⁵Now, both of them were naked, the man (*'ādām*) and his wife (*'iššāh*), and they were not ashamed.

152. *This short paragraph concludes the account of creation in Gen 2. Two main narrative moments follow one another: the first is the divine action which brings into existence a man and a* *woman; the second is the meeting of the couple, accompanied by human appreciation of the divine work. This narrative, as with the preceding one, does not intend to be a report of what actually happened, because the author uses a literary genre with symbolic value; an intelligent understanding of this biblical text is required. While all commentators agree in recognising the importance of its content, there are however differences in interpretation both as regards the passage as a whole, and in relation to the various particulars that the narrator details.*

A problem that we encounter straightaway comes from the terminology used to designate the main subject of the account. As is already evident from the above translation (with the Hebrew terms in brackets), there is a certain ambiguity in the term *'ādām*, used sometimes with the article, and sometimes without. In many cases, and certainly in the first part of Gen 2, the noun indicates the human being in general. This sense remains in the continuation of the narrative into the following chapter, as in Gen 3:9-10 when God comes to the garden to search for *'ādām*, or in Gen 3:22-24 when he expels him from Eden. It is also clear that the gift of food, the task of working, and above all the imposition of the command not to eat the forbidden fruit (Gen 2:16-17), as well as some consequences of sin (Gen 3:9-10,19,22-24) apply to humanity in general, without sexual distinction. In other cases, however, the same term *'ādām* is used to designate the male character, due to the explicit correlation with the "woman" (Gen 2:22-23, 25; 3:8, 12, 17, 20-21). This masculine sense is then confirmed by the fact that *'ādām* becomes, at some point in history, the proper name Adam of the progenitor of the human race (Gen 4:1, 25; 5:1-5).

153. *The ambiguity associated with the noun* 'ādām, *analogous to that which exists in English with the term "man", has facilitated two ways of interpreting this passage. The first is the reading that may be described as "traditional", according to which the account tells of the creation of the woman by the Creator using material (one of the ribs) taken from the male man. This is confirmed by the declaration of* 'ādām: *"she shall be called Woman, because* *she was taken from Man" (Gen 2:23). In this way, some exegetes suggest, the biblical author would have subtly overturned the evidence that all males come "from the" woman, narrating that in the beginning it is the woman who originates from the man. Paul takes this line, when he writes: "for just as woman is from man [ek tou andros], so man is by means of woman [dia tēs gynaikos], and everything is from God" (1 Cor 11:12). Going on what the Apostle wrote, a twofold teaching would result: on the one hand, that of reciprocal recognition, because "in the Lord neither is woman without man nor man without woman" (1 Cor 11:11); on the other, a scriptural basis would be given to the hierarchical order in the family and in the community (1 Cor 11:7-10), by reason of the fact that "Adam was formed first and Eve afterwards" (1 Tim 2:13).*

Such a sociological perspective is not universally accepted today, also because the biblical text offers a different, exegetically more rigorous reading. We have said that up to v. 20 the narrator speaks of 'ādām, without any specific sexual connotation. This generic presentation requires that we abandon imagining the precise configuration of such a being, while avoiding of course the "monstrous" form of the androgynous. In fact, we are invited to admit ignorance in relation to 'ādām so as to discover, by revelation, what the wonderful miracle wrought by God is (see Gen 15:12; Job 33:15). No one actually knows the mystery of their own origin. This phase of non-vision is symbolically represented by the act of the Creator who "made" 'ādām fall into a deep sleep" (v. 21): sleep in this case does not have the function of a general anaesthetic to allow a painless operation, but rather it evokes the presentation of an unimaginable event, by which from one being ('ādām) God forms two, man ('îš) and woman ('iššāh). This does not only indicate their radical similarity, but presents the prospect that the difference between them encourages the discovery of the spiritual good of mutual recognition, the principle of a communion of love and an invitation to become "one flesh" (v. 24). It is not the solitude of the male but that of the human being that is remedied by the creation of man and woman.

Similarity and difference

154. Starting from the accounts of creation in Gen 1-2 we can affirm that in order to classify the various beings created by God it is necessary to introduce both the concept of similarity with others, and that of diversity. All creatures are radically alike because of their perishability. In fact all living things die, things are consumed, and even the heavens "will pass" (Mt 24:29,35; cf. Is 51:6), despite being a conventional sign of what is lasting (Ps 89:37-38); the result is, therefore, that every creature is different from God, the only one who is eternal.

Creatures have elements of similarity between them, but also of diversity. In Gen 1 the description of creation in six days also has the function of grouping together things that have common characteristics, the waters, the lights, the plants, the living things; then on each single day there is diversity, between the waters above and those below, between the sun and the other stars, while the plants and the animals are created "according to their own kind"; finally, the human being, similar to and different from the animals, is the only one who is similar to the Creator, being created "in his image", although, as a creature, he is different from him. The author of Gen 1 has repeatedly stressed this aspect by using the verb "to separate" (Gen 1:4, 6, 7, 14, 18); every "confusion", a lack of respect for diversity, is equivalent to a return to primitive chaos (Gen 1:2). For this reason we find in the Torah various laws that prohibit mixing (cf. Lev 19:19; Deut 22:5, 9-11); thus, with symbolic practices, the believer recognises the significant differences that God made at the beginning of the world. More generally, a constant sapiential discernment is required in order not to give one creature the value of another.

Even in Gen 2, if with a different literary procedure and in a less systematic way, elements of similarity between beings are introduced, as when it is stated that 'ādām was shaped with the same material with which the animals were formed; but no animal is a "helper" that corresponds to the human being, who lives by the divine breath.

155. Now, this combination of similarity and difference is introduced within the reality of *'ādām*. In Gen 1 this is expressed in v. 27 where it is stated in the singular, as a mark of similarity, that the human being was created "in the image of God" (not only male, as suggested in 1 Cor 11:7), and, immediately after, the reality of male and female is specified with the plural, thus bringing out the difference within the common human nature. In Gen 2, to express the similarity between the two beings, the author uses the representation of their formation starting from the same material. The supposed etymological link between *'îš* (man) and *'iššāh* (woman), in addition to showing their "kinship", highlights at the same time the difference that leads to the spousal union (v. 24) that is necessary for the procreation of life.

The relationship of the couple must not be expressed as a "fusion" that nullifies the specific characteristics proper to each of the spouses. Where the biblical text says that the two "will be one flesh" (Gen 2:24), it must be understood that in the physical union the spouses are given a *sign* of their total, exclusive, lasting and inseparable love. This is a sign that is therefore perverted when it does not actually express mutual and definitive belonging; being a sign that expresses the reality of love for the other, it can, in the Christian tradition, be activated also in a different experience of corporality: all believers are called upon to unite themselves to Christ spiritually, but in the concreteness of the flesh, so as to form in him "one body" (1 Cor 10:17; 12:12-13; Eph 1:23; 4:4), in a way that implies respect for the diversity of the members (Rom 12:4-5; 1 Cor 12:14, 27; Eph 4:16).

According to the Scriptures otherness is inscribed in the bodily sign of sexuality, the value of which is to be accepted, understood ever more fully, and lived out with perfect justice. Perceived differences between man and woman are certainly bound up with the cultural history of various peoples, and among these there are some that are to be rejected because they contain negative judgements on the other sex (cf. Sir 25:24; 1 Tim 2:14) and seem to sanction oppressive and violent behaviour. A patient and loving effort of mutual listening is necessary between man and woman, an effort nourished by forgiveness, so that there arises in human history a more appropriate expression of the relationship between them, in particular in the spousal relationship as a type of the covenant willed by God.

156. *Some particulars of the creative act of the Lord God need clarification. First of all the CEI (Conferenza Episcopale Italiana) translation used in the Italian original of this document renders the Hebrew verb* lāqaḥ *with "to remove" (togliere; vv. 21-22, 23), conveying the sense of subtraction; it would be more appropriate to translate it with "take", as in the English translation, to bring out the semantic component of choice or election (cf. Gen 4:19; 6:2; 11:29; etc.). Furthermore, the ancient Greek version (LXX), followed by the Latin (Vulgate), translated the Hebrew term* ṣēlaʿ *with "rib" (vv. 21-22), which in all other biblical occurrences (cf. Ex 25:12, 14; 2 Sam 16:13; 1 Kgs 6:34; Ezek 41:5, 9; etc.) never designates a specific part of the human body, but simply a "side" of some object. If reference to an anatomical organ is avoided, as was already suggested above, the idea could be advanced that "man and woman" are "side and side", similar in their basic nature, and at the same time called to be "side by side", the one at the side of the other, as a help and an ally. We read in fact in Sirach: "The man who takes a wife has the makings of a fortune, a helper to match himself, a pillar of support" (Sir 36:24). In fact each of the two has a specific identity, evoked for the man in "closing the flesh up again" (v. 22), and for the woman expressed by the verb "to build" (bānāh: v. 22), which undoubtedly has the nuance of an operation concluded, so that its "being built" (bānāh; cf. Gen 16:2; 30:3) coincides with the potential to generate children (bānîm). The insistence on the specific identity of each of the subjects, revealed in their physical constitution, will ensure that the other is not intended as a remedy to fill a deficiency, or appreciated simply as a complementary support, but is instead longed for and welcomed, in amazed gratitude, as a person, who is not subordinate to the need of others, but praised as the perfect "good" created by God to complete his work.*

157. *The second part of the story focuses on the meeting of the couple (vv. 22b-25). Here it should be noted that it is the Lord who brings it about, since it is he who "brings" (literally "makes to* come") the woman to the man (v. 22b) with the implicit intention of promoting their union. The man speaks (v. 23), saying in the first place that "this time" the "good" that is able to overcome the solitude of the human being (v. 18) has been realised, a good that of course was accomplished by the Creator, but that is now welcomed in full awareness by the creature in a free decision of love. In the solemn words of vv. 23-24, in fact, not only is the equality of the two sexes affirmed, but the expression "bones of my bones and flesh of my flesh" reflects the language of "covenant" (cf. Gen 29:14; Jdg 9:2; 2 Sam 5:1-3; 19:13-14), attesting that the other will be considered as one's own body. Paul, in relation to conjugal love and making explicit reference to Gen 2:23-24, expresses himself in a similar way: "husbands must love their wives as they love their own bodies. A man who loves his wife, loves himself. No one has ever hated his own body, but he feeds it and looks after it, just as Christ does the Church, because we are members of his body" (Eph 5:28-30).

The call to institute the marriage covenant is a theme of v. 24 where the speaker brings out the purpose of the difference between man and woman: "this is why a man leaves his father and mother and becomes attached to his wife". The reference to parents is entirely incongruous in this narrative context, and compels the reader to see announced here the ideal path traced for man in general: the woman, led by God, goes towards the man (v. 22), and the man, recognising the gift, goes towards the woman (v. 24), each one leaving the reality they came from to bring about through their mutual "adhesion" that unity ("one flesh") that will be the beginning of new life, and will become in history a sign of witness to the one fatherhood, the one origin of all things.

The account concludes on a minor note, apparently, with the notice that nudity was not a cause of shame for the man and the woman (v. 25). This evokes not only the innocence of the beginnings, not yet spoiled by sin. It is also suggested that the sexual relationship of the spouses is pure insofar as in the flesh it expresses love according to the design of God. Since from this love life will begin, the relationship will be protected by modesty, as an expression of sacredness and mutual respect.

1. THE LOVE BETWEEN MAN AND WOMAN

158. According to the biblical narrative, the first words spoken by a human being to another who could understand are those of the man who recognises before him the woman with whom he will live in a covenant relationship of communion (Gen 2:23). These are poetic words that value and celebrate the gift. They are the beginning of a unending song that will leave its mark on human history (Jer 33:11) until "the bride", the Church, full of the Spirit of love, will say to the spouse, Christ: "Come" (Apoc 22:17), bringing to fulfilment the life of love and perfect joy.

The song of love

An entire book of the Bible, of a very particular literary genre, is offered to us as a model poem about conjugal love. This is the *Song of Songs*, so called because it is the greatest of songs, since it is the song of love of every man and of every woman who live to love one another and, in two voices, declare their affection and their happiness. He and she, the two lovers, are closely united with each other while conserving their own individual identity, indeed exalting it as something desired and attractive for the other (Song 7:11). The relationship is born of a mutually appreciated beauty, develops as a continuous searching and reciprocal knowledge, and is fulfilled in a longed for communion. This is how love is revealed, the love that is capable of generating people's happiness and of transforming everything in the world into a celebration that brings delight to all. The poetry of the Song is woven together by this miracle.

Beauty
159. Conjugal love springs from amazement at seeing the beauty of the other. The man is attracted by the grace of the woman, and she is seduced by his virile charm:

"How beautiful you are, my love,
how beautiful you are! Your eyes are doves.
How beautiful you are, my love,
and how you delight me!"

(Song 1:15-16)

The motif of beauty echoes repeatedly in the Song (Song 1:8; 4:1, 7; 5:9; 6:1, 4, 10): it describes a quality of the human body, admired in its splendour, without shame (cf. Gen 2:25), but above all appreciated because it makes one fall in love (cf. Sir 36:24), because it is a body that arouses love insofar as it speaks of love.

This could be a way of reading the history of salvation in which various individuals are remembered for their beauty: women, such as Sarah (Gen 12:11, 14), Rachel (Gen 29:17), Abigail (1 Sam 25:3), the three daughters of Job (Job 42:15), Esther (Est 2:7) and Judith (Jdt 8:7), and men, such as Joseph (Gen 39:6), Moses (Ex 2:2), David (1 Sam 16:12) and the high priest Simon (Sir 50:5-10); the beauty of these individuals, besides being a significant factor in the development of the narrative plot, arouses affection in the reader, who must feel fascinated by them, loving their story, and at the end being attracted by the Messiah, "the most handsome of the sons of men" (Ps 45:3).

Looking into each other's eyes, the lovers see sweetness, tenderness and passion; the pupils shine, silently expressing feelings and offering signals of love. More generally, all the limbs speak of attraction and readiness. The loved one describes his lover detailing poetically every part of her body (Song 4:1-5). At the same time he expresses his admiration and his desire:

"How beautiful you are, my love
There is no blemish in you" (Song 4:7).
"Come [...], look down [...],
you ravish my heart with one glance of your eyes,
with one jewel of your necklace."

(Song 4:8-9)

The woman who is loved responds with intensely lyrical images (Song 5:10-16), describing the features of him who is "better than other lovers" (Song 5:9) and called "the love of my soul" (Song 1:7; 3:2-4). The wonders of the created world with its fruits (Song 4:16; 2:3; 5:1; etc.) and its aromas (Song 2:12-13; 3:6; 4:6; 5:1; etc.) are used as metaphors to suggest the marvel of the person loved who, like an irrigated "garden", is a principle of life (Song 4:12, 15-16; 5:1; 6:2; 8:13). In an actual experience of God's Eden-like gift (Gen 2:8-25), the man exclaims:

> "I come into my garden,
> my sister, my bride,
> I pick my myrrh and balsam,
> I taste my honey and my honeycomb,
> I drink my wine and my milk."
>
> (Song 5:1)

Mutual searching and the desire for communion

160. Love expresses itself as a search, as anxiety to see, to meet and to embrace the loved one. The woman calls out: "Tell me, you whom my soul loves, where you pasture your flock" (Song 1:7), and she sets off:

> "On my bed at night I sought
> him whom my soul loves.
> I sought but could not find him!
> So I shall get up and go around the city;
> in the streets and in the squares
> I shall seek him whom my soul loves."
>
> (Song 3:1-2; cf. 5:6-8)

The man goes to meet his beloved (Song 2:8) and whispers to her:

> "My dove, hiding in the clefts of the rock,
> in the coverts of the cliff,
> show me your face,
> let me hear your voice,

for your voice is sweet
and your face is lovely."

(Song 2:14)

The lover comes, in fact, in the night of desire, knocking on the door of his lover (Song 5:2). He enters the secret room where life originates (Song 3:4; 8:5; cf. Gen 24:67), so that love is realised in the intimacy of mutual belonging:

"His left arm is under my head,
and his right arm embraces me."

(Song 2:6; 8:3)

"My love is mine,
and I am his."

(Song 2:16; 6:3; 7:11)

Love is reciprocal gift, free and generous; the one who tries to buy it destroys it (Song 8:7-12).

A unique relationship

161. Of the bride the beloved says, "My dove is my only one" (Song 6:9). She alone can satisfy with beauty and love the desire of her spouse (Song 4:10). There are countless girls (Song 6:8) but only one is chosen, the most beautiful (Song 1:8), the favourite, "as a lily among thistles" (Song 2:2), as splendid as the sun (Song 6:10), the star which on its own lights up the world. She is the exclusive possession of the beloved: "She is a garden enclosed, my sister, my bride; a garden enclosed, a sealed fountain" (Song 4:12). Similarly, the beloved is among young men as "an apple tree among the trees of the wood" (Song 2:3); he has something more than any other (Song 5:9); he is "known among ten thousand" (Song 5:10), and for him, therefore, the exquisite fruits of love are "stored up" (Song 7:14).

Precisely because the Song ideally draws its inspiration from the world of Solomon (Song 1:1, 5; 3:7, 9, 11), and hence from where polygamy is practised (Song 6:8-9), one is struck by contrast with the poet's intention to celebrate love in its exclusive and total form of belonging, that relationship towards which the biblical tradition converges, because it is the only one that fully satisfies.

A fragile love to be protected

162. The extraordinary passionate drive that pervades the Song of Songs clarifies one of its most celebrated affirmations, which is found at the conclusion of the poem:

> "For love is strong as Death,
> jealousy as fierce as Sheol.
> Its flame is a flame of fire,
> a mighty flame."

(Song 8:6)

Such a feeling, that nothing can extinguish or overwhelm (Song 8:7), could lead one to disregard its intrinsic fragility, since, in reality, love is an event of the human heart, and the heart goes through experiences of darkness, of uncertainty, of restlessness and of disappointment. Thus we see that the beloved searches in vain, in every place, for the love of her soul (Song 3:1-2), and the very moment of the meeting is presented paradoxically as that of his disappearance.

> "I opened to my love,
> but my love had turned and gone.
> My soul failed at his flight,
> I sought but could not find him,
> I called to him but he did not answer."

(Song 5:6)

Moreover, there are the threats that come from outside, represented both by the city guards who beat and injure the woman (Song 5:7), and above all by the "little foxes" who devastate the vineyard, because they are greedy for the bunches of ripening grapes (Song 2:15). With this last image the poet alludes to the forces of lust that violently destroy the blossoming of love. Without protection love reveals its vulnerability (Song 8:8-9). One does not love without protecting the person loved.

The feast

163. There is a festive atmosphere in the Song because the groom and bride convey their own happiness to others: "eat friends, and drink, drink deep with lovemaking" (Song 5:1); "the season of songs has come" (Song 2:12), declares the groom. The great day of the coronation of the king (Song 3:11; 7:6) and his wedding ceremony (Song 3:11; 8:8) are evoked: the golden canopy (Song 3:9-10) advances surrounded by a retinue of warriors (Song 3:7-8); elegant sandals trace out the steps of a dance (Song 7:1-2). The intimacy that is the code of the mystery of love is joined with a kind of public approval so that the joy of the heart is shared, and provokes unceasing universal acclaim (Song 6:9).

The beauty of the Canticle shines with the very beauty of love. It is suggestive that the woman on three occasions speaks of her beloved as "love" (*hā'ahăbāh*) (Song 2:7; 3:5; 8:4), while he responds to her in the same vein, saying, "How beautiful you are, how charming, my love (*'ahăbāh*), my delight!" (Song 7:7). One understands thus why this poem was read as a great allegory of the love between Israel, the bride loved by the Lord, and God, the spouse who is love itself. The prophetic traditions, as we shall see, will use the same symbolic device of spousal love to illustrate the story of God's attachment to his people. The New Testament will echo this in various ways, narrating, among other things, at the conclusion of the gospels, the encounter in the garden between the Risen Lord and Mary of Magdala (Jn 20:11-18).

The song of love becomes prayer

164. The person who prays contemplates the work of God, drawing lessons from it, reasons for praise and for heartfelt joy. Among the topics of prayer present in the *Psalter*, we find also the celebration of married love in its concrete realisation in which we can discover and celebrate the action of the Lord.

Ps 45, which is described in its title as a "song of love", almost like an echo of the Song of Songs, evokes the joyful moment of the marriage of a king and a young princess; we are reminded of the beauty of the spouses (vv. 3 and 12), the sumptuousness of their garments (vv. 4, 10, 14-15), the perfumes (vv. 8-9), the music (v. 9), and the procession that adds solemnity to the feast (vv. 10, 13, 15-16), in an atmosphere pervaded by joy (vv. 8, 9, 16). Unlike the Song, however, this poem does not highlight the amorous behaviour of the two lovers, but rather the divine intervention that bestows on the groom a blessing (v. 3) and consecration (v. 8), while for the bride it is a promise of fruitfulness (v. 17) and praise (v. 18). Furthermore, the king is presented as an ideal figure, of superhuman character, for to him are attributed qualities usually reserved for God: he is called "mighty" (v 4), endowed with "splendour" and "majesty" (v. 4), words of "grace" flow from his lips (v. 3), his progress brings "truth" and "justice" (v. 5), his right hand works "fearsome deeds" (v. 5); he is even called "God" (v. 7) and "Lord" of his bride (v. 12). One can understand then how this love song was read in a messianic sense, preparing for the wedding of the Davidic king of the end times, who in triumph is installed victorious on his throne of justice; and his bride represents Israel, called to forget her ancient origins (v. 11) and to surrender with reverence to the desire of her Lord (v. 12), entering the palace of fruitfulness and joy (vv. 16-17). The human figure of the royal wedding is thus taken up in prayer as a symbol of the story of love and triumph of the Messiah and of Israel. It thus becomes a song of praise and hope.

On another note, the spousal motif is taken up in Ps 128 as an expression of blessing (v. 1). In this psalm it is fruitfulness above all that is exalted with the images of the vine and the olive shoots (v. 3), kept in the intimacy of the home. It is a prayer because it celebrates the blessing of the Lord (v. 4), and because it invokes a blessing (v. 5), as it looks to an indefinite future in the knowledge that human effort, however arduous, will not be able "to build the house" (Ps 127:1-2) because the "fruit of the womb" is a gift of the Lord (Ps 127:3). The song of spousal love is in fact a celebration of the secret and powerful action of God in the love story of humanity.

The appreciation of the sages and their warnings

165. The wisdom literature of Israel includes books of different character, yet in all there is an unquestioning respect for the institution of marriage, as we have already seen in the Song of Songs and in the Psalter, both of which belong to the great collection of the "Writings".

One method used by the sages to promote the importance of conjugal love was to produce parabolic stories in which the protagonists would become iconic figures to be appreciated and imitated.

In the book of *Ruth*, which for the Jews belongs, with the Song of Songs, to the "five Rolls", the central character is a Moabite woman called Ruth, who, having become the widow of the Israelite, Mahlon, remains inextricably linked to her husband's family, and renounces her own homeland (cf. Ps 45:11) and her religious traditions, in tenacious fidelity to the bond of love contracted in marriage. Her declaration to her mother-in-law Naomi is well-known:

> "Do not press me to leave you and no longer to accompany you, for, wherever you go, I shall go, wherever you live, I shall live. Your people shall be my people, and your God shall be my God. Where you die, I shall die and there I shall be buried. Let the Lord bring unnameable ills on me and worse ills, too, if even death should part me from you!"
>
> (Ruth 1:16-17)

Together with Naomi, Ruth then emigrates to the land of Judah, and there her love story comes to fulfilment, as she meets Boaz, a near relative, who comes to the aid of the widow and makes her his wife (Ruth 4:10). The narrative complications of this edifying novella serve to highlight the merit of the protagonists, who, in a contest of mutual benevolence, show the power of the conjugal bond, which is capable of forging lasting connections between people of different ethnicities and traditions. This bond is ultimately rewarded by a marvellous outcome, given that from Ruth and Boaz was born Obed, "father of Jesse, father of David" (Ruth 4:17), figure of the Messiah. Death, in this touching story, does not separate families; and loving fidelity combined with responsibility, promoted by the levirate law, becomes a source of consolation and hope for individuals and for the entire community (Ruth 4:11-17).

In Greek we have another novella which tells of the journey of *Tobias*, the son of old Tobit, a deportee to Nineveh, and of his encounter with Sarah, the widow of seven husbands; their matrimonial union, which respects the law of Moses (Tob 7:11, 13) and is consecrated by prayer (Tob 8:4-8), gives rise to life and joy for the families of parents and in-laws alike (Tob 8:15-20; 11:17-18).

166. These stories with a happy ending seek to promote the love and fidelity of spouses, encouraging them to overcome hardships and sorrows so as to achieve a goal of happiness. Similarly, although on a different register, the book of *Proverbs* concludes its teaching with a poem dedicated to the "capable" wife, of whom it is said as a first quality:

> "Her husband's heart trusts in her,
> from her he will derive no little profit.
> She does him good, never harm
> all the days of her life."
>
> (Prov 31:11-12)

Having exalted the industrious and beneficial qualities of such a wife and mother (Prov 31:13-27) the writer concludes with an encomium:

> "Her children stand up and proclaim her blessed,
> her husband too sings her praises:
> 'Many women have done admirable things,
> but you surpass them all!'"
>
> (Prov 31:28-29)

167. Such an ideal picture does not exempt us from pointing out the possible problems of a couple's relationship. The sage is in fact fully conscious that life in marriage is not always perfect: the husband at times is lazy, a drunkard and foolish; and the wife bad-tempered, argumentative and even shameless, with disastrous and dishonourable consequences (Prov 12:4; 19:13; 21:9, 19; 25:24; 27:15-16; cf. Qoh 7:26-27; Sir 25:20). It is necessary, therefore, to "find" a good wife, because, if it is true that "a wife who is discreet" is "from the Lord" (Prov 19:14), it is up to the young man to know how to choose her (Prov 18:22), preferring interior qualities (Prov 31:30; cf. Sir 42:12) to exterior charm. Once married, the man is called to evade the seductions of the "foreign woman" (Prov 5:1-14, 20-21; 7:4-27; 23:26-28), and to maintain an exclusive bond with his wife:

> "Drink the water from your own storage well,
> fresh water from your own spring.
> Even if your fountains overflow outside,
> your streams of water in the public squares,
> let them be for you alone,
> and not for strangers with you.
> May your fountain-head be blessed!
> Find joy with the wife of your youth."
>
> (Prov 5:15-18)

Drinking the water from one's own well is a metaphor for desire satisfied according to justice, in a good relationship that is opposed to a sexuality without rules (Prov 31:2-3; cf. Sir 23:16-27; 47:19; Tob 8:7); the well, figure of the bride, is blessed by God, whose gaze rests on the entire life of the human being (Prov 5:21; Ps 1:6). Even if this genre of text can be read in an allegorical way, whereby the ideal bride would represent true wisdom, while the foreign woman would assume the value of worldly wisdom (Prov 2:16-17; 9:13-18), the fact remains that such a metaphor is based on the concrete reality of the matrimonial union, in its true meaning and in its requirements.

168. The book of *Sirach* also dedicates many of its teachings to the relationship between man and woman in the context of marriage. As often happens in the Hebrew tradition, the perspective is that of the man and the concern of the sage is to prepare young men to find a good bride (Sir 7:22; 26:13-18). The importance of this decision, which is not without risks (Sir 36:23-28), may perhaps explain some sayings of this wisdom collection that use very harsh expressions in relation to seductive and ill-intentioned women (Sir 23:22-23; 25:13-26; 26:7-12); this makes one appreciate, by contrast, the beauty of a happy marriage, where "a wife and husband....live in harmony" (Sir 25:1; cf. also 25:8; 26:1). The insistent stipulation to the husband is to be faithful to his wife, and to avoid any form of betrayal (Sir 9:3-9; 19:2; 23:16-21; 26:11-12; 42:12-13), while the father is urged to maintain special vigilance over his daughter (Sir 7:24-25; 22:4; 26:10; 42:11). Her vulnerability means that her father will always have a secret "worry" about her, whether she is a young girl or a married woman (Sir 42:9-10).

169. In this type of traditional literature we do not find the lyricism of the Song of Songs but a more concrete path to the wisdom necessary for that happiness that is possible for humanity on earth. *Qoheleth* also moves along these lines. Although sceptical about various aspects of human life, he recognises the goodness of the help that one receives from one's spouse, thus indirectly evoking Gen 2:18:

> "Two are better than one, for thus there is a rich reward for their work.
> If one should fall, the other helps up the first;
> but woe to the person who falls with no one to help!
> Again: if two sleep together they keep warm,
> but how can anyone keep warm alone?
> Where one alone would be overcome, two will put up resistance;
> and a threefold cord is not quickly broken."
>
> (Qoh 4:9-12)

Some will interpret this final proverbial expression, about the third element that strengthens the bond, as an allusion to the son of the couple, or a discreet evocation of God as custodian and support of spousal love. But the saying may perhaps simply suggest that "unity is strength", and marriage is a clear testimony to this.

Towards the end of his book, Qoheleth takes up one of his favourite themes, that of enjoying the simple joys given to the human being on earth, among which marital joy stands out:

> "Go, eat your bread in joy,
> drink your wine with a glad heart,
> since God has already approved your actions.
> At all times, dress in white
> and let your head not lack scent.
> Spend your life with the woman you love,
> all the days of the life of vanity
> which he has given you under the sun,
> since this is your lot in life
> and in the effort you expend under the sun."

(Qoh 9:7-9)

170. All this could appear almost trivial, although it is a kind of rereading of Ps 128; yet the simplest realities are also the most useful in envisaging what is valid for each person, as a context and a means of that human happiness that God has provided for his creatures. This explains why the spousal condition was taken up by the wisdom tradition as a great metaphor for the relationship between the individual person and wisdom, a relationship that is a source of blessing (Prov 3:17-18; Sir 15:2; Wis 8:18). The author of the *book of Wisdom* writes:

> "Wisdom I loved and sought from my youth;
> I resolved to have her as my bride,
> I fell in love with her beauty."

(Wis 8:2)

> "I therefore determined to take her to share my life,
> knowing that she would be my counsellor in prosperity
> and comfort me in cares and sorrow."

(Wis 8:9)

"When I go home I shall take my ease with her,
for her company has no bitterness,
a life shared with her has no pain –
nothing but pleasure and joy."

(Wis 8:16)

The ideal wife of the book of Proverbs (Prov 31:10-31) is probably a metaphor for wisdom, which, in the book of Wisdom, is in turn imagined as the exemplary wife (cf. also Sir 15:2): from this circle it is possible to draw out a full appreciation of marriage as a figure (event and symbol) of life and joy, when it responds to its innermost value, that desired by the Creator from the origin of the world.

The marriage union in human history

171. The anthropological perspective that the Bible promotes recognises in the loving relationship between a man and a woman the realisation of the design willed by the Creator for the human being (Gen 1-2). The constant and unanimous appreciation of the spousal relationship, with its culmination in the procreation and education of children, becomes a basic element in the ethical and religious framework of the inspired text. Scripture does not directly explain the reasons for such an approach, but it provides important insights that have been developed in doctrine and discipline in the Hebrew and Christian interpretative tradition.

It should be noted, however, that the ideal picture traced by the account of Gen 2, and developed later by the wisdom traditions of Israel, is not taken up in the same way in the other sections of the Old Testament. As will be shown especially in this section, the ancient Scriptures and the new which follow bring out problematic situations, inappropriate activities and improper behaviours that disfigure the perfect form of the spousal union set forth by God. The reasons that make the institution of marriage fragile are manifold and of varied relevance: these may include factors of economic order and social prestige, flawed customs handed on without a realisation of their limitations, and the passions of the human heart, so easily drawn to foolishness and violence. The biblical story traces a line that leads to a developing and, finally, to a full flowering of the spousal relationship; at the same time, by contrast, it expresses with increasing severity its condemnation of improper practices in the sexual sphere that are contrary to the law of God.

> In each part of this section, in order to have a certain consistency in the presentation, we will examine first what is attested in the Old Testament and then also the contribution of the New Testament, whenever it introduces important new elements.

A) Problematic Situations

172. Going through the biblical text, we find that marriage took on various forms in the history of Israel, with customs and practices sometimes differing from God's original design. In some cases this is attested in Scripture without explicit criticism.

It should be noted that in the Old Testament literary tradition the value of physical descent is privileged in an almost exclusive way. This is fully expressed in plentiful offspring (cf. Gen 24:60), especially those of the male sex (cf. Jer 20:15), because the realisation of the divine blessing is recognised in the multitude of descendants (Gen 1:27-28; 9:1; 12:2; 17:16, 20; 26:4; 28:14; Lev 26:9; Deut 28:4, 11; etc.). Procreation, therefore, constantly appears as a beneficial gift to be appreciated and as a value to be promoted. This explains why Abraham agreed to have a son from the servant Hagar (Gen 16:3-4), and why Jacob had children not only from his two wives, but also from their slaves (Gen 30:3-13). Alongside legitimate wives, "concubines" also frequently appear, whose status is neither defined nor clearly condemned (Gen 22:24; 25:6; 35:22; 36:12; Jdg 8:31; 19:1; 2 Sam 3:7; 16:22; etc.). The profile of the institution of marriage that emerges from the texts of the Old Testament is far from perfect. Among other things, marriage is routinely subjected to the will of the parents of those getting married (Gen 21:21; 24:51; 29:21-28; 34:8; Ex 2:21; Josh 15:16-17; Jdg 14:2; etc.), instead of depending on the free decision of the young people based on feelings of mutual affection (cf. Gen 29:15-15). Moreover, the subordination of the woman to the husband (*ba'al*, "lord", "master"), as a reflection of a patriarchal concept of society, and the estimation of the wife mainly in relation to her fertility, are today problematic aspects of the Old Testament model of marriage.

Polygamy

173. The sterility of wives (Gen 11:30; 25:21; 29:31; 30:1) and the desire for abundant offspring contributed if not to produce at least to favour the phenomenon of polygamy, recorded in the cases of Lamech (Gen 4:19) and Esau (Gen 26:34; 28:9; 36:2-5), but also for Abraham (Gen 25:1,6), Jacob (Gen 29:15-30), Gideon (Jdg 8:30), Elkanah (1 Sam 1:2), and later in relation to various kings of Israel, such as David (2 Sam 3:2-5; 5:13; 15:16), Solomon (1 Kgs 11:1-3) , Rehoboam (2 Chr 11:21), Abijah (2 Chr 13:21) and several others. For kings plurality of marriages (cf. Deut 17:17) served to establish useful alliances with the various countries of origin of the wives; the many children could then become instruments of the family's management of power (cf. 2 Chr 11:23). Polygamy, which in a patriarchal society could even be considered a means of protection for unmarried women, is indirectly recognised also by Hebrew legislation in the laws concerning the inheritance to be accorded to the children of two wives, "the one loved and the other unloved" (Deut 21:15-17), and also in the precept concerning the duties towards the slave, who is married and is later associated with a new wife (Ex 21:10); polygamy is also assumed in some rules regarding incest (Lev 18:18; 20:11; Deut 23:1; 27:20). Jealousy and rivalry between wives (Gen 16:4-6; 30:1; Lev 18:18; 1 Sam 1:7), often because of fertility, as well as disagreements between children of different mothers (cf. Gen 37:2-4), constitute a veiled criticism of the nonetheless accepted system of polygamous marriage. It seems clear, and it is recognised by students of the history of Israel, that there was a progressive evolution towards monogamous marriage. In the New Testament we do not find any clear mention of polygamy, nor an explicit condemnation in lists of immoral sexual behaviour. The texts of 1 Tim 3:2, 12 and Tit 1:6, which for the bishop, the priest and the deacon prescribe the statute "husband of one wife", seem to exclude from the church's ministry one who remarried after widowhood; but whoever thinks that monogamy is required of those in ministry should conclude that for other Christians such an obligation was not in force.

> The primary importance of offspring is to be seen also in the levirate law (Deut 25:5-10), which prescribes that, if a married man dies without leaving children, his brother should marry his wife. The firstborn she bears "will assume the dead brother's name; by this means his name will not be obliterated from Israel" (Deut 25:6). The punishment for the behaviour of Onan, who "spilt his seed on the ground" (Gen 38:7-10), is to be interpreted as the sanction for not fulfilling the law just mentioned; the condemnation should not therefore be generalised by applying it to other sexual transgressions. The levirate law, referred to favourably in Ruth 4, and to which the Sadducees refer in the controversy with Jesus in Mt 22:24, could have given rise to occasional instances of polygamy. One wonders, however, about the actual application of this law in the history of the Jewish people, since, among other things, it does not seem to take into account the feelings of the spouses at all. As with other Old Testament norms, the New Testament did not see fit to adopt this precept.

"Mixed" marriages

174. The narrator and the biblical legislator introduce a sometimes quite explicit critique of marriages between Israelites and other populations, especially those resident in the land of Canaan. It is narrated, for example, that the two Hittite wives of Esau "made life bitter for Isaac and Rebecca" (Gen 26:35); that the parents were not opposed to polygamy but to the union with foreign women is evident from the comparison with their attitude towards the twin Jacob, who was also the husband of two wives, but wives chosen from within the "family" (Gen 27:46; 28:1-69). The parents' initiative in procuring wives for their sons from their own relations is justified as preserving their own religious traditions and customs, which promote communion between the spouses; there is also the concern to safeguard membership of the "holy" people of Abraham, since the blessing promised him extends to all his descendants in the flesh, to his "seed". For this reason the Sinaitic law forbids alliances with the Canaanites, which in practice were made through marriages (Ex 23:32-33; 34:12-16; Deut 7:2-4).

This rule of separation was in reality largely ignored, and in certain cases the narrator does not spare censure (Jdg 3:5-6: 14:1-3; 1 Kgs 11:1-2; 16:31). On their return from exile in Babylon, in a context of the renewal of the covenant, the repudiation of foreign wives and the removal of their children were in fact imposed (Ezr 9:1-3; 10:18-44; Neh 10:31; 13:23-27). In other cases, however, no criticism is made of marriages with foreign women, marriages which were contracted even by important Israelites: from Joseph, for example, descend Ephraim and Manasseh who are children of an Egyptian mother (Gen 41:50-52); Moses married a Midianite (Ex 2:21-22), and was criticised, unjustly, because of his Ethiopian wife (Num 12:1); Boaz is praised for his marriage to Ruth the Moabite (Ruth 4:13-17), and it is also said that David had a foreigner among his various wives (1 Chr 3:2). These considerations lead us, therefore, not to overstate the normative force of certain legal prescriptions of the Old Testament.

In a Christian context this problem appears to be in the past insofar as the covenant with the Lord comes about through faith (Acts 3:25; Gal 3:6-7) and no longer demands belonging to a certain race according to the flesh. However, if the spouses are not both baptised or are not both "believers", similar difficulties and even serious disagreements may arise regarding the religious practice of individuals and the education of children. In his first letter to the Corinthians, Paul expounds the case of a "brother" married to a "non-believing" woman, recommending him not to repudiate her, if she agrees to stay with him; and the same criterion applies also to a Christian with a husband of another religious affiliation

(1 Cor 7:12-13); and this, says the Apostle, is because whoever is a believer sanctifies an unbelieving spouse, and even the children who are born are "holy". In this way the Old Testament categories of the covenant are revisited in the light of the Christian mystery. All this naturally presupposes a deep mutual respect between the spouses, with decisions shared regarding the children.

Divorce

175. Marriage is understood by spouses as a reality ideally destined to last a lifetime. In this it differs from occasional sexual relations and also from simple cohabitation. When juridical authority, whether family, state or religious, intervenes to define the status of marriage, the permanent stability of the relationship takes on a public dimension, with rights and duties institutionally protected. On the other hand, however, the spousal union is subjected over time to tests of various kinds which undermine the solidity of the bond: mutual affection can diminish; limitations can be discovered in a partner that are so serious as to be unbearable; instances of violence and behaviour harmful to the dignity and welfare of family members sometimes require distancing from a spouse. Moreover, a value "superior" to the very commitment of conjugal fidelity, such as the adherence of faith or moral demands, can be recognised by the individual, and sometimes also by religious law, so as to allow if not divorce then at least separation. In fact, several Hebrew legislative texts consider cases of repudiation, sometimes recognising it as legitimate (Lev 21:7, 14; 22:13; Num 30:10; Deut 21:14; 24:1, 3-4; cf. also Jdg 15:2; Ezek 44:22; 1 Chr 8:8), at other times prohibiting it (Deut 22:19, 29; cf. Mal 2:16). If it is definitely permitted to the believer of today, especially if Christian, to discuss the validity of individual provisions of the ancient law, nevertheless the principle of "discernment" of the greatest possible good remains valid in the various concrete situations, as indeed is the practice in moral casuistry and in courts of law.

In Israel, according to what we can deduce from rabbinic traditions, the sterility of the wife could constitute a valid motive for divorce. Given the primary task of procreation assigned to the couple, a new marriage was deemed desirable or even necessary.

In a clearly patriarchal society it was above all the right of the man that must be protected. Thus, for example, the adultery of the wife, whether real or suspected (cf. Num 5:11-31), could give rise to a procedure of repudiation (cf. Mt 1:19), while, as far as we know, an analogous power was not recognised in the case of the woman if her husband transgressed. Other more or less serious shortcomings or defects of the wife were probably taken into account to justify divorce in the legal practice of ancient Israel.

> **176.** The text that is cited also in the New Testament (Mt 5:31; 19:7; Mk 10:4) and that describes the procedure of repudiation in greatest detail is *Deut 24:1-4*. The norm, as usual, concerns the husband and grants him the right of repudiation, while forbidding him to go back on his decision, should the divorced woman be free again from the subsequent marriage contracted by her; the legislator takes care, therefore, to make the termination of the bond serious, since it is definitive, by prescribing, among other things, the putting into writing of the "writ of divorce" and its delivery to the woman (Deut 24:2; cf. Is 50:1; Jer 3:8). This entitles both spouses to enter into new marriages. The detailed procedure serves to protect the wife from arbitrary decisions of her husband. From a juridical point of view the least satisfactory element is found in the initial part of the law, where the reason for the act of repudiation is presented. It is stated in Deut 24:1: "Suppose a man has taken a woman and made her his wife, but she has not pleased him and he has found *something objectionable* (*'erwat dābār*) of which to accuse her". This final Hebrew expression has no parallel elsewhere, it is linguistically enigmatic, and therefore does not clarify for what reason the husband might no longer be pleased with his wife and decide to repudiate her; from here there arose a wide range of interpretations and legal practices regarding divorce in the Hebrew world.

We have no reliable data on the frequency and actual procedures of repudiation in ancient Israel; the biblical accounts are silent on the subject. The case of Michal, wife of David (1 Sam 18:27), who later became Palti's wife (1 Sam 25:44) and was finally claimed again by David (2 Sam 3:14-16), can hardly be considered typical, especially because it contradicts the norm of Deut 24:1-4 explained above. We also mentioned, when speaking of mixed marriages, the repudiation of foreign women imposed on those returning from exile (Ezra 9-10; Neh 9-10), with the supposed prospect of new marriages. In this case it was the "religious" motive that required divorce.

177. *The Teaching of Jesus* on the subject introduces radical new elements, since the Master emphatically asserts the indissolubility of marriage, prohibiting divorce and new marriages. The relevant gospel passages are Mt 5:31-32; 19:3-12; Mk 10:2-11 and Lk 16:18. While in Matthew and Mark the issue is dealt with in a context of controversy and in opposition to what "was said to the ancestors", in Luke we have only an isolated *logion*, which is apparently out of context. In John we find no trace of the issue, unless one evokes the critical reference of Jesus to the numerous husbands of the Samaritan woman in Jn 4:18.

To illustrate the teaching of the Lord, it is appropriate to comment on the passage *Mt 19:1-12,* which appears to be the most complete on the matter. There it is narrated that in Judea some Pharisees (Mt 19:1) wanted to put the Galilean master to the "test", in order to denigrate his teaching. Their question is a trap, in that it asks whether it is lawful to repudiate one's wife "for any reason" (Mt 19:3). Jesus, however, does not choose the path of casuistry, which would highlight the difference between various situations and motivations, but rather cites together Gen 1:27 and Gen 2:24, which attest the Creator's original will in forming the human couple (Mt 19:4-5). He then affirms, in no uncertain terms, "what God has united, no one may divide" (Mt 19:6). With this declaration not only is the fundamental rule dictated that prohibits human beings from "separating" the couple, but at the same time the reason for this is suggested, that marriage is not constituted just by the decision of the spouses, but involves also, as a foundational element, the divine act of "joining", an act not subject to human will. Since Jesus makes this declaration to Jews, indissolubility should not be restricted solely to the "sacramental" marriage of Christians.

The Pharisees react to the position taken by Jesus, and object

(Mt 19:7), following the style of doctrinal controversy. They make reference to a different scriptural passage, Deut 24:1-4, which contains the Mosaic "prescription" of repudiation. Jesus in turn replies, saying that rather than a disciplinary provision formulated by Moses in a given historical period, what God has established "from the beginning" (Mt 19:8) must be considered normative. Indeed, Jesus interprets the arrangement made by Moses as a "concession" due to the "hardness of heart" of the Israelites, a concession that has no value where the reality of a new heart, rendered docile by the Spirit of the Lord, is present. In other words, Jesus declares the ancient imperfect system to be ended, because with him and in him full obedience to the original will of God has become possible. In the new economy of the Spirit, repudiation is equivalent to adultery, and is therefore an act of grave transgression of the precept of love which requires perpetual fidelity in spouses. For this reason, the Lord says: "But I say this to you: anyone who divorces his wife – apart from an illicit marriage – and marries another, is guilty of adultery" (Mt 19:9).

> In Mk 10:12 repudiation by the woman is also declared to be adultery. In Mt 5:32, Jesus says that whoever divorces his wife "makes her commit adultery". This formulation differs from that of Mt 19:9, in that it considers seriously what happens to the spouse; moreover, anyone who marries a divorced woman, as in Lk 16:18, is also defined as an adulterer.

178. If the principal assumption is clear, there are, however, unresolved points. One may ask oneself, for example, what Jesus would say about situations in which there is clearly hardness of heart, such that innocent people become victims of violence or abandonment. The complexity of the problem appears already in the various formulations used to present the gospel norm of indissolubility. In some verses it seems that simple repudiation, that is, the forced removal of the spouse, is to be considered a sin, since it is a deliberate "separation" of what God has "united" (Mt 5:32; 19:6; Mk 10:9), while in other passages of a more detailed nature it is rather the subsequent marriage that is to be declared "adultery", for the supposed reason that the breaking of the bond is thereby made definitive and irrevocable (Mt 19:9; Mk 10:11; Lk 16:18a). This last aspect applies also to one who marries a divorced woman (Lk 16:18b), regardless of her possible innocence. In the norms of the Mosaic law, repudiation requires some "motivation"; and this principle is not only expressly formulated in Deut 24:1, but supposed in all the cases mentioned above in which the legislator allows or denies permission to divorce; this invites one to avoid putting every divorce case into the same category. We see then that, while in Mark and Luke the prohibition is formulated in an absolute manner, in the two passages of Matthew's gospel that prohibit divorce a phrase is introduced, expressed in Greek with *parektos logou porneias* (Mt 5:32) or *mē epi porneia* (Mt 19:9), which attaches an exception to the general prohibition of divorce with the words "except for the case of ...". But the term *porneia* is generic and imprecise, as also was the terminology in Deut 24:1: some interpreters suggest that it may refer to one of the cases of "illegitimate union", namely incest, as condemned by Leviticus in chapters 18 and 20, and considered, therefore, in the Jewish community, a proper reason for separation; for other interpreters, the term indicated adultery or some other serious sexual transgression, which made repudiation possible (cf. Mt 1:19).

We will not go into the details of this last debate. We will confine ourselves rather to a hermeneutical consideration of a general nature. Even in the case of a law considered "apodictic" (such as, "do not kill"), the legislator and, even more so, the judge must determine what is its correct application. Thus we find that in ancient law, and in recent secular or Christian law, the general prohibition not to suppress human life is qualified by a whole series of apparent "exceptions", which in fact express the proper interpretation of the same obligation in the complexity of concrete situations. If someone hits an attacker who is in the act of committing a murder and causes that person to die, the command not to kill is not transgressed. The intention in fact was to stop the attacker, protecting the life of the defenceless in the only way possible in those specific circumstances. When Jesus heals on the Sabbath day, he does not violate the law, but in his actions respects the value of liberation intrinsically bound up with the Sabbath precept. The apostles are told to shake off the dust from their sandals when they are not welcomed; they do not fail in their mission to bring the gospel of peace, because their action is an extreme way to bring home to the listeners their hardness of heart. The spouse who, on finding that the marriage relationship is no longer an expression of love, decides to separate from one who threatens the peace or the life of family members, is not acting contrary to marriage; indeed, paradoxically, this action attests the beauty and sanctity of the bond in actually declaring that it does not fulfil its meaning in conditions of injustice and abuse. In a pastoral context, it becomes fundamental to adopt this approach, in the form of practical discernment of the possible good, both to protect and promote the spousal union and to take into consideration the fragility of the human heart.

179. As regards the law of the indissolubility of marriage, we have an authoritative application of the principle of discernment in the first letter to the Corinthians (1 Cor 7:10-16). Paul begins by recalling the "order" of the Lord, even if he does not reproduce to the letter what we find in the gospels: "To the married I give this ruling, – not I but the Lord – a wife must not be separated from her husband, or if she is separated, she should remain unmarried or be reconciled to her husband, and a husband should not divorce his wife" (1 Cor 7:10-11). We note that the Apostle, in relating what the Lord has prescribed, distinguishes between the action of the wife ("to separate oneself") and that of the husband ("to divorce"), taking into account the differences in authority of the two spouses; he does attribute, however, a possible initiative to the woman, as in Mk 10:12. After the general assertion that prohibits separation, he immediately adds, however, that the wife is allowed to separate, provided that she does not remarry, so as eventually to return to her husband. This constitutes a particular way of understanding indissolubility, insofar as it accepts that marriage may be lived in separation. No criterion is provided that might justify the separation.

Paul then continues with his personal recommendations and

norms, saying: "In other cases I say – I and not the Lord" (1 Cor 7:12). We must assume that, while expressing his evaluation, the Apostle still intends always to obey the command of the Lord. He is, however, forced to deal with complex circumstances and to furnish directives not covered by the general rule. He does this by clearly linking the rules of behaviour with the person who has to observe them in his or her particular situation. When he refers to "others", he alludes to problematic matrimonial situations, in that they are contracted between a baptised "believer" and a pagan "non-believer". Here he forbids repudiation by the "believer", if the other "consents" to stay; "but if the unbeliever chooses to leave, then in these circumstances let the separation take place, the brother or sister is not tied. God has called you to live in peace" (1 Cor 7:15). It is thought that Paul is also authorising here a new marriage for the separated spouse.

180. Returning to the account of Mt 19, we see that it is Jesus' own disciples who react, showing their difficulty in accepting the Master's statements: "If that is how things are between husband and wife, it is not good to marry" (Mt 19:10). What the disciples' objection suggests is that by promoting the ideal of the indissolubility of marriage one ends up making the very institution of marriage less desirable. Jesus' final answer does not criticise the comment of the disciples; indeed in a certain sense he confirms its validity, when he says: "Not everyone can accept that saying, but only those to whom it is granted" (Mt 19:11). The Master does not speak of a lack of understanding, but of the inability of the heart to adhere to his message of demanding love. He makes the same observation for those who cannot give up wealth (Mt 19:23-24), or are confronted with the drama of the cross (Mt 16:22-23; 17:23; 26:31). We reaffirm, therefore, what we have already said, namely, that Jesus presupposes the gift of the Spirit who alone allows marriage to be lived in unfailing loving fidelity.

Biblical teaching leaves the field open to moral and pastoral theology: "hardness of heart" continues to be present, even in the baptised, and this requires wisdom and mercy from whoever must interpret the message of Jesus and his desire for good.

B. Improper behaviours

181. Scripture not only mentions problematic aspects of the institution of marriage, but also denounces negative behaviours, which, being contrary to the divine will, are sanctioned with whatever punishments are considered proportionate.

Incest

The Bible clearly condemns incest, understood as sexual intercourse, and obviously marriage too, between persons linked by close family ties. The reason for such legislation is not provided. We can suppose that, for the biblical tradition, spousal love should not be confused with other different emotional relationships, just as the difference between generations should be adequately safeguarded. It has not always been precisely defined which bonds of blood or affinity constituted a reason for prohibition; the biblical narratives are not consistent in supporting the norms of the legislation, which appears more rigorous in this regard, although not entirely uniform in its prohibitions. Abraham, for example, has his half-sister Sarah (Gen 20:12) as his wife, despite what Lev 18:9, 11 lays down; and Jacob marries two sisters (Gen 29:15-30), something that will be expressly forbidden by Lev 18:18.

Some accounts criticise incestuous behaviour when it causes offence to the father; these are cases where the honour to be shown to the parent as the origin of the child's life is lacking (Ex 20:12; Lev 19:3; Deut 5:16). This form of incest is attested in Gen 19:31-35, when Lot's daughters abuse their drunken father and justify their behaviour with the need to ensure descendants; it is also attested in Gen 35:22 and 49:4, when Reuben sleeps with the concubine of his father Jacob, and for this reason is excluded from the blessing (cf. 1 Chr 5:1). The episode of Absalom, who "went to his father's concubines" as a sign of a definitive break with his father David (2 Sam 16:20-22) should also be mentioned. According to some interpreters, a veiled allusion to incest may also be found in the episode of Ham who "saw the nakedness of his father" Noah (Gen 9:22), and for this reason was cursed (Gen 9:25).

182. The legislative provisions on this matter are rather restrictive; they thus promote respect for life, imposing precise limits on uncontrolled sexual impulse. The book of Leviticus details in an almost exhaustive way what the forbidden relationships are (Lev 18:6-18; 20:11-12, 17, 19-21), while Deuteronomy limits itself to a few prohibitions (Deut 23:1; 27:20, 22-23). The gravity of such a transgression is highlighted, first of all, by the qualifications that describe it as "a hateful thing" (Lev 18:26-27, 29-30; 20:13), "a perversion" (Lev 18:17; 20:12,14), "pollution" (Lev 20:21), "an outrage" (Lev 20:17); secondly, the penalties laid down, which are variously expressed as the death sentence, elimination from the people, and sterility, indicate how important the observance of these precepts was for the legislator.

In the New Testament we can consider significant John the Baptist's denunciation of Herod Antipas, who had married Herodias, wife of his brother Philip (Mk 6:17); it is probable that John believed that the king, who was both uncle and brother-in-law of the woman, was guilty of incest, contravening the prescriptions of Lev 18:13, 16; 20:21. Addressing the Christians of Corinth, Paul comes out strongly against an immorality (*porneia*) "that is not found even among gentiles", for one of them "is living with his stepmother" (1 Cor 5:1); for this person the Apostle imposes removal from the community (1 Cor 5:2, 11, 13), a provision that is seen as advantageous for the same culprit: "hand this man over to Satan for destruction of the flesh, so that his spirit may be saved on the day of the Lord" (1 Cor 5:5). The term *porneia* used by Paul in this condemnation of incest could favour those who interpret the so-called Matthean exception clause in the question of divorce as "illegitimate marriage" (Mt 5:32; 19:9). The request made to the gentile converts in Acts 15:20, 28 should be read in the same way.

Adultery

183. In Israel it is the guarantee of legitimate offspring, the right of every parent (Sir 23:22-23), rather than the protection of marital fidelity, that justifies the law strictly forbidding adultery (Ex 20:14; Lev 18:20; Deut 5:18), which is considered a transgression worthy of the death penalty (Lev 20:10; Deut 22:22-27; Ezek 16:38-41;

23:45-47; cf. Jn 8:5). The precept is inscribed in the Decalogue immediately after the prohibition on killing. It should be noted, however, that in the Old Testament adultery occurs only if a man has sexual relations with a married, or legally engaged, woman; the same rules do not apply, indeed the discipline appears rather mitigated, in the case of a man, even a married man, who has sexual relations with women who are not tied by the bond of marriage (cf. Gen 38:15-23; Ex 22:15-16 ; Lev 19:20-22; Deut 22:28-29).

> The wisdom tradition exalts the irreproachable woman. One need only think of the story of Susanna, who risks death in order not to commit adultery (Dan 13:22-23). The wisdom teachers, on the other hand, warn the young man that he might be seduced by the devious skills of a wife who is unfaithful to her husband (Prov 6:23-35; 7:1-27; 23:27-28; Sir 9:8-9), and they decisively condemn adultery (Prov 2:16-17; Sir 23:22-26; Wis 14:24,26), which, obviously, is committed in secret (Job 24:15) and may even be cleverly concealed. A well-known saying of Israel states: "This is how an adulteress behaves: she eats, then wipes her mouth and says, 'I have done nothing wrong'" (Prov 30:20).
>
> Adultery is clearly condemned by the prophets. Suffice it to recall Nathan's denunciation of King David, guilty of the relationship with Bathsheba, wife of Uriah (2 Sam 11:1-12, 15; cf. also Jer 7:9; Hos 4:2; Mal 3:5). In texts that use the spousal metaphor to speak of the relationship between God and Israel, adultery often has a metaphorical meaning, which expresses Israel's unfaithfulness to the Lord (Jer 3:8-9; Ezek 16:38; Hos 3:1; Mt 12:39; Apoc 2:22; etc.).

For the Torah the commitment to an exclusive sexual relationship is binding only on the woman, while it concerns the man only if he abuses the wife of another; in the New Testament, however, every betrayal by a married person is considered adultery, a sin that excludes one from the kingdom of God (1 Cor 6:9; Heb 13:4). Furthermore, referring probably to the last precept of the Decalogue (Ex 20:17; Deut 5:21), Jesus says that "anyone who looks at a woman lustfully has already committed adultery with her in his heart" (Mt 5:28; cf. also Mt 15:19). Finally, it should be borne in mind that, while the ancient law envisaged the death penalty for the guilty, Jesus forgives the adulteress (Jn 8:10, 11).

Prostitution

184. The term "prostitution" refers to the practice of indiscriminate sexual relations, mostly in exchange for some form of payment (cf. Gen 38:16-18; Ezek 16:31, 33). The story of Judah and Tamar (Gen 38), the story of Rahab the prostitute (Josh 2: 1-6), the nonchalant behaviour of Samson (Jdg 16:1) and the episode of the two prostitutes who present themselves to Solomon for a judgement (1 Kgs 3:16) show that prostitution was not considered misconduct worthy of public sanctions. From this we can perhaps deduce that the practice was tolerated. That it was seen as an improper act, however, is clear both from some narrative texts (cf. Gen 34:31; 38:23), and above all from the prophetic and sapiential traditions, which speak of it as despicable behaviour (cf. 1 Kgs 22:38; Is 23:15-16; Jer 5:7; Am 2:7; 7:17; Prov 7:10; 23:27; 29:3; Sir 9:6; 19:2), so much so that prostitution serves in all biblical literature as a metaphor for the infamous sin of idolatry (Ex 34:15-16; Lev 20:5; Deut 31:16; Is 1:21; Jer 2:20; Ezek 16:16; Hos 2:7; etc.).

It is surprising then to find the absence of a general prohibition of prostitution in Hebrew legislation. In the book of Leviticus, we find a rather intriguing precept addressed to the parent: "Do not profane your daughter by making her a prostitute, or the land itself will become prostituted and filled with depravity" (Lev 19:29). One can debate whether the norm should be interpreted literally, which would condemn the parent who takes advantage of his daughter for economic reasons, or whether it should be read metaphorically, with prostitution used as an image of idolatry, as in Ex 34:16 and in numerous prophetic texts (see, for example, Jer 3:1-3; Ezek 16:15-19; 23:43-44; Hos 2:4-7; 5:3-4). For the priest there are more stringent rules in this regard than for the ordinary Israelite; of him it is said that he must not marry a prostitute (Lev 21:7, 14), and for the daughter of the priest who prostitutes herself, thus dishonouring her father, the punishment is to be burnt alive (Lev 21:9).

The texts of the New Testament condemn those who give themselves to prostitution (1 Cor 6:15-20) and to any sexual immorality (Rom 13:13; 1 Cor 5:9-11; 6:9; Gal 5:19; Eph 5:5; Col 3:5-7; 1 Tim 1:10; Tit 3:3; Heb 12:16; 13:4; Apoc 21:8; 22:15). We should bear in mind, however, that Jesus showed mercy towards the public sinner (Lk 7:36-50), and praised the penitent attitude of the prostitutes, in contrast with the arrogance of those who believed themselves to be righteous (Mt 21:28-32).

Homosexual acts

185. The institution of marriage, constituted by the stable relationship between husband and wife, is constantly presented as obvious and normative in the whole biblical tradition. There are no examples of legally recognised "unions" between persons of the same sex.

For some time now, especially in western culture, voices of dissent have been raised in relation to the anthropological approach of Scripture, as it is understood and transmitted by the Church in its normative aspects; all this is seen as simply reflecting an archaic and historically conditioned mentality. We know that various biblical affirmations in the areas of cosmology, biology and sociology have little by little been seen as no longer relevant with the steady advance of the natural and human sciences; analogously, it is deduced by some that a new and more adequate understanding of the human person radically questions the exclusive evaluation of the heterosexual union, and invites similar acceptance of homosexuality and of homosexual unions, as a legitimate and worthy expression of the human being. In addition, it is sometimes argued that the Bible says little or nothing on this type of erotic relationship, which should not therefore be condemned, also because it is often wrongly confused with other deviant sexual behaviours. It would appear necessary, therefore, to examine the passages in sacred Scripture in which the topic of homosexuality is found, in particular those in which it is denounced and censured.

It should be pointed out straightaway that the Bible does not speak of the erotic inclination towards a person of the same sex, but only of homosexual acts. These are treated only in a few texts that differ from one another in literary genre and importance. As regards the Old Testament there are two accounts, Gen 19 and Jdg 19, that raise this issue indirectly, and norms in a law code (Lev 18:22 and 20:13) that condemn homosexual activity.

The accounts of Sodom (Gen 19) and Gibeah (Jdg 19)

186. The story of the sin of Sodom, on which divine judgement falls with the total destruction of the city (Gen 19:1-29), is well known; it has even become proverbial for the question of homosexuality. The episode belongs to the Abraham cycle. It constitutes a kind of contrasting counterpoint to the story of the blessings showered on Abraham, while Sodom becomes a paradigm for the curse of catastrophic punishment (cf. Deut 29:22; Is 1:9; 13:19; Jer 49:18; Ezek 16:56; Lam 4:6; Lk 17:29; etc.). For Abraham and his family, the blessing expresses itself in deliverance from every threat and danger, and above all in the gift of innumerable descendants (Gen 15:5; 17:4-5; 22:17); for the Canaanite city the curse is fulfilled in the total disappearance of life, leading to desolation and perpetual sterility.

The accursed fate of Sodom is motivated by its "sin", which is denounced from time to time as "very grave" (Gen 13:13; 18:20) and considered inescapable, since the minimum number of "just" people that could make plausible the suspension of divine judgement on the inhabitants of the city is not reached (Gen 18:32). The connivance of the whole population would seem to be a factor that aggravates the sin.

But what in reality was the sin of Sodom that deserved such an exemplary punishment? It should be noted first of all that, in other passages of the Hebrew Bible which refer to the sin of Sodom, there is never a reference to a sexual transgression carried out against persons of the same sex. In Is 1:10 the betrayal of the Lord is denounced, while in Is 3:9 a generically sinful conduct carried out in a blatant manner is evoked; in Jer 23:14 Jerusalem is compared to Sodom and Gomorrah because adultery is committed in her, her conduct is deceitful, and evildoers are encouraged, without showing any sign of conversion. Finally, in Ezek 16:49, the prophet asserts that the sin of Sodom was pride (cf. also Sir 16:8), pleasure-loving complacency and failure to assist the poor. It seems, therefore, that a significant biblical tradition, attested by the prophets, has labelled Sodom, and Gomorrah, with the emblematic but generic title of an evil city (cf. Deut 32:32-34).

There is, however, a different interpretation which is to be found in some New Testament texts, such as 2 Pt 2:6-10 and Jude 7, and which, from the second century of the Christian era onwards, established itself, becoming the usual interpretation of the biblical account. The city of Sodom is blamed for an improper sexual practice, called "sodomy", which consists in an erotic relationship with persons of the same sex. At first sight, this would seem to have clear support in the biblical account. In Gen 19, in fact, it is said that two "angels" (v. 1), given lodgings for the night in the house of Lot, are besieged by the "men of Sodom", young and old, all the population without exception (v. 4) with the intention of sexually abusing these strangers (v. 5). The Hebrew verb used here is "to know", which is a euphemism for sexual relations, as is confirmed by the offer of Lot, who, to protect his guests, is willing to sacrifice his two daughters who "are virgins" (v. 8).

187. The account, however, does not intend to present an image of an entire city dominated by overwhelming cravings of a homosexual nature; what is denounced rather is the conduct of a social and political entity that does not wish to welcome foreigners with respect, and therefore seeks to humiliate them, constraining them by force to suffer a shameful process of submission. Lot, who was responsible for the foreigners who had come "under the shelter of his roof" (v. 8), was also threatened with this degrading treatment (v. 9); this reveals the moral evil of the city of Sodom, which not only refuses hospitality, but will not put up with the presence within the city of one who provides an open house to the stranger. Lot, in fact, had shown the two "angels" the same traditional acts of hospitality (vv. 1-3) that Abraham had shown the three "men" who passed near his tent (Gen 18:1-8). Such hospitality obtains salvation for Lot (19:16) and the blessing of paternity for Abraham (Gen 18:10). Those who oppose and gravely offend the foreigner will suffer the curse, as it was spoken beforehand by the Lord to the patriarch, "I will bless those who bless you, and curse those who curse you" (12:3).

This way of reading the story of Sodom is confirmed by Wis 19:13-17, where the exemplary punishment of sinners, first Sodom and then Egypt, is motivated by the fact that "they had shown such bitter hatred to foreigners". Something similar may be deduced indirectly also from Mt 10:14-15 and Lk 10:10-12, where mention is made of punishment for the rejection of the Lord's emissaries, a punishment that will be more severe than that which befell the city of Sodom.

188. A further and stronger confirmation comes from the account of Jdg 19, which in a certain sense is parallel to that of Sodom: the theme of the chapter is the same sin, perpetrated, however, by "brothers" (Jdg 20:23, 28) against those who belong to a different tribe of Israel. The protagonist of the story is a Levite of Ephraim who comes to Gibeah of Benjamin with his concubine and is given hospitality by an old man (Jdg 19:16-21) whose actions recall those narrated about Abraham (Gen 18:1-8) and Lot (Gen 19:1-3). But some citizens of Gibeah, "worthless fellows", present themselves to the head of the house with the request to "know" the guest (Jdg 19:22). They subject the Levite's woman to their violence until she dies (v. 28), which shows that they were not sexually attracted by the male but only desirous of imposing themselves on the foreigner, humiliating him with shameful treatment, perhaps with the ultimate intention of killing him (cf. Jdg 20:5).

In conclusion, it should be said that the story regarding the city of Sodom, like that of Gibeah, illustrates a sin of denying hospitality, and showing hostility and violence to the stranger, behaviour judged to be extremely serious and therefore deserving of punishment of the utmost severity. The rejection of the one who is different, of the foreigner who is in need and defenceless, is the beginning of social breakdown, having within itself a murderous violence that deserves appropriate punishment.

We do not find in the narrative traditions of the Bible any pointers concerning homosexual practices, either as behaviour to be criticised or as attitudes that are tolerated or welcomed. Friendship between persons of the same sex, such as that of David and Jonathan, which is highlighted in 2 Sam 1:26, cannot be considered as an element favouring the recognition of homosexuality in Israelite society. The prophetic traditions do not mention practices of this nature, either among the people of God, or among the pagan nations; and this silence contrasts with the attestations of Lev 18:3-5, 24-30 that attribute to Egyptians, to Canaanites, and in general to non-Israelites unacceptable sexual behaviours, including homosexual relationships. This indicates, as we shall see, a negative evaluation of such activities.

189. The *Old Testament legislation* in this area is fairly limited. The norm of Deut 22:5, which forbids the woman to wear clothes, or objects, that are strictly male and the man to wear female clothes, or ornaments, is interpreted by some as a condemnation of abominable practices (*tô'ēbāh)*, such as the exchange of sexes that took place in Canaanite circles. Others think rather that this norm intends to clarify the strict distinction between man and woman, in conformity with the principle of "separation" and of difference, which is relevant, for example, to sowing seed or to the material used for clothing (Lev 19:19; Deut 22:9-11). Still others have proposed that the precept had the function of preventing disguises which might be used to avoid detection when committing crimes, such as adultery, stealing and even homicide.

Only in the book of Leviticus do we find a precise list of prohibitions relating to reprehensible sexual acts, and among these homosexual activity between males. In Lev 18:22 we have the command: "You shall not lie with a man as you would with a woman; this is a hateful thing (*tô'ēbāh)*"; and in Lev 20:13, the sanction is indicated: "The man who lies with a man in the same way as with a woman: they have done a hateful thing (*tô'ēbāh)*; they shall be put to death; their blood will be on their own heads". The prohibition of male homosexual practice is inserted between the prohibitions of incest (Lev 18:6-18; 20:11-12, 14, 19-21) and those of other sexual deviations, such as adultery (Lev 18:20; 20:10) and bestiality (Lev 18:23; 20:15-16). Apart from its qualification as a "hateful thing", the gravity of the act perpetrated is evident from the death sentence. There is no indication that this sanction was ever applied; it is clear, however, that such behaviour was deemed extremely shameful by Old Testament law.

190. The legislator does not provide reasons either for the prohibition or for the severe penalty imposed. Nevertheless, we can assume that the law of Leviticus intends to safeguard and promote an exercise of sexuality open to procreation, in accordance with the Creator's command to human beings (Gen 1:28), ensuring of course that such an act takes place within a legitimate marriage. The objective of procreation, which we assume is required by the law, would explain not only the condemnation of bestiality, but also the prohibition of having relations with one's wife during menstrual impurity (Lev 18:19; 20:18; cf. Ezek 18:6), in a condition therefore of infertility, in addition to that of "impurity" because of blood; this final law, of a ritual nature, is significant only if it is understood in its symbolic sense. Again with reference to Gen 1:28, one could also affirm that the system of "separation", and therefore of the diversities instituted by the creative action of the word of God, finds its key in the difference between man and woman, male and female; its symbolic value is contradicted and undermined by the union of persons of the same sex.

191. In the *New Testament* the motif of homosexuality is not mentioned in the gospels; it is present explicitly in only three texts of Paul (Rom 1:26-27; 1 Cor 6:9 and 1 Tim 1:10). The last two belong to lists of sins which recall, to a certain extent, the literary form of Leviticus; the first text is more important and will be treated in greater detail.

(a) In the *lists* that indicate forms of behaviour that prevent one "inheriting the Kingdom of God" (1 Cor 6:9-10; Gal 5:21; Eph 5:5; cf. also Tit 3:3), Paul includes also sexual sins, mostly with generic expressions, using, for example, the terminology of *porneia* (1 Cor 5:11; 6:9; Gal 5:19; Eph 5:5; Col 3:5; 1 Tim 1:10), and only rarely specifying particular acts, such as adultery (1 Cor 6:9) and, in two cases, male homosexuality (1 Cor 6:9; 1 Tim 1:10).

1 Cor 6:9-10

Those who commit improper acts attributed to the *pagans* are censured (cf. also 1 Cor 5:9-11) with the general term "evil-doers" (*adikoi*), in contrast to the "holy ones" (*hagioi*). Their distance from the Christian way of life is accentuated by the introductory rhetorical question "Do you not know that...?", used by the Apostle especially in the first letter to the Corinthians (1 Cor 3:16; 5:6; 6:2-3; etc.). The truth should be obvious to the recipients, who among other things are praised by Paul in the same letter for being richly endowed in "every kind of speech and knowledge" (1 Cor 1:5).

In 1 Cor 6:9-10 a list of ten transgressions is presented in two parts, almost a kind of Decalogue, adapted for the Corinthian situation: v. 9 refers mainly to sexual sins; v. 10 to sins of greed, which are more relevant to the context. In the first group we also have idolatry, located strangely among sins of a sexual nature. We will see that even in Rom 1 Paul will establish a link between the lack of recognition of God and transgressions in the sexual sphere. Homosexual activity (*arsenokoitai*) is found at the end of the first part, preceded by adultery and effeminate conduct (*malakoi*). As in the Decalogue and in other Old Testament lists, this list subjects all the guilty to the same sanction of exclusion from the Kingdom; some categories of sin, such as greed or slander, would be subject to discernment, because the gravity of the act could be very different from case to case.

1 Tim 1:9-10

192. Here, too, we have a very long list which designates the "wicked", the lawless (*anomoi*), in contrast to the one who is just (*dikaios*). One can see here perhaps a first group of five transgressions (v. 9) and a second (v.10) also of five; the Decalogue would seem to be in the background, since the list ranges from religious rebellion to the lack of respect for parents, from murder to sexual sins, concluding with perjury.

The context is that of an illustration of the deviant "doctrines" supported by those wanting to be "teachers of the law" (1 Tim 1:7), in opposition to the "gospel of the glory of the blessed God"

(1 Tim 1:11). Here too the list is introduced with "we know", as an illustration of something that is well-known.

From these lists we can conclude that for Christians homosexual practice is considered a serious sin. Paul does not provide explanations in this regard, implying that it was something quite well known and agreed, even if there may have been doctrinal positions outside the Christian community that promoted different views. A link back to the laws of Leviticus and to the tradition of the Old Testament in general may be noted, if for no other reason than the decalogical modes of expression, which reflect those known by tradition in Christian communities.

Rom 1:26-27

193. In an opening section of the letter to the Romans, designed to show the universal guilt of human beings, the object of the divine anger (Rom 1:18), for which reason all are in need of justification in Christ (Rom 3:21-26), Paul presents a general discourse (Rom 1:18-32) in which the question of homosexuality appears in such a way that reveals to us how this behaviour was understood and evaluated in the first Christian community.

The Apostle's reflection is introduced by a general consideration on "ungodliness and injustice", and on the "truth" suffocated by injustice (Rom 1:18). There are two elements here which we are invited to keep present in our analysis: on the one hand, the Hebrew-biblical concept of justice as related to the law and so to the rule and discipline of human behaviour; on the other hand, the concept of truth, contrasted with the lie (Rom 1:25), not missing from the Hebrew world but certainly very important in the Greek world. The text will then discuss unjust behaviours and will also be careful to denounce theories that justify evil (Rom 1:32). At the very beginning of his presentation, and indeed as a common thread running through his argument, Paul denounces the fact that the "reflections" of the pagans "became futile and their uncomprehending minds were darkened" (Rom 1:21); those who claimed "to be wise", became "foolish" (Rom 1:22), expressing in their behaviour their "unacceptable thoughts" (Rom 1:28).

194. The Apostle's denunciation takes place in three stages:

(1) The first regards the *relationship with God*, and here is denounced the fact that human beings, although having the reality of creation before their eyes and having the intelligence to understand, were not able to distinguish the creature from the Creator. Instead of rendering glory to God, they venerated "the likeness of the image" of men and of beasts (Rom 1:20-25). They did not perceive the difference, confusing distinct realities; from this arose an erroneous religious practice, which was identified with idolatry.

(2) From this lack of understanding, according to Paul, come consequences of an anthropological order, *above all in sexual deviations*. "Because they exchanged God's truth for a lie and reverenced and worshipped the creature more than the Creator" (Rom 1:25), they engage in "uncleanness" (*akatharsia*) that is seen as "dishonouring their own bodies" (Rom 1:24); and all this appears, almost emblematically, in the practice of female and male homosexuality. The fact that they "exchanged" God for an image (Rom 1:23), "having exchanged God's truth for a lie" (Rom 1:25), is presented as producing the "change" in sexual relationships, so that the relationship is described as "unnatural" (Rom 1:26). This expression is to be interpreted as something that contrasts with the concrete reality of sexual bodies, which have in themselves a difference and a purpose that are not recognised and respected in relationships between persons of the same sex. According to the Apostle homosexual relationships manifest only the "cravings of their hearts" (Rom 1:24), an unusual terminology that indicates unbridled passions and is described elsewhere as "passions of the flesh" (cf. Gal 5:16-17; Eph 2:3); indeed all this is described as "degrading passions" (Rom 1:26), "shameful things" (Rom 1:27), "perversion" (Rom 1:27). Paul thus follows closely the judgement of Leviticus but with an important difference, that of seeing such behaviour as a consequence of the foolishness, which in itself is a form of punishment: "God abandoned them to degrading passions [...] receiving in themselves due reward for their perversion" (Rom 1:26-27).

The human being therefore should see in the sexuality that no longer recognises "natural" differences the symptom of the distortion of the truth.

(3) Paul then adds that the lack of recognition of the true God always leads to the presence *in society of disordered and violent behaviours* that affect all interpersonal relationships. Here we find a rather varied list (Rom 1:29-31), similar to those given above, which denounces the grave situation of the world, seen with eyes illuminated by the Torah. Even the upheaval in the values of respect and of communion in community is interpreted as a "divine judgement" (Rom 1:32), which should open people's eyes to the lie that produced such injustice. The specific topic of relationships in society will be looked at in the following parts of this chapter.

195. *In conclusion*, the exegetical examination of the texts of the Old and New Testaments has brought to light elements that must be considered for an evaluation of the ethical aspects of homosexuality. Certain formulations of biblical authors, as well as the disciplinary directives of Leviticus, require an intelligent interpretation that both safeguards the values that the sacred text seeks to promote and avoids the literal repetition of culturally conditioned features of the time. The contribution provided by the human sciences, together with the reflections of theologians and moralists, will be necessary for an adequate exposition of the problem that is only sketched out in this document. Moreover, pastoral care will be required, particularly in relation to individuals, in order to carry out that service of the good that the Church is called to take up in its mission to humanity.

The marriage union in the prophetic perspective

196. The message brought by the prophets in the name of God obviously follows that of the Torah as regards its normative aspects. Fidelity in marriage is clearly considered a duty, and adultery is consequently condemned (2 Sam 12:1-12; Jer 7:9; 29:23; Hos 4:2; Mal 3:5). However, we do not find in this literature the condemnation of other inappropriate sexual behaviour; the frequent accusation of prostitution addressed to Israel refers metaphorically to idolatry (Is 1:21; Jer 3:6; Ezek 16:16; Hos 2:7; etc.); similarly, in most cases, the accusation of adultery should be understood as betrayal of the exclusive bond with the Lord (Jer 3:8; Ezek 16:32; Hos 2:4; etc.).

A more specific contribution regarding marriage is offered to us by a passage from the prophet Malachi, who criticises the practice of repudiation and advocates fidelity to one's first love, introducing the concept of the spousal "covenant" of which God is witness:

> "You cover the altar of the Lord with tears, with weeping and wailing, because he now refuses to consider the offering or to accept it from you. And you ask, 'Why?' Because the Lord stands as witness between you and the wife of your youth with whom you have broken faith, even though she was your partner and your wife by covenant (berît) [...] do not break faith with the wife of your youth. For I hate divorce, says the Lord, God of Israel."
>
> (Mal 2:13-16)

As may be seen, the prophet describes the marriage union as a covenant of eternal value between a man and a woman (cf. also Prov 2:17); this consideration helps us to understand better the choice of the prophets to describe the history of the Lord and Israel with the image of marriage. Hosea seems to have been the first to use such symbolism extensively (Hos 1-3). It was subsequently taken up especially by Jeremiah (cf. Jer 2–3) and Ezekiel (cf. Ezek 16 and 23) and by the later parts of the book of Isaiah (cf. Is 54 and 62).

The covenant of the Lord with Israel expressed in terms of marriage

197. Some exegetes have held that the spousal metaphor applied to Israel's relationship with God was used polemically against the religion of Baal, a name which in Hebrew signifies "husband", "master", or more generally in opposition to the various pagan deities who claimed the title of "husband" of the capital cities, which were designated as "virgin of ...", or "daughter of ...". However, the idea that marriage established covenant relationships between people and families was widely known (cf. Ex 23:32; 34:15-16; Deut 7:3), so that the aspect of religious polemic found, for example, in Hos 2:10 does not appear to be the only explanation for the use of marriage symbolism by the prophets to illustrate the Sinaitic covenant.

On the other hand, it is well-known that the biblical writers, when speaking of the history of the people of Israel with their God, adopted the idea of the "covenant" between the great king, "the lord", and his vassal, the "servant", which was governed by a treaty that listed mutual rights and obligations. The Decalogue would be the biblical equivalent of this process. There are important analogies between the covenant in the political sphere and that between spouses: for the two relationships the free consent of the two partners of the covenant is necessary as a constitutive element; the covenant imposes the essential obligation of loyalty and fidelity, which excludes duplicity and betrayal; finally, depending on the behaviour of the "allies", the end result is a story with either happy or destructive results to the point of considering even the annulment of the pact. This makes it clear why the two symbolic universes, the political and the matrimonial, frequently overlap in the prophetic literature, an overlapping also supported by the fact that the husband was seen as an authoritative figure towards his wife and children.

198. The fact that the institution of marriage is used to describe God's history with Israel is a sign that it possesses in itself an intrinsic value; once again the "similarity" between God and the human creature, between divine action and that decreed for human beings, is attested. The marriage covenant is implemented perfectly by the Lord, and this throws light on how it should be lived by the spouses. This is consequently the prophetic message intended indirectly for the couple. At the beginning there is always the initiative of love (Jer 2:2-3), caused not by self-interest, but by a pure desire of benevolence towards the spouse. The fidelity required by marriage, however, consists in maintaining over time the value revealed in the beginning, in the "time of youth". Even when serious sins, such as adultery and prostitution, threaten the existence of the bond of love, it is possible that the original love finds ways of reconciliation, through forgiveness, so as to reach an even deeper communion (Jer 4:1-2; Hos 2:16-22).

The example and teaching of Jesus

199. We have seen in the paragraph on divorce how Jesus shines new light on the status of marriage, by referring back to the design of the Creator who from the beginning desired the union of man and woman in one flesh to express a story of faithful love. Bearing in mind what was allowed in the Deuteronomic Code (Deut 24:1-4), and the various interpretations of his contemporaries, Christ brought to this issue a new and surprising stimulus, comparable to the best wine brought to the table on the wedding day (Jn 2:10). The newness of the gospel message also extends to other aspects of the man-woman relationship, some of which are truly remarkable.

Jesus and women

In contrast to a widespread underestimation of women in the society of his day, Jesus showed a special concern and regard for the women he met, sometimes causing shock and even indignation among his contemporaries (Mt 15:22-28; Lk 7:39; Jn 4:9, 27). Although he entrusted the Twelve with a privileged role in his Church, the Master welcomed among those who accompanied him also "many" women, among whom were Mary Magdalene, Joanna and Susanna, who not only provided for the material needs of the group (Lk 8:1-3; cf. also Mt 27:55; Mk 15:40-41), but also shared the same missionary vocation. Mary of Bethany is even presented by Luke as an exemplary icon of a disciple, listening at the feet of Jesus (Lk 10:39; cf. Acts 22:3). Luke highlights the role of Mary of Nazareth as the privileged witness of the mystery of the Incarnation of the Son of God (Lk 1:26-38), and associates with the beginnings of the gospel other female figures, such as Elizabeth (Lk 1:39-45) and Anna (Lk 2:36-38), as prophetic messengers of the consolation brought by the Saviour.

Some women were singled out by Jesus as models of generosity (Mk 12:41-44), of love (Lk 7:47), and of prophetic intuition (Mk 14:3-9). It is the women who follow Jesus to Calvary (Mt 27:55-56; Mk 15:40-41; Lk 23:49; Jn 19:25), and it is they who go to the tomb early in the morning (Mt 28:1; Mk 16:1-2; Lk 24:1; Jn 20:1), showing a courageous and loving faithfulness to their Master and Lord.

Above all, it should be stressed that the gospels report that it was women, and in particular Mary of Magdala, who were the first to meet the Risen One, receiving from him the task of witnessing to the brothers (Mt 28:1-8; Mk 16:1-8; Lk 24:1-12; Jn 20:1-13, 17). This fact is really remarkable given that at that time insufficient credit was given to the word of a woman (Lk 24:11; cf. also Mk 16:11). Christ will entrust to men, considered reliable witnesses, the task of announcing the Resurrection; the biblical narrative, however, leaves the door open to welcome the woman's voice of faith, once cultural conditions show her greater respect.

> Continuing the story of the life of the Christian community in the book of Acts, Luke points to the presence of women, together with Mary the mother of Jesus, in the community gathered in prayer waiting for Pentecost (Acts 1:14); others are remembered for their contribution to the life of the Church: Tabitha for her charity (Acts 9:36-42), Mary, mother of John, called Mark, for her open house (Acts 12:12), Lydia for her hospitality (Acts 16:13-15), and the four daughters of the evangelist Philip for their prophetic charism (Acts 21:9).

Celibacy for the Kingdom of God

200. The most clearly innovative contribution made by Christ relates to the practice of virginity consecrated to the Kingdom of God. The Old Testament recounts that the prophet Jeremiah was asked to renounce marriage as a sign of the imminent end of Jerusalem (Jer 16:2); and, as far as we know, other prophets, such as Elijah, Elisha and John the Baptist, did not marry, thus expressing a complete dedication to their ministry. Jesus places himself personally in this tradition of prophetic witnesses, while also assuming the role of the Bridegroom of Israel, a qualification which, as we have seen, was reserved for God in the prophetic tradition. Such an attribution to Christ is indirectly attested as when, to indicate the newness of his appearance, Jesus says to the disciples of John the Baptist: "Surely the bridegroom's attendants cannot mourn as long as the bridegroom is still with them? But the days will come when the bridegroom is taken away from them, and then they will fast" (Mt 9:15); Jesus alludes to himself as a bridegroom also in the parable of the wedding of the king's son (Mt 22:1-14; cf. also Lk 12:36) and in that of the ten girls who await the arrival of the bridegroom (Mt 25:1-12). More explicitly in the Gospel of John, the Baptist gives testimony to himself and to Christ using this symbolism: "He who has the bride is the bridegroom, and yet the bridegroom's friend, who stands and listens to him, is filled with joy at the bridegroom's voice. This joy of mine is complete" (Jn 3:29).

As for his disciples, the Lord did not give normative prescriptions that would induce them to imitate his choice of virginity. However, for the apostles and for those who followed him in his itinerant ministry, it seems that one should suppose that they took on the condition of celibacy or a personal status freed from the obligations of marriage. The passage of Lk 18:29-30, which in some way describes the condition of those who have followed the Master, should be interpreted in this sense, given that, in reply to Peter, Jesus declared: "Amen I say to you, there is no one who has left house, *wife*, brothers, parents or *children* for the sake of the kingdom of God who will not receive many times as much in this present age and, in the world to come, eternal life". The qualification of "eunuchs" "for the sake of the kingdom of heaven" (Mt 19:12) is applicable without a doubt also to those who choose not to marry and not to have children according to the flesh, in order to dedicate themselves body and soul to the community, giving birth through the Word to eternal life.

It is certain that the Lord Jesus came to inaugurate a new Israel, no longer procreated from human seed, but generated by the Word and brought alive by the Spirit (Jn 1:13; 3:5-6; Jam 1:18; 1 Pt 1:23). The Twelve, in a contrasting relationship with the twelve sons of Jacob, constitute the symbolic beginning of the new people of God, with "children" made such by the obedience of faith. Indeed, the Church of Christ constitutes a spiritual family (cf. Mt 12:46-50), in which God is the only true Father (Mt 23:9). However, all this does not impose the obligation of celibacy on all Christians. Virginity for the Kingdom of God is rather the fruit of a special "vocation"; on the one hand, it requires a specific call and a corresponding gift from the Lord, and, on the other, it is made in a free commitment of the single person, carried out in the name of Jesus and in imitation of him, so that one's whole existence assumes the prophetic form that announces the eschatological reality (cf. Mt 22:30).

The teaching of Paul

201. It is well-known that Christian faith undergoes an important theological development in the letters of Paul; and this applies also to the man-woman relationship. Although anchored in Jewish tradition, the anthropology of the Apostle comes with original interpretations, and with directives and counsels that have had a significant influence in the history of the Church; some of his pronouncements, however, arouse perplexities today, and they deserve to be highlighted.

On marriage
With regard to sexuality in general, the Pauline tradition insists on "holiness" of conduct, and consequently reproves every form of impurity (1 Cor 6:18; Eph 5:3; Col 3:5; Heb 13:4). Let it suffice to cite in this regard a passage from what is considered Paul's first letter:

"You know what instructions we gave you on the authority of the Lord Jesus. This is the will of God, your sanctification. He wants you to keep away from sexual immorality, and each one of you to know how to control the body in a way that is holy and honourable, not in the passions of lust like the nations who do not know God. He wants nobody at all ever to transgress by exploiting a brother or sister in these matters; the Lord always takes vengeance on sins of that sort, as we told you before emphatically. God called us to sanctity, not immorality (*akatharsia*); in other words, anyone who rejects this is rejecting not human authority, but God, who gives you his Holy Spirit."

(1 Thess 4:2-8)

"Purity" of the body is seen by Paul as the corollary of the person's belonging to the Lord:

"The body is not for sexual immorality (*porneia*); it is for the Lord and the Lord is for the body [...] Do you not know that your bodies are members of Christ? Am I to take the members of Christ's body and make them members of a prostitute (*pornē*)? Out of the question! Or do you not know that anyone who is united to a prostitute is one body with her? For it is said: the two shall be one flesh. But anyone who is united to the Lord is one spirit with him."

(1 Cor 6:13, 15-17)

The concept of covenant with the Lord serves then to prescribe the rules for the exercise of sexuality; as a consequence it follows that Christian "spirituality" manifests itself in the way in which one lives in the body.

202. The same symbolism of the covenant is applied by Paul to the condition of marriage in the well-known passage of Eph 5:22-33. It is here that the Apostle, once more quoting Gen 2:24, uses the category of "great mystery" (Eph 5:32) to characterise the marriage relationship as a perfect revelation of love. The prophets, as we have seen, had used the image of marriage to describe the story of the covenant between the Lord and Israel; now Paul, in a certain sense, actualises the ancient tradition, carrying out a double transposition. First of all, he attributes to Christ the image of the Bridegroom, as the maker of the "new covenant", which is ratified no longer in the blood of sacrificial victims, but in the gift of the person of Jesus himself, a gift that purifies and renders holy the Church his bride (Eph 5:25-27). The historic unfolding of love that the ancient prophecies ascribed to God, as for example in Ezek 16:8-14, is applied by Paul to the action of Christ, as the perfect fulfilment of the history of salvation. This first transposition of the prophetic metaphor is in continuity with the gospel tradition, in which allusion was made to the role of Christ as the Bridegroom of Israel.

The second transposition, more relevant in the field of anthropology, is made when the Apostle takes the Christological reality as a model for the marriage relationship between Christian spouses. It should not seem inappropriate or far-fetched to propose to the Christian husband the example of Christ, even when it includes the demanding duty of self-giving. In fact in the gospel the disciples of Jesus are asked to be "perfect" as the Father is perfect (Mt 5:48), and to do what Jesus did, to love as he loved (Jn 13:34; 15:12). The "great mystery" is actually accomplished when the human person becomes capable of complete likeness to God in love.

203. However, the deduction that, as Christ is the head of the Church, so too "a husband is head of his wife" (Eph 5:23), is problematic, and is challenged by the contemporary understanding of the marriage relationship. Paul intends, in this way, to provide the basis of the husband's authority over his wife, accepting probably what in the culture of his time appeared to be a "natural" fact, intended to guarantee order in the family, and conferring on this statute a high religious value. The relationship between husband and wife is therefore inserted in the list of asymmetric relationships, which therefore require a specific form of obedience. In the letter to the Ephesians the paragraph dedicated to the relationship between husband and wife is immediately followed by that concerning the relationship between parents and children (Eph 6:1-4) and that between masters and servants (Eph 6:5-9); the same thing happens in Col 3:18-22. We can ask ourselves, therefore, whether such an interpretative method respects the concept of equal dignity between the spouses, which among other things appears to be attested in Gen 2:22. To prescribe that "wives" should be subject "to their husbands in everything" (Eph 5:24; cf. also Col 3:18 and 1 Pt 3:1, 5) is not an adequate directive to define the relationship between spouses, where the perfection of love should express itself rather in dialogue, or better in the consensus of each person to the truth proffered by the other, so that both obey what God wants. "Docility" is requested therefore not only from the wife but also from the husband. And not only is the husband called upon to love, giving his whole self, but the wife also is called upon to make the same total gift expressed by Christ when he gave himself over lovingly to the Church.

204. From these reflections we draw two consequences: (i) The first is to understand in their cultural context the various pastoral pronouncements of Paul which, in the name of "tradition" perhaps (cf. 1 Cor 11:2), put the woman in a position of inferiority, both in the family and in the Church.

> The Apostle required that women should have their heads covered while praying and prophesying (1 Cor 11:5), which for the man was considered inappropriate (1 Cor 11:4), since, he affirms, "he is the image and glory of God, but woman is the glory of the man. For man is not from woman, but woman from man. Nor was man created for woman, but woman for man" (1 Cor 11:7-9). As we have been able to show in the exegesis of Gen 2:18-24, the biblical account of creation does not establish either the superiority or the authority of man over woman. The custom of veiled women in the community should not be maintained, therefore, if it expresses undue subjection.
>
> In a passage from the Pauline tradition we read: "During instruction, a woman should be quiet and respectful. I give no permission for a woman to teach or to have authority over a man. She should remain quiet, for Adam was formed first and Eve afterwards, and Adam was not led astray, but the woman was led

astray and fell into sin. She will be saved by childbearing, provided that they continue in a sensible life, constant in faith and love and holiness" (1 Tim 2:11-15). The scriptural basis of Gen 2-3 used to impose on the woman a general attitude of submission is presented in this letter as evidence; today, however, this reading is disputed. The disciplinary consequences for women, such as the obligation to keep silent, the ban on teaching, seen even as "dominating", and the duty to give birth to children, as a kind of expiation for the supposed sin of Eve, are therefore inappropriate.

In another passage from the first letter to the Corinthians, Paul reiterates the discipline outlined above: "for God is a God not of disorder but of peace. As in all the churches of the saints women should be silent in the churches, for they are not allowed to speak; they should be subordinate, as the Law also says. If they want something explained, they should ask their own husbands at home, for it is shameful for a woman to speak in the church" (1 Cor 14:33-35). It is possible that Paul alludes here to Gen 3:16 to affirm the submission of women to men; from this interpretation, however, it should not be inferred that it is improper for them to speak in assemblies, where they might teach their husbands with competence and wisdom. The Apostle's recommendations should be seen in the cultural context of the time, and considered above all to be an expression of his concern for order in ecclesial assemblies.

Several other anthropological considerations, made perhaps incidentally by Paul, are at least open to question. It does not seem satisfactory, for example, to tell the husband to love his wife because "a man who loves his wife loves himself" (Eph 5:28), just as it seems strange to assert that "the wife does not have authority (*ouk exousiazei*) over her own body, but the husband does; and in the same way the husband does not have authority over his own body, but the wife does" (1 Cor 7:4). The understanding of the nature of love, as well as the sense of the gift of one's body to one's spouse, require different formulations today from those found in the Pauline letter.

205. (ii) The second consequence goes, in a certain sense, in the opposite direction, and constitutes a question to be put to the model of equality required by the contemporary mentality as the proper relationship between husband and wife. In the quite frequent case of differences of opinion between spouses, how can a decision that obliges both, and perhaps even the children, be made? How will family harmony be preserved if no one "submits", in humble obedience, to the opinion of the other? Each social group would seem to require a figure of authority, exercising a function with the spiritual qualities of wisdom and love necessary to foster assent and a common purpose. But if, in a given cultural context, it is not considered appropriate that one of the spouses be delegated to exercise such an authoritative function, a strictly equal structure requires from each of the spouses attention to the common good of the family and a humble willingness to listen to the other, so as to "submit" lovingly to the truth and therefore to the will of God that is revealed in the patient dialogue of discernment. Otherwise, one of the two will prevail over the other in an underhand way, with inevitable negative consequences for the survival of the marriage bond.

On celibacy

206. Following the Lord Jesus Paul personally assumes the condition of celibacy as a radical surrender of himself to the service of the gospel. His disciples are his brothers and sisters and children (Rom 1:13; 1 Cor 4:14-15; Gal 4:19). The Apostle also furnishes a series of reasons to justify such a choice of life; it is appropriate to note also the aspects that are problematic.

> Replying to a series of questions of the Corinthians concerning marriage, Paul begins by saying: "Now about the questions about which you wrote. It is well for a man not to touch a woman; yet because of immorality (*porneia*) every man should have his own wife and every woman her own husband" (1 Cor 7:1-2). The general affirmation that it is well for a man not to touch a woman is to be understood as an endorsement of virginity, which could perhaps have been contested by anyone who understood the words of the Creator to *'ādām*, "be fruitful, multiply" (Gen 1:28), as a divine "commandment" imposed on all. It is, however, the second

phrase, "yet because of immorality ...", that raises doubts. It seems to present marriage not as a specific choice of love, but only as a protection against improper tendencies, as also in 1 Cor 7:8-9. In the rest of the letter an interpretation of marriage and celibacy emerges that, as Paul specifies, does not express a "command" (*epitagē*) of the Lord, but rather a personal opinion (*gnōmē*) of the Apostle (1 Cor 7:25; cf. also 1 Cor 7:40; Phlm 14). This difference should be carefully evaluated.

In relation to "virgins" (1 Cor 7:25) Paul writes: "Because of the impending crisis (*anankē*) I think it is good for you to stay as you are. Are you joined to a wife? Do not seek to be free. Are you free of a wife? Do not seek a wife. But if you marry, you do not sin, and if a virgin marries, she does not sin. Such people will have hardships (*thlipsis*) in the flesh, and I would spare you that" (1 Cor 7:26-28). Once again it is reiterated that celibacy is a good thing, indeed better than marriage. The reason given for this is the "difficulties" (cf. 2 Cor 12:10; 1 Thess 3:7), perhaps connected with the historical situation of the last times (1 Cor 7:29, 31; 2 Tim 3:1), marked by various kinds of "tribulations", as we also read in the eschatological discourse of Jesus (cf. Mt 24:9, 21, 29; cf. also 2 Cor 6:4). Paul would like his recipients to avoid these. The general advice of the Apostle is to remain in the condition in which everyone is (cf. 1 Cor 7:17, 20, 24). Changing one's life situation, however, can be a necessary response to a spiritual vocation; moreover, marriage cannot be legitimised simply by saying that "it is not a sin" (cf. 1 Tim 4:3), and the choice of celibacy cannot be a way of avoiding trouble.

207. Continuing his reflections, Paul provides an additional reason for preferring celibacy to marriage: "I want you to be free of anxiety. The unmarried man is anxious about the things of the Lord, how he may be pleasing to the Lord. The married man is anxious about worldly things, how he may be pleasing to his wife, and he is divided (*memeristai*). And the unmarried woman, and the virgin, is anxious about the things of the Lord, that she may be holy in both body and spirit, but the married woman is anxious about worldly things, how she may be pleasing to her husband. I am saying this to be helpful (*symphoron*) to you" (1 Cor 7:32-35). If it is right to see in virginity, freely chosen in obedient response to the divine call, a way of signifying and living an absolute dedication to the Lord, it is however highly problematic to consider marriage as an almost opposite way, in which the spouses would worry about the things of the world, trying to please one another instead of God alone. The "division" or splitting of the heart is not an inherent limitation of the spousal condition, in which it is indeed possible to live holy lives of true love, fully pleasing to the Lord. To consider that it is preferable not to marry one's fiancée, if this is the meaning of 1 Cor 7:36-38, or to tell the widow that it is better not to remarry, are corollaries of the previous Pauline arguments. In light of biblical revelation as a whole, in view of the beauty of marriage and its challenge of love, the vocation to consecrated virginity must find different motivations.

From the texts of Paul it has been deduced that the Christian is faced with two choices in life: that of marriage, which is simply permitted, and that of celibacy, preferable because it is more suited to living according to the gospel. Such a dichotomy needs to be reconsidered, especially if the exaltation of one of the two "ways" results in the devaluation of the other. In fact, each one must be seen as a "call" to holiness, with its own specific features; and each one can be lived in truth only through a gift of the Spirit of love. The satisfactory treatment of this issue should be entrusted to experts other than simple commentators on the biblical text. Among other things, the importance of the relationship between man and woman lived in chastity should be developed, both for those who are married and especially for those who have chosen virginity for the Kingdom of God. The example of Jesus could be the starting point of a process that discusses friendship between man and woman as a universal vocation of great spiritual richness.

2. LOVE BETWEEN PARENTS AND CHILDREN

208. The meeting between man and woman, as they come to know and appreciate each other, marks the start of a story of mutual love, which has its desired result in the generation of children. In Gen 4:1 we read: "The man had intercourse with his wife Eve, and she conceived and gave birth to Cain". The event of the birth is, in turn, the beginning of another story, marked by the relationship of the child with its parents, and rooted in a precise moment in time, so that every human being is a "child of man" and a "child of his time".

Such considerations find literary expression in the *"genealogies"* (Hebrew: *tôlᵉdôt*; Greek: *genesis*), through which the biblical narrator, using the list of fathers and sons, recalls in synthesis the different periods of the human story.

The genealogies

209. In the section that narrates the beginnings of humanity, having described the origin (*tôlᵉdôt*) of heaven and earth (Gen 2:4) and having listed the descendants of the first son of man, Cain (Gen 4:17-26), the book of Genesis establishes in three long genealogical lists (Gen 5:1-32; 10:1-32; 11:10-32) the coordinates of the primordial history of humanity, providing information regarding the diversified expansion of the various ethnic groups on the face of the earth. As is apparent from improbable dating, as well as from a certain fluidity in the identity of the people evoked, we are certainly not presented with a reliable report from a historical point of view; instead the biblical author aims to set out the "meaning" of history, understood as the truth and the ultimate purpose of human generation: the *truth* of history coincides with the revelation of the presence of God where human beings are active; this is programmatically declared by Eve at the birth of the first son of man, when she says: "I have acquired a man with the help of the Lord" (Gen 4:1). This is then made explicit in the numerous interventions of God, aimed at guiding the course of events in the direction of the blessing, the ultimate *purpose*, intended and brought about by the Lord.

In contrast to the lineage of Cain, which is, so to speak, interrupted insofar as it is marked by the curse (Gen 4:11), the first genealogy (Gen 5:1-32) presents the lineage of Seth the son of Adam, who replaced Abel (Gen 4:25). Of him it is said that "this man was the first to invoke the name of the Lord" (Gen 4:26), an anachronism with respect to Ex 6:3, yet a true religious attestation, which makes the point that, from the beginning, the true God was recognised and honoured, at least by some who acknowledged his presence. Ten names, from Adam, the sinner driven from Eden, to Noah, the "righteous" (Gen 6:9) and the "one who will bring us rest" (Gen 5:29), are enough to trace a story of many centuries, which flows into the new beginning of humanity, under the sign of an everlasting covenant and a renewed blessing of all creation, after the catastrophe of the flood (Gen 6–9).

210. The second genealogy (Gen 10:1-32), which differs from the first in that it does not have any indications of time, lists the numerous descendants of the three sons of Noah: Japhet (Gen 10:2-5), Ham (Gen 10:6-20) and Shem (Gen 10:21-31); reversing the order of their birth, the narrator focuses the reader on that patriarchal line in which the history of salvation will take shape. This is implemented in practice in the context of the "dispersion" of the peoples in the various parts of the world: the peoples who will have great importance in the continuation of the biblical story are mentioned here, almost as a preparatory showing of the different periods of the history of the people of God.

The last great genealogy of Genesis (Gen 11:10-32) concludes with the birth of Abraham, placed at the end of a list of ten names, which from Shem reaches the son of Terah. He will begin the history of his people, characterised by the covenant with the Lord. All the "generations" from the beginning of humanity thus lead to this central character, to a kind of promising beginning. In this "father", in fact, the original blessing of the Creator (Gen 1:28) becomes a marvellous historical truth (Gen 12:2), since the descendants of Abraham are the fruit not of the power of the flesh, but of the docile obedience of faith.

At the conclusion of the Hebrew canon, the first book of Chronicles, by way of an introduction to its historical account, takes up this literary genre (1 Chr 1–9), including in an almost exhaustive way all the various genealogies that we find scattered in earlier biblical books; in particular, the detailed enumeration of the descendants of the twelve sons of Jacob serves the narrator as a premise for the presentation of David as the messianic king, whose covenant with the Lord (1 Chr 11:1-3) is the beginning of everlasting hope for Israel (1 Chr 17:11-14).

211. Similarly, in the Gospel of Matthew (Mt 1:1-17), the person of Jesus Christ is seen as the final convergence of the entire history of Israel, arranged in three cycles of fourteen generations (v. 17), from Abraham to David (vv. 2-6a), from David to Jechoniah, king at the time of the deportation to Babylon (vv. 6b-11), and finally from Jechoniah to Jesus (vv. 12-16), "son of David, son of Abraham" (v. 1). The covenant, with its promises, finds fulfilment in Christ, as will be illustrated later in the gospel story: procreation according to the flesh is interrupted to give rise to generation through the Word.

The evangelist Luke, starting from Jesus, goes back to all his forefathers (Lk 3:23-38). The first of the "fathers" to be mentioned, Joseph, is only "considered" such (v. 23), however, because the birth of the son of the Most High is due to the intervention of the Spirit (Lk 1:31-35); among the other ancestors we find well-known people, interspersed with others whose history is unknown, in the universalistic concern to connect the "beloved Son" (Lk 3:22) with Adam, whose origin from God is specified (Lk 3:38).

212. Biblical genealogies constantly reproduce the patrilinear form. Some will say that this is a simple reflection of ancient patriarchal conceptions; others, however, will suggest that in this way the legal recognition by the father with the conferral of the rights due to the child was given preference over the physical generation by the mother. In the biblical tradition this essentially means welcoming the child into the community of the sacred covenant, as a member of a people who live for the divine promise. In fact, the male who is born in the "house" of

Abraham's descendants is, through *circumcision*, included among the sons of the covenant, from generation to generation: "This is my covenant which you must keep between myself and you, and your descendants after you: every one of your males must be circumcised" (Gen 17:10). The male line of the Israelites will therefore bear the "sign" (Gen 17:11) of an everlasting covenant (Gen 17:13). Jesus was circumcised on the eighth day (Lk 2:21), thus becoming son of Abraham, bearer of the definitive blessing to all nations (Acts 3:25-26; Gal 3:14).

Circumcision

213. Circumcision, which was practised by various peoples of antiquity, from Syria to Egypt (cf. Jer 9:24-25), seems originally to have been a marriage initiation rite; however, since in Israel it is prescribed as an act to be practised on the child on the eighth day after birth (Gen 17:12; Lev 12:3), its meaning changes considerably. Historians believe that in Israel this practice was established in exilic times as a sign of religious *affiliation*, when Abraham's children were deprived of other signs of identity, and found themselves living among uncircumcised Mesopotamian populations. It may be thought that the incision made on the male member had the practical function of freeing the sexual organ from any impediment, so as to facilitate procreation; but seen in the light of biblical revelation, circumcision becomes rather a sign of religious faith, which professes that *fruitfulness* and life come from the covenant relationship with God and not from human virility alone.

According to the prophets, the children of Israel did carry in their flesh the signs of their bond with the God of life, but their heart was uncircumcised (Lev 26:41; Jer 9:25); it did not belong to the Lord and was not bound to him with the fulness of love. The deceitful double standard between ritual obedience and a persistent inner rebellion could not be eliminated only by the urgent warning to "circumcise one's heart" (Deut 10:16; Jer 4:4). The intervention of God was necessary so as to inaugurate a *new covenant* (Jer 31:31-34), already announced by Deuteronomy in these terms: "The Lord your God will circumcise your heart and the heart of your descendants, so that you will love the Lord your God with all your heart and soul, and so will live" (Deut 30:6). It is no longer the physical parent who makes a cut in the flesh of the child, but it is the Father of life who puts his seal in the intimacy of the individual, so as to make his belonging to God everlasting; and this will not be reserved for males only, but given to every person, so that everyone, men and women, can love their Lord perfectly and live with eternal life.

214. In actual fact biblical genealogies do not always mention the father figure alone; in some cases *mothers* are cited who have specific relevance in the family line. This, among other things, is attested by Matthew in the genealogy of Jesus, where mention is made of Tamar (Mt 1:3), Rahab (Mt 1:5), Ruth (Mt 1:5), Bathsheba the wife of Uriah (Mt 1:6), and Mary, of whom "was born Jesus who is called the Messiah" (Mt 1:16). More generally, the biblical account often makes explicit the role of the mother not only for the events of gestation and childbirth, which are sometimes dramatic (cf. Gen 35:16-19), but also for the influence she exerts on the future of the offspring (cf. for example, Gen 27:5-17, 42-45; Ex 2:1-3, 7-9; 1 Kgs 1:11-31).

Furthermore, it is important to note how significant it is anthropologically that every human being originates from a dual principle, from a man and a woman together through the act of their joining together in love. Every separation between the spouses will constitute a laceration in the psychological identity of the person who receives life from the parents' communion. If it is through the loving union of the two that a child is born, it is in the harmony of the parents' feelings and in the convergence of their intentions that the child gains access to the meaning of existence, and grows as a person. This is expressed in the words that the father and mother direct to the child, so that the child may accept them as life-giving, since such words come from love and teach love.

This also has consequences of a religious nature. In fact, neither of the parents can boast of being on their own the origin of the child, a role which is reserved exclusively for God the Father; the coming together of man and woman to have a child is not enough, if God does not open the womb of the woman so that she can conceive and give birth (Gen 30:2); for this reason the Lord is blessed by believers, whom he has united (Tob 8:15-17), and to whom he has given the grace to bring to life a child of man (Ruth 4:13; 1 Sam 1:19-20, 27).

Actions of the parents

215. From the act of generation, a story unfolds in which father and mother perform acts of love for their offspring, through which the very meaning of being a parent and, by extension, of being a child is expressed.

(i) In the first phase of the child's life, the mother has an overriding importance due to gestation, childbirth, breastfeeding (2 Mac 7:27) and all the childcare activities that indelibly mark the emotional relationship between mother and child. However, the importance of the father must also be acknowledged, for it is he who "recognises" the child, registering him legally in the family and in the civil community. It can be said that, even though the father already participated in the generation "according to the flesh", he always performs a sort of "adoption", when, receiving the child born of a woman, he declares "this is my child". In ancient Israel the name of the child is sometimes given by the mother to the newborn (Gen 29:32-35; 30:6-24; 35:18; Lk 1:59-63); for the most part, though, it is conferred by the father at the time of circumcision, so that the infant is included in the genealogy of the people of the covenant. An eventual change of name indicates, in a certain sense, a new birth, because of a new spiritual paternity (cf. Gen 17:5).

(ii) The birth of the child makes it necessary that the parents undertake constant practical actions to foster the life of their child, who is dressed, nourished and protected from all kinds of danger. The child experiences the condition of the person in need, but this situation, far from being seen as humiliating, leads to a constant and joyful experience of being loved, day after day, in a free and generous way. At the same time, the parents accompany the acts of daily care with words, which tell the story of the child's beginnings, which transmit wise advice useful for the future, and which deliver the ethical and religious norms to be followed in order to nurture life. The parents rejoice if the child grows in obedience (cf. Lk 2:40, 51-52), because acceptance of the spiritual heritage of the parent is expressed in listening (Prov 10:1; 15:20; 23:24-25; 27:11; 29:23).

(iii) The young person becomes an adult, independent and autonomous, leaving father and mother to found a family. Parents support this moment by giving the child the inheritance due, and invoking on their child the blessings of prosperity, fruitfulness and happiness. The land handed on to be worked by the son will constitute in Israel an important symbol of the gift received from the ancestors. On it benevolent words of prayer and well-wishing will have the effect of a heavenly dew (Gen 27:28).

The reader of Scripture will not fail to notice how these parental acts are applied to God in his relationship to Israel. For God is Father, who generates with his Word of love, who nourishes and educates, who blesses and bestows the inheritance, for a life without end.

The duties of parents and children according to the Law

216. The human story narrated by the Bible is realistic; there exist various forms of relationship between parents and children, some commendable, others reprehensible. This may come as a surprise, since it is commonly believed that such a relationship should always be a natural channel of love, especially from the father and above all from the mother (Is 49:15).

But if affection appears to flow naturally from the parent's heart, this does not mean that it is always well controlled. In the history of the Patriarchs, we read that "Isaac loved Esau, for he had a taste for wild game; but Rebekah loved Jacob" (Gen 25:28); this imbalance will have an impact on the conflict between the two brothers. Similarly, "Israel loved Joseph more than all his other sons, for he was the son of his old age, and he had a coloured tunic made for him" (Gen 37:3); the consequence was that his brothers, "seeing how much more his father loved him than all his other sons, came to hate him so much that they could not say a peaceful word to him" (Gen 37:4). In other cases, the father lacks rigour in correcting his overbearing children: the priest Eli reproaches his sons, without however adequately sanctioning their wicked behaviour (1 Sam 2:22-25); Samuel was unable to educate his sons, and they exercised the office of judge in a perverse way (1 Sam 8:1-3); and David did not intervene appropriately against Amnon, who was guilty of rape against his half-sister Tamar, for "he would not upset his son Amnon, whom he loved because he was his first-born" (2 Sam 13:21).

Similarly, children do not always show respect and obedience towards their parents. Esau, for example, aggrieves his father and mother by marrying in a way contrary to their just desires (Gen 26:34-35); Jacob disrespects Isaac, getting out of him by deception the blessing reserved for the firstborn (Gen 27:33-35); the brothers of Joseph, by selling their brother, constrain their father to live in mourning (Gen 37:34-35).

From these stories one understands better the necessity of the Law of God, which serves as a directive, both for parents and children, so that the innate propensity to love unfolds in full truth and justice.

Rules for parents

217. In the heart of the Decalogue is formulated the norm on the Sabbath (Ex 20:8-11; Deut 5:12-15), which, among other things, asks the *pater familias* to be an instrument of liberation for his children, so that on the seventh day the whole family can symbolically experience the freedom that God had given with the emancipation from slavery in Egypt (Deut 5:15). It is important to note that, because he himself obeys the same precept, the father can be a model of obedience to the true authority, that of the Lord, who does not impose servile obligations to his own advantage, but calls for a discipline that expresses the authentic way of life. In the atmosphere of rest and celebration typical of the Sabbath the father, offering the children the joy of freedom, actually subjects them, at the same time, to the first of the commandments, causing them to remember and experience that every Israelite lives by renouncing the idolatrous work of his hands (Deut 5:8), so as to be free to serve the Lord alone. Every precept given by the father to the child must embody this same spirit, a spirit of freedom and obedience.

Starting from this central commandment of the Decalogue, one understands better how the essential duty of the parent is that of transmitting and inculcating the *Torah* of God (cf. Ps 78:3-7): the divine precepts, which the father has assimilated in his heart, become the subject of his "speaking" to his children, at home and on the way, from lying down to getting up to undertake work (Deut 6:6-7). Obedience lived practically by the father in the observance of the Law becomes an educational principle for the child (Deut 6:20), so that the justice implemented by the whole family has life and happiness as its fruit (Deut 6:24-25).

218. In this sense, the parent is the "teacher" more than any other, since he is the first to teach the meaning of life, through words of wisdom and through conduct that conforms to the good in obedience to God. The transmission of the Torah is based on the effective recognition of the child's freedom: it is not imposed through coercion, even though it is presented as a binding obligation; it is offered as a precious gift, even if it requires difficult decisions. The father encourages the child to make the right choice; he constantly takes up the words of Moses, who placed before Israel a radical choice: "Look, today I am offering you life and prosperity, death and disaster. [...] Choose life, then, so that you and your descendants may live" (Deut 30:15, 19). For the child the choice to be made is that of obedience, and obedience is practised in love for the Lord (Deut 30:16, 20).

Such love should be whole-hearted (Deut 6:5), exclusive (Deut 5:7), a gift of self. This last aspect is symbolically narrated in Gen 22. God asks Abraham to offer Isaac, his beloved son (Gen 22:2), as a sacrifice. The love of the father is put to the test here (Gen 22:1), because he is subjected to obedience to the divine will. By not considering the child as his possession, the father accedes to the full truth of his paternity. The Lord is not pretending to command the sacrifice, but really asking that the person of faith be ready to give up life to express devotion to the Lord of life. The martyrs in surrendering to the executioner explicitly express their faith in eternal life (2 Macc 7:9, 14, 23, 29; Wis 3:4-9), which is obtained only through choosing God before and above all else. Jesus himself will confirm this truth in an authoritative way (Mt 10:39; 16:25; Mk 8:35; Lk 9:24; 17:33; Jn 12:25). In Israel the handing over of oneself to God was symbolically expressed in the offering of the firstborn (Ex 13:2, 11-16; 22:28; 34:19-20; Num 3:13; 8:16-17), as Hannah did when she presented to the Lord her son Samuel whom she had so long desired (1 Sam 1:24-28), as did Mary and Joseph with Jesus (Lk 2:22-24). The rite intends to express the parents' gift of their only child to God, who accepts the offering and returns it to the donor. The Lord is different from Moloc who feeds on the victims. He does not want the killing of children, put to death to obtain some favour from the divinity (cf. Lev 18:21; 20:2-5; Deut 12:31; 18:10; 2 Kgs 3:27; 16:3; 23:10; Jer 32:35; etc.). Consenting to the "redemption", God accepts in return a humble offering, in order to show that the one who offers is given back to himself, sanctified by obedience, and made alive in the very act of self-giving to the Lord. Of Abraham, the letter to the Hebrews says, in fact: "By faith Abraham, when put to the test, offered up Isaac. Although he was waiting to receive the promise he was prepared to sacrifice his only son, of whom he had been told: through Isaac will your name be carried on. He reckoned that God had the power even to raise the dead, and from there, figuratively speaking, he did receive Isaac back" (Heb 11:17-19).

Rules for children

219. In imitation of the parent and through the parent's encouragement, the child is called to obedience. Children are formed by obedience, and the first obedience happens in listening to one's parents. As we said earlier, obedience is to be understood as the respectful assent to the word of those who, out of love for their children, transmit to them not their own opinion or will, but the beneficent law of God, which represents a call to authentic freedom, in that it indicates to the person the way of love. In this sense, whoever listens to the voice of parents listens to the voice of God; the child is called then to renounce any claim to be the exclusive principle of evaluation and decision, in order to welcome with humility, intelligence and creativity, the counsels of the witnesses of God, so as to appreciate them as a gift from which fruits of life pour out.

Still in the heart of the Decalogue, immediately after the commandment relating to the Sabbath which is addressed to the parent, we have the precept for the child: "Honour your father and your mother, as the Lord your God has commanded you, so that you may have long life and may prosper in the land ('ădāmāh) which the Lord your God is giving you" (Deut 5:16). A clearly recognisable feature differentiates this commandment from others in the list. This is its exclusively positive formulation, both in the presentation of the imperative, and in the consequences of observance. For the law relating to the Sabbath, the legislator furnished the reasons for the precept by going back to the origin of Israel, and in the Exodus version by recalling creation. No justification however is given regarding honouring parents, but the future is foreseen with a limitless promise of good. Now, to take advantage of the promise of life, it is necessary to understand what is laid down by the commandment.

220. The Hebrew verb used to indicate what the child's duty should be towards the parents is an intensive form of the verb *kābad*, which, due to the general meaning of the root, should be properly rendered with "giving glory". Frequently this verb, or its equivalents, with the noun *kābôd*, has God himself as direct object (Jdg 9:9; 13:17; 1 Sam 2:29; Is 24:15; 25:3; 29:13; 43:23; Mal 1:6; Ps 22:24; 50:15, 23; 86:12; Prov 3:9; etc.):

"To oppress the weak insults the Creator,
kindness to the needy honours the Creator (*kābad*)."
(Prov 14:31)

This leads one to believe that the honour given to parents has aspects of the sacred due to the fact that they constitute the historical mediation of the origin of life. In Lev 19:3, which is the first commandment of the so-called "Holiness Code" (cf. Lev 19:2), we find a complementary terminology: "Each of you shall respect father and mother", and the verb used (*yārē'*) generally expresses reverence for the Lord. Other precepts of the Torah denounce an attitude contrary to honour, and prescribe very severe sanctions against offenders: "Anyone who curses (*qālal*) father or mother will be put to death" (Ex 2:17; Lev 20:9); "Cursed be anyone who dishonours (*qālāh*) father or mother" (Deut 27:16); "Anyone who strikes father or mother will be put to death" (Ex 21:15). A similar terminology is taken up by the prophetic and sapiential traditions (cf. Mic 7:6; Mal 1:6; Prov 15:20; 20:20; 23:22; 28:7; 30:17; Sir 3:16).

While the basic attitude to parents is clear, the concrete acts that show honour are not clearly indicated, because they differ according to the age of the children, and undergo specific developments in various historical eras and in the varying cultures of peoples. The act of love and respect is in fact always symbolic, and this does not signify in any way something conventional or superfluous. On the contrary, in its simplicity it represents a concrete expression of values that have immense ethical and religious relevance.

It would be inappropriate to attempt to describe some of the manifestations of honour towards parents, because, as was mentioned, they vary from age to age, and according to cultures and traditions. We can, however, say that the act which most of all and universally expresses what the Decalogue requires is *obedience*; it is not prescribed only for children or minors, but for every son and daughter who, through their fathers and mothers, have received the word of the Torah, and through it access to the path of life.

Figures of authority in Israel

221. In the Deuteronomic Code other figures of authority are presented to the Israelite who, in the social sphere, require obedient consent. These are the judges (Deut 17:8-13), the king (Deut 17:14-20), the priests (Deut 18:1-8) and the prophet (Deut 18:9-22). For the first category, the judges, and the last, the prophet, it is explicitly said, almost by way of an inclusion, that every Israelite must obey the directives issued by them (Deut 17:10, 13; 18:15, 19); for the other holders of power, it is taken for granted, as is clear from the biblical tradition as a whole. We note, on the other hand, that the king has the duty to transcribe the law "in the presence of the levitical priests" and to read it every day of his life (Deut 17:18-19): in this way the legislator makes clear that whoever gives commands, whether in the sacred or the civil sphere, is in fact the first to obey, not indulging his will or pleasure, but submitting to the wise and beneficial will of God; whoever rebels against this human authority therefore disobeys God. It could be said that in Israelite society various instances of power are called to exercise a "paternal" function; for this reason the title of "father" is also given in Scripture to the king (1 Sam 24:12; 2 Kgs 5:13; 16:7; Is 9:5) and to the leaders of a community (2 Kgs 2:12; 13:14; 1 Chr 4:14; Sir 4:10). Accordingly, the subject must show respect and deference analogous to those required in the family; even if feelings of affection proper to the parental relationship are not required, practical acceptance of the provisions made by the one in charge will be necessary, also to encourage harmony and fraternal solidarity in each community. In the New Testament, obedience to religious leaders, to masters, as well as to political rulers will, as we shall see, be widely recommended. Naturally, those who have power are required to adhere absolutely to the sense of justice, which will have as a principal expression the defence of the weak (Deut 17:20; Is 10:1-2; Jer 21:12; Ps 72:1-4 ; Wis 1:1).

The teaching of the sages of Israel

222. The stories of the wisdom tradition, with their edifying purpose, present "fathers" who observe the dictates of the Torah and show themselves to be solicitous in inculcating good principles in their children. Tobit, for example, is more than generous with his advice for his son Tobias who is setting off on a journey (Tob 4:3-19); Mordecai reminds Esther, his adopted daughter (Est 2:7), of her responsibility towards her people (Est 4:13-14); and Job was concerned with performing the purification rites for his children who, when they feasted, had perhaps sinned against God (Job 1:4-5). The mother of the Maccabees even went as far as to encourage her seven sons to face martyrdom in order to maintain faithfulness to the Law of the Lord (2 Macc 7:20-23).

What is succinctly expressed in the actions and words of the characters in these stories finds confirmation and development in the wisdom collections. There we are given the opportunity to draw on that treasure of teaching which from generation to generation (Prov 4:3-5; Sir 8:9; 33:16-19) inspired and regulated the behaviour of the parent, and which, given the fruits obtained, is passed on to the child, an inexperienced disciple (Prov 1:4,22; 7:7; 8:5; 9:4), who is in turn enabled to distinguish truth from appearance (Prov 9:17-18; Sir 11:2-4; 19:22-30; Wis 2:1-22), the way of justice from that of oppression (Prov 1:10-19; 8:6-9, 20), and the demands of life which are opposed to the pleasure that leads to death (Prov 1:32-33; 2:11-22; 4:14-15; 5:3-6; 7:27; 8:34-36). The final aim of this transmission of wisdom is to make the child love what the father has loved (Prov 4:6; Wis 7:10-14), and so ceaselessly desire to acquire true wisdom (Prov 4:7; 9:9; Sir 6:18-19; Wis 6:17) and through it to come to the fear of the Lord (Prov 2:1-6; 9:10), the principle of all good (Sir 1:1; 11:14-15; 40:26-27).

The parent's love for the child is expressed then not so much in material gifts, however useful or even necessary they may be, but in the tireless outpouring of spiritual benefits, all focused on the purpose of providing a good "education" (Hebrew *mûsār*; Greek *paideia*). This task in essence takes two forms.

223. (i) *Counsels.* The first consists in the use of the *word*, as an authoritative offering of meaning, which requires listening and agreement:

> "Listen, my child, to your father's instruction (*mûsār*),
> do not reject your mother's teaching (*tôrāh*):
> they will be a graceful wreath for your head,
> a circlet for your neck."

(Prov 1:1, 8)

Moses, in the name of God, had encouraged the people to obey the wise law of the Lord (Deut 4:1, 5-6), and had enjoined them to fasten the precepts to hand and forehead as a memorial sign (Deut 6:8); now the father and the mother do the same, presenting their teaching as precious advice, exalting above all its beauty and richness, thus transforming the image of the Law from a "yoke" (cf. Jer 5:5; Neh 9:29; Mt 11:29-30; Acts 15:10) to a "jewel". Every proverbial counsel, in fact, is a pearl that contributes to the adornment of the person who welcomes it (Prov 4:9; Sir 6:29-31); it is a precious gift that enriches more than any other treasure (Prov 3:13-15; 8:11, 19); it is light on the way (Prov 6:20-23; Wis 7:29-30); it is the source of joy (Prov 2:10; Sir 6:28; 15:6); it is the way of life (Prov 3:2-4, 16-18) and of glory (Prov 3:16; 8:18).

Moses had asked that the words of the Lord be received in the "heart" (Deut 6:6); and the same thing is requested by the parent, asking for the free decision of the child (Sir 6:32):

> "My child, pay attention to what I am telling you,
> listen carefully to my words;
> do not let them out of your sight,
> keep them deep in your heart.
> For they are life to those who find them
> and health to all humanity.
> More than all else, keep watch over your heart,
> since here are the wellsprings of life."
>
> (Prov 4:20-23)

224. (ii) *Correction.* The second way in which the father educates the child is found in actions that seem contrary to love, and yet are in accordance with the wise intention of the parent (Sir 22:6). This is the use of the "*rod*", understood as the symbol of the instrument of correction which punishes mistakes, encouraging a change of conduct and inculcating right discipline (Prov 19:25; Sir 23:2-3).

In the Law of Moses the parent is asked to punish severely any gravely transgressive behaviour of the offspring: Deuteronomy even requires that the father be the first to stone the child who instigates idolatry (Deut 13:7-12; cf. Zech 13:3), and, in another case, the parents are required to become promoters of a public trial that results in a sentence of capital punishment for a "stubborn and rebellious son", "a wastrel and a drunkard" (Deut 21:18-21). Obviously these are extreme measures, but they are considered an indispensable deterrent by the legislator to safeguard the good of the community (Deut 13:12; 21:21). In the wisdom texts, despite the awareness that certain rebellious attitudes are destructive (Prov 1:32), a punitive discipline is advised which has the intention of preserving the life of the guilty (Prov 19:18; 23:13-14). It is worthwhile citing some sayings that demonstrate how the act of correction expresses love towards the child, who is helped thereby to walk in the right path:

> "One who is sparing with the rod hates the child,
> one who loves the child disciplines him."
>
> (Prov 13:24)
>
> "Folly is anchored in the heart of a youth,
> the whip of instruction will drive it far away."
>
> (Prov 22:15)
>
> "The rod and reproof bestow wisdom,
> a young person untrained shames the mother."
>
> (Prov 29:15)
>
> "Whoever loves a son will beat him frequently
> so that in after years the son may be a comfort."
>
> (Sir 30:1; cf. also Sir 30:9-13)

These words of wisdom compare the child perhaps too directly to an animal needing to be tamed (Prov 26:3; Sir 30:8; cf. also Jer 31:18); the use of coercive or violent practices cannot be accepted today. It remains important, however, to recognise that an effective education of the young person cannot neglect corrective and punitive aspects, entrusted to the wise and loving discernment of parents and educators. Moreover, this helps one to understand the way of teaching followed by the Lord towards human beings, his children (Deut 8:5; Job 5:17; Wis 11:10; Heb 12:5-11; Apoc 3:19):

"My child, do not scorn correction (*mûsār*) from the LORD,
do not resent his reproof;
for the Lord reproves those he loves,
as a father the child in whom he delights."

(Prov 3:11-12)

225. What emerges indirectly from all this is the fundamental duty of the child, called to "honour" the parents, in gratitude for the gift of life (Sir 7:27-28); this duty consists primarily in accepting respectfully and gratefully both words of wisdom and corrective actions, so that, in obedience and patience, the child learns to walk in the way of life, giving joy to father and mother:

"Listen to advice, accept correction,
to be the wiser in the time to come."

(Prov 19:20)

"Long life comes to anyone who honours a father;
whoever obeys the Lord makes a mother happy."

(Sir 3:6)

"Respect your father in deed as well as in word,
so that blessing may come on you from him."

(Sir 3:8)

"A wise child is a father's joy,
a foolish child a mother's grief."

(Prov 10:1; cf. also Prov 19:26)

Respect for parents is shown also in making allowances for the weakness of those in old age (Prov 23:22), and in providing for their necessities; the memory of what the father and mother have done for the child provides an incentive to repay them (Sir 7:27-28):

"My child, support your father in his old age,
do not grieve him as long as he lives.
Even if his mind should fail, show him sympathy;
in your full strength do not dishonour him;
for kindness to a father will not be forgotten."

(Sir 3:12-14)

The voice of the prophets

226. Unlike the sages of Israel, who are very attentive to family dynamics, the prophets do not deal extensively with the relationship between parents and children. Their specific mission is to guard or restore the covenant with the Lord, and in this regard they introduce the metaphor of divine paternity in order to foster love and encourage the conversion of hearts (Is 1:2; 45:10-11; 63:16; 64:7; Jer 3:19; 31:9, 20 ; Hos 11:1; Mal 1:6; 2:10; 3:17). Only occasionally do they denounce the bad behaviour of children towards their father and mother (Ezek 22:7), or blame the complicity of the family in doing evil (Jer 7:18; 12:6; Am 2:7).

Two oracles, however, deserve to be carefully considered, not least because they are taken up in the New Testament, where they receive a particular interpretation.

(i) In the eighth century, Micah describes the dissolution of Jerusalemite society, in which brothers are being killed (Mic 7:2), rulers driven by exorbitant greed distort the exercise of justice (Mic 7:3), and the betrayal of family members and friends brings about widespread lack of trust (Mic 7:5). The prophet concludes his denunciation, speaking of the moral degeneration within the family:

> "For son insults father,
> daughter rebels against mother,
> daughter-in-law against mother-in-law;
> a person's enemies come from within the household itself."
>
> (Mic 7:6)

Such a negative picture of society has its climax in the loss of feelings of respect that every child should have towards parents; the heart with its innate values is distorted; the situation as a result appears to be without remedy. The prophet, however, renews his trust in the Lord and in the hope of a salvation that cannot come except from a wonderful intervention of God (Mic 7:7).

In Mt 10:34-36, as in the parallel of Lk 12:51-53, the terminology of Mic 7:6 is taken up in a saying of the Lord, but with important variations and with different meaning. Jesus, in fact, presents himself as the one who "came" to bring "a sword" to the earth (Mt 10:34), that is, division (Lk 12:52) among family members: "For I have come to set son against father, daughter against mother, daughter-in-law against mother-in-law; a person's enemies will be the members of that person's own household" (Mt 10:35-36). From the gospel tradition as a whole we know that this saying of the Lord does not encourage rebellion and contempt of children for their parents; instead it brings out the need for preferential love for Christ (Mt 10:37; Lk 14:26), which imposes on everyone, parents and children alike, that type of "separation" that is a sign of an exclusive and all-encompassing love of God and adherence to the mystery of death and resurrection (Mt 10:21-23,39). It can also be assumed that from the preferential love for Christ flows a more truthful love towards the parents themselves. We will see later on how this issue is made explicit by the teaching of the Lord Jesus.

227. (ii) Several centuries after the prophetic ministry of Micah, in the time following the Babylonian exile, in a climate, therefore, of religious restoration, Malachi concludes his prophecy, and the prophetic canon, with an oracle of promise. Almost as if responding to the hopes of Micah, God says:

"Look, I shall send you the prophet Elijah
before the great and awesome Day of the Lord comes.
He will turn the hearts of parents to their children
and of children to their parents
so that I shall not strike the land with a curse of destruction."
(Mal 3:23-24)

On Israel, called to observe the Law of Moses (Mal 3:22), weighs the terrible threat of "destruction", once destined for the Canaanites (Deut 7:2), and now looming over the people of God. It is the Lord who acts, so that the day of judgement does not bring condemnation; and his work consists in sending the prophet Elijah, whose word will convert "hearts", restoring the relationship between "fathers" and "children". Once again, as already in the case of Mic 7:6, there is a profound discord between parents and children (cf. also Jer 31:29; Ezek 18:2-19); it seems to have come about from a marked generational gap that accompanied the dramatic event of the exile, which somehow distracted the fathers from the task of teaching the laws of the Lord and led the children not to believe in the promises contained in the Torah. To remedy this loss of trust in communication, God sends the prophet whose powerful word is capable of touching the intimate fibres of the heart, restoring the potential to hear and to transmit the will of God, and so receive the divine promises of life. It is prophecy, therefore, that heals the tensions in the family.

> In the gospel the prophet Elijah promised by Malachi (cf. also Sir 48:10) is identified with John the Baptist (Lk 1:17), whose mission of changing hearts prepares for the coming of salvation (Lk 1:76-77). The Baptist's preaching will not touch on the relationship between fathers and children; however, the appeal to personal conversion is the indispensable way to a fruitful relationship with one's neighbour, starting with the members of one's own family. This becomes particularly urgent when, for various reasons, the transmission of traditional values from one generation to the next is lacking.

The example and teaching of Jesus

228. The gospel of Luke is the richest source of information regarding the infancy of Jesus and his behaviour as a "son" towards Mary and Joseph. Particularly significant in this regard is the account of Lk 2:41-52, in which is narrated the annual pilgrimage of the family to Jerusalem for the feast of Passover, when Jesus was twelve years old. On that occasion the young man, considered perhaps of legal age and therefore subject to the Law, decided to stay in the Temple, engaging in discussions with the teachers who taught there; and he justified his decision, which surprised and pained his parents, by saying: "Why were you looking for me? Did you not know that I must be in my Father's house?" (Lk 2:49). With this declaration he indicated the obedience to which he gave absolute priority, revealing to his parents that he was first and foremost son of God, and that it was God's will that he pursue his prophetic mission. The sentence with which the evangelist concludes the episode, "He went down with them then and came to Nazareth and lived under their authority" (Lk 2:51), should not be seen to be in contradiction with what was previously narrated: submission to his parents can only be interpreted as a form of obedience to the Father's will, a means accepted and lived by Jesus which favoured his growth "in wisdom, in stature, and in divine and human favour" (Lk 2:52). The son of God, who amazed the doctors of the Law for the intelligence of his questions and responses (Lk 2:47), undergoes the process of growth of every son of man, in humble learning of the daily gift offered to him from the wisdom of his father and mother.

Once the moment of his prophetic ministry came, when Jesus was about thirty years old (Lk 3:23), the relationship to his parents changed, not through reaching maturity according to human criteria, but by a specific call of the Spirit (Lk 4:1, 14), which required leaving the environment of origin to establish a new family community. If the mother and brothers go looking for him to bring him home (Mk 3:21) or to claim some precedence in attention, Jesus proclaims the reality of a new community, founded on obedient listening to the Father's voice (Mt 12:46-50; Mk 3:31-35; Lk 8:20-21). The revelation of the "Father", with the need to obey him, undoubtedly constitutes the heart of Jesus' preaching. Even though he showed paternal feelings towards the children who were brought to him (Mk 10:13-16), even though sometimes, as Master, he addressed his disciples as "children" (Mk 10:24; Jn 13:33), Jesus always testified that the title of Father belongs only to God, whom all without distinction must acknowledge (Mt 23:9).

229. Blood ties and family obligations are relativised, therefore, or rather subjected to the call of the Kingdom. This is expressed in phrases that are harsh and disconcerting for the very reason that they call into question the supposed primary duty of care for parents. We read in fact that "one of the disciples said to him, 'Lord, let me first go and bury my father.' But Jesus said, 'Follow me, and leave the dead to bury their dead'" (Mt 8:21-22). Elsewhere this saying is attributed to Jesus: "Anyone who comes to me without hating father, mother, wife, children, brothers, sisters, yes and even life itself, cannot be my disciple" (Lk 14:26; see also Mt 10:37). The "hatred" should not be understood here as contempt or violence towards family members, but must be understood in the light of another affirmation of Jesus with which he highlights the need for the radical choice of God alone: "No servant can serve two masters: a servant will either hate the first and love the second, or be attached to the first and despise the second" (Lk 16:13; cf. also Mt 6:24). Even the deepest emotional bond, such as that with parents or between spouses, must not undermine full adherence to the Kingdom of God and to its demanding journey of love. This obviously does not mean that affection and care for the father and mother, as for all the other members of the family, cannot be an expression of love, and therefore constitute a way of following Christ.

In synthesis, what emerges from the gospel perspective is the call to loving obedience towards God, which relativises any other binding connection or obligation. This should be extended, by analogy, also to the forms of obedience required by civil and religious authorities. The response of Peter and John to the members of the Sanhedrin in Jerusalem should be understood in this sense: "You must judge whether in God's eyes it is right to listen to you and not to God" (Acts 4:19). This consideration is reiterated by Peter in response to the prohibition on teaching in the name of Jesus: "Obedience to God comes before obedience to human beings" (Acts 5:29).

Such a prophetic perspective should always be kept in mind, even when we are faced with instructions given in the letters of Paul and Peter regarding submission to parents and to political authorities.

The pastoral instructions of the apostolic tradition

230. In the letters sent by the apostles to the communities entrusted to their care we find some instructive advice regarding family discipline and how one should behave before the public authorities. Four groups may be identified, each characterised by precise internal relations, and, consequently, by specific duties, even if, as we shall see, the theme of "obedience" is constantly laid down for all those who are in any way liable to it. The purpose of social order seems paramount.

(i) *Parents and children.* The first group is composed of parents and children (Eph 6:1-4; Col 3:20-21). The limited presence of this issue in the pastoral guidance of the Pauline letters – it is absent in the letters of the other apostles – and the rather summary treatment of the duties of the subjects involved suggest that in the communities of the early Church it was not considered necessary to insist on encouraging a good relationship between parents and children. The generic statements about "children rebellious to parents" in Rom 1:30 and 2 Tim 3:2 seem to refer to situations outside the Christian world. Today, however, we feel the need for a more detailed discussion on the theme, because children's trust in their parents has been widely undermined, and the parents' diminished authority has an effect on the education of the young.

In the two texts just cited we have only one command for the *children*, that of "obeying" the parents "always", as Col 3:20 specifies, because this is "right" (Eph 6:1) and "pleasing to the Lord" (Col 3:20). The explicit reference to the precept of the Decalogue (Eph 6:2-3) constitutes for the Apostle a solid foundation for the instruction, such that no further comments are required. The identification of "honouring", in the Decalogue, and "obeying", in Paul, largely follows the interpretative tradition of the Israelite world of wisdom, which constantly requires that one heed and consent to the teachings of the father and mother. The Apostle, however, makes clear that the child is called to obey "in the Lord" (Eph 6:1), thus giving the submission a specifically Christian value, since in the background there is the example of the Lord Jesus, the Son who became obedient to the Father "unto death, death on a cross" (Phil 2:5, 8). If in the act of obeying, the "son", as we shall see, is no different from the "servant" (Gal 4:1-2), there is nonetheless a great difference: the spirit with which a son obeys is that of a trusting love, different, therefore, from the simple acceptance of an imposed duty.

Parents are advised not to "exasperate" their children (Eph 6:4; Col 3:21), imposing excessive obligations on them or subjecting them to punishments that are too severe and which could lead to rebelliousness or at least discouragement (Col 3:22): wisdom requires moderation and patience in the sometimes coercive exercise of authority (cf. Wis 12:16-21). Paul adds: "nourish them with discipline and the instruction of the Lord" (Eph 6:4); if then the parents should avoid an improper rigour, they should not however avoid the "discipline" (*paideia*) indispensable for the formation of the young; the inculcation in their minds of the "teaching" (*nouthesia*) of the Lord concerns not so much doctrinal content, but rather the spirit of humble and helpful love.

231. (ii) *Masters and servants.* A second group, situated also within the family of the apostolic times, is constituted by "masters" (*kyrioi, despotai*) and "servants" (*douloi*). This group is strictly linked to the first, not only on account of its close literary proximity, but also because of a certain similarity in content (Eph 6:5-6; Col 3:22-25; see also 1 Tim 6:1-2; Tit 2:9-10; Phlm 8-21; 1 Pt 2:18-25). A more widespread and varied scrutiny shows that the relationship between masters and servants required a particular pastoral approach. Today such teaching can provide useful suggestions for the relationship between employers and employees, even if the context is no longer that of the family environment.

The *subordinates* may be "slaves", in a condition of permanent servitude, opposed to the "free" (cf. 1 Cor 12:13; Gal 3:28; Eph 6:8; Col 3:11), or they may simply be "servants" or "domestics" (*oiketai*), whose duties are temporary and paid. In the Greco-Roman world the practice of having slaves to perform various domestic tasks, not necessarily the most humble, was widespread; and this practice was also accepted in Hebrew (Sir 33:25-33) and Christian families. It is quite surprising that the apostles did not invite masters, as disciples of the Lord, to emancipate their slaves, in conformity with the prescription of the ancient Law which called for their release in the seventh year (Ex 21:2-4; Deut 15:12-15). To be exact, this discipline seems to have been limited to Hebrew slaves, and did not apply to those taken "from the nations" (cf. Lev 25:44-46); for a Christian, however, the consideration of the "brother or sister", even if pagan, for whom Christ had died could prompt actions of unexpected generosity. The process of recognition of the radical injustice of slavery has in fact required many centuries and innumerable sufferings to establish itself as a universal cultural heritage. Consequently, the interpreter of the Bible is required to have a critical and at the same time respectful view of the historical situations, so as to draw from the pages of Scripture the right directives of justice and love, which are meaningful for the people of today. This principle should be kept in mind in all the following considerations. To give an example, the advice given by Paul to remain in the state in which one finds oneself (1 Cor 7:17) should not, it seems, be taken literally. Instead of saying "If you were called as a slave, that is of no concern. If you can gain your freedom, make use of the opportunity" (1 Cor 7:21), it seems more just to favour the process of emancipation, so that all may consecrate themselves to service through a decision of love (cf. Ex 21:5-6) and not through obligation imposed by others.

232. "*Slaves*" are commanded to "be submissive" (Tit 2:9; 1 Pt 2:18) and to "obey" (Eph 6:5; Col 3:22) in everything (Col 3:22; Tit 2:9) their "earthly masters" (*kata sarka kyrioi*) (Eph 6:5), showing them respect (1 Tim 6:1; 1 Pt 2:18), not for the purpose of pleasing people, but with a willing disposition and attitude of fidelity, as if serving the Lord (*kyrios*) (Eph 6:6-7; Col 3:22-23), who will reward both the slave and the free person equally (Eph 6:8; Col 3:24-25). Whoever must suffer from overbearing masters is called to accept this condition as a "grace" (*charis*), following the example of the Lord Jesus, who, when suffering, entrusted himself to the one who judges with justice (1 Pt 2:19-25). The opposite attitude, driven by rebelliousness or revenge, would lead to blaspheming the name of God (1 Tim 6:1) and would be harmful to the Christian "teaching" (*didaskalia*) (1 Tim 6:1; Tit 2:10). From this set of instructions there emerges quite clearly the intention of not leaving oneself open to the accusation of subversion, which would undermine the preaching of the gospel.

Christian "*masters*" are advised to put threats aside (Eph 6:9) and to treat their servants justly and fairly (Col 4:1). Philemon is asked by Paul to welcome his fugitive slave Onesimus, no longer as a slave, but as a "dear brother" (Phlm 16). This expression suggests an emotional attitude of great value with practical implications in real life; the assumption of a fraternal dimension is superior even to the act of emancipation of the slave, if this is carried out without love, but because one is forced to do so by legislation or by social pressure.

In these pastoral instructions we undoubtedly discover significant points of spiritual understanding concerning the attitude of "service" which in many cases Christians are obliged to adopt, sometimes even in humiliating or painful conditions. The apostles thus point to a "spirit" with which to live the conditions of submission, experienced in various contexts, both social, as in the relationship between workers and employers, and political, involving subjects and rulers. It is clear that the loving wisdom that comes to us from the gospel, combined with a more precise consideration of human rights, will call for an increasingly more appropriate regulation of the discipline of work, as well as of submission to the laws of the state, from which a long desired social harmony will arise.

233. (iii) *Shepherds and the flock.* A third group of people placed in an asymmetrical relationship is that found in Christian communities, presided over by a "*bishop*" or by a "*presbyter*" (elder) as figures of religious authority, to whom the *faithful* must pay obedience and respect. We read, for example, in one of Paul's first letters: "We appeal to you, brothers and sisters, to be considerate to those who work among you, and who are your leaders in the Lord and admonish you. Esteem them especially highly, because of their work" (1 Thess 5:12-13). This recommendation is taken up again in the first letter to the Corinthians, where the Apostle asks his recipients to "submit" to those who dedicate themselves to the "service of the saints" (1 Cor 16:15-16); this is confirmed by the letter to the Hebrews: "Obey your leaders and submit to them; they watch over your souls because they will give an account of them; make this a joy for them to do, and not a grief – this would do you no good" (Heb 13:17; cf. also 1 Pt 5:5). From these quotations there appears, if not a reversal of perspective, at least a significant variation of it: in fact, if the idea remains that the subject is called to obey, it is nevertheless stressed, as the gospel teaches (Mk 10:42-45), that the "leaders" are "servants" who toil for the benefit of the community, and who will have to account for their commitment to the Lord; the result is a less unilateral idea of obedience, a virtue which therefore characterises all believers, and not only in relation to God, but also in relation to one's brothers and sisters.

The guidance given to the "shepherds" that their ministry (*diakonia*) should be deployed for the good of the flock (cf. Jn 21:15-17) is consequently quite substantial. Paul presents himself to his communities as a father (1 Cor 4:15; Gal 4:19; 2 Cor 6:13; Phil 2:22; 1 Thess 2:11) or a mother (1 Thess 2:7), and offers his example for imitation (1 Cor 4:16-17). The Acts of the Apostles recall his guidance given to the elders (*presbyteroi*) of the Church of Ephesus: "Be on your guard for yourselves and for all the flock of which the Holy Spirit has made you the guardians (*episkopoi*), to feed the Church of God which he bought with the blood of his own Son" (Acts 20:28; cf. also 1 Pt 5:1-4). Such vigilance involves scrupulous attention to the truth of the gospel against perverse doctrines (Acts 20:29-31), but also total unselfishness and confident generosity (Acts 20:32-35). An echo of this exhortation is found in 1 Pt 5:1-4. Many other valuable counsels are given in the letters to Timothy (1 Tim 3:1-7; 4:6-16; 5:1-3, 17-22; 6:11-16, 20; 2 Tim 1:6-8, 14; 2:1-7, 14-16, 22-26; 3:14–4:15) and to Titus (Tit 1:5-9; 3:8-11), to encourage them to exercise their mandate as shepherds according to the spirit of Christ. The loving exercise of authority by the leaders of Christian communities can become a paradigm offered to those who exercise power in civil society, suggesting to them ways of peace, collaboration and promotion of the common good that arise from ministry exercised according to the dictates of the gospel.

234. (iv) The last group concerns civil and political life, in which Christians are obviously present, and for which they are subject to a specific form of obedience. The apostles do not have the opportunity to give advice to public authorities, but they can address themselves to Christians as *citizens*. The most detailed instructions are found in Rom 13:1-7, in which Paul expounds his idea, highly positive towards the civil power, which requires that "Everyone is to obey the governing authorities" (Rom 13:1). Some statements seem to us perhaps too unambiguous, as when the Apostle says: "because there is no authority except from God, and the existing authorities have been ordained by God. So anyone who disobeys authority (*exousia*) is resisting God's ordinance (*diatagē*)" (Rom 13:1-2). Jesus himself had said to Pilate: "You would have no authority (*exousia*) over me at all if it had not been given you from above" (Jn 19:11); the question remains, however, of the tyrannical exercise of power, whereby submission could betray a shameful complicity with evil (Apoc 13:3-4, 8, 12-17), while, on the contrary, "civil disobedience" would be a duty for the citizen committed to truth and justice. Paul then from his general premises derives the rules of behaviour in the public sphere: "You must be obedient, therefore, not only because of this wrath, but also for conscience's (*syneidesis*) sake. And this is why you should pay taxes, too, because the authorities are all serving (*leitourgoi*) God as his agents, engaged upon the same task. Pay to all what is due, tax to whom tax is due, toll to whom toll is due, fear to whom fear is due, honour to whom honour is due" (Rom 13:5-7). Jesus also said: "Pay Caesar what belongs to Caesar, and God what belongs to God" (Mk 12:17), and he invited Peter to pay the temple tax (Mt 17:24-27); the reasons given by the Master do not perfectly match those of the Apostle, but the operational direction is the same, with its recognition of the value that public service renders both to the community and to individuals, provided that it carries out its task according to justice and remains within its limits, not infringing on what is proper to God.

In addition to obedient submission (Tit 3:1-2), Paul also requests, as something pleasing to God, that there should be prayer for those in power, so that Christians can "live peaceful and quiet lives with all devotion and dignity" (1 Tim 2:1-3). Peter, for his part, reiterates the Pauline command to submit to human authorities (1 Pt 2:13-14, 17), and introduces a further objective, apologetic in nature, to obedient conduct: "It is God's will that those who do good should silence the ignorance of fools. As free people, but not using freedom as a cover for evil, but as slaves of God" (1 Pt 2:15-16); it is clear that freedom, which is a characteristic of the citizen, is subordinated to the service of God and the exercise of the good.

235. At the end of this wide-ranging treatment concerning asymmetric relationships in the family and in society, it emerges that, despite the variety of situations, a humble attitude of obedience is always requested of the child, the servant, the believer, or the citizen. The virtue of obedience is not considered very attractive in our day, yet it expresses a dimension of loving service which lies at the heart of the most authentic gospel tradition, and which finds in Christ the perfect example to imitate (Mk 14:36; Jn 4:34; 5:30; 6:38; 8:29; 14:31; Phil 2:8; Heb 5:8).

Those who hold authority in the home or in society are asked for something similar (Eph 6:9), in the sense that the exercise of power must always be understood as "service", as an obedient submission not only to the will of God the Father, but also to the brother or sister, before whom one kneels to wash their feet (Jn 13:13-17).

3. LOVE OF BROTHERS AND SISTERS

236. Whether it concerns the blood family, or those belonging to a community or to a people, "brotherly" love represents a fundamental dimension of authentic life in society. It is not easy, however, to see in the other a brother or sister, just as it is not easy to recognise that everyone's freedom must take into consideration the identity and the rights of the neighbour. And yet, only this kind of love gives access to a freedom and equality respectful of the human person, since, even if such values can be promoted and controlled by laws, brotherly and sisterly love in its fullness requires a personal choice, the fruit of an inner conviction, indeed of a gift from God. This is what we see when reading the Scriptures, in which, despite the ideals promoted, tales of harmony between brothers are rare. We begin with three stories narrated in the book of Genesis.

(1) Cain and Abel (Gen 4:1-16)

237. From the first story of the sons of Adam and Eve, conflict between brothers appears, without any indication that this is due to an innate predisposition to evil on the part of one of the two, as interpreted by 1 Jn 3:12.

> *Diversity between brothers.* While the birth of Cain, the firstborn, is celebrated by the mother as an event of almost divine significance: "I have acquired a man with the help of the Lord" (Gen 4:1), for the other son the narrator simply says: "she gave birth to a second child, Abel, the brother of Cain" (Gen 4:2). The name of the younger suggests in Hebrew the idea of breath, of what is ephemeral, as if that individual were simply another, a second, the brother of the first. The temporal succession between the brothers, therefore, must always be considered as significant; from it, in fact, priority, superiority and privileges are determined which contrast with the supposed equality between children of

the same parents. In other words, brothers are never equal. To this first temporal asymmetry is added that of place and occupation, since Cain naturally becomes the owner of fertile lands, while Abel will have to assume the condition of a shepherd, with an arduous nomadic life. Their respective cultic activities correspond to the status of farmer and shepherd; even in this case it does not follow from the text of Genesis that the offering of Cain was less valid than that of Abel, as asserted in Heb 11:4: both rites, in fact, will be fully recognised in the worship of Israel. Yet "the Lord looked with favour on Abel and his offering. But he did not look with favour on Cain and his offering" (Gen 4:4-5). Biblical revelation will regularly return to this intriguing literary motif, affirming that God acts in surprising ways, benefitting those whom he wishes, without taking account of the supposed rights or merits of the various protagonists of history. In many cases one can observe the Lord's predilection for the little ones (Deut 7:7), the humble and the disadvantaged (Lk 1:51-53), since these people allow God to express more clearly his generous compassionate love; nevertheless God's decisive choice of one person rather than another constitutes a mystery of that divine freedom (Ps 78:67-68; 87:2; Mal 1:2-3) which humanity must accept with reverence and trust.

Envy. We are not told by the text of Genesis how the two brothers recognised the Lord's "favour" or disfavour; perhaps it was different levels of prosperity, or perhaps some other circumstance that produced disappointment and sadness in Cain (Gen 4:5). Those who find themselves less favoured spontaneously demand equal justice, which alone it seems could satisfy everyone; and so the feeling of jealousy, internally justified, moves to restore the equality of the subjects. Envy of the good things granted to another becomes, therefore, a threat to brotherly love. With the voice of God, the biblical text brings out this danger, which is likened to an animal crouching at the door; although threatening, it can however be "tamed" (Gen 4:7). The voice of God is the voice of conscience which urges discernment, responsibility and truth; it is a word directed to the human heart, so that it may know how to decide to "act rightly", overcoming temptation.

Violence. But from the heart comes violence (Mk 7:21-22). Cain speaks to his brother, but, as far as we know from the biblical text, which is ambiguous at this point, only to arrange to meet in the open country. There, without witnesses, brother puts brother to death (Gen 4:8). The crime of fratricide involves not only the exercise of violence, but is disguised by deceit, subterfuge and falsehood. According to the narrative of Genesis, it is as if the crime was not discovered by the parents, nor by others, who are nevertheless mentioned by Cain in Gen 4:14 as possible agents of retaliation; but God makes himself present with the question, "Where is your brother Abel?" (Gen 4:9a), in order to impress upon the killer the absence of the one who had been given to him to be kept safe. Cain declines all responsibility with the famous reply: "I do not know. Am I my brother's guardian?" (Gen 4:9b). It is absurd to attempt to deny the facts before the one who is able to hear the silent cry of the blood that rises from the earth up to the Creator (Gen 4:10). With another question, "What have you done?" (Gen 4:10), the Lord wants to arouse in the one responsible awareness of the gravity of the crime, immediately pointing to the consequences of the evil he has done: the curse of the earth, made unproductive, will force the killer to become a "homeless wanderer" (Gen 4:11-12), threatened with revenge from anyone who encounters him (Gen 4:14). From Cain descends Lamech, from violence descends violence, in a frightening crescendo of threats and retaliations, intended paradoxically to defend life (Gen 4:23-25).

(2) Esau and Jacob (Gen 25:19-34; 27:1–28:9; 32:4-22; 33:1-17)

238. With a similar but more complex literary plot, the rivalry between another two brothers is narrated. The twins Esau and Jacob struggle with each other already in the womb of the mother (Gen 25:22), with the younger trying to grab the heel of the older one to get ahead of him. This is a symbol of the innate craving of every person who wants to take precedence by displacing the one in front of him.

The various features that distinguish between the two brothers are listed from the beginning by the narrator: Esau is "red" and hairy (Gen 25:25), dedicated to hunting as "a man of the open country", while Jacob is "a quiet man", who leads a protected life (Gen 25:27). The father preferred the elder, while the mother favoured the younger (Gen 25:28). The former does not seem to profit greatly from his activity, since we see him, hungry, asking his brother for a bowl of soup (Gen 25:29-30), and hastily giving up his right as first-born (Gen 25:31-34). The differences between the two do not justify their rivalry, which is born of jealousy; once again, it is envy that is the secret driving force of dishonest actions, so that the second takes the place of the first, pretending to be him, and snatching by deception what was reserved for the other (Gen 27:1-29). There naturally arises the desire for revenge by the brother who has been cheated, and who consequently, as his father attests (Gen 27:39-40), will be destined for a future of scarce resources and humiliating subjection. The brooding anger of Esau will force the two sons of Isaac to separate (Gen 27:42-45), a sign of the failure of their relationship.

The continuing story will involve a long exile for Jacob, forced to work hard for his father-in-law for twenty years (Gen 31:28-41); on his return, however, and despite the threat of Esau who comes to meet his brother with four hundred men (Gen 33:1), the story ends positively, when, in a surprising turn of events, the one who had been wronged unexpectedly presents himself with acts of moving tenderness: "he ran to meet him, took him in his arms, threw himself on his neck and kissed him, and they wept" (Gen 33:4). Esau does not want compensation, because, unlike his brother, he is happy with what he has (Gen 33:9); but he accepts the gift that Jacob insists on offering him as a sign of peace and renewed communion (Gen 33:11). The two then separate (Gen 33:12-17), perhaps because Jacob does not feel fully reassured, and probably doubts the sincerity of his brother. This incomplete picture, typical of human affairs, of a burgeoning reconciliation, will have its seal in the presence of both brothers at the burial of their father Isaac (Gen 35:29).

(3) Joseph and his brothers (Gen 37; 39–48)

239. The third story of the book of Genesis is well known: it tells of brothers who join forces against the youngest, of the misfortunes and success of the slave sold into a foreign land, and finally of everyone coming together in the forgiveness granted by the victim. The sapiential tone of the whole story leads the reader to discover here an exemplary path of fraternal reconciliation.

The sons of Jacob were born to several mothers, both wives and concubines, who were often in conflict with each other (Gen 30:1-24). Their rivalry is then reflected at the level of the children, also because the father loved Joseph more than all the others (Gen 37:3), for he was the son of his old age, and born to Rachel, his favourite wife (cf. Gen 29:30). The gift of a special tunic made by Jacob for the son he loved, because it expresses a clear preference, unleashes the jealousy of the brothers (Gen 37:4), which was fuelled by the speeches Joseph gave implying his superiority and based on his dreams (Gen 37:5-11). Envy turns into hatred (Gen 37:4, 8), and hatred leads to violence. The ideal opportunity comes when there are no witnesses, and the brothers can get rid of their brother. The initial plan to kill him (Gen 37:18-20) changed with the decision to sell him so as to earn something (Gen 37:26-27); the tunic, the reason for the jealousy, is taken back to the father torn and stained with blood, as a false proof of a disaster (Gen 37:31-33), but in reality it is the undeniable sign of a definitive fracture of brotherhood. The father's inconsolable grief (Gen 37:34-35) is not enough to bring out the truth and touch the hearts of the guilty.

The story of Joseph in Egypt is quite complex; in short it is designed to illustrate the wonderful parable of the victim of injustice who manages through the wisdom inspired in him by God (Gen 41:39) to rise to an authority inferior only to Pharaoh (Gen 41:40-44). His personal triumph, however, is not the conclusion of the story, which awaits a propitious moment for the reconciliation of the brothers. This takes place many years later when famine in the land of Canaan forces the sons of Jacob to come to the country of the Nile to buy grain. Joseph, without being recognised, sees his brothers before him, and, in place of planning revenge, he uses his power and various stratagems to arouse in the hearts of those who had sold him feelings of compassionate love towards Benjamin, his younger brother, and towards his father (Gen 44:20-34). Despite the absence of an explicit confession, as an expression of repentance for the crime committed against him, Joseph lets his tenderness burst into tears (Gen 45:1-2, 14), forgetting his past suffering which is eclipsed by the joy of finding his brothers again; and together with them he rereads the whole story as a marvellous salvific plan of God: "Joseph said to his brothers, 'Come closer to me.' When they had come closer he said, 'I am your brother Joseph whom you sold into Egypt. But now, do not grieve, do not reproach yourselves for having sold me here, since God sent me before you to preserve your lives [...] it was not you who sent me here but God'" (Gen 45:4-8).

This hidden action of God to restore brotherhood turns out to be a key for reading all the stories of brothers. Christians will see in the story of Joseph a prefiguration of the revelation of Christ, the brother put to death out of envy, who as Lord returns to reconcile sinners to himself and to the Father, reuniting them in one family.

The history of the peoples

240. The relationship problems within the community of blood brothers, illustrated in the book of Genesis, are reproduced in the biblical narratives which follow at the level of clans, ethnic groups and nations. Universal fraternity is an integral part of humanity's common origin, since all human beings are thought to descend from Adam and Noah; yet this brotherhood is not adequately recognised, and it is constantly undermined by multiple special circumstances and social differences, which offer a pretext for the exercise of the violence that lies in the human heart. The identity of one group is expressed and consolidated often in polemical opposition to another. From the very beginning, therefore, history will be marked by rivalry and by war; and human beings will have to escape from the rubble each time as they try to mend the fractures and redesign plans for peace and solidarity. Scripture in fact bears witness to a historical process that starts with conflict and results in great suffering; yet it lays down a path of ideals, with exemplary proposals and behaviours, with laws and institutions that give hope to believers, above all because every human affair is subject to the divine action, in a horizon of the eternal covenant between the Lord and humanity.

Violent rivalry is a constant phenomenon visible to all; it frightens us, and even leads us to doubt God, God's power over history and compassion for victims (Ps 73:1-14; 94:3-7; Job 24; Lam 2:20-21):

> "How long, O Lord, am I to cry for help
> while you will not listen;
> to cry, 'Violence!' to you
> though you will not save?
> Why do you show me wrong-doing,
> make me see evil?
> Plundering and violence confront me,
> contention and discord flourish.
> And so the Law loses its grip
> and justice never comes out,
> since the wicked outwits the righteous
> and so justice comes out perverted."

(Hab 1:2-4)

What is the remedy for all this? According to what the Bible says two ways lie ahead, that of the world and that of God.

Imperialism and the Kingdom of God

241. The Bible describes the history of the world as the constant emergence of dominant powers, who, by their political organisation and above all by their technological and military ability, impose their dominance and their despotic rule on peoples, while at the same time claiming to bring peace and progress. This is discreetly suggested already by the short story of the origin of *Babel* (Gen 11:1-9), the city-state that will determine the end of the kingdom of Judah, with which the narrative cycle of Israel's historiography officially ends (2 Kgs 25; 2 Chr 36). The legendary character of Gen 11 is quite evident, but this does not prevent us from seeing foreshadowed here the way empires arise, their motivations and the impact they have.

The beginning of the narrative introduces the motif of "uniformity": "The whole world had a single language, with a single vocabulary" (Gen 11:1). This could be interpreted as a sort of historical truth, deduced from the fact that the inhabitants of the earth were all descendants of the sons of Noah, who all, one supposes, had the same language. But the previous chapter had stated that after the flood the nations scattered over the earth (Gen 10:32) and each people had, in addition to its own territory, also its own particular language (Gen 10:5, 20, 31). It is more convincing then to understand the initial affirmation of our account as the starting point of an imperialist project that consists in imposition of a single language, as a basis of understanding and a foundation for the construction of a uniform community.

Subsequently a migration is announced and a settlement in the plain (Gen 11:2), symbol of a territorial conquest, which, thanks to favourable resources, allows for the realisation of civic structures, a utopian vision which is both unique and universal. Technology, represented by the manufacture of bricks, is put at the service of the project of building a "city", an entity of a political order, which unites all citizens under the same aegis, subjecting them to an identical law, to a common economy and to the same provision, with "a tower with its top reaching heaven", a supreme element of defence which is not only earthly, but also religious, if we accept an allusion to the Mesopotamian ziggurats (Gen 11:3-4a).

The project is presented as highly desirable, since, on the one hand, it allows them to "make a name" for themselves, that is, to become famous, with enduring glory, and, on the other, not to be "scattered all over the world", because unity gives strength, and security is guaranteed by internal cohesion (Gen 11:4b).

The biblical narrator, in an allusive way, thus brings out the problematic elements that are found in the various empires with which Israel had to deal in its millennial history, from Egypt to

Assyria and Babylon, from the Ptolemies to the Romans, suffering the threat of annihilation since its particular character was difficult to assimilate. The story of Gen 11 inserts at this point God's evaluation of the human project and its partial realisation; we are told that the Lord finds that "they are all a single people with a single language", and that this, instead of being a "good thing", is judged harmful. The Lord intervenes, therefore, to shatter the planned construction from within through the "confusion" of languages, by which the programme that those people had set themselves becomes impossible (Gen 11:5-7). The kingdom divided against itself faces ruin (Dan 2:41-43; cf. Mk 3:24). The "dispersion" brought about by the Lord is the condemnation of the imperialistic dream, and, at the same time, is the beginning of a new and different way of unifying human society, which, according to the New Testament, takes place at Pentecost, when all peoples, each with its own language and dialect, are brought together by listening together to the prophetic word, instigated by the outpouring of the Spirit (Acts 2:1-11): the Kingdom of God, the community of brothers and sisters, is built up in a way that is opposed to the totalitarian model. The apocalyptic writings, which express a global reading of the entire human history, will describe, with images taken also from the animal world, the monstrous rise of empires (Dan 7–8; Apoc 13); and, for the consolation of believers, they will announce their end (Apoc 14:8; 18:2-3; 19:11-21), with the humble but powerful manifestation of an eternal Kingdom (Dan 2:44-45), of a "holy city", in which men and women of every nation, tribe, people and language are united in love, as the wonderful work of God (Apoc 7:9-10; 21:1-4).

Israel, a people of brothers and sisters

242. The Old Testament is the written witness of the history of a particular people, whose specific characteristic consists in its covenant with the Lord of all the earth (Ex 19:5-6). If Israel, presenting itself as the offspring of Abraham, Isaac and Jacob, expresses its unity starting from a "carnal" principle, this represents only one sign of its profound identity, which arises from united listening to the one true God. In fact, only if Israel obeys the word of the Lord will it be different from all other peoples (Deut 4:32-40), and will its history be the principle of blessing for all humanity; only by being personally docile to the Torah will each Israelite contribute to being a seed of hope for the world.

Israel, in fact, is a nation like any other, made up of people with different aspirations, composed of many tribes and families, often endowed with particular traditions and with privileged roles in the context of the nation; its history will show that individualistic forces and particular interests can threaten the concord of the nation.

> A couple of examples, taken from a complex story lasting many centuries will suffice to illustrate the point.
>
> The tribe of Benjamin refused to hand over the guilty of the town of Gibeah (Jdg 20:13), and found itself fighting against the coalition of the other tribes of Israel (Jdg 20:14-48); its defeat and the decision to ostracise the tribe risked the disappearance forever of a component of the people of God (Jdg 21:3).
>
> Due to the bad government of Rehoboam, son of Solomon, who rejected the advice of the elders to "become the servant" of his people (1 Kgs 12:7), the northern tribes formed themselves into the kingdom of Israel, separate from the kingdom of Judah (1 Kgs 12:19). The split was permanent, with episodes of serious hostility, as during the Syro-Ephraimite war, which threatened the continuation of the Davidic dynasty in Jerusalem (2 Kgs 16:5-9; Is 7:1-9). The enmity between Samaritans and Jews will last up to the time of Jesus (Lk 9:52-53; Jn 4:9); an extraordinary intervention by God, announced by the prophet (Ezek 37:15-27), will be needed to unite the two sceptres into the one rod of the Davidic shepherd.

We have already established how difficult it is to live as brothers and sisters, even among children of the same father, in the context of a blood family; it is clearly even more difficult to unite individuals and groups that are distant from each other in terms of ancestry, interests and conditions of life. This is the role of the

Law, which, with its rules and sapiential teachings, intends to foster unity, respecting the diversity of the members, supporting the rights of all, and promoting solidarity with the poor, irrespective of their merits. The Torah, in fact, prescribes "justice" that is not limited to mere respect for the rights of others, but seeks the full promotion of the life of others. Rooted in the experience of the Lord's love for the fathers (Deut 7:8; 10:15, 18), fed by the memory of divine help when Israel was threatened (Deut 6:21-24), the Law takes the form of legal precepts, but addresses itself to the heart of the Israelite (Deut 6:6; 30:14), demanding in essence love of God (Deut 6:5) and love of neighbour (Lev 19:18).

A people in solidarity

243. In the eyes of the Law every person has the same fundamental rights as all others; consequently, every person is called to recognise such rights in others. Such a universal scope already finds expression in the command given by God to the descendants of Noah after the flood (Gen 9:6) not to shed the blood of human beings (*'ādām*): respect for life is, in concrete terms, the sign of the absolute value of those created in the image of God.

The Decalogue, synthesis of the religious and ethical prescriptions given to Israel, lists the duties towards others by resorting to the category of "*neighbour*" (*rēă'*) (Ex 20:16-17; Deut 5:20-21), that is, one who lives in the same living space (Ex 22:6,9,13). This makes clear the concreteness of the relationship. Indeed, the Hebrew term reported above has the nuance of "companion" (Deut 19:5; 1 Kgs 20:35; Zech 3:8) and even "friend" (Ex 33:11; Deut 13:7; Ps 35:14) and lover (Jer 3:1, 20; Hos 3:1); this invites us to consider the other not as anybody or as a stranger, but rather as a companion, whose presence has positive effects. For this reason, the Law prescribes not a detached respect, but lays down: "you will love your neighbour as yourself" (Lev 19:18).

The concept of "neighbour" can be extended indefinitely, since it applies to any person one meets, regardless of specific ethnic, confessional or cultural credentials. A similar consideration, though in a more restricted way, should be made also for the category of the *"poor"* (*'ānî, 'ebyôn, dal*), with which one defines the person who is in need of especially beneficial attention. For the biblical tradition, poverty is almost inherent to the status of the "widow" and the "orphan", who are deprived of a regular income, but it is also recognised as the normal condition of the "Levite" priest, who possesses no land in Israel, and of the "foreigner" or "immigrant" (*gēr*), who is also without agricultural land, and therefore forced to work precariously as a farm labourer, daily worker, or domestic servant. Since the Lord "sees justice done for the orphan and the widow; he loves the foreigner and gives the foreigner food and clothing" (Deut 10:18), it follows that the Israelite is called to imitation: "Love the foreigner then, for you were once foreigners in Egypt" (Deut 10:19). Even those who suffer from a disability, such as the blind and the deaf, must be respected and assisted beyond any legal requirement. One understands then how Elijah helped a poor widow of Zarephath in Phoenicia (1 Kgs 17:7-16), and how Elisha healed a pagan leper (2 Kgs 5:1-19); Jesus did the same, without discrimination. The Torah insists therefore on the duty to avoid any kind of exploitation of anyone who is destitute or in need:

> "You must not exploit a poor and needy labourer, whether one of your own people or a foreigner resident in your community. You must pay the wages each day, not allowing the sun to set before you do, since the labourer, being poor, depends on them and otherwise may appeal to the Lord against you, and you would incur guilt."
>
> (Deut 24:14-15)

> "You shall not pervert justice to a foreigner or an orphan; you shall not take a widow's clothes in pledge. Remember that you were once a slave in Egypt and that the Lord your God redeemed you from that. This is why I am giving you this order."
>
> (Deut 24:17-18; cf. also Deut 27:19)

244. The Law not only strictly prohibits oppression and every form of injustice, but also requires engagement in countless initiatives left to the generosity of the Israelite in order to give generous help to the poor. Thus one is invited to leave part of the harvest in the field, so that the destitute can come to feed themselves, without having to beg (Lev 19:9-10; 23:22; Deut 24:19-22); it is laid down that those who celebrate a feast should share the meal with those without resources (Deut 16:11, 14; cf. Neh 8:10-12); one is urged to assist the needy with the offering of first fruits (Deut 26:11) and with the annual and triennial tithes (Lev 27:30-33; Deut 14:22-29; 26:12-15); one is commanded to make loans to those in need, without receiving interest (Ex 22:24; Lev 25:35-38; Deut 23:20), accepting even the risk of not being compensated (Deut 15:7-11), in the hope of contributing to the disappearance of poverty (Deut 15:4) and giving the poor the possibility of starting up some economic activity with their self-respect intact.

In these last prescriptions of Deuteronomy, another concept appears, in parallel or co-related, that of "*brother*" (*'āh*), a term which, in the Law, describes the fellow citizen and fellow believer, not the blood relative. The bond of "brotherhood" is a factor that requires greater solidarity; these rules do not apply on some points to the "stranger" (*nokrî*), that is, the merchant or the official passing through Israel (cf. Deut 14:21; 23:21), not because respect should not be shown, but because such a person is not considered poor and needing protection. Deuteronomy often invites consideration of "*your* brother" (Deut 15:3, 7, 9, 11, 12; 17:15; 22:1; etc.), emphasising the responsibility of the believer, and calling for a generosity that is independent of feelings of sympathy, gratitude or self-interest.

The relationship with one's neighbour, however, can in practice be very difficult, due to wrongs suffered, damage sustained, insults, bodily injuries or other acts that are offensive. For this reason, the Law regulates compensation procedures, which contribute to putting an end to disputes and creating the conditions for social harmony. Situations of hostility among brothers may persist. Nevertheless, even if he is an "*enemy*" (*'ôyēb*), the other always remains a "brother", a "neighbour" to love. This is expressed in two prescriptions of the Torah, which by what they suggest may be applied analogically in different circumstances of life.

245. The first concerns the assistance to be given to someone who is in difficulty. The image, symbolic in nature, is that of the farmer who has either lost a head of cattle or has overloaded his pack animal, risking losing his load and the animal itself. The Deuteronomic Code describes the person in difficulty as "your brother" (Deut 22:1-4) and repeatedly urges that you should not pretend not to have seen him; this same norm is already found in the Covenant Code, with the specification, however, that the person to help is "your enemy":

> "If you come on your enemy's ox or donkey straying, you will take it back to him. If you see the donkey of your enemy collapsed under its load, do not stand back; you must go and help him with it."
>
> (Ex 23:4-5)

From this we can deduce that the Israelite is always asked to "give a hand", to help a neighbour, without harking back to past animosities, but seeing in that person the brother or sister in need.

The second important prescription is to be found in the so-called Holiness Code (Lev 19:17-18). The subject of the regulation here is the person who believes he has been wronged and who thus considers the other an "enemy". The context, therefore, is that of a hostile relationship that risks engendering "hatred" in the heart against the brother or sister; God asks that the other should be "firmly reproved" so that the offence is recognised, and truth and justice restored, without acting vindictively and without bearing a grudge, so as to obey the commandment that says "you shall love your neighbour as yourself" (Lev 19:18).

We can conclude, therefore, that the Torah does not say "You will love your neighbour and hate your enemy"; this dichotomy of opposing feelings is the result of an interpretative tradition (Mt 5:43) which Jesus will radically oppose.

A people at war

246. The just person, through word and deed, is a promoter of peace. However, one often finds oneself in situations where it is the other, whether sibling or stranger, who does not share the same principles and rules of behaviour, with the result that one is forced into a confrontation, undertaking a conflict or even a war, ideally unwanted, while behaving always according to justice. In the face of an adversary who threatens violence the Law requires conduct inspired by mildness.

CONFLICTS BETWEEN CITIZENS

The latent rivalry between people and groups, due to differences of interests, divergent ideologies, humiliations or misunderstandings, can easily explode with aggressive claims and actions. Open rivalry must then be resolved and defused according to justice, not by the use of force. The fundamental rule is that in conflict one should not take the law into one's own hands in the name of one's own convictions and according to personal criteria of vengeance, such as Lamech unjustly claimed, demanding "seventy-sevenfold" vengeance (Gen 4:24). It follows that, instead of private revenge, with which the presumed victim becomes an executioner, a procedure must be adopted that best promotes a consensual resolution of differences.

247. (i) The first way is to establish a *dialogue* between the litigants. By speaking and discussing between themselves, the adversaries can find forms of compromise and reasonable agreements, which ideally result in alliances of peace, based on commitments of mutual respect. This is how Isaac behaved in the conflict with Abimelech (Gen 26:26-31), and Jacob with Laban (Gen 31:43-54). As we said above, this is what the Law of Moses teaches (Lev 19:17-18), and this is what Jesus invites us to do (Mt 5:25; 18:15-18).

> The gospel brings to perfection this discipline of dialogue. The Christian is called to an attitude of total gentleness (Mt 5:5), renouncing the symmetrical response, according to the rule of an

"eye for an eye" (Ex 21:24-25) to become a "peacemaker" (Mt 5:9), assuming a disarmed and disarming benevolence (Rom 12:17-21). The justice which surpasses "that of the scribes and Pharisees" (Mt 5:20) is that which puts back the sword in its sheath (Mt 26:52) and presents the other cheek to the aggressor (Mt 5:39); it is that which submits willingly to harassment and revilement (Mt 5:39-41) for the love of the enemy (Mt 5:44), transforming resentment into blessing (Lk 6:28), and countering the offence with prayer for the aggressor (Mt 5:44-47). Christ embodied this conduct in his Passion (1 Pt 2:23), leaving an example that inspired the martyrdom of Christians (Acts 7:59-60). To forgive those who have offended seventy times seven (Mt 18:22) is equivalent to offering the violent the final word for reconciliation.

248. (ii) In certain cases, indeed frequently, the path of dialogue and pure meekness is not viable, because it would harm innocent victims, or because it does not satisfy both parties. The Law then asks that the conflict be resolved by resorting to a *mediator*, individual or collective, with the power to decide fairly in relation to the dispute, so as to restore harmony among the citizens. In the villages of Israel, it seems, the elders acted as justices of the peace, or rather as conciliators, determining the amount of compensation for wrongs provoked intentionally (Deut 22:18-19) or for damage caused unknowingly (Ex 21:22, 30).

> This strategy of the mediator is suggested by Jesus in Mt 18:16-17, using authoritative witnesses and the intervention of the whole community as a way to put right an unsuccessful interpersonal dialogue. Paul, too, asks that disputes be resolved, not by going to the pagan tribunal, but by submitting the case to someone in the Church who can arbitrate between brothers and sisters (1 Cor 6:1-8).

249. (iii) This type of conciliatory mediation, desirable for its customary placid wisdom designed to win people over, is not always successful. It is at this point that the Law calls for the intervention of the *judiciary*, which is entrusted with the task of settling disputes between citizens, with the forced imposition of its irrevocable verdicts.

The importance given to the judicial institution in the Old Testament is unquestionable; this is underlined by the fact that, in the book of Exodus, the establishment of a college of judges, who work alongside Moses in the jurisdictional task, takes place even before the people reach Sinai (Ex 18:13-27), the place where the Law will be promulgated (Ex 20–23). Something similar happens in Deuteronomy: the beginning of the book recalls the origin of the judicial institution (Deut 1:9-18), and only afterwards are the rules to be followed explained (Deut 5:6-22; 12–26). With such a narrative device, Scripture makes it clear that the Law has no social efficacy without the figure of the judge who should make decisions in accordance with the established laws, and decree punishments for transgressions in a proportionate way.

From this one understands the concerns of the biblical tradition for those who take on the role of magistrates. In Ex 18:21 it is prescribed that "men of strength who fear God, men trustworthy and incorruptible" should be chosen; and in Deut 1:13, for the same assignment, "wise, shrewd and experienced men" are recommended. The Law requires, therefore, both moral integrity, and competence and wisdom. It is these qualities that confer authority on the judicial institution.

NATIONS IN CONFLICT

250. Within civil society it is not weapons that resolve controversial issues according to justice; private vendettas and civil wars are not tolerated in a society governed by law. In the relationship between nations, however, in the case of serious disagreements and in the absence of tribunals of impartial mediation recognised by the contenders, *war* is unfortunately resorted to, which, although seen as a defeat for reasonable dialogue, is nevertheless considered an extreme means for restoring rights that have been trampled. There is a great deal of talk about war in the Bible, especially in the Old Testament; hence the charge addressed by many to the Hebrew people of being internally cohesive and belligerent towards others. It is true that the history of Israel, like that of many other nations, is a succession of conflicts, some provoked by the people of God, others endured often with catastrophic results. With the actual outbreak of violence, events of unbearable ambiguity are inevitable; every reasonable person who reads the biblical stories will find elements that are unsatisfactory and open to criticism. It seems opportune, therefore, to provide some guidance for a correct interpretation of the relevant biblical passages.

Throughout the Ancient Near East, and therefore also in Israel, war was generally conceived of as an *ordeal*, an event by which the just judgement of God was realised in the case of the two contenders, whether two kings or two armies, each claiming to be in the right: the divinity, from the heavenly throne, seat of the supreme tribunal (Ps 9:5, 8; 11:4), grants victory to those who are right, and brings about the defeat of those who are wrong. Impartiality is the key to this commendable justice (Deut 10:17; Sir 35:12-13). Divine intervention is made clear by the fact that often the triumph and humiliation of rivals are brought about by striking cosmic phenomena, such as when the sea opens and closes at the Lord's command (Ex 14:21-29), when huge hailstones rain down from heaven on the enemy (Josh 10:11), and when the sun stops to allow the "just" to complete a successful military operation (Josh 10:12-14). In any case, with different nuances and in different ways, the conviction is reinforced that whoever gains the victory is not the most warlike, but the one who is in the right; this idea is an expression of faith in the almighty and just God, who, in due course, will restore justice on earth, giving to each one according to their deeds (1 Kgs 8:32; Jer 32:19; Ps 62:13; Prov 24:12).

251. A similar concept applies to the whole of human history and to its turning points. It dominates not only the interpretation of the origins of Israel, where a people of slaves gets the better of Pharaoh's chariots, but also the course of the so-called "conquest" of Canaan. The latter is considered by some to be an injustice, but the biblical text presents the whole story as an act of justice. The Canaanites, in fact, are found guilty of very serious crimes according to the judgement of God (Gen 15:16), and the Israelites, whose right of settlement is recognised, are entrusted with the task of carrying out justice by bringing down the wicked. They could not have done it if it had not been right. The whole affair, in fact, is continuously marked by a striking disparity of military forces in the field (Num 13:31): the "wicked" are equipped with imposing systems of defence (Deut 1:28) and are very well armed (Josh 11:4; Jdg 1:19; 4:3), while the "just" are defenceless or have insufficient weaponry; yet the ones who win are the weaker, because it is God who gives the victory. The didactic purpose of the biblical stories accentuates the wonderful and unexpected aspect of the conquest: the walls of Jericho collapse on themselves (Josh 6:20), without a military attack, but simply with a procession of the ark around the city (Jos 6:12-16); Gideon, at war with the Midianites who are as numerous as locusts (Jdg 7:12), is invited by God to reduce his army from thirty-two thousand to three hundred soldiers (Jdg 7:3,8), and these, without fighting, but simply blowing their horns, cause the enemies to kill one another (Jdg 7:22). David, who defeats Goliath, is a sign of the truth that it is the Lord who gives the victory (1 Sam 17:41-51).

> Only in this sense can one speak of "holy war", which is in no way that undertaken in the name of a religious ideology, perhaps to make others submit to one's own belief, but is instead the battle in which the Holy One triumphs by means of the person who is gentle and just. Such a war will be waged by a deployment of people who will move in procession, preceded by the ark of the Lord and by the Levites who sing the divine praises (2 Chr 20:21); the fighters will gain victory in a surprising way, remaining unharmed even without defending themselves, and defeating the enemy without doing violence. Such an image is found only very imperfectly in the reality of war; instead it has its full truth in spiritual combat (Lk 21:18-19), where the believer has the upper hand against the evil one and his flaming darts (Eph 6:10-17).

Narrating history in such a way undoubtedly has parabolic value: on the one hand, it seeks to arouse faith to overcome the fear of facing a dangerous enemy (Deut 1:29); on the other hand, it shows how people should behave when called to wage war as an act of justice.

The laws of war

252. The essential rules on how to proceed in an enterprise of war are laid down in Deut 20:1-20. The legislator first of all acknowledges that the encounter is terrifying, since the opponent has superior forces at his disposal (Deut 20:1); we are indirectly told that a war, far from being a display of power, must be based exclusively on faith in God, the only one who can grant victory (Deut 20:4); for this reason the Law prescribes that whoever is afraid should be dismissed (Deut 20:8), because his lack of faith would bring discouragement to the other fighters.

It does not matter then if only a few stay; faith in God requires that one does not rely on the number or equipment of the soldiers. Those recruiting will dismiss anyone who has recently built a house or planted a vineyard or has recently contracted to marry (Deut 20:5-7). The purpose of this is to avoid the risk of premature death for those who represent the hope of the people, and also to declare that the future is not in the booty taken fighting in a distant place (Deut 20:14-15) but in the gift already present in the land of Israel.

It is then also made clear how the war should be conducted. The first thing to do is to offer peace (Deut 20:10-11). In the context outlined above, it is assumed that the attacker laying siege is driven by a just grievance; he therefore offers his opponent, who is deemed guilty, a way to repair the wrong by surrendering so that no blood is spilled. It is paradoxical, however, that peace is proposed by the one who is in a position of military inferiority, even if sure of achieving victory; the combatant's "primary" desire is to reach an agreement without violence. If the proposal is not accepted, armed conflict becomes inevitable and the deaths of many (Deut 20:13), together with looting (Deut 20:14), point to the dramatic and unsatisfactory nature of a relationship in which recognition of truth and justice has ceased. War involves massacres, reprisals and destruction; for this reason, in recent times, people have tried to regulate its brutality, introducing rules of respect for the opponent and of *pietas* towards the defeated; biblical guidance and above all the Christian spirit can be a ferment of wisdom and goodness in this regard in a scenario that is in itself inhuman.

These latter considerations require us to give an explanation for the divine command which imposes the "extermination" (*ḥerem*) of the Canaanite populations (Deut 7:2; 20:17-18). Such a provision is explicable only in the light of the ancient system of justice, which envisaged the death penalty for those guilty of very serious crimes, and required absolute rigour by the one enforcing justice (Deut 7:16; 13:9-11; 19:13, 21; 25:12). It is clear that one should not derive from these accounts an endorsement of aggressive conduct towards other peoples. The image of an intolerant and merciless God, which some deduce from the texts of the "conquest", must certainly be corrected; the reader is called instead to understand the need for justice (cf. for example, Mk 12:9), but the way to implement it will have to be in accord with criteria of universal law and of gospel teaching, inspired by respect for life, mercy and a desire for reconciliation (cf. Lk 23:34).

It should be remembered that the same Hebrew people, whom the Lord chose as an instrument of justice against the Egyptians and the Canaanites, found themselves on the side of the guilty, and had to undergo the judgement of God, carried out this time by pagan nations (Is 10:5-6; 47:6; Jer 50:23; 51:20-23). Moses had foretold this (Deut 8:19-20; 32:21), and it was definitively accomplished with the fall of Jerusalem (Jer 1:15-16). A small remnant, humiliated and suffering (Zeph 3:12-13), will become a witness of divine justice in history, when the humble king (Zech 9:9) will establish on earth the kingdom of universal peace (Zech 9:10).

The teaching of the sages

253. The very rich patrimony of wisdom teaching that we find in the Bible seeks without a doubt to promote harmony in society, on the one hand, by warning against quarrels among the citizens (Prov 3:29-30; 6:19; 30:32-33; Sir 28:8-12), and, on the other, with the invitation to a generous benevolence towards one's neighbour (Sir 22:23; 37:6). It is significant that the first concrete precept of the book of Proverbs requires prompt assistance to those in need:

"Refuse no kindness to those who have a right to it,
if it is in your power to do it.
Do not say to your neighbour, 'Go away!
Come another time! I will give it you tomorrow,'
if you can do it now."

(Prov 3:27-28)

These verses should not be read as a mere recommendation of reasonable courtesy between neighbours; they are rather a call on the wealthy not to disregard the serious duty of solidarity (Prov 22:9; Sir 4:1-10; 29:8-13; Tob 4:7-11). The rich person is for the most part a predator rather than a benefactor (Prov 21:26; Sir 13:3-9). Sirach writes: "What peace can there be between hyena and dog? And what peace between rich and poor? Wild desert donkeys are the prey of lions; so too the poor are the quarry of the rich" (Sir 13:18-19). The work of the sage in this regard is by no means secondary. True, he does not have tools that are immediately effective, since instead of money and the sword he makes use of the word, of counsel, of parables and of irony; the wisdom communicated to others, however, is an indispensable element for the formation of conscience, and for the education that restrains instincts and gives the person a human face and a human heart.

254. The sage, by encouraging benevolence and fraternal communion, calls for an ever higher quality in the relationship with one's neighbour. Real solidarity towards others, faithfully practised over time, especially when the relationship is undermined by adversity (Sir 6:8-10; 12:8-9), is a factor of growing cohesion between people (Sir 22:23), which leads to the precious experience of *friendship,* the value of which is greater than the bonds of kinship (Prov 18:24; 27:10). We can understand the good it brings between individuals, and appreciate it when it takes place between groups and nations. It is affirmed by the sayings of the sages:

"A friend is a friend at all times,
it is for adversity that a sibling is born."

(Prov 17:17)

"A loyal friend is a powerful defence:
whoever finds one has indeed found a treasure.
A loyal friend is something beyond price,
there is no measuring such worth.
A loyal friend is the elixir of life
and those who fear the Lord will find one."

(Sir 6:14-16)

In the biblical tradition we have no accounts of friendship, except the very beautiful one between Jonathan and David. A very close bond was established between the two after the victory over Goliath: "Jonathan's soul became bound to that of David; Jonathan loved him like his very self" (1 Sam 18:1). The verb "to love" certainly expresses an emotional nuance, but it must be seen, also in the political context of the succession to the throne, as an alliance; in fact "Jonathan made a pact with David" (1 Sam 18:3), giving him his cloak, together with his sword, his bow and his belt (1 Sam 18:4): in this way the king's son excluded all rivalry, and ceded to his friend the opportunity to accede to the throne. Jonathan's loyalty was shown in the defence of his friend even in the face of Saul's insinuations and anger (1 Sam 19:1-7; 20:1-42); and in the funeral lament David recognised the quality of their friendship, expressing his own words of love: "I am desolate for you, Jonathan my brother. You were the dearest to me, your love more wonderful to me than the love of a woman" (2 Sam 1:26).

Fraternity and hostility in the prayer of the Psalms

255. The one who prays brings before God the condition of a person living in a community of human beings. This, as we have seen earlier, brings contrasting situations that lead to different ways of praying.

The first way is expressed in joy, arising from the experience of a real fraternity which has liturgical manifestation in the pilgrimage of everyone to the sanctuary of Jerusalem, where believers gather to invoke peace for family and for friends (Ps 122:6-9). The feeling of spiritual joy is admirably expressed in Ps 133:

"How good (*ṭôb*) and how pleasant it is,
when kindred live in unity!
It is like precious (*ṭôb*) oil upon the head
running down upon the beard;
running down upon Aaron's beard,
upon the collar of his robes;
like the dew of Hermon, which runs down
on the mountains of Zion.
For there the Lord bestows his blessing:
life for ever",

256. The second manner of prayer is in a certain sense the opposite of the first. Human beings, in fact, do not frequently experience the pleasure of fraternal harmony, but more often the bitterness of feeling surrounded by numerous and cruel "enemies" (Ps 3:2-3; 7:2-3; 25:19; 69:5). The one praying feels abandoned (Ps 69:9), betrayed (Ps 41:10; 55:13-15), threatened by his own companions (Ps 35:7, 11-12, 15), and as a result reveals his suffering to God, seeking an immediate intervention to resolve the situation (Ps 3:8; 104:35; 143:12). This type of prayer, widely attested in the Psalter, arouses unease and confusion for many. The tones of the prayer are the very opposite of the sentiments of love that those praying, especially Christians, should express; the difficulty is such that quite a few verses or whole psalms are omitted in liturgical recitation.

The objections find their justification in the particularly crude language that is used at times by the psalmist. When generic or metaphorical expressions are used, the one praying does not in fact feel revulsion. Hence if the faithful recite, as "the Lord's revelation", that God makes the foes of David his footstool (Ps 110:1) and will "shatter kings in the day of his wrath" (110:5), the person praying recognises with joy the realisation of the divine action that scatters the proud to raise up the humble (Ps 68:7; 145:9; 147:6; Lk 1:52); that same person, however, will find it unseemly that in the same psalm it is said that the Messiah "heaps the bodies high; he shatters heads throughout the wide earth" (Ps 110:6), and consequently will omit this verse, without realising that this is a repetition with different if more realistic words of what was said previously. Furthermore, no one who suffers the experience of being threatened will hesitate to say with the Psalmist "Let there be shame and confusion on those who seek my life" (Ps 70:3), but could never pronounce the words of Ps 137:8-9: "O daughter Babylon, destroyer, blessed is the one who repays you the payment you paid to us! Blessed is one who grasps and shatters your children on the rock!" It is necessary then that we know how to understand and adequately grasp the meaning of forms of biblical prayer which, in a concrete and even brutal way, put into words the desire to see evil disappear from the earth.

The literary genre of these supplications is the "lament", which is ideally spoken by one who is persecuted to death, tortured and despised (Ps 10:7-11; 17:10-12; 22:17-19); it is the prayer of a person who has suffered and still suffers without anyone coming to help (Ps 7:3; 22:12; 25:16). The Christian takes up this prayer in the light of Christ on the cross. The prayer is like a cry (Ps 22:2; 39:13; 40:2), powerful and dramatic, which invokes help from God, imploring freedom, victory, life; it asks in a compelling way that the adversary should cease to attack and to rage. The meaning of the petition will be accepted by all; it will be difficult though to take up the prayer when it expresses feelings of rancour and revenge, as in the so-called "imprecatory psalms" (cf. Ps 83; 109). We will consider three aspects that can help us to interpret in a more satisfactory way these "inspired" texts that have come down to us as examples of prayer.

257. (i) *The one who raises the lament is one who suffers.* The person who prays the psalms of lamentation, as we have said, is someone who is suffering, or rather is a person terrified by threat and worn out by pain, who uses exaggerated and exasperated language both in the description of suffering (Ps 22:17-18; 69:5) and in the plea for a speedy and definitive release. The gravity of the evil, which produces unbearable pain in the innocent, is expressed with hard and harsh language. Anyone who, in prayer, takes up the words of the Psalmist, almost never experiences this desperate condition personally; but that person can raise a lament in the name of brothers and sisters who are persecuted (Ps 94:5-6), and can be the pleading voice of many who have no voice because of their terrible suffering. Those who know how to identify with the martyrs will not be afraid to let the cry of the martyrs of the Apocalypse come out of their mouths: "How long, holy and true Lord, will you wait before you judge and avenge our blood on the inhabitants of the earth?" (Apoc 6:10).

(ii) *The psalmist asks: "deliver us from evil".* Every psalm is a prayer. It is not an outburst against enemies calling desperately for retaliation but is essentially an invocation addressed to God, to whom the individual entrusts the task of doing justice. The victim renounces personal revenge (Rom 2:19; Heb 10:30), but desires that justice should assert itself in history, and accordingly turns to the Lord as judge of the world, in the confidence that he will act by doing good, so that evil is forever annihilated (Ps 3:8; 137:9) and the innocent can see their triumph, which is also the triumph of God (Ps 35:27; 59:14). Every petition has in itself something improper, when it seems to presume to dictate to the Lord how to act; in reality, if properly understood, it expresses, even if in inadequate terms, the desire for liberation and life that God rewards with fulfilment. Jesus promised it: "Will not God grant justice to his chosen ones who keep calling to him day and night even though he delays? I promise you, he will grant justice to them, and speedily." (Lk 18:7-8).

(iii) *Who are the "enemies" of the psalmist?* The psalms speak of nations that rise up against God and the Messiah (Ps 2:1-2), they evoke coalitions made up of disparate people, such as the Amalekites and the Assyrians (Ps 83:6-9), who have already disappeared from history, and they use harsh words against Edom and Babylon (Ps 137:7-9); now it is clear that these names and these presumed historical peoples are meant only to be "figures" of the present enemy of the person praying (cf. Acts 4:23-30). For the most part, however, the adversary of whom the psalms speak has no face, or precise ethnic identification, and is only presented as arrogant, wicked, a blasphemer, cruel. Who then are the enemies of the person who is praying? It is necessary to identify, with a prophetic spirit, who in the history of the individual person or of the entire people of God, appears as a hostile, dangerous, unjust and reprehensible force. It is certainly possible, in specific circumstances, to give a name to these enemies, asking the Lord that they cease from doing harm for ever. A certain spiritual progress can be made, however, in identifying the "true" enemy, who is not only someone who threatens physical life (Mt 10:28) or people's dignity, but above all someone who undermines the spiritual life of the person who prays, who urges people to commit injustices, who seduces and drags into evil. It is these occult forces that strike deceptively in the shadows (Ps 10:8-9; 59:4); they prowl about like lions ready to maul (Ps 17:12; 1 Pt 5:8); they are like snakes with deadly poison (Ps 58:5; 140:4); they pretend to be angels of light when in fact they are satanic forces (2 Cor 11:14) and must be radically opposed (Ps 26:5; 139:21-22). We remember then the words of Paul in the letter to the Ephesians: "For our struggle is not against human enemies, but against rulers, authorities and the cosmic powers of this darkness, the spirits of evil in the heavenly places" (Eph 6:12). Satan is the Hebrew name that means "adversary"; he is the enemy; hence the urgent need to ask God that he be destroyed for ever.

The message of the prophets

258. Knowledge of God, who revealed himself in his compassionate goodness towards the destitute, should have produced in the people of Israel not only love of neighbour but also concern for the poor and the disadvantaged. But here instead there is the terrible reality of kings, judges, priests and the rich who subvert people's rights and gravely offend against justice (Jer 5:28; Zech 7:9-11): all are corrupt (Jer 5:1-9); they despise the widow and the orphan (Is 1:23; 10:2; Ezek 22:7, 25; Mal 3:5); they exploit the weak (Ezek 22:29; Am 2:7; 4:1; 5:11; 8:4, 6); they take possession of the goods of their neighbour (Is 5:8; Am 2:8; Mic 2:1-2), because they think only of their unjust profit (Jer 6:13; 8:10; 22:17; Ezek 22:27; 33:31; Hab 2:9).

History is not a place of brotherly love, but of hatred: "each cave in the land is a place where violence makes its home" (Ps 74:20). The prophets then raise their voices to denounce, to warn, to threaten, since criminal acts undermine the essence of the people of God, its vocation to unity and its mission to become a sign of blessing for the nations. Raised up tirelessly by the Lord (Jer 7:25; 25:4; 29:19), his messengers appeal to human freedom, calling for that conversion which consists in committing oneself to accomplish what is good (Is 1:16-17). Unfortunately they are not heeded (Is 6:9-10); on the contrary they are resisted (Jer 1:19; 11:19; Ezek 2:6; Am 7:12-13).

The prophetic voice then can only announce the punishment of God, who not only destroys unjustly accumulated riches (Jer 15:13; 17:3; 20:5; Hos 13:15; Am 3:11), but by a miracle establishes justice by the coming of a descendant of David, who will bring back justice and kindness to the earth (Is 9:6; 32:1; Jer 23:5; 33:15-16), and will ensure universal peace (Is 32:16-18; 57:14-19; 66:12; Jer 33:6, 9; Zech 9:9-10).

> "Then he will judge between the nations
> and arbitrate between many peoples.
> They will hammer their swords into ploughshares
> and their spears into sickles.
> Nation will not lift sword against nation;
> no longer will they learn to make war."
>
> (Is 2:4)

The ancestors lived from this messianic expectation, from this hope, and with the same hope the humble and the oppressed live today. Christians see this hope fulfilled in Jesus of Nazareth and in those who live by his spirit.

Jesus and his "brothers and sisters"

259. Being born into a family, Jesus is inserted into a community of brothers and sisters: some are his relations (Mt 13:55-56; Mk 6:3; Jn 7:3, 5, 10; Acts 1:14; etc.), while others represent the wider circle of those who share traditions, laws and religious faith with him (Mt 5:22-24, 47; 7:3-5; 23:8; etc.). Brother among brothers and sisters (Heb 2:11-12, 17), he does not undervalue such bonds; it is sufficient to recall his affection for Lazarus and his two sisters (Jn 11:1-3, 11, 36), or his tears for the misfortune of Jerusalem (Lk 19:41). Nevertheless, Christ relativises earthly links, subjecting them to criteria of greater value, and opening up dimensions of greater love.

For the Lord the blood relationship is not the fundamental element for the establishment of a community of brothers and sisters; it is necessary instead to listen obediently to the will of the Father; this is what he tells his relatives who come to look for him, pointing to his disciples as his true brothers and sisters (Mt 12:46-50; Mk 3:31-35; Lk 8:19-21). He will confirm and exalt this reality in his appearance as the Risen One (Mt 28:10; Jn 20:17). The choice of the Kingdom is expressed characteristically in the choice of love for the Lord rather than the duty of solidarity towards the family (Mt 10:21; Lk 14:26).

We can see that this perspective was already somehow foreshadowed in the old covenant; the Master accepts the demands of the Torah, bringing them to perfection (Mt 5:17). In particular, he receives from tradition the first commandment, which calls for total love of the Lord, and the second, which prescribes love for one's neighbour; his contribution is to bring them together in unity (Mt 22:37-39; Mk 12:29-31; Lk 10:26-28), affirming that in their unbreakable union they represent the whole Law and the Prophets (Mt 22:40; see also Mt 7:12; Rom 13:9; Gal 5:14; Jam 2:8). The joining together of the two commandments ensures that the second, described as "similar to the first" (Mt 22:39), is deemed sacred, and that love for one's neighbour unfolds with the same potential and fulness that marks love for God.

260. The teaching of Jesus, composed of words and exemplary deeds, will develop this fundamental nucleus. He will insist, in particular, on the very high demands of love for "one another", thus making the "ancient" commandment "new" (Jn 13:34; 2 Jn 5). For Jesus, love requires that one never offends one's neighbour with contempt and insult (Mt 5:22); love demands that one does not judge one's neighbour (Mt 7:1-2; Lk 6:37); love rules out acts of vindictive retaliation (Mt 5:39-41), and love requires that one should cease to aspire to be the "first" at the expense of others (Mt 20:25-27; Mk 10:42-45; Lk 14:7-11; 22:24-27). But above all, the true fulfilment of the precept takes place in concrete acts of *giving*. The disciple, as the parable of the Samaritan teaches (Lk 10:30-37), is one who makes himself neighbour to the person in need, going beyond confessional affiliations, and displaying a depth of generosity that does not expect earthly rewards (Lk 12:33-34; 14:12-14). Love is true, in fact, only if it is the humble "service" of others, as the Master and Lord showed in washing the feet of the disciples (Jn 13:1-5), setting the example, so that what he did becomes a paradigm of Christian conduct (Jn 13:12-15; cf. also Mt 20:25-28; Mk 10:42-45; Lk 22:25-27). The giving of material goods and the provision of service are in reality signs of giving one's life for others (Jn 15:12-15; cf. 1 Jn 3:16). Universality and total generosity clearly distinguish the Christian commandment of love for one's neighbour.

The Lord Jesus humbled himself before human weakness, bringing assistance without sparing himself to all kinds of diseases and needs; he sent his disciples to do the same (Mt 10:8; Lk 9:1; 10:9); he even asked them to divest themselves of their possessions to help the poor (Mt 19:21; Mk 10:21, 28-30; cf. Heb 13:16; 1 Jn 3:17-18). Anyone who comes to the aid of the hungry, strangers and prisoners (Mt 25:31-46), anyone who gives even a cup of water to a child in need (Mt 10:42), becomes like Christ, an authentic embodiment of love of neighbour, whatever other qualities this person possesses. To establish such welcoming kindness, God, at the beginning of the history of the covenant, appeared in the form of three travellers in need of refreshment (Gen 18:1-2); and, without knowing it, Abraham became the generous host of angels (Heb 13:2). In the revelation of the end times, Christ himself, the Lord of history, the king who judges the world, takes the form of the destitute, and says to everyone: "In so far as you did this to one of the least of these brothers or sisters of mine, you did it to me" (Mt 25:40).

Christian love extends to everyone, even to the most distant and hostile. Christ, in fact, asks that the brother or sister who has sinned always be forgiven (Mt 18:21-22; Lk 17:3-4), and sets fraternal reconciliation as a prelude to any act of worship (Mt 5:23-24), so that the Father may bring his saving mercy to all (Mt 6:14-15; 18:23-35). He asks for kindness with no exclusions, and thus invites people to do good even to the enemy, in imitation of the "perfect" magnanimity of the Creator (Mt 5:43-48). While all this may appear difficult to implement, it becomes possible for those who live by the Spirit of love given by God (Rom 5:5; Gal 5:22).

The community of Christians

261. The book of the *Acts of the Apostles* offers us an idealised picture of the early church, which is born from the powerful gift of the Spirit of love at Pentecost. We are told that many people, of different races and languages (Acts 2:6-11), were converted at the witness of Peter (Acts 2:37-41) and persevered in listening to the teaching of the apostles (Acts 2:42), united among themselves by adherence to the Word of God. As a result they were of "one heart and mind" (Acts 4:32), and the convergence of their feelings expressed itself in common prayer (Acts 2:42, 46-47), reflecting their communion in the Lord (cf. Mt 18:19-20). Moreover, they held their goods in common, sold their possessions and shared the proceeds with brothers and sisters in need (Acts 2:44-45; 4:32), so that no one was in want (Acts 4:34-35). The ending of poverty, which the Torah had envisaged as a blessing of God on his people (Deut 15:4-6), is brought about in a marvellous way through the work of people moved by the Spirit of goodness; what Jerusalem symbolised, as a city of origin for every people (Ps 87:4-6) and as a pole of peace, attracting all nations (Is 2:2-5; 56:6-8; Zech 8:20; 14:16), finds its full truth in the Church of Christ. Such a perfect scenario is not a utopia; it describes the profound mystery of the Christian community, visible wherever one breathes the spirit of the gospel in the multiple and creative forms of brotherly and sisterly love.

262. In his letters *Paul* allows us to have a real insight into his communities, in which such a powerful ferment of good is at work (Rom 15:14; 1 Cor 1:4-7; 2 Cor 8:7; Phil 1:3-11; etc.), even amid the tensions and conflicts that arise from the human heart, which can often be petty and provocative. The Apostle ceaselessly reaffirms that the unity of Christians is not rooted in the goodwill of human beings, but is the fruit of the event of grace of Christ, who broke down the dividing wall between Jews and Gentiles, eliminating in himself the enmity, so as to "make the two into a single unit" (Eph 2:14-18). We know that for Paul the communion of the children of Israel with the Gentiles in their recognition of the only Saviour represents the heart of his gospel; the unity of the two in one body brings about the "new man" (Eph 2:15), that new creation where "there is no Greek and Jew, no circumcised and uncircumcised, no barbarian and Scythian, slave and free, but Christ is all and in all" (Col 3:10-11; cf. Gal 3:28).

The principal sign of this profound unity is to be found in the communion of all in the one bread and the one cup: "The cup of blessing which we bless, is it not a fellowship in the blood of Christ? The bread which we break, is it not a fellowship in the body of Christ? As there is one bread, so we, though many, are one body, for we all share in the one bread" (1 Cor 10:16-17). What Christians celebrate, eating the body of the Lord and drinking his blood (1 Cor 11:26; cf. Jn 6:53-58), is the sacrament of their communion. Because of this it does not allow divisions (1 Cor 11:18).

Paul, therefore, constantly and insistently encourages the strengthening of the bonds of fraternal communion and the elimination of dissensions and divisions among Christians. There is, in fact, a risk of parties or cliques being formed, due to the influence of the various *leaders* of the community. It must not be said: "I belong to Paul", "I belong to Apollo", "I belong to Cephas", because Christ is not divided, and only he has been crucified for all (1 Cor 1:12-15). Hence the pressing admonition of the Apostle: "Brothers and sisters, I urge you, in the name of our Lord Jesus

Christ, all to be in agreement. There should be no divisions among yourselves, so that you are united in your beliefs and judgements" (1 Cor 1:10; cf. also Rom 15:5-6). Communion in "belief" is not a purely ideological conformity but is expressed rather in the concrete practice of love, taking on, according to the example of the Lord Jesus, the attitude of "service" (Gal 5:13-15; Phil 2:1-8), carrying one another's burdens (Gal 6:2), and forgiving, as Jesus did, so as to sow seeds of peace (Eph 4:1-3; Col 3:12-15).

263. An innovative image, dear to the Apostle, which illustrates in a significant way how the community of brothers and sisters in Christ is to be understood, is that of the "*body*". There are two elements of major importance in this symbolism. (i) The first is that of the necessary *cohesion* between the members, because of everyone's participation in the same "divine" life (1 Cor 6:15; 12:27): "one body, and one Spirit, just as you were called in the one hope of your calling, one Lord, one faith, one baptism, one God and Father of all, who is over all, through all and in all" (Eph 4:4-6). Each member, though different from the others, is part of the one body, and exercises a specific function in it with its own usefulness (1 Cor 12:14-26). If a member suffers, the whole body suffers, and if a member is honoured, all the members rejoice together (1 Cor 12:26). Hence the missionary importance of "saving" each person (1 Cor 9:19-23) to give fulness to the organism of the Church (Eph 1:23). (ii) The second element to underline, in the image of the body, is even more important for Paul. It is that of the *diversity* of the members, indispensable for the vitality of the organism: "Just as we have many members in one body, and the members do not have the same function, so we, though many, form one body in Christ, each individually members of one another" (Rom 12:4-5). What from the outside can be seen as a principle of division, in particular the superiority of some over others, is instead interpreted by the Apostle as a charismatic gift to be placed at the service of the entire body (1 Cor 12:4-11):

"having different gifts (*charismata*) according to the grace (*charis*) given to us; maybe prophecy (*prophēteia*) in proportion to our faith, maybe serving in ministry (*diakonia*), maybe the teacher in teaching (*didaskalia*), maybe the encouraging person in encouraging (*paraklēsis*), the generous person in simplicity, the leader in enthusiasm, the compassionate in exercising compassion."

(Rom 12:6-8; cf. also 1 Cor 12:27-30; Eph 4:7, 12-16)

264. The law in the Deuteronomic Code calls on the king not to become proud, and to remember that he is brother to his subjects (Deut 17:20); but in the community of the new covenant brotherhood is exercised in becoming the servant of others (1 Cor 12:22-25). This applies to all, because each person has a divine gift for the building up of the whole body; each, according to function, cooperates in the growth of the body until it has reached the perfect state willed by God (Eph 4:13, 15-16; Col 2:19; cf. also 1 Pt 4:10-11). What enlivens and gives cohesion to the body of the Church is *love* (*agapē*), the perfect charism, the only lasting virtue (1 Cor 13:8) which Paul points out as a supreme good (1 Cor 13:13) to be desired above every other charism (1 Cor 12:31; 14:1; Col 3:14-15), and which he admirably describes in its qualities and expressions:

"Love is patient; love is kind; love is not jealous; love is not boastful, or puffed up or rude; it does not insist on its rights, it does not take offence, it does not plan evil, it does not rejoice at wrongdoing but rejoices in the truth. It puts up with everything, it believes everything, it hopes everything, endures everything."

(1 Cor 13:4-7)

In another of Paul's letters we read:

"Let love be genuine. Hate what is evil; stick to what is good. Be affectionate to one another with fraternal love, outdoing one another in showing honour, not holding back in enthusiasm, being ardent in spirit, serving the Lord, rejoicing in hope, steadfast under trial, persevering in prayer, sharing the needs of the saints, cultivating hospitality. Bless any who persecute you, bless them and do not curse them. Rejoice with any who rejoice, weep with any who weep. Share the thoughts of one another; do not have exalted ideas, but associate with the lowly. Do not act as though you were wiser than you are. Repay no one with evil for evil, but purpose what is good in everyone's eyes. As far as you can, be at peace with everyone. [...] Do not be conquered by evil, but conquer evil by good."

(Rom 12:9-21)

In the letters of the other apostles also, although with different metaphors and emphases, we have a unanimous insistence on solidarity and on fraternal love. In his first letter Peter echoes the preaching of Jesus and that of Paul: "you should all be of one mind (*homophrones*) and be sympathetic (*sympatheis*); love the brothers and sisters (*philadelphoi*), tender hearted and humble. Do not repay one wrong with another, or abuse with abuse; instead, repay with a blessing, for you were called to this in order to inherit a blessing" (1 Pt 3:8-9). And John, in conformity with the teaching of Jesus, insists on the fact that love of God, the first commandment, demands love of one's brother and sister: "Anyone who says 'I love God' and hates a brother or sister is a liar, since whoever does not love the brother or sister whom he has seen cannot love God whom he has not seen. This is the commandment we have received from him, that whoever loves God loves also brother and sister" (1 Jn 4:20-21; cf. also 1 Jn 2:3-11; 3:10-11, 16-18, 23-24; 4:11-12; 5:1-2).

CONCLUSION

265. The whole course of this chapter, complex in its details, has *love* as a common thread, whether it is expressed in the precious form of the marriage union, or in the dedication of father and mother to their children, or in the obedient respect of children for their parents, or in the solidarity, service and forgiveness that distinguish fraternal relationships. It could be said that Scripture teaches that love is the spiritual dimension that makes a human being human, because it makes the human being similar to God. Even where there is a certain parity or "equality" between individuals, as in the relationship between husband and wife, or between members of a civil or religious community, the Bible points out that there is always some difference or "inequality" that can give rise to envy, rivalry, and abuse; love will show itself not only in not giving way to the temptation of contention and intimidation, but also in transforming one's talents and qualities into a means of cohesion, so that one person's gift is constantly at the service of the neighbour. The confident hope of believers is that love will invade the consciences of all, making human history wonderful, in obedience to the divine command.

Love is in fact *commanded* by the Torah and by the Gospel. While there are times when it springs spontaneously from the heart, it remains a duty that requires free decision as well as effort, patience and courage, together with trust in God and in God's promise. Love is a virtue that men and women refine in the daily commitment of life. But love is not only commanded; love is *given* to whoever seeks it. It is not just an aspiration and a dream; it is also something that becomes real in history. The Spirit of love is communicated to the community in prayer, making it capable of love which is amazing, dynamic and attractive.

CHAPTER FOUR

The Human Being in History

266. The human being is a historical being. Like all creatures human beings have a beginning, which constitutes the first sign of their "historicity", understood as finiteness, a dimension that differentiates them from the One Being who has no beginning or end (Is 41:4; 44:6; Ps 90:2; 93:2; Sir 42:21; Apoc 1:8; 21:6; 22:13). According to the text of Gen 1, *'ādām* comes to exist in a world that, created before him, welcomes him generously, to enable him to live. Human beings are not the first of the creatures, but the primary role of human beings in history is revealed to them. The temporal span that gives structure to the first story of creation in seven days, with the evening and morning following one another, that is, with the unfolding of reality in the form of a "before" and an "after", will be perceived by the individual in the rhythm of the breath and in the beating of the heart, and will be regulated for all by the cycles of the sun and the moon (Gen 1:17-18); the flow of days and years, of which on earth only human beings are aware, constitutes a component of their nature and their responsibility in history.

The human being is a historical being, because every person is born of a mother and father who precede their child in time and are for the child the sign of the Origin that no one can know: "You do not understand", Qoheleth writes, "the path of the wind or the growth of an embryo in the womb: no more can you understand the work of God, the Creator of all" (Qoh 11:5). Something of our origin can be recounted by a witness who participated in or assisted at the birth, especially the parent, but the sense of the origin of the world can only be revealed by God and by his spokespersons. This is why it is in these sacred texts that the secret truth about the human being is made known to every person.

267. Despite its fragility, the child of Adam is a protagonist of history, capable of influencing events and with the power to guide the future in a life-giving direction by listening to the witnesses of God; but by refusing to obey the child of Adam can also drag everything into death. Unlike all other creatures, the destiny of *'ādām* and, in part, that of others, can be decided by *'ādām*. Created in the image of God, *'ādām* carries within a powerful potential, which will be described as *freedom*, an essential quality of the spiritual being. Even if in a form that is not always complete, this freedom constitutes an essential component of the human being, which God desired and which God tirelessly supports so that it develops on the way of life.

> In biblical Hebrew we do not have an abstract term that expresses the concept of freedom; the reality, however, is clearly suggested by other linguistic means, as we shall see directly, providing the reader with a precise illustration of the responsibilities that belong to the human being. The noun *eleuteria* is occasionally found in the LXX, as in relation to emancipation from slavery (Lev 19:20; Sir 7:21), whereas by contrast the terminology of freedom, which defines the independence of choice without external pressures, is very frequent in the New Testament (cf. Jn 8:32; 1 Cor 10:19; 2 Cor 3:17; Gal 2:4; 5:1, 13; etc.) also through the influence of contemporary Greek literature.

From the very beginning the biblical account brings out the aspect of freedom by narrating that the Creator speaks to the human being and gives a *command*. The voice of God in Gen 1 expresses itself as an imperative addressed to the other creatures also, because it "commands" that everything should exist (Ps 33:9; 148:5); however, the appearance and action of the various beings, even if sometimes presented as an act of obedience to a divine order (1 Kgs 17:4; Job 28:26; 38:10-11; Bar 3:35), are not the fruit of free consent, but rather the result of the divine will that imposes itself by pure authority (Ps 115:3; 135:6-7). Only human beings can listen to the command, and, through the autonomy that belongs to them, they can obey or disobey.

> In some cases, domestic animals seem to have a similar capacity, and "human" talents and feelings are attributed to them. The similarity with the human being must not however obscure the differences. In any case, the Bible narrates that God speaks to human beings, revealing his will to them and asking them to carry it out. It is made known to us, therefore, that it is the human being, and the human being alone, who is the recipient of the divine command.

The choice of whether to consent or to disobey emerges as the fundamental way in which human beings express their freedom. The importance of the thematic motif of the commandment, which makes real the act of freedom, is confirmed by the prominence given to it by the whole of Scripture. This will be the subject of the first part of this chapter, which is entitled "Human beings under the Law".

268. Freedom of choice is concretely implemented in decisions that actually take place in history and from which consequences for the future emerge. Human beings make many and varied decisions throughout their lives, but the most decisive ones are those that respond or do not respond to the divine command. The Bible, in fact, shows that, despite having enigmatic aspects, due also to the surprising actions of God (Is 45:15; Ezek 18:25; Hos 14:10; Ps 92:6-7; Job 28:12-13; Qoh 3:11; Sir 11:4; Wis 17:1), the human story can be read with the interpretative key of obedience or disobedience to what God has ordered. This hermeneutical principle substantially controls the entire biblical historiography. More specifically, Scripture attests that human beings rarely obey and almost always rebel, using their freedom as dissent and opposition to God; indeed the Bible speaks of an "original" disobedience, of a transgression that is placed at the beginning, as the starting point of human history. How such a perspective, with its dramatic implications, should be understood will be treated in the second part of this chapter, entitled "Obedience and transgression".

The human being is the summit of creation, because the earth is entrusted to the children of Adam; however, because of the improper exercise of their freedom, because of their disobedience to the will of God, the world risks destruction (Gen 6:5-7). This would have happened but for the providential intervention by the Father of life, the main protagonist of history. The Creator does not create and then abandon his creatures to themselves; on the contrary, as Scripture repeatedly makes clear, God holds the cosmos (Ps 95:4) and the fate of human beings in particular in his hands; and thus God acts in a mysterious but effective way to ensure that history becomes a history of grace, a history of salvation. How this happens, how this constitutes the message of hope for believers, is illustrated in the last part of this chapter, which is called "The intervention of God in the history of sinners".

To facilitate a thematic presentation anchored to the biblical accounts of creation, we will present at the beginning of each part of this chapter the relevant verses of Gen 2-3 with an exegetical comment that leads on to the relevant development provided by the various literary collections of the Old and New Testaments.

1. HUMAN BEINGS UNDER THE LAW

269. In the accounts of Gen 1-2, the actions performed by God are accompanied by God's words, which help us to understand the meaning of creation. In Gen 1 exegetes have noted that God pronounces ten words, a kind of original Decalogue, and almost all, except the soliloquy of Gen 1:26 and the offering of food in Gen 1:29, have a jussive linguistic form; injunctions are directed to the light (Gen 1:3), to the firmament (Gen 1:6), to the waters

(Gen 1:9), to the earth (Gen 1:11, 24), to the stars (Gen 1:14), to the animals (Gen 1:22), and finally to humans (Gen 1:28). We can say that, in this first story, the divine command intends to make known the will of the Creator in the very act of his work, as happens explicitly for the creation of man in Gen 1:26. A similar stylistic device is found in the pithy verse of Ps 33:9:

> "He spoke, and it came to be.
> He commanded; it stood in its place."
>
> (cf. also Is 48:13; Ps 148:5)

One cannot say, therefore, that, in the "imperative" formulations of Gen 1, "commandments" are actually given, not even with regard to the words addressed to humankind, "be fruitful, multiply" (Gen 1:28), because they are presented as a "blessing" and not as a precept; this, moreover, is confirmed in the parallel of Gen 1:22, where the same terminology is applied to fish and birds. In other words, human fertility and "dominion" over the earth and over animals are to be regarded as the original gift of God, rather than, as sometimes interpreted, the first precept to be implemented. We can however add that inherently intrinsic to every gift of the Lord is the invitation to welcome it according to its meaning; only human beings are capable of accepting this divine call in a manner that is conscious, intelligent and free.

270. The perspective of Gen 2 is considerably different, since, in this second account, the imperative dimension of the action and the word of the Lord, both delivered to the human being, appears to be clearer. We have above all an indirect way of putting forward a command, analogous therefore to the case in Gen 1, in which the divine gift is linked to a goal desired by the Creator, which the human being is called to fulfil. This is expressed in Gen 2:15, where we read that God placed *'ādām* in the garden, assigning him the task of working and keeping the land.

This way of expounding the duty that flows from the divine initiative is found in other passages of Scripture, too; the accounts of the origins are in fact like the premise for the commandment. Thus in

Gen 1 the creation of the universe in six days and the Creator's rest on the seventh are recounted; this is the basis for the prescriptions of Ex 20:8-11 regarding weekday work and abstention from work on the Sabbath, by which man celebrates the divine work. Or again, the narrative of the liberation from Egypt (Ex 1–15) constitutes the theological premise of the Decalogue in Deut 5:6-21: not only does it facilitate the understanding of how idolatry is equivalent to falling back into slavery (Dt 5:9), but it confers on the Sabbath precept the significance of celebrating freedom, as well as demanding freedom from servitude for members of the family (Deut 5:12-15). Another characteristic example is that of Is 5:1-4: here the prophet, using the form of a parable set in an agricultural context, makes it appear that the divine action obviously expects fruits, produced specifically by human activity, as is seen also in Mt 21:33-41.

In Gen 2 the manner in which the command is addressed to man in an explicit way deserves a more extensive comment.

Gen 2:16-17

[16]Then the Lord God gave the man this command, "You may eat of all the trees in the garden. [17]But of the tree of the knowledge of good and evil you are not to eat; for the day you eat of that you shall die."

271. The command. *The terminology of the commandment appears here for the first time with the verb* ṣāwāh; *used always in an intensive form, it is taken up later in Gen 3:11, 17 in the context of divine "judgement". The verb appears in the Decalogue (Deut 5:12, 15-16) and widely in the law Codes (Ex 23:15; Lev 24:23; Deut 19:11; etc.). The noun* miṣwāh *is one of the technical terms for the divine command (Ex 15:26; 16:28; 20:6; Lev 4:2, 13, 22, 27; Deut 6:1; 7:9; etc.).*

A wealth of terms convey the sense of "commandment" in Hebrew; they are largely synonymous, even if some exegetes seek to specify nuances for the various verbs and nouns. The most frequent terms are: *tôrāh* (instruction, norm), *ḥōq* (decree), *mišpāṭ* (decision, judgement), *ʿēdāh* or *ʿēdût* (attestation), in addition to *dābār* (word), a generic but important term which refers among other things to the "ten words" of the Decalogue (Ex 34:28; Deut 4:13; 10:4).

The command is expressed with the verbal form of the imperative, both in the positive form of the prescription ("remember", "observe", "do", "honour"), and above all in the negative form of the prohibition ("do not kill", "do not steal", "do not make an image"). In some cases the two forms are joined in a single precept, as in the command of the Sabbath: "For six days you will labour and do all your work, but the seventh day [...] you shall do no work" (Ex 20:9-10).

272. *The order given by the Lord in Gen 2:16-17 has formally a two-part structure; to the normative injunction, which expresses the divine will (Gen 2:16-17a), a "motivation" is added ("because ..." Gen 2:17b). The command itself is twofold, because the prohibition ("you must not eat") is preceded by a solemn positive invitation (ʾākōl tōʾkēl "you may / must eat"), expressed in a linguistic form used elsewhere for normative assertions (cf. Ex 21:28; Deut 6:17; 7:18; 1 Kgs 3:26; Prov 27:23); it follows from this that insofar as nourishment is concerned the human being is comprehensively subjected to obedience, both in abstaining from what is forbidden, and in eating what God offers. The motivation of the commandment in Gen 2:17b, which uses the formula of the verdict that imposes the death penalty (môt tāmût, "you shall die"), reveals the tragic consequences of the transgression. The threat of death constitutes a deterrent, and is therefore a help for human beings to obey; on the other hand, the consequence of "dying" makes it clear how transgression is directly opposed to the work of God who with his breath gives life to man (Gen 2:7).*

Different forms of "motivation" appear in the legal formulations of the Codes. Some provide the justification for the precept, illustrating its meaning in relation to some significant event in the history of salvation, such as when one is ordered to love the foreigner, because the Lord loved Israel when Israel was a foreigner in Egypt

(Deut 10:19). More often, the motivation brings out the negative consequences of disobedience, as in Gen 2:17b; a typical example is that of the prohibition on taking the name of the Lord in vain, "for the Lord will not acquit anyone who misuses his name" (Ex 20:7; Deut 5:11). In positive commands, the legislator highlights mainly the prospect of life and happiness that flows from obedience (Ex 20:12; Deut 5:16; 30:19-20). Most times, however, the command does not have a justification, and, when it is expressed, it does not develop an argument capable of showing the reasonableness of the prescript. Such a way of "commanding", therefore, seems to ask for great trust in the One who gives the orders.

273. *The command presents itself essentially as the expression of an "extraneous" will, as an external imposition. It is the voice of another demanding a certain action or laying down some limit. Even when the request has immediate positive aspects, when it presents itself as a call to live (Ezek 16:6), to enter into the possession of something good (Gen 12:1; Deut 1:21), to nourish oneself on exquisite food (Is 55:2), the simple fact that this imperative comes from outside is problematic for human beings: if, on the one hand, the command is perceived as an annoying interference, nevertheless, on the other hand, it offers an opportunity to the individual both to show intelligence in discerning the value of the command, and above all to trust the legislator. For God, the command is a "gift" (Deut 5:22; 9:20; 10:4; Neh 9:14), while for human beings it takes on mostly the aspect of a "test" (Gen 22:1; Ex 15:25; 16:4). In practice, the individual rarely grasps immediately the "goodness" of what is prescribed; a person demonstrates faith, therefore, by obeying while not fully understanding the good of what is being prescribed (Heb 11:17-19).*

274. The prohibition. *The command of Gen 2:16-17 focusses on food, the importance of which for human beings has already been illustrated in the second chapter of the Document. The goodness of nourishing oneself is particularly enhanced here by the divine command to eat of "all" the trees in the garden: what the Creator had done by planting every type of fruit tree (Gen 1:11-12; 2:8-9) is now shown to be an abundant and generous gift; but a limit is placed on* *the gift. God asks the human being to refrain from eating the fruit of one particular tree, situated next to the tree of life (Gen 2:9), but quite distinct from it. The prohibition is always a limitation placed on the desire to have everything, on that craving, once called concupiscence, that the human being feels as an innate drive for completeness. To consent to such a craving is the equivalent of ideally doing away with the reality of the donor; it eliminates God, therefore, but, at the same time, brings about the end of the human being, who lives only because he is a gift of God. Only by respecting the command, which forms a sort of barrier to the exclusive exercise of one's own will, does the human being recognise the Creator, whose reality is invisible, but whose presence is signalled in particular by the forbidden tree. It is forbidden not out of jealousy, but out of love, to save humanity from the folly of omnipotence.*

275. The knowledge of good and evil. *The command given to* 'ādām *appears arbitrary in itself. Its popular interpretation, which speaks of the apple as a forbidden fruit, makes the prescription appear even ridiculous. But, with his symbolic language of the tree, the fruit, and the eating, and with the significant concept, the knowledge of good and evil, the sacred author introduces a fundamental concept regarding the nature of human beings and their responsibility in history. What is forbidden to human beings? And why is this particular tree taboo for them? The tree of the knowledge of good and evil is the symbol of the origin of ethical and religious values, and therefore a sign of the reality of God as origin of the Law and regulator of the good. Deciding to take its fruit from the tree as an act of theft is equivalent to wanting to be like God (Gen 3:22); it means, in other words, that one intends to live by self-determination. The knowledge of good and evil can only be given by the one who is its source, by God who possesses it to communicate it to his children; human creatures receive knowledge through obedience, by which they affirm that God gives, and that his gift brings life.*

History. *Obedience and disobedience to the divine command, as we will see, are the factors that determine the profile of history. Israel will testify to this, in particular as it narrates its history as the people of the Lord.*

God's command at the beginning of the history of the people of Israel

276. The Pentateuch is the section of the Bible in which the relationship between human beings and the divine Law is structurally developed; the other sections of the Old Testament, as well as the New Testament writings, constantly refer to the Torah as a foundational and normative text (Mal 3:22; Ps 1:2; Sir 2:16; Mt 5:17-19).

Covenant and Law

As in Gen 2, so in the sweeping narrative that follows, the commandment comes after the gift and is joined to it: it is in fact the same original action of God that creates the relationship with the human being, from which rights and duties necessarily arise. In biblical literature this relationship is called "covenant" (*berît*), a legal institution that throughout the Ancient Near East served to regulate interpersonal relationships, and also relationships between groups and nations. This institution essentially involves three constituent elements: (1) the benevolent initiative of one of the two contracting parties who has superior authority and grants favours to the subordinate; (2) the regulation of the friendly relationship through legal dispositions; (3) the positive consequences, blessings, or negative consequences, curses, that will flow from faithfulness or betrayal. It can be said that the concept of "pact" lies at the foundation of the narrative and legislative framework of the Bible. Although particular nuances are found in the presentation of the different covenants, such as that with Noah in Gen 9:8-17, with Abraham in Gen 15 and 17, with the people of Israel in Ex 19–20 and 24, or that with David in 1 Sam 7 (cf. Ps 89:4), all of them will be characterised, in the first place, by a gratuitous divine gift, bestowed without any motivation other than the free decision of love of the Lord (Deut 4:37; 7:7-10; Ps 89:2-5), and, secondly, by a binding commitment from the two parties involved, both called to "maintain" the covenant bond, through a behaviour marked by fidelity in love (cf. Deut 7:7, 9,

12; Ps 89:29; Neh 9:32; and also Gen 17:9-10; Ex 19:5). Infidelity will bring with it tragic consequences (Lev 26:4-33; Deut 8:19-20; 11:16-17; 28:15-68; 29:18-27).

The pact is drawn up in specific temporal circumstances, but its authenticity is demonstrated concretely in the course of history. The biblical narrative therefore will reproduce the history of the covenant between God and humanity, between the Lord and his people Israel, a history conditioned by fidelity or infidelity to the duties that govern this relationship. Divine blessings and curses will be repeatedly remembered, and will testify to the permanent validity of the agreement which has been forged.

Narrative and Law

277. The narrative of the Torah, from the creation of the world to the death of Moses, witnesses first and foremost to the originating action of God, and as such introduces the very foundation of the Law put before humanity, pointing out why it is necessary and what it means. Responsibility arises from the gift. The commandment does not impose on humanity the obligation of some service to be offered to God, according to the principle of reciprocity (*do ut des*); this would be incompatible with the purity of love shown by the Father (Deut 32:6). Rather fidelity to the gift is required of the child, and this consists in keeping it. The gift must be recognised, welcomed and lived, and it is actually in this that the observance of the commandment consists.

The gift of the Law

The Law does not present itself therefore in Israel as a tiresome burden imposed by kings on their subjects with the aim of protecting their own rights (cf. 1 Sam 8:11-17); on the contrary, God reveals his will by showing it to be the way of life and of happiness, available to anyone who wants to follow it (Deut 5:32-33; 6:1-3, 17-19; 11:8-9; etc.).

Even if he affirms explicitly that the norms are achievable or perhaps easy (cf. Deut 30:11-14), the legislator, aware of their importance, enhances the commandment with a promise of life and blessedness (Lev 26:3-13; Deut 4:1, 40; 28:1-14; 32:47), in order to encourage obedience, and he also adds ominous threats of misfortune in order to ward off the temptation of transgression (Lev 26:14-38; Deut 28:15-68). The divine act of communicating the Law is seen then as a means of educating humanity, as a process of instruction that creates a just society and fosters universal happiness.

The forms of the Law

278. Every commandment given by the Lord to Israel expresses a concrete form of action for good. There are, however, precepts of greater importance, because they concern fundamental aspects of the relationship with God and with one's neighbour; other precepts seem more limited, however, either because they relate to secondary issues, or because they are addressed to limited categories of people, as in the case of liturgical rubrics. Exegetes have attributed greater importance to the so-called "apodictic laws", which are expressed as absolute prohibitions, which have no justifying motivation due to their intrinsic importance, and which are without exceptions, as in the Decalogue: "You shall have no other gods", "You shall not murder", "You shall not steal", etc. Other norms have the "casuistic" form, and so present themselves with different directives according to the circumstances and the subjects involved, as in the case of an ox that injures a person (Ex 21:28-32); a closer look reveals, however, that there is no deviation from the norm, but guidance for a correct interpretation of the command, in this case, not to kill.

The distinction between laws of a religious and ethical nature and prescriptions of a symbolic type seems more significant. The former have a perennial and universal validity, they do not undergo changes over time, and can be insisted upon for every person on the face of the earth: the adoration of God, respect for life, for the property of others, for the truth. Other rules, which are very useful for giving identity to a people, are by contrast only a provisional way of expressing a certain value; they can be modified, therefore, according to suitability and efficacy in society. Precepts such as circumcision, the observance of the Sabbath, rules relating to purity, norms on pure or impure foods, and so on, certainly contain praiseworthy aspects, but may undergo variations in application or even be abolished, if new measures of a symbolic order are considered to be more suitable for expressing adherence to the Lord and love for one's brothers and sisters.

In Scripture we see that God sometimes requires obedience to a single commandment, such as when he imposed the practice of circumcision on Abraham (Gen 17:9-14), or when he ordered the sacrifice of Isaac (Gen 22:1-2). The biblical tradition, however, provides the believer with the precepts of the Lord in organic form, through collections that allow one to take on all the requirements of the covenant. This seems to be inspired by the structure of the treaties that were made between rulers in the Ancient Near East. We have, for example, the form of the "*Decalogue*"; the most famous (Ex 20:1-17; Dt 5:6-22) is that pronounced and delivered by the Lord at Sinai (Dt 4:13; 5:22), generally seen as the synthesis of the will of God for Israel, for it forbids not only evil deeds, but also words and desires contrary to the good. Other forms with ten or twelve commands (cf. Ex 34:12-26; Lev 20:9-21) gather together norms regarding a specific sector of religious or moral life.

A somewhat systematic arrangement governs the legislative collections contained in the three main Torah *Codes*. The so-called "Covenant Code" (Ex 20:22–23:33), which seems to be the oldest collection of norms, concerns various aspects of a cultic, moral and civil nature. The "Deuteronomic Code" (Deut 12–26) is much longer and more elaborate, and, in addition to offering a broad prospectus of legal material, it includes, in keeping with the pedagogical approach of the book, paraenetic elements, to encourage a more authentic obedience; primary elements of originality are, on the one hand, the prescription of the unity of the place of worship, as a sign of adhesion to the one Lord (Dt 12:2-28); and, on the other hand, a series of measures favourable to those in need, such as widows, orphans, Levites, and immigrants. The "Holiness Code" (Lev 17–26), so called because of its repeated invitation to holiness, contains norms inspired by priestly spirituality, where purity and cultic devotion receive particular emphasis. Some laws supplement or correct previous regulations, due to changed social and economic conditions, or because of a more developed understanding of the good, as will appear in the section on the prophets.

The multiplicity of precepts and the unity of the Law

279. The Hebrew interpretative tradition, with the precision that characterises it, recognised in the Torah 613 precepts issued by the Lord. This figure was often considered particularly onerous, without perhaps considering that in modern life the citizen is subjected to an infinitely greater number of laws, and the Christian has to follow canonical norms and liturgical rubrics that are much more numerous. The complexity of life requires in fact a multiplicity of commandments, through which is expressed the variety of cases, circumstances and situations which must all be orientated towards justice. If rightly understood, even the minor precepts, such as taking birds from the nest but letting the mother go (Deut 22:6-7), symbolically indicate to the believer how to make a good decision which is supportive of life in the reality of everyday situations.

On the other hand, Scripture itself, especially in the Torah, but also in its other sections, helps the reader to focus attention on what is essential in the meticulous observance of the individual commandments. Deuteronomy, in particular, insists on the fact that there is, in reality, only one commandment, namely, to adhere with total fidelity to the Lord. This is expressed in two literary forms of equal value.

(i) The first is composed of a verb with relational meaning and which has the Lord as its object; the best known expression is found in Deut 6:5: "You shall love the Lord, your God, with all your heart, with all your soul, with all your strength" (see also Deut 10:12, 15; 11:13, 15, 22; 13:4; etc.). To replace or complement the verb "to love", we can find synonyms, such as "to serve", that is to humble oneself (Ex 23:25; Deut 6:13; 10:12,20; 11:13; etc.), "to fear", that is, to respect and to revere (Lev 19:14, 32; 25:17, 36, 43; Deut 5:29; 6:2, 13, 24; 10:12, 20; etc.), "to hold fast to" (Deut 10:20; 11:12; 13:5; 30:20), and the like. One can thus recognise that God asks people to take on the attitude of the "child" towards the Father (Mal 3:17-18).

(ii) The second way of unifying the Law consists of a verb that expresses the act of obedience, such as to listen, to observe, to keep, to remember, to practise, to do, etc., and which has as its object one of the many terms denoting laws: command, precept, norm, statute, prescription, word of God, etc. We read in Deut 4:1-2:

> "And now, Israel, listen to the laws and customs that I am teaching you, so that, by observing them, you may survive to enter and take possession of the land which the Lord, God of your ancestors, is giving you. You must add nothing to what I command you, and take nothing from it, but keep the commandments of the Lord our God just as I lay them down for you."
>
> (cf. also Deut 4:5-6, 14; 5:1, 32-33; 6:1-3; etc.)

This type of commandment is not comparable to the precepts that prescribe or prohibit a specific act; what is implicit in every law is made explicit here, namely, that the fundamental act desired by God is that of obedience. The whole life of the believer is thus interpreted as assuming the condition of the "servant", willing in everything to do the will of the Lord.

Finally, we should remember that, especially in the prophetic literature, a single commandment can be seen as able to express symbolically the whole meaning of the Law, so much so that on its observance or non-observance depends the entire fidelity to the covenant. In the case of Amos, for example, the pursuit of what is good lies in re-establishing justice in the courts (Am 5:15) and not in pilgrimages to the sanctuary (Am 5:5), even with abundant ritual offerings (Am 4:4-5; 5:21-25). After the exile, however, it is the care of the temple that represents a fundamental duty for the community. For Haggai the divine blessing is connected with the decision to rebuild the house of the Lord (Hag 1:3-11). For Jeremiah, the salvation of Jerusalem, besieged by the Babylonian army, is bound up with the release of the Hebrew slaves (Jer 34:8-22). And finally, at the time of the Maccabees, the legislation relating to clean foods came to assume a decisive value, so that Israel's martyr is the one who dies because he refuses to eat pork (2 Macc 7). Hence, even a ritual precept can express, in certain circumstances, full adherence to the will of God and faithfulness to the covenant.

Hierarchy in the commandments and their purpose

280. All the individual precepts are to be observed; however, the gradation in punitive sanctions for transgression, from the death penalty to a simple monetary fine, shows the different value of one norm compared to another. In the legislation of the Old Testament, and more generally in all biblical literature, the greatest importance is given to the honour to be attributed to God, because the obedient adherence to all other duties depends on respect for the divine law and for God's will. Among the areas that define interpersonal relationships, primary value is given to the protection of life; the family, too, is considered a fundamental good, and for its protection strict rules on sexual matters are prescribed. The obligations of justice towards the vulnerable are set out extensively, but there is no system of sanctions in case of non-fulfilment. A proper exercise of justice in court is certainly demanded from the judges (Ex 23:1-2,6; Deut 1:17; 16:19-20), but we do not find rules that can guarantee in general the protection of the weak. This activity thus appears as a horizon of justice offered to the generous commitment of the believer, whom God will appraise for blessing or curse (cf. Ex 22:25-26; Deut 24:10-15; Mt 25:31-46).

One can deduce from the very presentation of the Law of Israel the purpose of *educating* consciences so that, from the knowledge of the good, the believer is led to decide freely to implement justice, motivated more by love than by fear of punishment.

"Look, today I am offering you life and prosperity, death and disaster. If you obey the commandments of the Lord your God, which I am laying down for you today, if you love the Lord your God and follow his ways, if you keep his commandments, his laws and his customs, you will live and grow numerous, and the Lord your God will bless you in the land which you are entering and make your own. [...]. Choose life, then, so that you and your descendants may live, in the love of the Lord your God, obeying his voice, holding fast to him; for in this your life consists, and on this depends the length of time that you stay

in the land which the Lord swore to your ancestors Abraham,
Isaac and Jacob that he would give them."

(Deut 30:15-16, 19-20)

God himself is seen as the protagonist in this work of the formation
of minds, both with the wisdom of the norms and with the assertion
of his activity of control, evaluation and sanction of human actions.
Blessings and curses, realised in historical time, also become
instruments of wisdom to inculcate in human hearts devotion to the
true good. To encourage the remembrance and the exact knowledge
of the Law, the biblical tradition also indicates how it was written
down: the commandments of the Decalogue are engraved on stone
(Ex 24:12; 34:1, 4; Deut 4:13; 5:22; 9:9-11; 10:1, 3), underlining their
eternal validity; the Israelite is required to write down the precepts
so that they can be tied to the hand and placed on the doorposts
(Deut 6:8-9); the king is asked to rewrite the Law and to read it
every day in order to administer justice properly (Deut 17:18-19).
But only when the Law is inscribed by the Lord in the hearts of all,
from the smallest to the greatest (Jer 31:33-34), only then will the
work of God have fully achieved its intention.

The Law in the wisdom traditions

281. The world of Israel's sages holds in the highest regard the
Law of the Lord, which is an "incorruptible light" for the world
(Wis 18:4); parents and teachers together promote moral and
religious teaching clearly inspired by the revelation of the God
of Israel (Prov 2:1-6; 3:11; Sir 17:9-12; 24:23-27; cf. Bar 4:1-4). In
the texts of "traditional" wisdom (Proverbs, Sirach, Wisdom),
we find many exhortations that follow those of Moses in the
Torah; the values proposed are rooted in the Decalogue and more
generally in the biblical rules, which are imbued with wisdom
and transmitted from generation to generation. The "just" person
(ṣaddîq) is identified with the one who is religious, "who fears the
Lord" (yᵉrē' 'ădōnay), and with the one who is "wise" (ḥākām)
(Prov 1:1-7; 28:4-5; Sir 15:1; 19:20; 24:10-12; Wis 6:1-4; 9:9-17).

"My child, if you take my words to heart,
if you set store by my commandments,
tuning your ear to wisdom,
opening your heart to understanding [...],
then you will understand what is the fear of the Lord,
and discover the knowledge of God [...].
Then you will understand righteousness, equity and fair
    dealing,
the paths that lead to happiness."

(Prov 2:1-2, 5, 9)

The specific contribution of the wisdom literature is to encourage the practice of the Law (Sir 15:1-6; 19:20) through the testimony of parents (Prov 1:8; Sir 2:1), who encourage love for the commandments (cf. Prov 31:2; Sir 3:1); moreover, the acuteness of the sayings and parables, the very expressive metaphors together with the incisiveness of the aphorisms, contribute to encouraging the acceptance of the Torah and to forming people in the discipline of obedient listening, because "an attentive ear is the sage's dream" (Sir 3:29). Frequently the sage does not present teaching in the form of an explicit command; but every word is offered to the disciple with the intention of eliciting a good decision (Sir 15:15-20); the good suggested is in itself an invitation and a necessity, a driving force to choose justice and life.

282. To this traditional wisdom teaching the critical contribution of the books of Job and Qohelet must be added. In the book of *Job*, the human claim and even God's explicit promise of just "retribution" are contested; in other words, the consequential link between acting justly and the deserved fruit of such behaviour in life and well-being is radically denied (Job 9:22). We know that the protagonist of the story is presented as just and irreproachable (Job 1:1, 8; 2:3), and he himself will not cease to declare his innocence to his friends who question it (Job 6:29-30; 13:23; 23:10-12; 27:5-6; 29:14-17; 31:1-40); yet unspeakable misfortunes and sufferings fall upon him. Job's complaint, his request for an explanation from God, is a criticism of those who claim to judge automatically every event in history, and, more generally, it represents a questioning of the way one understands the divine promise which results from obedience to the commandments. God himself will not condemn Job's words at all (Job 42:8), even if they were spoken with a little presumption (Job 38:2; 40:2, 8); his grievances, steeped in pain, should not be read then as the protest of a rebel, but as a necessary question to the Lord who knows the ways of wisdom (Job 28:23-28).

The book of *Qoheleth* reiterates in its own way the questioning of the book of Job: the just and the unjust, the wise and the foolish do not in fact seem to have a different fate in life, and all are indiscriminately condemned to an existence without satisfaction, which will inevitably end with death (Qoh 2:15-16). On the other hand, if there is no one so righteous to do only good without ever sinning (Qoh 7:20), what is the meaning of the retributive system?

For this reason, perhaps, the wise "king in Jerusalem" (Qoh 1:1), opposed to any excess, introduces moderation even in the exercise of justice, which he understands as moral perfectionism pursued with the scrupulous fulfilling of so many external practices; and he criticises, too, the pretensions of wisdom obtained with so much effort and study (Qoh 1:18; 2:11), without his teaching giving rise to wickedness and foolishness as alternatives:

> "Do not be righteous to excess
> and do not make yourself unduly wise:
> why should you destroy yourself?
> Do not be wicked to excess
> and do not be a fool:
> why die before your time?"

(Qoh 7:16-17)

We are urged then by this master of wisdom not to promise success to those who commit themselves to virtuous conduct, nor to establish a close correlation between good fortune and virtue; the wicked do indeed prosper (Qoh 3:16; 4:1; 5:7; cf. also Jer 12:1-2; Ps 73:2-12; Job 21:7-33). However, with his insistence on the "fear of God", understood as an attitude of humble appreciation of the wisdom and greatness of God (Qoh 3:14; 5:6; 7:18; 8:12-13), Qoheleth invites us to welcome the joys of life as a free gift from God, without considering them a reward for good conduct. This of course applies to what is visible "under the sun". The commandment is certainly a bringer of life, but it is necessary to understand precisely what kind of life it is. It is the book of Wisdom which, without denying the concrete good that flows from virtue, opens up to a vision beyond this world, a sure reward for the righteous (Wis 3:1-9; 5:15-16).

The commandments of the Lord as prayer in the Psalter

283. The Psalter presents itself as if it were a Torah, being divided into five books like the Pentateuch; for this reason, it very frequently leads the person praying to appreciate, eulogise and praise (Ps 56:5, 11) the Law of God, seen always as a precious good and an inexhaustible treasure. It is sufficient in this regard to refer to three psalms (Ps 1; 19; 119), which, as if in a crescendo, celebrate the Torah, and place on the lips of the believer full adherence to the will of God (Ps 40:8-9).

Psalm 1

Introducing the entire collection of prayers, Ps 1 announces the blessedness and fruitfulness of the "just" one who meditates day and night on the Law of the Lord, because of the delight he finds in it (vv. 1-2). The "way" of the just one is opposite to that of the "wicked" and the "sinner" (vv. 1, 6), both as regards conduct, and as a result of what follows: fidelity to the Torah in fact brings with it lasting vitality and success (vv. 3, 6), while those who travel on a different road will be blown away like chaff in the wind (vv. 4-6). The psalmist, then, does not receive a simple instruction in the form of a programme for life, but, in the very act of pronouncing the words of the psalm, the person praying consecrates the truth of the Law and its power of blessing.

Psalm 19

284. This is exactly the case also with Ps 19, where the person reciting it concludes the canticle by offering to God the words of his mouth to be accepted as a sacrifice (v. 15); the praise of the Law is interpreted, therefore, as a hymn to God and a thanksgiving for his gift:

> "The law (*tôrāh*) of the Lord is perfect;
> it revives the soul.
> The decrees (*'ēdût*) of the Lord are steadfast;
> they give wisdom to the simple.
> The precepts (*piqqûdîm*) of the Lord are right;
> they gladden the heart.
> The command (*miṣwāh*) of the Lord is clear;
> it gives light to the eyes.
> The fear of the Lord (*yir'at 'ădōnay*) is pure,
> abiding for ever.
> The judgements (*mišpāṭîm*) of the Lord are true;
> they are, all of them, righteous.
> They are more to be desired than gold,
> than quantities of gold.
> And sweeter are they than honey,
> than honey flowing from the comb.
> So in them your servant finds instruction;
> great reward is in their keeping."
>
> (Ps 19:8-12)

While eulogising the precepts of the Lord, the psalmist at the same time savours them, almost tasting the sweetness of honey, and assimilates them, experiencing refreshment (v. 8a) and joy (v. 9a). The "profit" derived from them (v. 12b) is that of being enlightened (vv. 9b, 12), made wise (v. 8b), because of the clear truth of the Lord's commandments (vv. 9-10).

And as always happens in contemplating the mystery of God, prayer is added to praise for the good received (vv.13-14). In particular, the psalmist seeks pardon for hidden sins, not yet revealed to the believer's heart, and above all invokes from God freedom from pride, a serious sin (v. 14), especially for those who expect to take advantage of their adhesion to the commandments of the Law.

The first part of Ps 19, at first sight very different in content, evokes the celestial world (v. 2), and in particular the daily cycle of the sun (vv. 6-7); this establishes a sort of parallel or better, a symphonic accord, between the praise that occurs in the firmament and that of the person praying on earth. There is a cosmic revelation, which everyone can access, a kind of silent word that "narrates" the glory of the Creator (vv. 2-5); the psalmist is able to listen to it and make it heard for every creature, even for those who have not had the gift of the Law that Israel received (Ps 147:20). The task of the stars to transmit the knowledge of God (Ps 19:3) is taken up by the psalmist being illuminated by the contemplation of the Torah, brighter and more life-giving than the sun.

Psalm 119

285. It is in Ps 119 that the Psalter expresses the most complete celebration of the Torah of God, with an elaborate literary composition that intends to symbolise totality, through the use of the acrostic, so that every letter of the alphabet introduces not a verse (as in Ps 25; 34; 37; 111; 112; 145), but an "octave", in which the Law is proclaimed and exalted for its priceless value (Ps 119:14, 72, 99-100, 127). In each single stanza of eight verses and for the twenty-two letters of the Hebrew alphabet, the various terms that define the Law are mentioned, verse after verse (cf. Ps 19:8-10, cited above), so as to display the wonderful aspects of the Word of God and the various attitudes that the person praying shows towards the divine will.

> The term *tôrāh* (instruction) is attested twenty-five times and is the first to be used (Ps 119:1); and, as appears already from the first verse, it is associated successively with various synonyms: *'ēdāh* (testimony), *derek* (way, conduct), *piqqûdîm* (dispositions), *ḥōq* (decree), *miṣwāh* (command), *mišpāṭ* (judgement), in addition to *dābār* and *'imrāh* (word) (Ps 119:9, 11). Nouns are used sometimes

in the singular to suggest that the will of the Lord is one; they appear more frequently in the plural, to recall the complex multiplicity of the commandments that regulate the life of the believer.

This repetitive literary arrangement aims to make it clear that there is no other reality to meditate upon than the Word of God given as Torah to Israel. The author of Psalm 119, however, has introduced continuous variations on the theme, which point to the luminous facets of the Law and are useful for savouring and assimilating the fruits of life that derive from it: this occurs through verbs that describe the attitudes of the person praying with regard to the Torah as "to walk" (vv. 1, 3), "to keep" (vv. 4-5, 9), "to learn" (vv. 7, 33-34, 73), "to recount" (v. 13), "to ponder" (v. 15), "to remember" (vv. 16, 52, 55), "to long for" (vv. 20, 40), "to taste" (vv. 66, 103), "to rejoice" (vv. 14, 16), and, ten times in all, "to love" (vv. 47, 48, 97, 113, 119, 127, 140, 159, 163, 167). The various feelings of the soul are subjected to the will of God, so that the whole person (vv. 2, 34), at all times (vv. 20, 44, 97), has no other focus than the Lord and his commandments, in supplication (vv. 5, 12, 22, 25) and in praise (vv. 7, 62, 89), as a renewed commitment of fidelity (vv. 8, 11, 30-32) and as confident trust in the action of the Lord (vv. 42-43, 49, 74).

Compared to Ps 1, where the "way" of the righteous ran in the opposite direction to that of the wicked, in Ps 119 the two roads intersect and collide. The person praying invokes not only salvation (vv. 117, 121-122) in the face of the violence of the wicked, but, while expressing sadness (vv. 28, 143), boldly proclaims that joy is present at the very moment of adhering to the commandments of the Lord:

"Your statutes have become my song
wherever I dwell" (Ps 119:54).
"Had your law not been my delight,
I would have died in my affliction."

(Ps 119:92)

The Psalter's insistent appeal to be instructed and guided by the Lord (cf. Ps 25:4-5, 9; 86:11; 94:12; 143:10) is most strongly expressed in our psalm (Ps 119:12, 26, 64, 66, 68, 99, 108, 124, 135, 171). The Word of God, especially in its aspect of revealing their duty to human beings, requires a continuous meditative reflection, but it is the Lord himself who illuminates, showing clearly which is the path to follow. It is in this sense that we can speak of the "interiorisation" of the Law in the human heart.

The prophets, proclaimers and interpreters of the Torah

286. The voice of God heard at Sinai, transmitted and codified by Moses, continues to be heard in the history of Israel, through the word of the prophets, who, like Moses (Deut 18:15), are witnesses of the Lord's faithfulness to the covenant and to the commandments that make it effective. There is a significant inclusion between the first page of the prophetic collection, where we have the invitation to "give ear to the Torah of our God" (Is 1:10), and one of the last verses of the same collection, where we read: "Remember the Torah of my servant Moses to whom at Horeb I prescribed decrees and rulings for all Israel" (Mal 3:22). The prophets, in fact, have the task of calling the people to observe what God has prescribed as a condition of the covenant (Mic 6:8); and, following the example adopted by the promulgator of the Sinaitic Law, they accompany their urgent injunctions with threats and promises, so as to encourage obedience. In some cases we note that a rather explicit reference is made to the Decalogue (Jer 7:1-15; Ezek 18:5-18; Hos 4:1-3); more generally, the duty of adhering exclusively to the Lord is invoked, against every form of syncretism and idolatry (1 Kgs 18:18, 21; Is 1:2-4; Jer 2:11-13), together with the need to do justice towards the poor and disadvantaged (Is 1:17; 3:14-15; Jer 5:28; Mal 3:5).

The mission of the prophets is not limited, however, to recalling what God had commanded, because they have to deal with rebellious and obstinate people (Is 1:2-4; 6:9-10; 30:9; Jer 5:1-

5,21; Ezek 2:3-5), and their task is to call them to change their lives (Is 1:16-17; Am 5:14-15), convincing those who have abandoned the Lord to return to him with true repentance (Jer 2:19; 3:10,12-13; Ezek 3:16-21); their purpose is to renew reverence for the Lord who was despised (Is 1:4; Jer 3:22-25; Hos 2:9) and thus disobeyed. Here, then, the prophetic word is clothed with precious literary qualities, not for an aesthetic purpose, but to make the truth shine through poetry and rhetoric, with linguistic devices designed to touch the heart and persuade. With the wisdom given them by the Lord, the prophets thus make the value of faithfulness to God more understandable, through the use of metaphors, parables and ironic reasoning. Isaiah composes the "love song" for the vineyard, in order to denounce the oppression of the poor (Is 5:1-7); Jeremiah, with evocative images, shows the gravity of the foolishness of Israel who traded the glory of its God for a useless idol (Jer 2:11), and abandoned the well of living water to dig worthless cisterns (Jer 2:13); Hosea and Ezekiel make use of the marriage metaphor to show how shameful the betrayal is (Hos 2:4-15; Ezek 16:1-43), and Amos intones the funeral lament over the prosperous city of Samaria (Am 5:1-3). Examples could easily be multiplied. In short, while recalling the ancient precept, the prophetic word is replete with new elements not of style but of content; not only does it recall the past, but it takes forward the listeners' knowledge of God with an enlightening word, which shows how the divine Torah continually arises to brighten the darkness of the heart (Is 2:3,5; 42:6-7; 58:8; Hos 6:5; Mic 7:9; Zeph 3:5). Here too we see at work the desire to make the command of the Lord reach the depths of people's hearts.

287. Furthermore, inspired by God, these prophets help people understand the meaning of the Law, ranking the precepts correctly, so that people can discover, in the face of unwarranted falsifications, what the will of God really is (Jer 8:8-9). One of the most frequently occurring motifs in this regard concerns the rejection of sacrifices, which, although prescribed by the Lord, are prone to mask injustice. Samuel condemned Saul's decision to offer burnt offerings, because he had disobeyed the Lord's command regarding the booty:

"Is the Lord pleased by burnt offerings and sacrifices
or by obedience to the Lord's voice?
Truly, obedience is better than sacrifice,
submissiveness better than the fat of rams.
Rebellion is a sin of sorcery,
presumption a crime of idolatry!"

(1 Sam 15:22-23)

Worship is characterised as idolatry, if it does not conform to what God wants. Similar assertions are taken up by the prophets: almost identically in Hos 6:6, and with various expressions and different motivations in almost all the prophets (Is 1:11-15; 43:22-24; 58:3-5; Jer 6:20; 7:21-22; 14:12; Am 4:4-5; 5:21-23; Mic 6:6-7; Zech 7:4-6). This constitutes a severe warning to reflect on the intolerable duplicity of conscience in those who take pleasure in devout practices but neglect the duty of justice.

And finally, the prophets intervene in history to teach the discernment of God's will in some particular circumstances, which require an interpretation of events according to the thought of God, and not that of humans, with decisions that cannot rely on codified norms. In this case they call for obedience to their directives on the basis of what the Lord has revealed to them. It is Isaiah who tells Ahaz what to do when the army of the enemy coalition is marching on Jerusalem to overthrow the royal line (Is 7:1-9); it is Jeremiah who reveals to Zedekiah his duty to surrender to the king of Babylon in order to save his life (Jer 38:14-23), and it is he, too, who makes known to the deportees the surprising will of the Lord regarding a long exile, demanding among other things that they "seek the welfare of the city" of Babylon (Jer 29:4-7).

Without the prophets we would therefore not have a full understanding of the divine precepts, nor would we know how to interpret them adequately; and we would not be aware what God's will might be when explicit commandments are lacking.

Jesus and the commandments of God

288. Jesus was recognised as a prophet (Mt 21:11, 46; Lk 7:16; 24:19; Jn 4:19; 6:14; 7:40; 9:17). Similar to Moses and prophesied by him as the fulfilment of revelation (Lk 24:44; Jn 1:45; Acts 3:2-23), he makes known the will of the Father as only the Son can (Mt 11:27; Jn 5:20; 8:28; 12:49-50; 14:24; 15:15; 17:6-8). He did not come to abolish the Law of the Lord or the message of the prophets (Mt 5:17; 7:12), for his mission consists rather in bringing everyone, not only the children of Abraham, to obey fully the will of the one God. Continuing the line of the prophets, from Samuel to John the Baptist (Lk 16:16; Acts 3:24), he cannot but reiterate the value of the commandments, even the least of them (Mt 5:19), so that, understanding and loving even the smallest letter or the simple stroke of the commandment, people become great in the Kingdom of Heaven (Mt 5:18-19). For what counts is the great love that is shown in humble observance of even a minor rule.

Jesus, like the ancient prophets, taught the "observance" of the Law, not in words, by saying "Lord, Lord", but by putting the words of the Lord into practice (Mt 7:21-27; 21:28-31; cf. 1 Jn 3:18). Unlike the scribes and Pharisees, who teach the rules, imposing on others heavy burdens, while they do not practise what they teach (Mt 23:2-4; Jn 7:19), the Master lives a life of total obedience to the will of God, because he loves the Father (Jn 14:31); he is the "just one" (Mt 27:19; Lk 23:47; Acts 3:14; 7:52; 22:14; 1 Pet 3:18; 1 Jn 2:1, 29), who is willing to die to fulfil God's will (Mt 26:39; Jn 4:34; 5:30; 6:38; 18:11; Rom 5:19; Phil 2:8; Heb 5:8). He knew how to identify in the precept of love for God, combined with love of neighbour, the synthesis of all the Torah and of all the prophets (Mt 22:40); and since it is the way of love, his yoke is easy, and the burden laid on the disciples is light (Mt 11:30).

289. Jesus was fully faithful to his prophetic charism also in knowing how to point to the true meaning of God's commandments, countering the interpretative deviations that had distorted the clarity of the divine prescriptions. He asserted, therefore, that it was not enough to follow what was said "to the ancestors", who, perhaps to satisfy their disciples, or perhaps simply because they did not have the Spirit of the Son of God, had favoured an accommodating and imperfect reading of the commandments; the Lord proclaims with messianic authority: "But I say this to you ..." (Mt 5:22, 28, 32, 34, 39, 44), and reveals that high demand for love, which makes the disciple similar to the heavenly Father (Mt 5:48). By asking people to love as he loves the Father, he intends to call for a perfect observance of his commandments (Jn 14:15, 21; 15:10; cf. 1 Jn 2:3-6; 5:2-3; 2 Jn 6), understanding them, however, in a perceptive way. This is how one explains his "non-traditional" reading of the Law (Mk 7:5, 8): the Sabbath is made for man, and not man for the Sabbath (Mk 2:27), and that day is "sanctified" when experienced as an opportunity of salvation for the enslaved (Mk 3:4); the temple of Jerusalem will be destroyed (Jn 2:19; cf. Jn 4:21-24), because it has ceased to be a house of prayer and has become a marketplace (Jn 2:16), or rather a den of thieves (Mk 11:17); the rules on clean and unclean foods are only intended to remind the faithful of the call to "holiness" that flows from a pure heart (Mk 7:14-23); the sacred offering to God is reprehensible when made for the perverse purpose of not helping one's parents (Mk 7:9-13; Mt 15:3-6); the almsgiving loved by the Lord is that which renounces all earthly approval (Mt 6:1-4), and the fasting desired by God, carried out with a joyful face (Mt 6:16-18), is to be practised only when the bridegroom is absent (Mk 2:19).

290. This last comment leads us to another aspect of the prophetic revelation of the Lord Jesus, which provides the light to be able to discern "the signs of the times", recognising what the will of God is at a given moment in history (Mk 13:18; Lk 12:54-59). Jesus said to the Pharisees and Sadducees:

"In the evening you say, 'It will be fine; there's a red sky', and in the morning, 'Stormy weather today; the sky is red and overcast'. You know how to read the face of the sky; can you not read the signs of the times?"

(Mt 16:2-3)

The light for this act of discernment comes from the one who is the true light (Lk 2:32; Jn 1:4-5, 9; 3:19-21; 8:12; 9:5; 12:46), able to give more light than the precepts of the Torah, because Jesus is the Master who makes his disciples the "light of the world" (Mt 5:14; Jn 8:12; 12:36). In fact, as happened with Moses and the elders of Israel (Num 11:16-17, 25-29), and as Elijah did when taking leave of Elisha (2 Kgs 2:9-15), Christ gave the Spirit to his disciples so that they could not only do God's will out of love and with perfection, but that they would also be able to go into the world as prophets and teachers (Mt 21:34) showing the way of love and transmitting the same Spirit with which they are filled.

Paul and the Law

291. The Christian Church, formed by the preaching of the apostles and by the gift of the Spirit, stands out in the social landscape of the time because of its strong ethical and religious character. What the various communities scattered throughout the world of that time have in common is their acknowledgement of the gift of salvation brought by the redemptive Passion of Christ, which, by regenerating believers, enables them to behave in a new way (Rom 6:19; Eph 4:17-32; cf. also Eph 5:1-20; Col 1:21-23; 3:1-10; 1 Pet 1:14-16; 4:1-6), that of "new creatures", who leave behind forever sinful vices and practices in order to conform to the will of God, expressed by his precepts of holiness (2 Cor 5:17; Gal 6:15; Eph 2:15; 4:24).

Such a picture is envisaged in the apostolic preaching narrated in the Acts of the Apostles (Acts 2:37-41; 3:19, 25-26; 5:31; 8:18; etc.), as well as in the laudatory and paraenetic sections of the letters of the apostles. The incessant exhortations found in these texts make it clear, however, that "conversion" is a process to be activated repeatedly as the spiritual dynamism of the Christian communities. The letters that John sends to the seven churches (Apoc 1:4) contain praise for faith and perseverance in trials, but also reproaches of various kinds (Apoc 2:1–3:22), with a repeated invitation to a change of life, a sign that the gospel ideal had to be continually re-proposed to the attention and practice of believers. We read, for example, in the warning to the angel of the church of Sardis:

"I know about your behaviour, how you are reputed to be alive and yet are dead. Wake up; strengthen what remains; it is near death. So far I have failed to find any of your works perfect in the sight of God; remember how you received and listened to the message. Hold on to that. Repent! If you do not wake up, I shall come to you like a thief, and you will have no idea at what hour I shall come upon you."

(Apoc 3:1-3)

292. Something similar is also found in the apostolic letters, as if it were necessary always to put before the eyes of Christians the prescriptive instructions given by God and by Christ to reach life. In these letters only rarely are there explicit references to the law of Moses as the norm to follow (Rom 10:5; 1 Cor 9:9; cf. Jam 2:8-11; 4:11), probably because this could have given rise to a judaizing interpretation of the Torah; however, the fundamental precepts of the Decalogue and the appeal to love of God and of one's brothers and sisters represent the essential context of all Christian preaching.

Obedience to God and to his commandments is recommended also by Paul, who insistently calls for the practice of what is good (Rom 6:16; Eph 4:20-24), and in particular encourages "love", which is the "fulness of the Law" (Rom 13:8, 10; 1 Cor 13:4-7). None of his injunctions would make sense, if the duty to submit to God's will in all aspects of one's existence were not valid and permanent (Col 4:12); and this not with a servile attitude, but as a realisation of being children of God (Gal 3:26; 4:6-7), loving and grateful, in imitation of Christ (Rom 5:19; Phil 2:5). A very significant text in this regard is Rom 8:14-17:

"All who are guided by the Spirit of God are children of God; for you did not receive a spirit of slavery to bring you back into fear, you received the Spirit of adoption (*pneuma hyiothesias*). Whenever we cry out, '*Abba*, Father!', that very Spirit is joining with our spirit to bear witness that we are children of God. And if we are children, then we are heirs, heirs of God and joint heirs with Christ, provided that we share his suffering, so as to share his glory".

293. Certain statements of Paul on the Law are well known, and are often interpreted as if he had adopted an attitude of opposition in its regard. This interpretation relativises and even forgets the fact that the Apostle himself not only declares explicitly that "the Law is holy", but also that the precept in which the law finds its concrete expression is "holy and righteous and good" (Rom 7:12). Moreover, immediately after having enunciated the doctrine of justification by faith without the works of the Law (Rom 3:28), Paul asks himself whether, by presenting faith as the origin and exclusive means of justification, the Law is not deprived of all its value, and he responds emphatically: "Out of the question! We are setting up the Law" (Rom 3:31).

In this document we can only make some considerations of a general nature in order to clarify matters to some extent, and, first of all, in relation to the term "law" (*nomos*).

The use that Paul makes of *nomos* is by no means univocal. It is used, in fact, for disparate realities, and this can lead to interpretative misunderstandings. In certain cases the noun signifies the Pentateuch (Rom 3:21) or even the whole of the Old Testament (1 Cor 14:21); in other cases it refers more specifically to the legal prescriptions of Moses (Rom 2:12; 4:13; 1 Cor 9:8-9, 20), while sometimes it alludes to the duty that a person perceives in conscience (Rom 2:14-15; 7:23). The meaning is different again, of course, in expressions such as "the law of Christ" (Gal 6:2), "the law of faith" (Rom 3:27), "the law of righteousness" (Rom 9:31), and "the law of sin and death" (Rom 8:2; cf. 7:25) in opposition to "the law of the Spirit of life" (Rom 8:2).

Despite the complexity of the terminology, the texts in which the term *nomos* refers to the Mosaic Law in the letters of Paul stand out in terms of number and importance of content. Among them, in particular, there are those that deny the value of the works of the Law for justification. This denial, reaffirmed in the letter to the Romans (Rom 3:28), had had its first formulation in an earlier writing addressed to the Galatians (Gal 2:16). The circumstances evoked here help us to understand exactly such a denial. Some Jewish Christians, coming from Jerusalem, sought to impose circumcision on the Christians of Galatia of pagan origin (Gal 6:12-13); this demand, which for the Apostle implied submitting to the whole of the Torah (Gal 5:3; cf. 4:21), meant attributing to the Law a justificatory value, and, ultimately, affirming that Christ had died in vain (cf. Gal 2:21). It is in this context, and because of the extreme consequences of the demands of the Judaizers, that Paul denies to the Law and the works it requires any value in relation to justification, which is the foundation of a person's existence before God. This foundation can only be the Son of God sent by the Father, born of a woman under the Law to redeem those who are under the Law (Gal 4:4-5); faith in him, and not the works of the law, is the only way, the only means by which God justifies us (Gal 2:16).

294. Confirming this doctrine in the Letter to the Romans (Rom 3:28), Paul will assert, as mentioned above, that if faith is the only way of justification, this does not deprive the Law of its value (Rom 3:31). As an essential component of Scripture, the Torah is God's revelation which has its fulfilment in Christ (Rom 1:1; 3:21); this is demonstrated by the story of Abraham, who "put his faith in God and this was reckoned to him as righteousness" (Rom 4:1-25; cf. Gal 3:6-29); he thus became the father of believers, who are justified by faith "in the one who raised from the dead our Lord Jesus, who was handed over to death for our sins and raised for our justification" (Rom 4:24-25). According to the Apostle, the condemnation of sin in the flesh assumed by the Son of God had as its purpose that "the Law's requirements might be satisfied in us who live our lives not according to the flesh but according to the Spirit" (Rom 8:4). Thus, the revelation of God's justice by faith in the death of Christ (Rom 3:21) and liberation from the law of sin and death by the Spirit (Rom 8:2) have made it possible for believers to be able to fulfil the just demands of the Law, by submitting not to the letter but to the power of the Spirit (Rom 2:29; 7:6; 2 Cor 3:6), which is received as a gift (Rom 5:5). Relying on this conviction, Paul urges Christians to undertake an unceasing process of discernment of the will of God, a fundamental element of the believing experience (Rom 12:2; Phil 1:10; cf. Eph 5:10, 17; Col 1:9-10), orientated towards obedience not to sin but to justice (cf. Rom 6:15-23; 8:5-13).

2. OBEDIENCE AND TRANSGRESSION

295. The commandment is an integral part of the creation story. From this point history begins, interpreted by Scripture in terms of obedience to or transgression of the will of God. We pass from the first two chapters of Genesis to the third, which serves as a kind of transition. On the one hand, the text envisages something primordial, since the human beings are placed in the garden of Eden, in a situation once described as "paradise", and the narrative method used belongs to a literary genre that cannot be defined as "historical", reporting a specific event that really happened: putting in the scene a talking snake, describing trees with special powers, presenting God walking in the garden and making leather tunics, or cherubim barring access to the garden with the flame of the blazing sword, all these things invite us to read the narrative as a symbolic presentation with programmatic value. On the other hand, in the third chapter of Genesis the human beings become protagonists because it is their actions and their words that largely determine the narrative flow. It is therefore a "human" story that is told, a "true" story, because it really makes us understand what the human being is; the true meaning of the story will be substantiated by the whole of the biblical narrative, in which, repeatedly, though with many variations, it will be shown how sin constitutes a constant in the human story.

In Gen 3 there are two narrative sequences: (i) the first is constituted by vv. 1-7, in which the sin committed by the progenitors is recounted; (ii) the second, vv. 8-24, tells of God's intervention as a consequence of the transgression. These two sections provide the subject matter for the remaining two parts of this chapter.

Gen 3:1-7

[1]Now, the snake was the most cunning of all the wild animals that the Lord God had made. It asked the woman, 'Did God really say you were not to eat from any of the trees in the garden?' [2]The woman answered the snake, 'We may eat the fruit of the trees in the garden. [3]It was of the fruit of the tree in the middle of the garden that God said, "You must not eat it, nor touch it, under pain of death."' [4]Then the snake said to the woman, 'No! You will not die! [5]God knows that the day you eat it your eyes will be opened and you will be like gods, knowing good from evil.' [6]The woman saw that the tree was good to eat and pleasing to the eye, and that it was desirable for the wisdom that it could give. So she took some of its fruit and ate it. She also gave some to her husband who was with her, and he ate it.[7] Then the eyes of both of them were opened and they realised that they were naked. So they sewed fig leaves together to make themselves loincloths.

296. *The narrative has two stages: first we have the dialogue between the snake and the woman (vv. 1-5), in which what God has prescribed is recalled; then follow the actions of the woman and the man (vv. 6-7).*

The text begins with a surprise, introducing as it does a specific animal, not mentioned before, the "snake" (nāḥāš), which has a decisive role in the story (vv. 1, 2, 4, 13, 14). The narrator describes it as "the most cunning of all the wild animals that the Lord God had made" (v. 1), and this initial description suggests that the whole story should be interpreted as a sapiential comparison between "cunning", which evokes a commendable quality, but with traces of subterfuge and deception, and "intelligence" or "wisdom", which is not mentioned here, because, though a quality of the human being (Prov 2:2-3; 3:13; 4:1, 5, 7; Sir 14:20-21; 17:4-5) which gives the ability to reflect, discern and choose the good, it is unfortunately absent, and with dramatic consequences.

With a suggestive play on words, the narrator points out the presence on one side of a "clever" "character" ('ārûm) (v. 1) and facing him two "naked" beings ('ărûmmîm) (Gen 2:25). If nudity without shame (Gen 2:25) could be interpreted as innocence and even as the intimacy of love between man and woman, here it suggests a vulnerability which is not physical but intellectual and moral, a weakness that will become obvious to the human beings themselves after the sin (v. 7).

The cunning of the serpent, as we shall see, is expressed as questioning an aspect of the truth, and precisely some of its attractive sides; but this is like bait that hides the insidious hook. The serpent was made by God (v. 1), to be, like all the animals, a "help" to man (Gen 2:1); here, however, it shows itself as the "enemy"; and this demonstrates how the gifts of God can become an occasion for evil, when they are not subject to obedience to the Lord. In this way, the human being is being put to the test, and will display wisdom if the trap is recognised and rejected. In other texts of the Bible this situation is called a temptation (in Hebrew with the root nāsāh, in Greek especially with the noun peirasmos).

297. *The narrative presents a debate between the serpent and the woman. A first aspect to consider is that of the opposition between the animal and the human being; some might see presented here the conflict between instinct and rationality. It is true that the individual experiences an inner struggle between the "carnal" urges and the spiritual dimension, as Paul also describes in Rom 7:7-25 in Gen 3, however, the serpent speaks as if he wished to awaken the woman's intelligence in the desire for "knowledge" and not for satisfaction of the senses.*

The devil

The interpretative tradition of the story sees in the serpent a representation of the evil spirit (Apoc 12:9), which receives various names, such as Satan (the adversary), the Devil (subversive), Belial (the wicked one), Belzebub (the lord of the flies) or Beelzebul (the lord of the dung). Although Paul calls him "the god of this world" (2 Cor 4:4), Scripture never asserts that this "figure" is a kind of bad divinity, an antagonist of the good God, because everything that exists outside of God can only be one of his creatures. Since a powerful force is envisaged, capable of taking different and multiple forms (Mk 5:9), the Christian tradition has thought of "fallen angels", that is, spiritual beings who rebelled against God, and for this reason were ousted from the celestial kingdom, and left on earth to exercise a certain dominion over the world. From this arises the designation of Satan as the "Prince of this world" (Jn 12:31; 14:30; 16:11). The biblical passages that speak of rebel angels are 2 Pt 2:4 and Jude 6, where it is asserted, however, that they were cast into the abyss and held prisoner for the judgement, not left to wander on earth, therefore, to seduce and dominate human beings (Mt 12:43; Lk 11:24-26). In the book of Tobit the demon Asmodeus has the power to kill Sarah's various husbands (Tob 3:8; 6:14-16; 7:3). In the New Testament demons even take possession of people, provoking them to inhuman actions (Mk 5:2-5) or suicide (Mt 17:15); and the devil acts as a "tempter" who leads people to evil (Mt 4:3; 1 Thess 3:5; 1 Pt 5:8). Throughout history the voice of the serpent is often assumed by human voices like false prophets and false teachers who interweave their words with lies (Deut 13:2,4; Is 9:14-15; Mt 7:15; 24:11; 2 Pt 2:19; 1 Jn 4:1); for this reason even Peter was called Satan by Jesus because he opposed the promptings of the divine will (Mk 8:33). In the book of the Apocalypse, the eschatological triumph of God occurs with the annihilation of Satan and his "angels" (Apoc 12:9; 20:2-3, 10).

298. *A second aspect that merits consideration is the choice of the narrator to use the woman instead of the man, or both human beings, as interlocutor of the serpent. The text does not explain* this detail so that various interpretations have been developed, including seeing the woman as more vulnerable and more easily deceived. It is true that the tempter tries to discover a weakness in order to strike, but attributing to the woman less intelligence or vigilance represents an unacceptable prejudice denied by Scripture itself. We should remember that Wisdom is usually depicted as a female character (cf. Prov 1:20-21; 8:1-4; Wis 8:3), and this is not because of the grammatical gender, but because the woman is able to express a rich sapiential activity, in giving life, warmth and joy to all (Prov 31:10-31). Many women in biblical history have proved themselves wiser and more courageous than men. If one assumes this perspective, the confrontation in Gen 3 does not take place between a very astute being and a foolish one, but rather between two manifestations of wisdom, and the "temptation" engages with the mind of the human being, who, in the desire to "know", risks the sin of pride, and pretends to be a god, rather than realising that one is a child who receives everything from the Creator and Father.

Another way to understand the choice of the female person as interlocutor is to consider that the woman is the one who gives life by becoming a mother; this aspect is explicitly evoked in the sentence given in Gen 3:16, but also in the promise that her "race", literally "her seed", will triumph over the serpent (Gen 3:15). The figure of the woman, who will be called Eve, "mother of all living beings" (Gen 3:20), must be seen as revealing a potential that resembles that of God in being able to give life. The desire to "be like God", on which the temptation will be based, is rooted in a gift of which the woman is the privileged recipient.

299. The temptation occurs by means of words, which deceive and seduce. The first of the serpent's statements (v. 1) appears as a provocation, which, with some exaggeration, nevertheless touches on a crucial point, that of the limit imposed by God without justification. It is generally interpreted as a question, although in Hebrew the form seems rather an assertion, and it can be translated in two ways. (i) The first is the one more commonly attested: "Is it true that God said:'you must not eat of any tree'?"; the serpent is clearly lying, insinuating that humans are forbidden any fruit, and in this case the temptation lies in making God appear not to want to feed human beings and so keep them alive. (ii) The second way of translating formulates the question in a more subtle form: "Is it true that the Lord said: 'You must not eat from all the trees'?", and in this case the snake is not lying, but brings out the fact that human beings are faced with a limit, being denied access to all the trees, because something has been banned by God. The temptation then focusses precisely on the prohibition as such, and indirectly raises the question "why" there is such a ban.

The woman's reply (v. 2) seems at first sight to be a necessary and respectful clarification, as it distinguishes between the fruits of the trees in the garden that human beings can eat, and what, by contrast, is prohibited. Without realising it, however, she confirms that something is prohibited, adding some details to God's command, showing her inadequate perception of what is prohibited. The woman does not say that the forbidden tree is that of the "knowledge of good and evil", but that it is the tree which stands "in the middle of the garden", almost confusing it with "the tree of life" (Gen 2:9), the only one whose location was specified by the narrator. And of this so "central" tree the woman adds that God has forbidden them to "touch it" under pain of death, a clarification that does not conform to the word of God. This apparently superfluous addition is symptomatic of the feeling of someone facing a taboo, the reason for which is not known.

The reply of the serpent (vv. 4-5) marks a definite turning point in the dialogue; the serpent passes from the "question" to the categorical affirmation, claiming a knowledge of reality that is not at all warranted, but that appears convincing due to the emphatic nature of the pronouncement. The tempter radically reverses the outcome of the forbidden action, which instead of bringing death, as was laid down by God in Gen 2:17, produces an extraordinary boost to life, the quality of "being like God". All this comes about from feeding on that fruit that gives "the knowledge of good and evil", whereby the eyes open so as to see ... that one is God. The seductive power of the serpent's words is based on two elements: the first is the suspicion about God, the second is the attractive prospect of human progress. A vicious circle is established among these elements: the lack of trust in God makes the tempter's word *convincing, while the offer of tangible goods, even if only imaginary, undermines faith in the words of the Lord.*

300. *The effectiveness of this diabolical deceit can be seen from the result it produces in the woman's conscience (v. 6a). The subtlety of the biblical narrative allows us to understand better the insidious nature of temptation. The lying words of the serpent, in fact, apparently have the same effects which in the wisdom and prayer traditions of Israel are attributed to the precept of the Lord: the eyes are, as it were, illuminated, almost as if they had previously been blinded by a presumed naivety, and the woman can see what is "good", "attractive" and within her grasp. But what seems good in the eyes of the human person who is deceived is radically different from what is good in the eyes of God. Instead of the desire for God and for the true good (Prov 11:23; 13:12), the craving for things to consume is unleashed (Num 11:4; Ps 78:29-30; 106:14). Instead of seeing all the trees in the garden as a gift from God, and in the forbidden tree the sign of a salvific truth, the woman believes she has discovered that in everything there is only the dishonesty of the Creator, who was hiding his jealousy of human beings. In this distortion of values, one can guess how the "diabolical" suggestion operates. Sin has already happened in the heart (cf. Mt 5:28) before it is visible externally.*

The act in which the transgression takes place consists in "eating" the fruit of the forbidden tree (v. 6b). The importance of the motif is evident from the numerous occurrences of the same verb in Gen 3, not only in the first part of the account (vv. 1, 2, 3, 5, 6), but also in the second, both in the interrogation (vv. 11, 12, 13, 17), and in the sanctions (vv. 14, 17, 18, 19, 22). On the one hand, eating the forbidden fruit is to be understood in its metaphorical sense (cf. Prov 30:20), in symmetrical opposition to feeding on what God offers to sustain life (cf. Deut 8:3); on the other hand, the even daily experience of a food earned in hardship (Gen 3:17-19) will be understood as an incentive to seek the true nourishment of joy, not in the produce of the soil, but in the spiritual gift of God.

Sin also develops in the changed relationship between man and woman. The Creator had wanted that the woman be a "help" for man; now "the man who was with her" (v. 6b) is instead made an accomplice of the transgression, through the woman's act of "giving" the forbidden fruit. The first occurrence of the verb (nātan) having as subject the human person thus expresses the distortion of the concept of gift, because what is offered is a leaven of death.

The account concludes with the experience resulting from disobedience (v. 7). Both transgressors have a new vision of things: it becomes clear to them that the serpent's promise to become like God was not true, because they see they are "naked". Nakedness here highlights the condition of fragility; it reveals also perhaps "shame" for the guilt, or at least for the disastrous result of their behaviour. But unfortunately, instead of recognising their mistake, human beings pitifully cover the signs of their foolish transgression with "fig leaves", a useless protection against the threat of death, a ridiculous remedy to hide their disobedience from God.

Transgression and obedience in human history

301. The account of Gen 3 presents the reader with an image of the human being marked by profound foolishness, which gives rise to the act of disobedience to the divine commandment. Scripture does not wish in this way to deny the responsibility of the human being by taking sin to be a fatal consequence of imperfect human nature. If this were the case, there would be neither a precept nor a punishment, which in fact presuppose the real possibility of making a good choice. In actual fact the path of good opposed to the path of evil is a recurring motif in biblical tradition. This is explicitly formulated at the conclusion of the Torah, where the Lord declares:

"Look, today I am offering you life and prosperity, death and disaster. If you obey the commandments of the Lord your God, which I am laying down for you today, if you love the Lord your God and follow his ways, if you keep his commandments, his laws and his customs, you will live and

> grow numerous, and the Lord your God will bless you in the
> land which you are entering and make your own [....]. Choose
> life, then, so that you and your descendants may live."
>
> (Deut 30:15-16, 19)

The sapiential world and the prophetic tradition, as we shall see, inherit this principle, and make it a cornerstone of their teaching (Is 1:16-20; Jer 21:8; Ezek 18:26-28; Am 5:14; Mic 6:8; Mal 2:22-24; Ps 1:6; Prov 8:32-36; Sir 7:1-3; 15:11-20). Revealing that the progenitors, from the beginning, have been victims of seductive deception, the sacred author admonishes and educates, inviting us to beware of the deceitful attractions that lead to death (Prov 2:8-19; 5:1-14; 9:13-18), and indirectly brings out the need for a "saviour" for those who fall into temptation.

The proliferation of evil

302. The continuation of the biblical narrative will confirm what is expressed in symbolic form in the foundational account. As if it were a historical constant, the attestation of the divine gift is followed repeatedly by the denunciation of a sinful action of the human being, for the most part merely stated without a precise explanation of the cause that provoked it, even if one can surmise that, at the root of everything, there is generally a foolishness always ready to be misled. The seducer, who in the Gen 3 account had the voice of the serpent, will later take the form of unreliable foreign wisdom traditions (Ex 23:32-33; Josh 23:12-13; 1 Kgs 11:1-8; Jer 10:2-5; Prov 7:4-5; Col 2:8), of false prophecy (Deut 13:2-6; Is 9:14-15; Jer 14:13-16; 23:9-32; Ezek 13:2-23; 14:9; Mic 3:5-8; Zech 13:2-6; Mt 24:11; 2 Tim 3:13), and of the perverse passions of the heart (Jer 17:9; Ps 36:2-5; Prov 26:23-28; Wis 4:12; 5:2; 6:2-4; 18:30-31; Sir 5:2; 9:9; Eph 4:22; Jam 1:13-15). Although one can say that envy induced Cain to kill Abel (Gen 4:8), as it moved the brothers to sell Joseph as a slave (Gen 37:28), although one can think that Lamech carried out a disproportionate vendetta (Gen 4:23-24), dishonestly claiming to protect his life, such assertions do not resolve the enigma of evil, and they do not explain why people do not resist temptation, allowing themselves to be "dominated" by "sin crouching at the door" (Gen 4:7). The Creator himself, according to the biblical narrator, is amazed at this:

> "The Lord saw that human wickedness was great on earth and that the human heart contrived nothing but wicked schemes all day long. The Lord regretted having made human beings on earth and was grieved at heart."
>
> (Gen 6:5-6)

Even after the flood, when humanity receives, as it were, a new beginning, starting from a "just" progenitor (Gen 6:9), the appearance of evil, perpetrated by individuals or entire populations, punctuates the rhythm of history: Ham despises his father (Gen 9:22-25), and nations proudly join forces to build "a tower with its top reaching heaven" (Gen 11:4). The account of the origins of humanity would thus seem to show that the "children of Adam" express their freedom in the transgressive act of ingratitude and foolishness, of pride and violence, rather than testifying their likeness to God. History unfolds then as a proliferation of evil, and Scripture expresses its dramatic quality with a great variety of terms, rendered in modern translations with: sin, guilt, rebellion, wickedness, impiety, impurity, abomination, foolishness, deceit, perversion, etc. For their part, the legal codes of the Torah make explicit the different forms of transgression that the biblical narrative, and common experience too, show to be in no way theoretical.

The presence of the "just" one

303. The biblical tradition of the origins does not consider sinfulness as a congenital inheritance transmitted by the "fathers". In the same history there appear surprisingly some exemplary figures: "Enoch walked with God [...] then he was no more, because God took him" (Gen 5:24); "Noah won favour in the sight of the Lord [...]. Noah was a good man, a righteous and blameless man among his contemporaries, and he walked with God" (Gen 6:8-9). Abraham was recognised by the Lord as just (Gen 15:6) and obedient, so that he became the father of a blessed people (Gen 22:15-18). It is therefore through the juxtaposition of two contrasting facts, on the one hand, the spread of a contagious evil, and, on the other, the presence of people of integrity, that Scripture attests to the reality of human freedom. The two ways placed before the creature are not only a theoretical perspective, for they are actually followed by good people and bad.

> The motif of the "two ways" is widely present also in the New Testament and with a great variety of images. Jesus spoke of the narrow door and the wide one (Mt 7:13-14), of the wise person who builds on rock and the foolish one who builds on sand (Mt 7:24-27), of the good seed and the darnel (Mt 13:24-30), of the good fish and the bad (Mt 13:47-50), of the son who obeys and the one who disobeys (Mt 21:28-31), of the wise girls and the foolish ones (Mt 25:1-13), of the sheep separated from the goats (Mt 25:31-46), of the Pharisee and the tax collector (Lk 18:10-14), and so on.

The appearance of the just person, instigator of justice and goodness for the children, is unpredictable and mysterious, but for the reader this is a reason for hope, as well as a model to imitate. For it is in the very appearance of the obedient and good person that the discreet but powerfully effective intervention of the Lord of history is revealed, working so that a path of salvation is possible for his children. It is through the just Noah that the human race is saved; and through Abraham that the nations will all be blessed. As is narrated in the story of Joseph, at the end of the Genesis cycle, God is capable of transforming a sinful conspiracy into an incredible outcome of life for the guilty (Gen 45:4-8; cf. Wis 9:17-18). So when the Bible uses expressions such as "a twisted and perverse generation" (Deut 32:5), a "race of wrongdoers" (Is 1:4), as if evoking a hereditary defect, and even when it accuses the people of treachery from the womb (Is 48:8; Ps 51:7) and confirms the truth of the proverb "like mother, like daughter" (Ezek 16:44), the intention is to encourage human beings to decisions of justice (Ps 78:8), and, more radically, to open the heart to faith in the wonderful intervention of the Lord, who, as St. Paul will say, "has imprisoned all human beings in their disobedience to show mercy to all" (Rom 11:32), so that "where sin increased, grace was superabundant" (Rom 5:20). In this perspective, the Messiah represents that just one who gives rise to a new humanity, regenerated and made capable of faithful love.

In the history of Israel

304. The combined dynamic of sin and justice is repeatedly evident in the history of Israel. With the liberation from Egyptian slavery, this people experiences a kind of birth as a nation (Ex 14-15). Such an event of grace, mediated by the faithful activity of Moses (Deut 34:10-12), instead of producing a harmonious and enduring docility to the will of the Lord, was followed by an uninterrupted series of rebellions (cf. Ps 78 and 106). Moses said to his people: "From the very day that you came out of the land of Egypt until you arrived here [in the land of Moab, at the Jordan border], you have been rebels against the Lord" (Deut 9:7; cf. also 9:24). Among the countless acts of grumbling and rebelliousness that punctuate the forty years in the desert, one remembers in particular the sin of idolatry perpetrated at the foot of Sinai (Ex 32:1-6), in the very aftermath of liberation and of their acceptance of the covenant with the Lord, which had been ratified by the solemn commitment to obey the words of the Law (Ex 19:8; 24:3, 7). Set at the beginning of the history of the people, the adoration of the golden calf represents a kind of prototype of the sin of Israel; this transgression will manifest itself repeatedly in different forms throughout history and will bring about the final catastrophe (2 Kgs 17:14-23; 24:3-4; Jer 1:15-16).

On the other hand, the sign of human freedom, expressed in full obedience to the Lord, is represented by the uninterrupted series of "servants" of the Lord, and in particular by the prophets, whose word, the fruit of listening to the Lord, intervenes to save, calling tirelessly to conversion that can take place at any moment in history (Ezek 18), so that God has the opportunity to forgive and restore the covenant.

The contribution of the wisdom traditions

305. In the wisdom writings we find a general consideration of human behaviour, evaluated in relation to *justice*, which is regulated by the commandments of the Lord. The sages do not explicitly cite the precepts of the Torah, and do not promote the implementation of the specific ritual prescriptions of Israel, because their perspective aims to be universal, and they therefore use generic categories along with assertions that are valid for every age and for any person.

Temptation and test

A first contribution of this literature consists in focusing in various ways on the experience of human beings faced with two different prospects, with two types of discourse, with two opposite attitudes to life. The sages start by inviting reflection on the condition of the conscience called to evaluate, distinguishing between appearance and truth, and to make a choice that is favourable to life.

There are books that illustrate this motif extensively, presenting it as the experience of *temptation*, and therefore in harmony with Gen 3. This comes in the form of a wide-ranging and articulated discourse, more or less directly opposed to that of the Torah, with which a deceiver holds out in an attractive way a future of pleasure, wealth and social success. We see a symbolic example of this from the first page of the book of *Proverbs*, in the proposal of the "wicked" (Prov 1:10-14) who put forward a plan of violent conquest; this is taken up in a similar way in the honeyed words of the foreign woman, adulterous and seductive, who promises secret pleasures (Prov 5:3-6; 7:4-27), and finally in the invitation of the silly woman (Prov 9:13-18), so similar to that of "Wisdom" (Prov 9:4-6), that it could easily trap the naive. The boundary between wisdom and arrogance, between worldly success and divine blessing, between truth and lies is not at all easy to discern; the duty of the sage is precisely that of helping to make things clear, so that the disciple may make a choice that leads to life.

306. *Sirach* does not resort to the same literary method, even if his sayings implicitly suppose opposition between the wisdom he transmits and that advocated by "sinners" (Sir 1:24; 3:27; 5:9; 13:17; 15:19; etc.). The sage warns the disciple of the apparent success of the wicked (Sir 9:11); indeed from the outset he encourages the disciple to face the "test" (*peirasmos*), which is present in the service of the Lord (Sir 2:1; 4:17), a test that is revealed in "painful events" which have the beneficial function of refining the just one, like gold in the crucible (Sir 2:4-5).

The *book of Wisdom* in a certain sense makes a synthesis of the two approaches just summarised. Firstly, it reflects the expressive form of Proverbs, with the contrast between the discourse of the wise, in this case Solomon, and the perverse reasoning of the wicked (Wis 2:1-20), who "call death upon themselves with deed and word" (Wis 1:16), because, having made a covenant with death (Wis 1:16), instead of directing their desire towards the immortality promised by God (Wis 2:22-23), they want to drag human beings into the fleeting intoxication of dissolute pleasure (Wis 2:5-9). At the same time, taking up the suggestion of Sirach, the author of this book shows that the wicked, unwilling to tolerate the just one who "reproaches" them for their "sins against the Law" (Wis 2:12), take action against him with "insult and torture" (Wis 2:19), putting his faith in God the Father to the "test" (Wis 2:16). In fact it is the Lord who thus "tests" his chosen ones, trying them like "gold in the crucible" (Wis 3:5-6), so as to find them worthy of an eternal prize (Wis 3:7-9; 5:15-16). Echoes of these texts are found in the gospels, in the story of the Passion (cf. Mt 27:43).

The unjust

307. The biblical wisdom traditions quite uniformly put before the reader the way of good juxtaposed to that of evil, inviting one to choose justice as one would choose wisdom and life (Sir 17:6-7). In fact:

> "A human being is presented with life and death
> and will receive whichever is preferred."
>
> (Sir 15:17)

The sages establish that there are the wicked and sinners (Prov 1:31), the violent (Prov 4:17; 10:11; 28:15), the proud (Sir 10:12-13), the insolent (Prov 3:34; 19:29; Sir 15:8) and fools (Prov 1:22; Qoh 7:5); they also identify some causes of this distortion of intelligence and of the heart. Simplifying somewhat, we can say that a frequent motivation for sinful conduct is the attraction of pleasure, of immediate satisfaction (Prov 1:13-14; 7:18; Sir 6:2-4; 18:30-33; 23:5-6). This is quite easy to recognise. A different motivation, found especially in Sirach, explains instead the orientation towards evil with the lack of the "fear of God", which is indeed "the beginning of wisdom" (Sir 1:14; cf. also Sir 1:20; 15:1; 19:20), and, consequently, inspires righteous conduct (Sir 2:15-17). Today the motif of "fear" does not meet with a ready assent, because it appears contrary to the dignity of the human being and opposed to the way of love taught by the gospel. The "fear of God" can, however, be a preparation for higher spiritual qualities; and, in many cases at least, since it brings with it the consideration of God's "judgement" on the conduct of every person (Sir 1:8, 40; 4:19; 5:6; 12:6; 16:11-14; 17:23; cf. also Qoh 5:5-6; 12:13-14), it can constitute a restraint on immorality and therefore a stimulus to make responsible choices. Moreover, the lexicon of "fear" in Old Testament texts also serves to express the idea of "respect" for the person in authority, and therefore also just reverence towards the Creator and Lord, which leads one to obey his precepts. The "fear of the Lord", in fact, is not an expression of fear, but rather a source of joy in the heart (Sir 1:12, 16, 18; 23:27), caused by trust in the divine protection and in the gift of life granted without fail to the just (Sir 1:13, 17; 34:14-20). Where this inner attitude is absent, where God is ignored or even despised, it is not surprising that instances of injustice multiply. This seems clear enough also in contemporary society.

There is no one who is just before God

308. Finally, in the wisdom literature we find a motif with clear relevance, even if it is perhaps perplexing. From the observation of the imperfection of the human being, and of a profound foolishness and moral fragility, the generalised conclusion is reached and formulated as an important religious truth, namely, that "no one can be considered just before God". Among the sayings of Proverbs we read: the just one falls "seven times" (Prov 24:16), and Sirach warns: "remember that we all are guilty" (Sir 8:5). This is asserted to encourage humble, penitent and compassionate conduct.

The theme is taken up in the book of Job, with different nuances, found in the following quotes, which are placed on the lips of Job's "friends":

"Can anyone be righteous before God,
any person be pure in the presence of their Maker?
Even in his own servants he puts no trust,
even with his angels he finds fault.
What then of those who live in houses of clay,
whose foundation is mere dust [..]?"

(Job 4:17-19)

"How can anyone be pure,
anyone born of woman be righteous?
God cannot rely even on his holy ones,
to him, even the heavens seem impure.
How much more, this hateful, corrupt thing, humanity,
which soaks up wickedness like water?"

(Job 15:14-16)

"How can a human be righteous before God,
one born of woman be pure?
See, even the moon is not bright,
and the stars are not pure in his sight.
How much less a human, a maggot,
the son of man, a worm!"

(Job 25:4-6)

We have included these substantial quotes in order to show how the motif of human sinfulness can certainly lead to a humble attitude towards God (cf. Ps 143:2) and the beginning of a penitential journey (Sir 17:24-27); this must not serve, however, as in the case of Job's friends, to justify every misfortune that befalls people by considering it a divine sanction against the guilty (Job 32:2-3). In any case, every contempt for human beings, creatures of God, must always be avoided because such lack of regard does not lead to true praise of the Lord.

The severe verdict of the prophets

309. In order to communicate his word of life in various historical circumstances, the Lord had promised Israel that he would raise up a prophet like Moses (Deut 18:15). A speaker and a reliable mediator, God and the prophet, cannot fail to transmit the same message. The infidelity that Moses had foreseen before he died (Deut 31:16-18, 27-29) is confirmed by his successors, and related to specific events and to individual protagonists of history.

The prophets "see" the rebellion of Israel, but also that of the nations, because the Lord reveals to his servants the evil hidden under the cloak of devout practices (Is 1:10-15; Jer 7:8-11), combined with actions which are oppressive yet legally approved (Is 5:20-23; 10:1-2; Am 2:6), immorality accepted without criticism (Jer 5:7-8; Am 2:7; 6:1-6), and violent ideologies promoted as submission to a divine plan (Is 10:5-11; 14:12-17; 47:6-8; Hab 1:7-10). Moved by God's desire for justice, the prophets speak and cry out. Their voice generally challenges the statements of rulers, priests, false prophets and traditional sages, who often reassure consciences with illusory promises. The prophetic word, therefore, meets regular opposition, also because it announces in a dramatic way a future of disaster brought about by the presence of grave evil that involves the whole of society. The purpose of such ominous predictions, however, is paradoxically positive since they draw everyone to conversion; returning to the right path is possible, because God shows himself willing to forgive and to renew his covenant with gifts even greater than those granted in the past.

Although "dated" and referring to a specific historical moment and to figures from a particular period, prophetic literature highlights aspects of sin that are found in different eras and committed by the most varied characters. For this reason the oracles of the prophets are preserved, and are reread to draw from them lessons and instructions. Moreover, although aimed at specific recipients and assuming different literary styles, while developing themes that are also very specific, the oracular collections agree, however, in presenting a vision of history in which disobedience to the Law of the Lord predominates. It would be simplistic nevertheless to assert that the prophet is called exclusively to denounce transgressions and predict their punitive consequences, because in reality God speaks also, and above all, to offer new covenants, as with David and his descendants, to encourage initiatives for good, such as the construction of the temple, or to stimulate attitudes of faith, when danger is faced by the people, and to open up unheard of horizons of hope for those who experience desolation and failure. However, one can hardly question that an orientation of the prophetic preaching that condemns a generalised infidelity to God is an interpretative key to the understanding of history. In this regard, we can highlight some features that are common to the various prophetic books.

Total infidelity

310. The prophets sometimes attribute to their society responsibility for the transgression of all the main commandments of the Decalogue (Jer 7:8-9; Hos 4:1-3), or at least of a whole series of sins, perpetrated in various related contexts (Is 5:8-24; Am 2:6-8). More frequently they denounce in a comprehensive and generalised way the abandonment of the Lord (Is 1:4; Hos 4:10) with the practice of idolatry (Jer 1:16; 2:11-13), disobedience to the word announced by the prophets (Jer 11:7-8; 13:10; Ezek 20:8; Zech 1:4; 7:11-12), disregard for benefits received (Jer 2:32; 18:15; Ezek 23:35; Hos 2:15), with the consequent breaking of the covenant (Jer 11:10; 31:32; Ezek 16:59). In certain cases, the prophet sees in a specific unjust practice the clear sign of contempt for God, as with the sale of innocent people (Am 2:6), the violation of the Sabbath (Jer 17:27), the use of rigged scales (Mic 6:10-11) or the offering of poor quality animals for sacrifices in the temple (Mal 1:6-8). Over and above the reproach for isolated transgressions, the prophets deplore the condition of a stubborn conscience, which makes the very word of God ineffective (Is 48:4; Jer 4:22; 13:23; 17:1; Ezek 2:4; 3:7; Zech 7:12). The reassuring voices of the false prophets prevail (Is 28:15; Jer 6:14; 23:17; 29:8-9; Ezek 13:8-10; Am 9:10), while the bearers of the severe message of truth are ridiculed or silenced (Jer 26:7-9; Hos 9:8; Am 2:11-12; 7:12-13).

All are responsible

311. The prophets often assert that all humanity is corrupt: Israel above all (Is 1:21-23; 24:4-5; Jer 6:28; 9:1; Hos 9:1, 9-10; Am 9:8; Mic 1:5; Zeph 3:1-2; Zech 7:11-12), more seriously responsible as the first beneficiary of the Lord's saving actions (Am 2:9-11; 3:1-2); but then all the nations too, without exception, as is clear from the prophetic collections (Is 13–21; Jer 46–51; Ezek 25–32; Am 1:3–2:3; etc.). In Israelite society, not one, from the smallest to the greatest, acts properly (Jer 5:1-5; 6:13; Ezek 22:30; Mic 7:2), and it is precisely the institutional figures of the king, the priests, the judges and the prophets, who are supposed to promote fidelity to the covenant but who instigate the systematic distortion of the values desired by the Lord (Is 5:20-23; Jer 2:8; 5:31; Ezek 22:25-28; Mic 3:1-5; Zeph 3:3-4).

The prophets, sent by the Lord for the conversion of the people, declare the failure of their mission (Is 6:9-10; Jer 6:27-30; Ezek 2:1-7). From their words emerges a dramatic vision of history, sometimes summarised in the form of a parable with an unhappy outcome, due to a foolishness and an obstinacy that cannot be reformed (Is 1:2-4; 5:1-7; Ezek 16; Hos 11:1-4; etc.).

Yet, just when everything seems to be leading inexorably to the final catastrophe, the prophets announce a wonderful and unimaginable event of salvation which the Lord carries out by virtue of his eternal love and omnipotence as Creator. God does not abandon, God does not break his covenant. History does not end with punishment, but with the advent of grace. This latter aspect will be discussed in the final part of this chapter.

The reception of the divine message in prayer

312. The Psalter is comparable to a sacred container, in which is condensed everything the Lord has made known to Israel through the Torah, the sages and the prophets; it receives the Word and transforms it into prayers to be put on the believer's lips so as to assimilate the Revelation in the course of meditation. Two practices in which this process of internalisation of the divine message in prayer takes place should be highlighted, with specific reference to the motif of the manifestation of sin in human history.

The first practice incorporates the *wisdom* motif of the "two ways", the way of the sinners and the way of the just; this recollection serves to reaffirm the believer's attachment to the sanctifying source that is the Law of the Lord, as we have seen with Ps 1. But it is above all the presence of the "wicked", so well attested in the sapiential writings, that is continually evoked in the Psalms, both because the success of the arrogant presents a temptation for the faithful (Ps 37:1-14; 49:6-13; 73:2-13; 125:3), which can be overcome only in the confident expectation of God's judgment, and because the violence of the wicked puts the poor to the test, and requires, therefore, that prayer becomes a supplication for the restoration of the good (Ps 2:8; 5:10-11; 10:1-18; 35:4-10; 120:2; etc.). It is by invoking divine intervention that the believer brings about justice.

The second practice of prayer is the fruit of listening to the word of the *prophet*, which by revealing sin, even that concealed by devout actions, calls everyone to a sincere conversion (cf. Ps 50:7-23). Many psalms describe the opening of the heart, which humbly confesses guilt and asks the Lord for forgiveness and salvation; whoever prays obeys the prophetic command (cf. Jer 3:21-25; Hos 14:2-4). The Christian tradition has identified seven "penitential psalms" (Ps 6; 32; 38; 51; 102; 130; 143), which are considered suitable words to address to the Lord in the act of individual repentance; Ps 103 could also be added to these psalms. In addition to this "personal" form, we also have the collective supplications, where a person praying, interpreting the voice of all the people, as in Ezr 9:6-15, Neh 9:5-36 and Dan 9:4-19, confesses not only past and present faults (Ps 78 and 106), but recognises the repeated appearance in history of God's mercy and his unfailing loyalty to the covenant; in this way the lips of sinners can already celebrate in praise the goodness of the Lord (Ps 106:1-2,47-48; cf. Is 63:7-9).

Jesus, the just one who saves

313. The gospels all begin with the presentation of the prophetic figure of John the Baptist, who, in the role of Elijah (Mt 3:4; cf. 2 Kgs 1:8), proclaims in the desert the need for "conversion" (Mt 3:2, 8, 11) to escape the divine judgment (Mt 3:7, 10). The appeal, addressed to all (Lk 3:10-14), was not accepted, however, by those who, as descendants of Abraham (Mt 3:9; Lk 3:8), thought they did not need it. While the tax collectors and prostitutes, that is, the public sinners, believed the preaching of John (Mt 21:32; Lk 7:29), the chief priests and elders of Jerusalem, together with the scribes and Pharisees, did not listen to the voice of the prophet (Mt 21:23, 31; Lk 7:30), considering themselves "just" (Mt 23:28; Lk 16:15; 18:9).

The necessity of conversion

The same mission was pursued by Jesus when the Baptist was imprisoned (Mk 1:14-15), and, according to the Gospel of Matthew, he took up again the announcement of the precursor: "Repent, for the kingdom of heaven is close at hand" (Mt 4:17; cf. Mt 3:2). The call of sinners defines the task that Christ assumed (Mk 2:17; Mt 19:13; Lk 5:32); his warnings, therefore, are severe towards those who refused his message (Mt 11:20-24; 23:13-36; Lk 13:2-5), while his words addressed to sinners, the humble and the penitent are full of compassion (Mk 2:15-17; Lk 15:2; 19:1-10; 23:39-43). The gospel paradox will be that of establishing that the "last" will be the first to enter the Kingdom of God (Mt 21:31; Lk 18:14), while those who considered themselves the "first" by right will remain excluded (Mt 8:11-12; Lk 13:28-29).

The disciples of Jesus were sent to continue the mandate

of their Lord by calling on people to repent in order to be saved (Mk 6:12; Lk 24:47; cf. Acts 2:38; 3:19; 17:30; 26:20). The process of conversion from sin to justice thus represents a constant dimension of human history; and it concerns everyone, at least in the form of a repeated call to perfection.

Overcoming temptation

314. Of course the gospels do not only present the reality of "sinners", some obstinate, while others are repentant; there are also "just" persons such as Mary, the servant of the Lord, docile to his Word (Lk 1:38, 45), Joseph her husband (Mt 1:19), Zechariah and Elizabeth (Lk 1:6), Simeon and Anna (Lk 2:25), John the Baptist (Mk 6:20), Joseph of Arimathaea (Lk 23:50) and many others. And, of course, Jesus of Nazareth himself, who is before all others the Just One.

But the just, too, are put to the test; their fidelity to God is tested and proved and praised when they are asked to make a choice between obedience and rebellion, between trusting love for God and surrender to a specific wordly attraction. This finds expressive form in the life of Jesus in the account of the *temptations* (Mt 4:1-11; Lk 4:1-13; cf. Mk 1:12-13). It is not only an early episode in the life of the Lord, but rather the paradigm of his historical activity (Heb 12:2), which will be confirmed by the development of the gospel story.

We can see then a "typological" relationship between the beginning of human history, with Adam and Eve being deceived by the serpent, and the new Adam (Rom 5:14; 1 Cor 15:45) victorious against the devil. The analogy between the two stories can be identified in the motif of food, object of disobedience of the progenitors, who ate the fruit of the forbidden tree, while Jesus, hungry after the long fast, renounces the "bread" to adhere exclusively to the word of God (Mt 4:4). Even more striking is the fact that in Gen 3 disobedience consists in wanting to be "like God" (Gen 3:5), and for Jesus the temptation regards his identity as "son of God" (Mt 4:3,6; Lk 4:3,9), which however is experienced by Christ as obedience to the Father.

The Gospels of Matthew and Luke describe a triple temptation and locate it in the desert (Mt 4:1; Lk 4:1; and also Mk 1:12). In the background another "typological" contrast appears, that between the people of Israel, the firstborn of the Lord (Ex 4:22), rebellious for forty years (Deut 9:7), and the Son of God, who in the forty days in the desert, which symbolise his existence, shows himself to be docile and just. Israel grumbled for food other than manna (Ex 16:2-3; Num 11:4-6), tempted the Lord in their lack of faith (Ex 17:2,7; Num 14:22), and prostrated themselves before the golden calf (Ex 32:1-6); the Lord Jesus overcomes the temptation of Satan, affirming that he is nourished by the word of God (Mt 4:4; Lk 4:4), that he fully trusts in the Lord (Mt 4:7; Lk 4:18), and that he renounces all forms of idolatry to worship God alone (Mt 4:10; Lk 4:8).

Luke concludes his account without reference to the intervention of the "angels" who, as a sign of his victory, come to serve Jesus (Mt 4:11; Mk 1:12), instead he notes: "Having finished every way of putting him [Jesus] to the test, the devil left him, until the opportune moment (*kairos*)" (Lk 4:13). An allusion is thus made to the time of the "test", when the tempter will reappear (cf. Lk 22:3,31; Jn 13:27), and Christ will make the definitive choice of obedience to the Father.

Victory over Satan

315. Jesus is not only a model to imitate, because he does not limit himself to resisting the temptations of the devil, but also intervenes in history to fight against and defeat that force of evil that deceives human beings and even enslaves them (Mt 12:28-30; Lk 13:16; Heb 2:14-15). The gospels report frequent episodes of exorcism (Mk 1:23-27; 3:11; 5:1-20; 7:25-30; 9:14-29), where the powerful authority (*exousia*) of Christ brings about the liberation of the person who is healed (Mt 4:24; 9:32-33; 12:22; cf. Acts 10:38), who is made capable of doing good (Mk 5:15-20). In this it is shown that Jesus is Christ the Saviour. The "just" of old had also brought about the salvation of the people entrusted to them, like Noah who saved his family in the ark, or Moses who with his intercession deflected the anger of the Lord against Israel, or like the various judges and leaders who courageously freed the people from foreign domination. But only Jesus is the true Saviour, because, by expelling from the hearts of people that powerful presence that leads to evil, he gave human beings the freedom to choose the good and adhere to the will of God. The conversion advocated by all the prophets is not brought about, therefore, only by the goodwill of the individual, but is realised jointly through the redemptive work of Christ.

A similar power to drive out demons is given to his disciples (Mt 10:1; Mk 3:15; Lk 9:1), who exercise it "in the name" of Jesus Christ (Mk 16:17; Lk 10:17). We can see in this one of the signs of the enduring mission of the Christian community; in history, in fact, the struggle against Satan will be constantly repeated (Rom 16:20), until God himself will destroy forever the adversary of the human race.

Justification brought about by Christ

316. The apostle Paul confirms the role of Saviour that the gospels attribute to Christ; and with a complex doctrinal development, the main lines of which can only be briefly summarised here, he makes explicit its significance in relation to "sin", a reality that is opposed to "justice". Paul's aim is to make known the gospel which is "God's power for salvation to everyone who has faith" (Rom 1:16); in other words, he intends to show how the justice of God, which was revealed in Christ, makes sinners just (Rom 3:21-26).

All are sinners

One of the main statements of the letter to the Romans says: "all have sinned and fallen short of God's glory" (Rom 3:23; cf. also Rom 3:9); this assumption is firstly maintained to some degree by scrutiny of the human reality, fruit of a prophetic "vision" of history, in which is revealed "the ungodliness and injustice" of human beings (Rom 1:18), idolaters, depraved and violent people (Rom 1:19-32); and even those who are instructed by the Law of the Lord and are convinced that they are "a guide to the blind and a light to those who are in darkness" (Rom 2:17-19) offend God by transgressing the precepts of the Law (Rom 2:23). Thus Paul takes up in universal terms what the prophets of Israel had declared and more generally the tradition of ancient Scripture; as a scriptural proof, in fact, he cites a chain of quotations from the Psalms and Isaiah, introduced by a paraphrase of Ps 14:3 or Ps 53:4: "there is no one who does any good, no, not even one" (Rom 3:10-18), in order that "every mouth may be silenced" and "the whole world brought under the judgement of God" (Rom 3:19).

Paul reaffirms his analysis with his particular reading of Gen 3, referring to the origin of human history. He notes that the entry of sin into the world occurred "through one man" (Rom 5:12; cf. also 1 Cor 15:21), clearly referring to Adam (Rom 5:14; cf. 1 Cor 15:22), who, however, because of the use of the noun *anthropos*, is to be understood as a "human being" inclusive of man and woman. To the first "man" is attributed the "disobedience" (*parakoē*) (Rom 5:19), the "transgression" (*parabasis*) (Rom 5:14), and the "fall" (*paraptōma*) (Rom 5:15, 18, 20), which provoked condemnation (*katakrima*) (Rom 5:16-17) and death (*thanatos*) (Rom 5:12, 14, 17, 21), which is extended to all (Rom 5:15).

Christ justifies

317. Paul's purpose throughout this long and complex argument is to reveal the gift of "grace" (*charis*) poured out in abundance on all by the Lord Jesus Christ (Rom 5:2, 15, 17, 20). Adam is a "figure (*typos*) of the one who was to come" (Rom 5:14), and Christ is the anti-type of Adam, because with his "obedience" (*hypakoē*) (Rom 5:19) he brought "justification" (*dikaiōma*) (Rom 5:16,18) and life (*zōē*) (Rom 5:17-18):

> "Just as by one man's disobedience many were made sinners (*hamartoloi*), so by one man's obedience are many (*hoi polloi*) to be made righteous (*dikaioi*)" (Rom 5:19), "so that as sin reigned in death, so grace was to reign through righteousness leading to eternal life through Jesus Christ our Lord" (Rom 5:21).

Paul calls the recipients of his letter to obedience, but not by reproducing exactly the exhortations of the ancient covenant, as we read them, for example, in Deuteronomy; the Apostle, in fact, speaks more specifically of the "obedience of faith" (*hypakoē pisteōs*) (Rom 1:5; 16:26; cf. also Mk 3:15; Rom 15:18), which is therefore submission to the gift of grace, which transforms human beings by making them capable of observing the commandments of the Lord (Rom 8:3-4), without having any reason to boast (cf. Rom 3:27; 4:2).

And with these contributions from the New Testament, in which the salvific intervention of God in human history appears, we come to the last part of the chapter, which will develop this theme extensively.

3. THE INTERVENTION OF GOD IN THE HISTORY OF SINNERS

318. Let us return to the account of the origins (Gen 3:8-24) to learn what happened after the transgression committed by the man and the woman. What we read has usually been interpreted as the punitive intervention of God, which determined the mortal condition of humanity, as well as a certain human weakness more easily drawn to sin. As we will make clear in our commentary, the text presents the Lord in the act of promulgating painful measures, which, however, cannot be reduced to a simple act of punishment in a judicial process. In particular, the death penalty, that according to the commandment of the Lord (Gen 2:17) would be applied "on the day when" the progenitors had eaten from the forbidden tree, is not in fact carried out immediately; the other punitive measures are less onerous. Moreover, from the account of Gen 3 it does not seem possible to deduce that human beings would also have been struck by an inner weakness, making them more inclined to evil; if it is common experience that every sinful act leaves a trace that negatively influences the future, it does not seem acceptable either to affirm that God produces this, for, as we will see, God always acts to favour the good in humanity, nor is it right to maintain that a hereditary moral flaw permanently conditions people's freedom.

Every divine act in the history of human beings is constantly directed to their good, starting from the punishments that follow sin; it is not the death of the sinner, but the sinner's life that the Lord desires (Ezek 18:23, 32; 33:11), as shown by the tunics of skins with which the Creator clothes the wretched nakedness of the progenitors.

Gen 3:8-24

[8] [The man and the woman] heard the sound (*qôl*) of the Lord God walking in the garden in the cool of the day, and the man and his wife hid from the presence of the Lord God among the trees of the garden.

[9] But the Lord God called to the man. 'Where are you?' he asked. [10] He replied, 'I heard the sound of you in the garden. I was afraid because I was naked, so I hid.' [11] He said, 'Who told you that you were naked? Have you been eating from the tree from which I forbade you to eat?' [12] The man replied, 'The woman you gave (*nātan*) to be with me, she gave me (*nātan*) fruit from the tree, and I ate it.'

[13] Then the Lord God said to the woman, 'What is this that you have done?' The woman replied, 'The snake tempted me and I ate.'

[14] Then the Lord God said to the snake, 'Because you have done this, cursed are you of all cattle and wild animals! On your belly you shall go and on dust you shall feed, all the days of your life. [15] I shall put enmity between you and the woman, and between your offspring and hers; he will bruise your head and you will strike his heel'.

[16] To the woman he said: I shall give you intense pain in childbearing, in pain you shall give birth to children. Your

yearning shall be for your husband, and he shall rule you'.

[17] To the man he said: 'Because you listened to the voice (*qôl*) of your wife and ate from the tree from which I had forbidden you to eat, cursed be the soil (*'ădāmāh*) because of you! In pain you shall get your food from it all the days of your life. [18] Brambles and thistles shall it yield for you, as you eat the produce of the land. [19] By the sweat of your face shall you earn your food, until you return to the ground (*'ădāmāh*), for from there you were taken. For dust you are and to dust you shall return.

[20]The man named his wife 'Eve' because she was the mother of all those who live. [21]The Lord God made tunics of skins for the man and his wife to clothe them.

22 Then the Lord God said, 'See, the man has become like one of us in knowing good from evil, he must not be allowed to reach out (*šālaḥ*) his hand and pick from the tree of life too, and eat and live for ever!' 23 So the Lord God expelled (*šālaḥ*) him from the garden of Eden, to till the soil from which he had been taken. 24 He banished the man, and in front of the garden of Eden he posted the cherubim and the fiery flashing sword, to guard the way to the tree of life.

The text can be divided into three sections: (1) God questions the man and the woman (vv. 8-13); (2) subsequently he issues decrees to the protagonists of the story, beginning with the serpent, then the woman and then the man (vv. 14-19); (3) finally, he takes immediate decisions in relation to the transgressors, clothes them with leather tunics and excludes them from the garden (vv. 20-24). In the translation we have included some Hebrew terms in brackets to underline connections that are not evident in modern translations.

(1) The conversation between God and the human beings (vv. 8-13)

319. *God takes the initiative in meeting the human beings; this is done discreetly, allowing God's presence in the garden to be heard (v. 8). God was not called upon, nor sought out. But God comes to the place where people have failed. One should certainly discard the* portrayal of the Creator who "strolled" in the garden, as if he were in the habit of taking a breath of fresh air at a certain time of the day. The text states literally that he is accompanied by the "wind of the day" (v. 8), an expression not attested elsewhere, but which is significant for the symbolic value of the terms used. The "wind" (rûǎḥ) suggests the occurrence of an event of "justice" (Is 4:4; 11:4; 28:6), which will evaluate and disperse what is evil (Ps 1:4). The "day", as a manifestation of the light, indicates in Scripture the right time to do justice (2 Sam 15:2; Zeph 2:3; 3:5, 8); on the other hand, the "day" which because of sin was a harbinger of death (Gen 2:17) coincides with that of the advent of the Lord to remedy the folly of human beings.

The human beings "hear" (šāma') a "noise" (qôl) produced by God's coming into the garden (vv. 8, 10); precisely because they did not listen to the voice of God, but that of deception (v. 17), the presence of God brings fear and leads to flight. Instead of coming to the light (Jn 3:20), the man and woman hide among the trees (v.8), as if this preserved them from the divine gaze that sees everything.

God then makes his voice heard and "calls" (v. 9), that is, he calls them to a confrontation with the truth. The word of the Lord takes an interrogative form: "where are you?" (v.9); "who told you [...]?" (v.11a), "have you been eating [...]?" (v. 11b); "what is this you have done?" (v. 13); this does not imply that the Creator does not know where 'ādām is, or needs to inform himself about what has happened in order to pronounce a verdict. In a court, the judge's interrogation has the function of ascertaining the facts and establishing the responsibility of the guilty; but in our account the Lord intends rather to bring out from the mouths of the transgressors the confession of their errant behaviour so as to make them aware of the evil that he already knows perfectly well. The questions, in fact, are addressed only to the man and the woman, the only ones called to admit their sin, as a way to justice.

To the man the Lord addresses several questions, which might also have been addressed to the woman (vv. 9, 11); they bring out the experience of "fear", and shame for their "nakedness", which move them to avoid the face of the Lord. Some sense of guilt seems to emerge; however, while acknowledging that he "ate" the forbidden *fruit, the man blames the woman and, indirectly, God, who gave her "to be with" him (v. 12). A sincere confession is lacking, therefore, as are any actions seeking mercy.*

The same thing happens in the case of the woman (v. 13), who admits to having eaten, but justifies herself by saying that she was deceived by the serpent, alluding perhaps to its creation by God who endowed it with dangerous cunning. None of this expresses repentance. This is why the intervention of God takes on corrective forms.

(2) The decrees made by the Lord (vv. 14-19)

320. *The man had blamed the woman, and she the serpent; God then turns to the protagonists, proceeding in reverse order, starting with the last.*

We note two literary devices, which demonstrate the stylistic skill of the editor. (i) The first is that of establishing precise relationships between the recipients of the divine injunctions: in the words to the serpent (vv. 14-15) the woman is evoked (v. 15), and in the dispositions for the woman (v. 16) the man is mentioned (v. 16b). As a counterpoint to what has been done, the serpent, who had prevailed by deception, is told that the woman will prevail through her descendants (v. 15); to the woman, who made the man complicit, it is announced that the man will "dominate" her (v. 16b); and on the man, who had received food from the woman without effort, it is imposed that he will eat bread by the sweat of his face (v. 19). (ii) The second device is rhetorical; the composition presents an inclusion between the condemnation of the serpent (v. 14) and that of the man (vv. 17-19): in the verses cited the motif of the "curse" appears, the punishment concerns "eating", and is to last "all the days of your life", and it ends with the reference to "dust". Only for the serpent and for man is the divine declaration introduced by a motivation: "because you have done this ...", "because you listened to the voice of the woman...". These phenomena, which highlight the relationships between the protagonists, mean that God's declarations are not to be considered in an isolated way, as limited to a single figure.

The serpent is "cursed" by God (v.14), because it represents the enemy of human beings, and, as such, is condemned to "feed on dust", and so to feed on what is a sign of death and what kills instead of nourishing. Although the serpent is still able to attack the human race in insidious ways, its defeat is already decreed, because its head, the vital principle for this animal and also the organ of seduction, will be crushed by the woman who is victorious through her race. Christians will see in this announcement a prophecy of the Virgin and of Christ who together bring about the annihilation of evil.

For the human beings God announces "suffering" ('iṣṣābôn) (vv.16-17), which affects the abilities that bring glory and pride to the person of the woman and of the man. For the first, it is bringing children to birth, and, for the second, it is work that leads the creatures to imagine they are like the Creator; God now marks these activities with a sign of pain and fatigue to remind human beings that they are not God.

321. Two additional observations are necessary.

(i) To the woman it is said she will be "attracted" by the man (v. 16b). The noun tᵉšûqāh (craving, passion) can have a negative connotation, as in Gen 4:7, where it is attributed to "sin" crouching at the door, ready to attack the human being; but it also has a positive significance, as in Song 7:11, where it expresses the love of the groom for the bride. Since the expression of v. 16b follows immediately the statement on maternal procreation (v. 16a), we can take it that there is an allusion to the woman's drive to seek the man who can make her mother, something that is widely attested in biblical stories. This impulse, which also expresses the search for protection, is juxtaposed with "domination" (māšal) on the part of the man (cf. also Gen 4:7), almost as a restraint on something dangerous. The authority of the husband over the wife is often seen to be affirmed here, and this provision would be interpreted as a punishment for the woman; more generally, it is believed that sin has altered the relationships between man and woman, introducing the domination of one over the other. It may perhaps be added, as is clear from Song 7:11, that sexual attraction also belongs to the man, as well as the desire for fatherhood; now, if the "domination" is not intended as oppressive, but also as fostering good relations, *we could conclude that the husband, too, in some way, will have to be controlled by his wife, in order to bring about mutual consent. This way of understanding the text will be seen as less forced, if we go on to consider also the consequences announced for the man.*

(ii) The fatigue of work (vv. 17-19a) cannot be a male prerogative, even if, in ancient times, cultivation of the fields was carried out mainly by men; the pain of daily work is actually common to all humans, and, according to Prov 31:10-31, it is above all the woman who is given to untiring activity. Moreover, the "return to dust" (v. 19b) is obviously not reserved for the male, and, as already seen, the serpent does not attack and threaten the woman alone (v. 15), but every child of man. With these observations we intend to invite an interpretation of these texts of the origins that does not endorse improperly customs or rules which, upon careful examination, are not substantiated by the word of God.

And lastly, it should be noted that God does not in fact decree the death penalty for human beings. Although this has been the regular interpretation, based probably on Wis 2:23-24, the text of Gen 3 says that man (ʾādām) will struggle to obtain food every day of his life "until you return to the ground (ʾădāmāh), for from there you were taken". Immortality, difficult to imagine for a fragile being, should not be considered a good thing which has been lost, but rather a future promise, which human beings will reach by humbly submitting to the destiny of death.

(3) Measures taken by God (vv. 20-24)

322. *Actions follow the words. They are not what one would expect based on the divine pronouncements. Among other things, the first act is performed by the man, and is surprising, and apparently out of context. The man gives the name Eve to his wife, thus calling her "the mother of all those who live" (v. 20). Indeed, what is anticipated here in delightful recognition will be narrated immediately afterwards (Gen 4:1; cf. also Gen 4:25) with the birth of the children of the woman. The narrator's remark shows that the immediately preceding pronouncement of the Lord (v. 19) does not impede life, since here is announced, in an almost prophetic way, an indefinite line of living beings (cf. Gen 2:7), generated by human beings. Furthermore, it* *is the husband who attributes to his wife a glorious title: she who could have been humiliated by the pain of childbirth and by male "domination" is instead exalted in her fertility. And finally, instead of a change in the relationship between man and woman (cf. v. 16b), the glory of the woman is proclaimed by the man. This already helps us perhaps not to introduce into human history signs of systematic and inevitable degeneration; the sin of the past does not always make subsequent actions morally impoverished.*

Two actions are then announced by God (vv. 21, 22-24). The first is diametrically opposed to the simply punitive interpretation of the preceding divine words (vv. 16-19), because it clearly reveals the intention of protecting human beings through the symbolic act of preparing for them tunics of skins with which they can be clothed (v. 21). Even after the fratricide committed by Cain the Lord places a mysterious protective sign on the perpetrator so as to safeguard his life (Gen 4:15).

323. *Clothing* in the biblical tradition has various functions, some practical, others of symbolic value; it is included among the primary needs of human beings (Sir 29:21; cf. Gen 28:20), and at the same time differentiates the human person from the animal.

The human body must be clothed because of the cold. The newborn is wrapped in swaddling clothes (Ezek 16:4; Lk 2:7, 12), as the first act of care for the baby; the poor person's cloak is a blanket for warmth (Ex 22:26), while those who are "naked", "denuded" perhaps by the abuse of others (Job 24:7, 9-10), risk death. God ensured that the clothing of the people of Israel did not wear out during the forty years in the desert (Deut 8:4; 29:4), and this despite the "fathers" being rebellious. The fact that the Creator clothes the progenitors just after the transgression had made their nakedness evident is a clear sign of mercy. Clothing the naked will be included among the works of mercy (Is 58:7; Mt 25:36), because, in a certain sense, it imitates the action of God.

The garment worn by human beings also protects the person's sexual intimacy; it is like a barrier of modesty placed against unbridled lust. The biblical expression "to uncover someone's nakedness" alludes to an improper sexual relationship (Lev 20:11-

21). The behaviour of Ham who "sees" Noah's nakedness (Gen 9:22) is to be interpreted as an act damaging to the dignity of his father, while respect is shown by Shem and Japheth, who "walking backwards, covered their father's nakedness" with a cloak (Gen 9:23). The tunics of skins of Gen 3:21 could be seen also as pointing to what in the sexual sphere needs to be protected.

Finally, clothing confers a "status" on the individual, distinguishing one person in relationship to others (Is 3:6-7). The male dresses differently from the female (Deut 22:5; Is 3:18-24); rich clothes are worn by rich people (Lk 16:19), and considered a possession of value (Jdg 5:50; 14:12-13, 19). The king will be distinguished by his attire (1 Sam 28:8; 1 Kgs 22:30-33), the queen by her splendid garments (Ezek 16:10-13; Ps 45:14-15), the priest by his robes (Ex 28:31-35; 39:22-29; Sir 50:11) and the prophet sometimes for his strange garb (2 Kgs 1:8; Mt 3:4). Proper dress is required to attend the king's wedding banquet (Mt 22:11-12). Putting on sackcloth and tearing one's clothes are humble penitential signs (2 Kgs 19:1-2; Is 37:1; Jer 4:8; Jon 3:5-8). Stripping someone naked may constitute a shameful additional penalty for those condemned (Jer 13:22, 26; Ezek 16:39; Hos 2:5); Jesus was derided when he was clothed in a purple cloak (Mk 15:17-20), and humiliated when he was stripped for the crucifixion (Mk 15:24). The father in the Lucan parable has his errant son clothed with a beautiful robe (Lk 15:22), restoring his dignity as son; the tunics of skins of Gen 3:21, which replace the fig leaf loincloths (Gen 3:7), can be interpreted as a symbol of forgiveness and rehabilitation.

324. *The account concludes with God's expulsion of the man and woman from the garden (vv. 22-24). The motivation for this decision emerges from the soliloquy of the Lord which establishes that the human being, through the knowledge of good and evil, has become "like" a divine being. The "nature" of the human being has clearly not changed for the better with the transgression; the Creator, however, sees that the human being, by taking the forbidden fruit, has become like God. This determines the divine decision to "drive them out" so that they no longer have access to the tree of life; the cherubim are posted at the entrance to guard the* *way barred to human beings. In keeping with our interpretative process this last decision of the Creator should also be considered providential insofar as it makes the human creatures understand that they should not "stretch out the hand" to grab the desired fruit, which can be life-giving only if it is given. Quality of life for the human being, therefore, is rightly pursued when one does not try to force the limits imposed by God, but is prepared to wait for the garden doors to reopen, so as to receive, by grace, what one wanted to take by foolish pride and greed.*

The testimony of the Law and the prophets

325. Following what is attested programmatically in Gen 3, biblical tradition denounces the fact that human beings express their freedom in transgression; not all human beings are sinners nor are they always, yet universal human guilt is, according to Scripture, a historical reality with disastrous consequences. And so the Creator and Father intervenes in human history to restore justice.

When a crime is committed in society, all agree that compensatory action is necessary; this is identified with a specific punishment, decided by a judge, who, with both fairness and rigour, hands down the punishment deserved to the guilty person. In the interpretation of biblical texts, "judicial" action is therefore seen as an appropriate interpretation of God's way of acting in history, and, consequently, it is identified as the discipline to be used in human systems for pursuing justice. Sacred Scripture, in the Old and especially in the New Testament, however, envisages the action of God not only as as Judge, but also as Father; in other words, the inspired word actually indicates *two procedures*, two ways of intervening by the Lord when people disobey the Law, two distinct modes, related to each other, both used as ways of justice, and therefore to be accepted in their complementarity as expressions of the will for good which is inherent in the very essence of God. The first is the mode of "judgement" (*mišpāṭ*), in which God intervenes as Judge; the second is that of the "lawsuit" or "controversy" (*rîb*), in which the Lord acts as Father.

Although expressed by the biblical text with a common legal vocabulary, these two ways of implementing justice involve a specific series of normative provisions, with distinct procedural disciplines. It should be borne in mind also that, applied to God and his actions, these procedures belong to distinct "literary genres", the meaning of which should be grasped without falling into fundamentalist readings, which take literally what needs to be interpreted.

(1) God as Judge

326. It is right to recognise the concept of God as Judge every time God intervenes to resolve, in justice, a situation of *conflict* which has arisen between two subjects, of whom one assumes the role of the innocent party (the injured person, the victim, the sufferer), while the other fulfils the role of the guilty one (wicked, aggressive, even violent). The legal structure thus outlined involves three actors: judge, defendant and plaintiff; the judge is asked to "judge between the two" (cf. Gen 16:5; Deut 1:16; Jdg 11:27; 1 Sam 24:13, 16; Ezek 34:20; Ps 75:8), establishing who is in the right and who is in the wrong, and handing down a sentence according to their actions (Ps 28:4; Prov 12:14; 24:12; Sir 16:13,15; Rom 2:6; 1 Pt 1:17; Apoc 20:12; 22:12). This institutional arrangement allows the authority, equipped with legitimate power, to operate in two directions: on the one hand, to *save* the victim, whose rights have been trampled upon, and, on the other, to *punish* the one who is guilty, preventing that person from continuing the abuse, delivering punishment for the evil perpetrated (cf. 1 Kgs 8:32; Ps 9:4-5; Qoh 3:17; Sir 35:21-25), and, when possible, imposing a fair compensation (Ex 21:18-19; 22:2b-3; Deut 22:18-19). The biblical author often formulates only one of the two directives of divine judgement, explaining for the most part the application of punishment; the other directive, which suggests the healing dimension of the intervention, is implied, or is mentioned in the wider literary context.

The value of this literary genre

327. Since God is perfect in all his works (Deut 32:4; Ps 33:4; 89:15), his activity as judge can only be an irreproachable expression of the promotion of the good. The throne of God, in fact, is conceived as the *supreme* location of justice (Ps 9:5, 8; 47:9; 97:2), in that (i) God is eminently capable of carrying out his task (Ps 7:12; 45:7; 82:8), since God knows everything, even the secrets of the heart (1 Kgs 8:39; Jer 17:10; Ps 94:9; Prov 5:21; 15:3; 17:3; Wis 1:6-10; Sir 15:18-20; 23:19-21), and no one who is guilty, however high-ranking, can resist his power (Nah 1:6; Ps 10:18; 66:7; 76:8-9,13; 82:1-8); (ii) God's court represents a sort of court of appeal, which repairs every unjust human verdict (Is 3:14-15; Ps 82:2-7); and finally (iii) because the judge of all the earth (Gen 18:25; Deut 10:14) extends his jurisdiction to the whole universe, subjecting every people to his judgement, in all epochs of history (Ps 9:8-9).

Problems and limits of the idea of God as Judge

328. The image of God as Judge, when applied indiscriminately, does not fail to arouse perplexity and even criticisms, which are to be found in the actual biblical text itself.

The sages of Israel, above all, contest the idea that every misfortune is tantamount to a specific punitive divine sanction. The book of Job, as a whole, presents an intense appeal for the recognition of the integrity of the protagonist, who had to suffer many misfortunes without the possibility of a fault proportionate to his sufferings being attributed to him. To refine a rigid and systematic theory of retribution, therefore, a different line of thought is developed, which interprets the privations and sufferings of the just man as a *test*, desired and carried out by the Lord specifically in relation to the "just one", from Abraham (Gen 22:1) to the "suffering servant" (Is 53:7-10), to the persecuted one of the book of Wisdom (Wis 2:19), in order to put the faithfulness of human beings to the test, and bring out their sincere and selfless relationship with God (Deut 8:2; 13:4; Jdg 2:22; Is 53:4,12; Ps 66:10; Job 1:9-11).

Furthermore, in the wisdom tradition in particular, there is the tendency to express the dynamic of punishing evil without the direct intervention of the judicial authority; the idea is introduced that the criminal, by his action, produces a result detrimental to himself, according to the proverb: "One who digs a pit falls into it; the stone comes back on the one who rolls it" (Prov 26:27; cf. also Ps 9:16-17; 35:8; 37:15; 57:7; Prov 1:18, 32; 8:36; 11:27; Job 4:8; Qoh 10:8; Wis 1:16; 11:16; Sir 27:25-27).

However, the same sages of Israel, and sometimes even the prophets, attest that, on closer examination, there is in fact no justice on earth: the wicked thrive undisturbed, while the victims suffer without escape, and this lasts a long time, indeed it seems to be a constant of history (Jer 12:1-2; Hab 1:2-4,13; Ps 13:2-3; 73:2-12; Job 9:7; 21:5-18; 24:2-17; Qoh 7:15). Such a dramatic observation calls into question not only the justice of the Lord in his role as judge (Zeph 1:12; Mal 2:17; Ps 10:13; 73:11; Job 21:7-21; Wis 2:18-20), but even challenges his presence in the world (Mic 7:10; Ps 10:4; 14:1; 42:4, 11). Why does God not intervene? Why does God not listen to the cry of the victims? Why does God allow the wicked to act with violence? (Hab 1:2-4; Ps 94:20). Such questions return rather frequently in the biblical text.

The free initiatives of God

329. A significant line of response to this questioning consists in saying that, in reality, God does not always act as judge in human history: in regard to sinners, in fact, his way of intervening does not always follow the rules of criminal procedure, because in his unfathomable wisdom God works constantly, always respecting human freedom, with the aim of achieving the greatest possible good for all the protagonists of the human story.

In fact, instead of intervening immediately with punishments, God raises *prophets* to become mediators of justice through their word (cf. Gen 18:17, 22-33; Ex 32:7; 1 Sam 3:11-14; Jon 1:2; 3:4; 4:11). This is not done by the Judge, but by the Saviour.

The main task of the prophets is to make sinners aware of their iniquity, because they obstinately deny it, hide it, and do not recognise its gravity. But this is not intended as a premise for condemnation; the prophetic mission has in fact always aimed at the *conversion* of the wicked, their return to God and to the practice of the good. In this perspective, the prophets have, therefore, an intrinsic "intercessory" function, as interpreters of the will of salvation of their Lord, who "does not take pleasure in the death of the wicked, but in the conversion of the wicked who changes path and so lives" (Ezek 33:11).

To understand adequately the divine action towards sinners in human history, one must not resort only to the judicial process, implemented by a just judge, perhaps with some leaning towards indulgence, but it is necessary rather to see a different way of acting, that of the Father towards his disobedient children.

(2) God as Father

330. If we consider attentively the duration of "history", of the time in which the human being is allowed to exercise free decisions, we must recognise that for the most part the image of God conveyed by the biblical text is not that of the judge who decides between two contenders, imposing his will against that of the wicked. In a specific and systematic way in the prophetic literature, which expresses the word of God in history, the Lord presents himself, in fact, as the partner in a covenant, who, in the name of the laws and the duties inscribed in the freely agreed pact, reproaches the other partner, Israel, about a series of reprehensible behaviours. In this perspective, God therefore assumes the role of accuser, not that of judge.

Such a manner of proceeding, which has a judicial character and therefore has rules respectful of law and justice, is not modelled on the forensic judgment that takes place in a law court, but is instead to be likened to the "dispute" (*rîb*) that takes place in a family context. The quarrel in this case is between two subjects, without the involvement of a third party, either because there is no legal entity superior to the two contenders, or because they are reluctant to make the disagreement public with the risk of a definitive breakdown of the relationship. The dispute will not be truly resolved except with agreement between the covenant partners. Since we are considering how God intervenes in the case of sinners, we must remember that the covenant was established out of pure love (Deut 7:7-8; 10:15); and, therefore, in the name of his fidelity to the commitment assumed, God does not want the breakdown of the relationship, but the affirmation of justice in truth; what the divine accuser pursues is consequently reconciliation, achieved with the forgiveness of the Lord, as the principle of human conduct drawn to obedience and right behaviour. In conclusion, it must be said that the family controversy, in its dynamics and in its purposes, is the "literary genre" that interprets in a more adequate way the *historical action* of the Lord towards his sinful people.

Scripture uses different images to represent the Lord in his role as accuser: at times he is seen as the ruler who denounces the unfaithful behaviour of his vassal (Is 1:24; Mic 1:2-7; 6:1-8; Mal 1:6; Ps 50:1-6); in other cases, he presents himself as a husband betrayed by his wife (Jer 3:1-4; Hos 2:4); in still others he is compared to a father dealing with rebellious children (Deut 32:5-6; Is 1:2-4; Jer 3:19; Hos 11:1; Mal 1:6). The paternal image of God allows us to understand better the various aspects of the family legal dispute; it was the father who gave rise to the relationship on his own initiative, as an act of free love, without conditions; moreover, he enjoys a publicly recognised authoritative role as *pater familias*; on the other hand, he is primarily responsible for the behaviour of his children, and has the legal, sapiential and emotional means necessary to restore the right relationships between family members. The image of the father, in his merciful role, will find its fulfilment in the New Testament revelation, as an expression of the new covenant.

The dynamics of the family dispute between the Lord and his people can be briefly summarised in a succession of three interventions of God.

(a) Words that promote a change of life

331. Unlike the judge who, having established guilt, pronounces the sentence, imposing silence on the contenders both for the prosecution and the defence, the father intervenes in the quarrel, provoking and demanding the response of the guilty (Mic 6:3). He speaks in denunciation of the evil, of which he is perfectly aware, with the intention of bringing the rebels to "recognise" their guilt (cf. Josh 7:19; Is 59:12; Jer 2:19; 3:13; 14:20; Ps 32:5; 51:5; Prov 28:13). The purpose of the word is to make people think, to touch them, to encourage a reasonable decision. The prophetic word of the Lord is not, therefore, the emission of an irrevocable sentence, as in the law court, but always an offer of new life.

In certain cases, the sinner admits guilt with an explicit confession (Jer 3:22-25; Ps 106:5; Neh 9:33; Dan 9:5-11), and prepares acts that publicly demonstrate repentance such as putting ashes on the head, tearing clothes, fasting, offering expiatory sacrifices (Is 1:11-13; Jer 4:8; Joel 1:13-14; 2:15; Jon 3:5-8). All this is for the purpose of obtaining forgiveness (Hos 14:3-4; Ps 51:1-6). God, however, often sees that the heart of the wicked one has not really been converted; the verbal declarations are not sincere, and the penitential rites are only a show, not accompanied by an authentic change of life with fidelity to God and justice towards one's neighbour (Is 1:16-17; 58:3-7; Jer 6:20; 7:21-23; Am 5:21-24). What the Lord asks, in reality, as a sign of authentic repentance, is typically expressed in Mic 6:8: "You have already been told what is good and what the Lord seeks from you: only this, to do what is right, to love loyalty and to walk humbly with your God".

(b) Warning actions, and the use of correction

332. The words of the divine accuser, however wise and however driven by anger, are in many cases, or even almost always, ineffective. The father then resorts to punishment because he really loves his child (Prov 3:12; 13:24; 19:18; 22:15; 23:13-14; 29:15, 17; Sir 22,6) and wants to save the child from being lost. This course of action, seemingly far from benevolent, aims to make the guilty understand the error of their ways and, consequently, to arouse the desire to return to the covenant relationship (Is 1:5; 27:7-9; Jer 2:30; Hos 2:9; Am 4:6-11). Punishment has medicinal value; it is not the punishment that concludes the legal process, as occurs in the judicial procedure, but it is instead a passing intervention, a sort of preparation for forgiveness and reconciliation (Deut 32:39; Jer 33:4-9; 2 Chr 7:13-14; Wis 16:10-13; Tob 13:2).

(c) Forgiveness and the new covenant

333. The father achieves the result of his juridical act of accusation when he is able to forgive. He has always wanted it, but the act of forgiveness takes place when the sinner welcomes it with repentance and gratitude, mindful of an undeserved grace. Repentance is expressed, in fact, in the recognition of sin and in entrusting oneself to the Lord's great mercy (Ps 51:3), and is accompanied by the sincere purpose of obedience to the commandments.

The final event of the *rîb* is realised, therefore, as a renewed encounter between the beneficial will of the father and the free consent of the child, a meeting of truth that highlights the love and the saving power of the Lord. The whole prophetic message of the Old Testament is a pledge of this event, and the whole New Testament is the attestation of the joyful fulfilment of what had been announced as the meaning of history, with a revelation that is not limited to Israel alone, but extends to all peoples, gathered under the same seal of mercy, in a new and enduring covenant.

334. Biblical history is narrated by prophets, that is, by authors who "see" how God conducts events, and can therefore show how God operates in relation to the actions of human beings, sometimes showering abundant blessings, and sometimes generously putting right mistaken actions. In concrete terms, the inspired narrators *interpret* what happens: they describe the facts precisely, selecting and ordering them among themselves, in order to make "visible" the presence of God, who, although invisible, "makes himself seen" by those with a pure heart willing to listen. If history is human reality, because it is lived and suffered day after day by parents and children with successes and failures, in truth, according to the Bible, it is a history of God with human beings, a history of a covenant in which is revealed the eternal fidelity of the Father to human beings, his children.

A cycle of events

335. In keeping with this overall view, the prophetic narrative presents itself as a sort of cyclical, or rather repetitive, movement, as if the diversity of peoples and the changing conditions of time were not relevant while the same spiritual conditions persist regarding both humans beings and God. This is attested in a paradigmatic way in the book of Judges, which begins to narrate the events of the people of Israel, who have become autonomous after their settlement in the land of Canaan. A rather stereotypical "literary scheme" serves as a key to understand all human affairs, because human beings and the Lord are always the same, and history proves it.

A clear example of this literary model is found in the opening pages of the book of Judges, in Jdg 2:1-16, which we summarise under three main headings.

(i) *The sin of idolatry*: "The Israelites did what is evil in the Lord's eyes and served the Baals. They deserted the Lord, God of their ancestors, who had brought them out of the land of Egypt, and they followed other gods, from those of the surrounding peoples" (Jdg 2:11-12). The betrayal of the Lord is, so to speak, justified by forgetfulness of the benefits received (Jdg 2:10); there is also a break between the generation of the parents and that of the children, who adopt the practices of the surrounding peoples, precisely those whom God had told them to eliminate so that they would not be a seductive trap for them (Ex 23:33; Deut 7:25). The starting point therefore is the transgression, which comes with the lack of recognition of the gift of God and with the loss of identity which arises out of a desire to be like others.

(ii) *The anger of God*. The sinful choice of the people "provokes" God (Jdg 2:12) and unleashes a reaction: "Then the Lord's anger grew hot against Israel. He handed them over to plunderers who plundered them; he delivered them to the enemies surrounding them, and they were no longer able to resist their enemies" (Jdg 2:14). With the anthropomorphic image of anger, the Lord is compared to a person deeply offended, who considers the situation unbearable and therefore takes action to change it. This is achieved not with the death of the guilty, but with their humiliation, with a kind of reduction to slavery, expressed in our passage with the image of the "deliverance" to foreigners. Here a historical process appears, which is the complete opposite of the original event of salvation carried out when God had freed his people from Egyptian oppression, a terrible event for the image of God it portrays, even if it is laid down among the "curses" of the

Sinaitic covenant (Lev 26:17, 33; Deut 28:64-68). Likewise there is the unveiling of evil, because idolatry is in reality enslavement to idols (Deut 5:9; Jdg 2:11, 13, 19), while the surrounding nations, with whom an alliance has been made, show themselves in fact to be violent enemies. This stage is not, however, the final act of history, because it is only a "test" for sinners (Jdg 2:22) to make them return to the source of life.

(iii) *The salvific intervention.* Slavery is a pitiful condition; the people are "in great distress" (Jdg 2:15) and "groaning" because of the oppression and ill-treatment suffered (Jdg 2:18). The lament expresses the suffering which arouses the "pity" of God (Jdg 2:18); at the same time, it is always, at least indirectly, a "cry" asking for help (cf. Ex 2:23-25; Deut 26:7-8; Jdg 3:9, 15; 4:3; 6:6; 10:10, 12), and the merciful God responds to their appeal: "The Lord then appointed them judges, who rescued them from the hands of their plunderers" (Jdg 2:16). The final salvific event spelled out here makes the whole story a "history of salvation". God works through intermediaries, here called "judges", not because they are appointed to judge in the court of law, but because they are entrusted with the task of justice which consists in freeing the oppressed, through combat carried out in obedience, according to God's rules.

The cycle that goes from sin to salvation is repeated, with some variation, from age to age (Jdg 2:17-20; 3:7): on the one hand, it is shown that human beings are easily deceived, as is attested in the story of Gen 3; on the other hand, it is revealed to the reader that the Lord continually transforms evil into good through forgiveness. But his saving gift introduces into history some elements of newness that are surprising and promising; thus not only do we have the repetition of the same, but a dynamism of grace that aspires to fulfilment.

The progress of history and its fulfilment

336. Looking at the passing of the days, the prophets observe that time is marked by unique and unrepeatable events. This had already happened at the very beginning of humanity, when, because of the total perversity of the human heart, the Lord decreed the flood to destroy every living thing on earth (Gen 6:5, 17); on that occasion, however, a "covenant" with Noah and his family is established (Gen 6:18; 9:8-11), which is defined as eternal (Gen 9:16), with the sign of the rainbow that will recall that "never again shall all living things be destroyed by the waters of a flood, nor shall there ever again be a flood to devastate the earth" (Gen 9:11). For the first time in the biblical narrative, the idea of an eternal covenant and an irreversible act of mercy appears.

Subsequently, the biblical narrator will speak of definite moments in history, in which the Lord will declare that he is making a specific covenant with other individuals, marking his intervention on the human story, so that things are new, no longer like those of the past. The whole history of Israel is based on three specific events, as on focal points: three covenants set in train a time distinguished by special promises, not known before.

(i) Israel defines itself as the people of the covenant, first of all, in reference to Abraham and the oath of blessing (Gen 22:16-18; 26:3; 50:24) that the Lord pronounced, establishing with him and his descendants an eternal covenant (Gen 17:7, 13, 19). This occurs at a specific moment in history, without what precedes being considered to have caused this new event. Compared to the cyclical scheme previously noted, God in this case does not intervene to deliver from the painful consequences of sin; his manifestation happens unexpectedly, like the making of a promise that anticipates the need, and fills the flow of time with hope, because he raises up one who is the bearer of blessing for all the families of the earth.

(ii) The Sinaitic covenant is grafted on to this covenant (Deut 7:7-8; 29:12); it too is seen by the biblical narrator as a surprising gift of revelation, as a founding experience that is unique (Deut 4:32-38) and everlasting (Deut 29:28; Sir 17:10; Rom 11:29). This is not because the Israelites are capable of absolute fidelity, but because God will not cease to "keep" his commitment in favour of the people he has chosen.

(iii) The third decisive covenant, that between the Lord and David, will be established to carry to fulfilment the promise made to the fathers to give them the land of Canaan as an inheritance; it comes unexpectedly, however, as a free choice of God, and will be declared an "eternal covenant", because it is completely founded on the divine benevolence, so that the Lord, in the case of the sin of the king's children, will intervene with a salutary punishment, but will never withdraw his faithful love from them (2 Sam 7:14-16; 23:5; Ps 89:31-38; Sir 47:22).

337. By virtue of these covenants the history of Israel will become testimony to the way in which God acts in history. An intrinsic component of hope will thus be inscribed in the hearts of believers, together with the confidence that the Lord will give complete fulfilment to his surprising initiative for good. Thus, even when, with the end of the kingdom of Samaria and then with the fall of Jerusalem and the painful Babylonian exile, the children of Abraham were bewildered, fearing the end of their history and of the covenants with God, the prophets are raised up by the Lord to announce the arrival of a "new covenant", fulfilment of all the divine oaths and of his promises. It is a definitive turning point in human history (Is 42:9; 43:18-19; 48:6-8; 65:17-20), because in this covenant it is God who forgives sin forever, and who creates a new people capable of loyalty and love never before realised:

> "Look, the days are coming, declares the Lord, when I shall make a new covenant with the House of Israel and the House of Judah [...]. Within them I shall plant my Law, writing it on their hearts. Then I shall be their God and they will be my people. They will no longer teach one another, saying, "Learn to know the Lord!" for they will all know me, from the least to the greatest, declares the Lord, since I shall forgive their guilt and never more call their sin to mind."
>
> (Jer 31:31, 33-34)

> "I shall pour clean water over you and you will be cleansed; I shall cleanse you of all your filth and of all your foul idols. I shall give you a new heart and put a new spirit in you; I shall remove the heart of stone from your bodies and give you a heart of flesh. I shall put my spirit in you and make you keep my laws and respect and practise my judgements. You will live in the land which I gave your ancestors. You will be my

people and I shall be your God."

(Ezek 36:25-28; cf. also Ezek 11:19-20).

The history of salvation is fulfilled then in this wonderful miracle of grace. Christ will declare it a reality in his person, and the evangelists will witness to it as the unique event of universal salvation.

History seen by the sages of Israel

338. As we have mentioned several times, the sages have a view of reality that considers its universal and permanent elements; history is thus seen more in its repetitive nature, because human beings always remain the same, even as the seasons change. In this regard, the prologue of the book of *Qoheleth* is emblematic:

> "A generation goes, a generation comes,
> yet the earth stands firm for ever."

(Qoh 1:4)

> "What was, will be again,
> what has been done, will be done again,
> and there is nothing new under the sun!
> There is something of which it is said, 'Look here!
>   This is new!'
> It existed in the ages before us."

(Qoh 1:9-10)

Such an observation undoubtedly has its own truth. It is contradicted, however, by the prophetic voice that proclaims the rise of the new and unheard of in the time of human beings:

> "No need to remember past events,
> to harp on what was done before.
> Look, I am about to do something new,
> now it is springing up; can you not see it?"

(Is 43:18-19)

Similarly, there are wisdom traditions that reflect on the various events of history; the understanding of the human being is enriched by the light that comes from the particular interventions of God in the human story.

339. *Sirach*, at the end of his collection of proverbial sayings, after recalling the works of the Lord in creation (Sir 42:15–43:33), goes on to list illustrious characters of history, made glorious by the Lord (Sir 44:2); he mentions people spoken of in the biblical tradition. From Enoch (Sir 44:16) to Simon, son of Onias, high priest in Jerusalem (Sir 50:1-21), a series of characters, with unique and, in general, admirable qualities, are listed, as evidence of a story full of extraordinary events. There is no shortage in this review of references to human sinfulness (Sir 45:18-19, 23; 46:7, 11; 47:11; etc.), but the repeated covenants, from Noah (Sir 44:18) to Abraham (Sir 44:20-21), and from Moses (Sir 45:5) and Aaron (Sir 45:7, 15) to David (Sir 45:25; 47:11), attest to a salvific history, which invites praise of the Lord, "the doer of great deeds everywhere" and who "has acted mercifully towards us" (Sir 50:22).

But it is above all in the *book of Wisdom* that the sage considers the course of history, seeing at work the wisdom of the "Lord, lover of life" (Wis 11:24, 26), described as the "Saviour of all" (Wis 16:7). Since the primordial age, the divine intervention presents itself as a saving act: with Adam (Wis 10:1-2), with the land submerged by the flood (Wis 10:4), with Lot (Wis 10:6), and so on, each episode illustrating that "wisdom delivered those who cherished her from all their troubles" (Wis 10:9). The author is interested above all in how God treats sinners; he notes that the Lord uses "mercy" towards the Israelites, who are "tested" as by a father who wants to correct, while he judges the enemies of his people in anger, acting like a stern king (Wis 11:9-10). This dichotomy would be awkward, if it were not supplemented by the affirmation that God always acts "with measure, number and weight" (Wis 11:20), making use of gradual punishments (Wis 12:2) which are designed to induce sinners to reflect (Wis 11:15-16; 12:25) and to repent (Wis 1:23; 12:10, 19-20). The history of salvation is, therefore, the work of God, but it requires that human beings understand it and accept it.

The salvific path in prayer

340. The psalms constitute the road that the believer follows in order to experience the salvific intervention of God in a personal story of sin or in that of the people, with whom one feels solidarity. First of all, the psalmist listens to the reproaches of the Lord and God's appeal for conversion (cf. Ps 81:9-14; 95:8-11) and, recognising them as true, is consequently led to a confession of sin and a plea for the mercy of the Lord (cf. Ps 6:2-3; 32:5; 38:5; 130:3-5). A typical example of this spiritual journey is provided by Psalms 50 and 51, which should be read together to respect their intrinsic relationship, marked as it is by significant lexical repetitions.

Ps 50 is an anomaly as a text of prayer; it presents itself as a prophetic pronouncement, because it is the Lord who manifests himself in full splendour (vv. 2-3), summoning the cosmic witnesses of the covenant (v. 4), to give solemnity and justice to a procedure of accusation (v. 6) filed against those who along with him sanctioned the covenant through sacrifice (v. 5). It is God who speaks (vv. 1, 7); the person who prays this psalm assumes the truth of the divine words, repeats them to appreciate them more deeply and to recognise the path to be taken in obedience to the will of God. As we read in the prophetic oracles, the Lord dismisses the sacrifices, which are judged useless and even offensive, as if the Creator needed to eat the offerings of the worshippers (vv. 8-12); and, in the commandments that prescribe justice towards brothers and sisters (vv. 16-20), the Lord points out the condition for obtaining salvation (vv. 22-23). Twice the invitation to offer the sacrifice of the *tôdāh* to God resounds (vv. 14 and 23); and with this expression, rather than with an invitation to praise, the Lord asks that the wicked make the "confession" of sin, as an initial step on the "right way" that leads to salvation (v. 23) and therefore allows one to give glory to God (v. 15).

In Ps 51, known as the *Miserere*, it is the human being who speaks, responding to what was heard from the Lord. And the one praying asks, first of all, for mercy, and, more specifically, that the Lord show his compassionate love by granting the forgiveness that destroys sin (vv. 2-4, 11); the request is accompanied by a full and total admission of guilt (vv. 5-8), because it is this "sincerity" and this paradoxical "wisdom" that is pleasing to the Lord (v. 8). The individual praying, aware of being born "in guilt" (v. 7), asks God to be recreated with the gift of a new "heart" and a "spirit" of holiness which will allow a resolute pursuit of the good (vv. 12-14). From here pours forth praise for God (v. 17), which rises as the sacrifice pleasing to the Lord, because it is offered by a broken and humbled heart (v. 19).

The coming of mercy in the person of Jesus

341. Divine prophecies are fulfilled, humanity's long wait comes to an end and is filled with joy, the advent of grace becomes a historical reality, which can be seen, heard, and touched by human hands (Mt 13:16-17; Jn 4:25-26; 9:35-37; 1 Jn 1:1-4). The past is marked by sin, but the present is now made luminous by the Kingdom of God that has come closer (Mt 4:17); indeed it has come with all the saving power of the Almighty (Lk 11:20). All this, because:

> "The Word became flesh,
> and lived among us,
> and we saw his glory,
> the glory as of an only-begotten Son of the Father,
> full of grace and truth. [...].
> Indeed, from his fullness
> we have all received,
> grace upon grace, [...],
> No one has ever seen God;
> it is the only-begotten Son,
> who is close to the Father's heart,
> who has made him known."

(Jn 1:14, 16, 18)

The name of the Son of God is Jesus, the Saviour (Mt 1:21).

Christ reveals the mercy of the Father

342. The gospels testify that Jesus is the Messiah, that is, the Christ, of whom the ancient Scriptures had spoken (Jn 1:41, 45); it was he himself who opened the mind of his disciples to understand the prophecies, which announced the painful death and the resurrection of the Christ, from which flowed conversion and forgiveness of sins for all peoples (Lk 24:46-47). The salvation of God is in fact available for all who believe (Mk 16:16); starting from Jerusalem, the message will reach the ends of the earth (Acts 1:8; 13:47). The fulfilment of grace extends from Israel in blessing to all peoples, so as to make *universal* the gift of God which is "for all" (Acts 10:34-36).

God's initiative is revealed in Jesus; he does not wait for sinners to return to him, but goes *looking for them*, like the shepherd who leaves the ninety-nine sheep in the desert to go and find and bring back the one that was lost (Lk 15:4-6). Jesus himself declares that he has come for sinners (Lk 5:31), to "seek out and save what was lost" (Lk 19:10); for this reason he is pleased to eat with tax collectors and sinners (Mk 2:15-17; Mt 11:19; Lk 5:29), scandalising those who did not understand mercy (Mt 9:13), and celebrating as they celebrate in heaven over one sinner who repents (Lk 15:7). God's anticipatory mercy is manifested in the fact that forgiveness is granted even when feelings or acts of repentance are not expressed. It is so in the case of the woman caught in the act of adultery (Jn 8:10-11), or the paralysed man lowered from the roof (Mk 2:5). Jesus washes the feet of his disciples (Jn 13:1-11) before they understand the meaning of his action (Jn 13:7); and he does the same for Judas who will betray him (Jn 13:21). The Lord's forgiveness does not require exhausting penitential procedures, but a simple request for mercy, as made by the tax collector in the temple (Lk 18:13-14), and by the thief crucified with Jesus, who simply said: "remember me when you come into your kingdom" (Lk 23:42). Again in the Gospel of Luke Jesus prayed from the cross saying: "Father, forgive them; for they do not know what they are doing" (Lk 23:34).

In the parable of the son who returns to the father's house after squandering all he had, we do have a confession of guilt (Lk 15:21), but the declaration expresses an imperfect repentance, motivated rather by the desire to have some food to feed himself (Lk 15:17-20); yet the father seems not to notice either the unsatisfactory motivation for the return, or the words that lack authenticity. With staggering generosity, not only does he welcome the one who was lost, but he clothes him with dignity and makes him a sharer in the festive banquet (Lk 15:22-24). It is no surprise that this does not satisfy the religious types who are smugly proud of their own works; the elder son in the Lucan parable, who prides himself on never having transgressed his father's orders, does not understand and does not accept that a feast should be provided for one who has led a dissolute life (Lk 15:29). But the father goes out to look for him too (Lk 15:29), begging him to accept the dynamic of divine mercy, anxious that this presumptuous son too, once he has understood, will enter into the house of joy, where the wonderful gift of coming back to life is being celebrated.

343. The fulfilment of the prophecies, the perfect and definitive manifestation of the Lord in human history, has, as we have just shown, features of overwhelming fulness. The images used by the prophets to indicate the advent of salvation often have a hyperbolic character, and obviously are not to be taken literally, as when Isaiah states "then moonlight will be bright as sunlight, and sunlight itself will be seven times brighter" (Is 30:26), a promise to be read in relation to another passage of the book: "No more shall the sun give you light by day nor the moon be your light in the night, but the Lord will be your light for ever, your God will be your splendour" (Is 60:19; cf. Apoc 21:13; 22:5).

The salvation brought about by Christ, therefore, is not to be admired only in the visible manifestation of a power that heals the sick and raises the dead, or in the ability to curb merely with a word the storm at sea, but rather in the penetrating and gentle communication of his Spirit of love, which brings authentic healing and true rebirth for people, with a heart of love similar to that of God.

In fact, one of the most important features, little stressed in the interpretation of New Testament texts, is to see that what in the Old Testament was reserved for God, now, in the new covenant, is being done by human beings. A decisive demonstration of this extraordinary transformation is seen in the power to forgive. The evangelist Mark tells us that when Jesus said to the paralysed man: "My child, your sins are forgiven", the scribes said in their hearts: "How can this man talk like that? It is blasphemy! Who can forgive sins, but God alone?" (Mk 2:6-8). Jesus makes clear that "the Son of man has authority to forgive sins on earth" (Mk 2:10), because he has been filled with the Spirit, which makes him merciful like the Father.

And, perhaps even more astonishingly, the fulfilment of the history of salvation takes place when Christ gives the same "power" to Peter, as the rock on which the Church is founded (Mt 16:19), and also to all the apostles (Jn 20:22-23), and to the entire Christian community (Mt 18:18). Indeed, forgiving one's brothers and sisters and even one's enemies is presented by the Lord Jesus as a "commandment" (Mt 5:44-48), because he gives the commandment to love as he has loved (Jn 13:34). Now, if the precept of forgiving, which in a certain sense forms the pinnacle of love, is being taught, this means that it is possible to fulfil it because the Holy Spirit is poured out into the hearts of believers. Indeed, the salvation of God, that is, his forgiveness, is not received by a person unless that person forgives the brothers and sisters (Mt 6:14-15; 18:28-35; Lk 6:37). Forgiveness is received in forgiving. What seems impossible to human beings, because it is too "divine", is in fact made possible through the gift of grace. Those who believe will therefore invoke the Spirit, the one principle of divine love, and will pray to the Father to grant forgiveness, so that they may become children of God, similar to God in love and capable of mercy, which is the light of salvation for all humanity (Mt 5:14).

Universal salvation

344. The apostolic preaching has as its central nucleus the announcement of salvation brought about by Christ:

> "But God, being rich in mercy, through the great love with which he loved us, even when we were dead by our sins, brought us to life in Christ – it is through grace that you have been saved – and raised us up with him and seated us with him in heaven, in Christ Jesus, so that for ages to come he might show the overflowing richness of his grace in his kindness towards us in Christ Jesus."
>
> (Eph 2:4-7)

The apostle Paul, as we have shown earlier, focuses his message on the announcement of the "justification" of sinners, one of the ways in which the forgiveness that saves is described. Here we add only a few remarks, in order to highlight the specific contribution of his "gospel".

The first point is to emphasise the absolute priority of grace, repeated with insistence by Paul, against any self-satisfied claim to be saved by one's own works. In the fulfilment of the history of salvation in Christ, a "new creation" takes place (2 Cor 5:17; Gal 6:15), which involves the whole of creation (Rom 8:18-25); the concept makes it clear that it is the work of God that gives reality and life to his new creatures, and certainly not the moralising effort of human beings (Eph 2:8-10). And this supreme gift is not presented by Paul as a simple remedy for the failed historical adventure of sinful humanity, but instead as the realisation of the "purpose of God" (Rom 8:28), desired by him before the creation of the world (Eph 1:1-14). The Apostle writes, "those he foreknew he also predestined to be conformed to the image of his Son, so that he should be the eldest among many brothers and sisters; those he called he also justified, and those he justified he also glorified" (Rom 8:29-30). The "glory" that the Creator had given to the "son of man" (Ps 8:6) is actually fulfilled in the final event of saving grace. History reveals the triumph of God as the triumph of love, because no force in heaven or on earth or in the depths "will be able to separate us from the love of God in Christ Jesus our Lord" (Rom 8:39). This is the eternal, indestructible covenant. If it is true that all human beings are sinners and in need of forgiveness, it will not be their efforts or their merits that will save them, because by God "all are freely *(dōrean)* justified by the gift of his grace *(charis)* through the redemption which is in Christ Jesus" (Rom 3:24). Indeed, God "proves his love for us, that while we were still sinners, Christ died for us" (Rom 5:8; cf. Eph 2:11-18). And through this death for love, the Spirit was poured into the hearts of believers, so that they can live according to the desires of God, producing the fruits of "love *(agapē)*, joy, peace, patience, kindness, goodness, faith, gentleness and self-control" (Gal 5:22).

345. And such an immeasurable gift has been made not only to the people of Israel, but to all peoples (Acts 10:34-35). This is a cornerstone of Paul's message, on which he fought, not only to remove the boast of those who gloried in circumcision, but also to exalt to the maximum the gratuitousness of salvation in Christ. Faith is possible for everyone, and it is by faith, not by obligations or practices of any kind, that one reaches grace and fulness of life (Rom 5:1-2; cf. Rom 3:27-30). A dynamic and creative faith will be "working through love" (Gal 5:6).

Paul will by no means neglect the paraenesis, which exhorts us to adopt a conduct worthy of God and of the grace received. But what precedes and grounds the exercise of love is the forgiveness of the Lord, with which he reconciles all humanity to himself (Rom 5:11; Eph 2:16; Col 1:20). The apostolic ministry will become an instrument of this saving dispensation:

> "Everything is from God, who reconciled us to himself through Christ, and gave us the ministry of reconciliation, because God was in Christ, reconciling the world to himself, not reckoning their sins to them, and entrusting to us the message of reconciliation. Therefore we are ambassadors for

Christ, since God is appealing through us: on Christ's behalf we beg you, be reconciled to God."

(2 Cor 5:18-20)

CONCLUSION

346. From a particular reading of Gen 3 a rather negative concept of humanity has been affirmed, which is marked from the beginning by a situation of sin. Before the transgression, however, comes the commandment, which is beneficial, illuminating and attractive, since it reveals what is good, and the very command shows that it is possible. God made known the commandment to human beings; they are the only ones called to obey, because they alone are free, made in the image of God. Even before the commandment there is the divine gift, with the endowment of God's life-giving breath, the gift of a spirit that can express itself as wisdom, prophecy, justice and love; there is also the gift of placing all the creatures of the earth at the service of human beings, because only human beings are able to embrace all things, transforming them for beneficial service to the praise of the Creator. Before sin there is the covenant, desired by God and made known in his gifts; before sin there is God's faithfulness, loving and unfailing.

If human beings, fragile and inconsistent, foolish and ungrateful as they are, prove over time to be unable to maintain the role of partner in a wonderful communion with God, this must not lead to a systematic devaluation of humanity, with a radical pessimism about the course of history. For this would mean that we forget God, the God of history, the God who is faithful in love, and who, where sin abounds, makes grace abound all the more (Rom 5:20). The history of salvation exalts God in his free, generous, inexhaustible love (Rom 8:31-38); but it also exalts human beings, made capable by the Lord of truly expressing their nature as God's "children", not only recipients,

357

but also promoters of love, bringers of hope, therefore, for every generation that comes into being, until there will only be love, because everything will be subject to God who will be "all in all" (1 Cor 15:28).

CONCLUSION

347. In these concluding pages the reader will be expecting a synthesis of our journey. Some may wish to be spared the effort of detailed analysis, and consider it sufficient to gather, in a simple summary, what the author has illustrated in great detail. In our times communication takes place in the form of short messages, slogans almost, without explanations, without nuances; and from such small doses many nourish themselves. In other cases, more rare and deserving, the reader seeks a summary, not to avoid reading the whole book, but to have one's attention directed to the points that are crucial for the author; in this case, the conclusions provide a useful orientation to start the long process of reading in an intelligent and focused way.

The guidelines of this document have already been provided in the Introduction, as is appropriate. To summarise at the end what has been the object of multiple investigations would be contrary to what we sought to achieve in the previous pages. Indeed, it would be unworthy of humanity and of God himself to reduce the biblical message on anthropology to a few formulations, when it was said, from the beginning, that the human being is a mystery, within which lies hidden the marvellous plan of God, which everyone is personally called to explore, so as to discover its meaning and to live.

In more explicit terms, our text throughout has sought to show the extraordinary richness of Revelation, made up of different facets, contrasts, developments and suggestions, which the wise person will not claim to have assimilated. It is in the ability to cope with the complexity, without being afraid of the effort, without pretending to have understood the whole extraordinary divine work, that the authentic act of reading is realised, not only of these pages, but of the entire Bible. The act of reading is in itself a dynamic process, as the reader grows in the intelligent appropriation of the message, without ever exhausting it. The question will always remain before us *"What is man?"* and with Sirach we are called to recognise that as regards this mystery of wisdom "the first man did not finish discovering about her, nor has the most recent tracked her down" (Sir 24:28).

348. The various chapters with their parts, and also the individual paragraphs of the Document are doors, which aim to open onto a biblical text that is complex, varied and allusive, often perceived as discordant by our universe of thought. But it is there that we have access to the Word of God to which we can listen. The numerous citations of Scripture that accompany the exposition are not a display of erudition, nor a simple proof of the formulations proposed, but, as they provide assistance for the personal appreciation of the subject, they are further doors that lead into the contemplation of the consoling truth about human beings in the light of God. In fact, many other themes, aspects and problems should be added to our discussion; other paths might have been taken; and other interpretative proposals are not only legitimate but necessary to give a less approximate idea of what, for the Bible, is the human being, created by God as a child, yet sharing in an amazing covenant with the Father.

Wanting to define what a human being is with a formula is like taking a picture of an individual at a certain moment of life, and pretending that the "image" can be adequate to express the whole story and account for the totality of what has been lived. We could perhaps then say that the various chapters and paragraphs of this Document are representations of the human being taken one by one from particular angles and with particular approaches, with the aim of presenting biblical anthropology in a less summary fashion. In these pages, moreover, instead of a static image, we have constantly proposed a journey, an *"itinerary"*, based on the memory of the beginnings and followed through in listening to historical testimony, with multiple and varied contributions, without identifying the truth in a single point, not even in the final one, which, among other things, would not make sense without what precedes it.

349. But above all our presentation, multifaceted and developing as it is, comparable to the flame of the Spirit, seeks to show that the truth of humanity is not really "visible". This is not because the inner and spiritual dimension is obviously removed from sensory perception, which, however, can at least be evoked through metaphors and symbols; but more radically because what a human being is cannot be adequately represented even by a very accurate description of the individual's historical trajectory, traced with the most complete documentation of "objective" facts (Qoh 3:11). The mystery of humanity has its foundation in the dark depths of its origin, imagined like the extraordinary formation of the embryo in the womb of a woman, where from a few cells a child is formed, without the mother herself knowing how this happens within her (2 Macc 7:22), because in that secret place it is God who acts (Jer 1:5; Ps 119:73; 139:13-14; Job 10:8). This original event is a "figure" of the entire human trajectory, since it prophetically shows that, in the complicated vicissitudes of human lives, there is at work a powerful creative reality that is concealed from all (Jn 1:31); it is the *becoming*, secret and promising, only partially understood, of the development of the child, which is the true reality of every human being. Birth, as when a woman brings a child to the light, is always a revelation, an unimaginable vision, a disconcerting and consoling discovery; so it will be for us, at the end of our being "formed" and shaped as new creatures, as children of God (2 Cor 5:1-5). Indeed, Scripture says that what we are has not yet been fully revealed (Col 3:3-4). John writes:

> "My dear friends, we are already God's children, but what we shall be has not yet been revealed. We know that when he appears we shall be like him, for we shall see him as he is."
>
> (1 Jn 3:2)

What we are, the truth therefore of the human being, finds expression in the fact of being called and truly being "children of God" (1 Jn 3:1). Not only creatures, not only intelligent and free beings, not only children of human beings, but also children of the Most High, similar to him, with a resemblance difficult to understand and put into words, but which will be fully revealed in the fulfilment of existence, when parable will give way to reality, and humanity's resemblance to God will reach its fulness in the face-to-face vision, like that of the only-begotten Son, who, gazing at the Father, receives from him the supreme revelation of love, which is the substance of likeness to God (Jn 1:18).

350. It is then by looking at Jesus and meditating assiduously on his story, that some understanding can be gained of that greatness with which the son of man was clothed (*Gaudium et Spes* § 22), when he was made "little lower than the angels" (Ps 8:6). It will not be enough to seek in the gospels some edifying saying or some consoling event; it will not be sufficient even to assimilate its mysteries of light. It will be necessary to enter the darkness of humiliation; it will be necessary to fix one's gaze on the disfigured face of Christ, which has lost all beauty (Is 53:2), because it is on the path of humiliation, of suffering, of injustice suffered for love that one can glimpse the sublime greatness of the human being in the mystery of being regenerated by God. It is not after the passion, but at the heart of the cross that Christians come to see the truth (1 Cor 2:2). Pilate, without knowing it, had affirmed it when he presented Jesus to the crowds and said: "Here is the man" (Jn 19:5). Like Christ, the believer, too, will follow the same path, so as to be transformed into the same image of the Son, by the action of the Spirit of the Lord (2 Cor 3:18).

Thematic Index

Numbers refer to the numbering of individual paragraphs or groups of paragraphs.